DATE DUE			

WEST CAMPUS

GAYLORD

Monsters in the Mirror

Monsters in the Mirror

REPRESENTATIONS OF NAZISM IN POST-WAR POPULAR CULTURE

Sara Buttsworth and Maartje Abbenhuis, Editors

AN IMPRINT OF ABC-CLIO, LLC
Santa Barbara, California • Denver, Colorado • Oxford, England

Library of Congress Cataloging-in-Publication Data

Monsters in the mirror : representations of Nazism in post-war popular culture /
Sara Buttsworth and Maartje Abbenhuis, editors.
  p. cm.
  Includes bibliographical references and index.
  ISBN 978-0-313-38216-1 (alk. paper) — ISBN 978-0-313-38217-8 (ebook)
1. National socialism in popular culture. I. Buttsworth, Sara. II. Abbenhuis,
Maartje M.
  JC481.M555   2010
  320.53'3—dc22   2010021209

ISBN: 978-0-313-38216-1
EISBN: 978-0-313-38217-8

14   13   12   11   10   1   2   3   4   5

This book is also available on the World Wide Web as an eBook.
Visit www.abc-clio.com for details.

Praeger
An Imprint of ABC-CLIO, LLC

ABC-CLIO, LLC
130 Cremona Drive, P.O. Box 1911
Santa Barbara, California 93116-1911

This book is printed on acid-free paper ∞

Manufactured in the United States of America

To our students, who inspired our questions

Contents

Illustrations and Tables

Acknowledgments

It may seem somewhat odd that two historians without research interests in the Nazi era—one of us is a historian of European neutrality, the other an expert in war, culture, and gender—would embark on editing a collection of essays dedicated to the uses and abuses of Nazism in postwar popular culture. Having both taught the history and the legacies of Nazi Germany and the Holocaust to various levels of university students, having engaged in numerous conversations about our students' misconceptions about the Third Reich, and having sought appropriate resources to explain the ways in which Nazism is communicated to us and our students in everyday ways, we were acutely aware of a gap in the available scholarship. This book is an attempt to start to fill that gap. Our call for papers was enthusiastically taken up by a host of emerging scholars in a range of disciplines as well as a few established experts. Choosing what to put in and what to leave out was difficult, but we hope that this collection will inspire more researchers to take up the challenge and critically engage in the analysis of this under-studied (and, in so many ways, frightfully disturbing) aspect of western popular culture.

Of course, we could not have completed this collection without the help and support of our friends and colleagues, particularly in the Department of History at the University of Auckland. We cannot thank our Praeger editor, Michael Millman, enough for his support of the project. We would also like to extend our gratitude to Purdue University Press, the editors of *Shofar: An Interdisciplinary Journal of Jewish Studies,* and Professor Lynn Rapaport for allowing us to republish her article "Holocaust Pornography." A similar debt of gratitude goes out to collection technician and photographer, Shaun Higgins, and the Auckland War Memorial Museum for allowing us to print two photos of their Second World War "Scars on the Heart" exhibition in our introduction.

Above all, we thank our partners, Brady and Gord, for being our kindest critics, our keenest editors, and our rocks in what has been the most difficult of years.

Sara Buttsworth and Maartje Abbenhuis
December 2009

Introduction

The Mundanity of Evil: Everyday Nazism in Post-War Popular Culture

Maartje Abbenhuis and Sara Buttsworth

In October 2009, a small group of students from one of New Zealand's most prestigious secondary schools for boys, Auckland Grammar, posted pictures on a social networking web site. These photographs were taken during a visit to a Second World War exhibition at the Auckland War Memorial Museum, titled "Scars on the Heart." The students photographed themselves bowing to, kissing and saluting (in *"Heil Hitler!"* fashion) a giant swastika flag painted on one of the walls of the exhibition. A frenzy of media attention ensued with the press and the public consumed with the apparent insensitivity shown by the boys toward the history of the Second World War, the New Zealanders who fought in it, and the victims of the Holocaust.[1] This incident occurred only a few weeks after a group of university students were severely reprimanded by Lincoln University's disciplinary committee for wearing Holocaust outfits and t-shirts emblazoned with Nazi slogans and imagery to an Oktoberfest party on campus.[2] The Auckland Grammar incident resulted in a barrage of public questions about how it was possible that New Zealand teenagers were not properly educated about the Second World War and the Holocaust. The students were made to apologize to museum staff, a war veteran, and a Holocaust survivor for their behavior.

What is most telling about the media coverage was that it fixated on the shortcomings of New Zealand society at large for not properly educating its youth. After all, so many surmised, the boys must have been ignorant of the horror of the war, otherwise they would never have acted in such an offensive and thoughtless manner. What the media, and all those concerned citizens, failed to even question was how, in a society that takes due care to inculcate a historical understanding of both the war and Holocaust in its education system—the principal of the school assured the public that his students did have some knowledge of these events—and gives due attention to the Holocaust and war memory, it is possible for a group of young men to visit a war memorial museum and salute the Nazi flag? In many ways, this question underpins the existence of this collection. Given the manner in which Nazism and the Nazi past is generally represented in popular culture, it does not strike either of us as surprising that these teenagers would act in the manner they did. What is far more disturbing, from our perspective as historians who wish to teach an appropriately contextualized understanding of the past, is that so little attention is given to the manner in which the Third Reich has become part of our everyday lives. Why is Nazism part of the furniture of living in our popular culture and why has the continued presence of Nazism in popular culture not been questioned in a systematically critical way?

This collection springs from our concerns about how the representation of Nazi Germany in western society complicates our ability to effectively historicize the Nazi past and its most important legacy, the Holocaust. To illustrate our concerns, consider the following questions: if you were born after 1945, how old were you when you first became aware of the Second World War and Nazi Germany? And what was the vehicle for this introduction? Was it a conversation with a family member who had experienced the war? A subject introduced by a teacher? Or was it a comic book or cartoon? A novel or a feature film? The further we are removed in time from the events of the first half of the twentieth century, the more likely it is that we have been first introduced to ideas about Nazism through popular culture and only later had the subject introduced by a teacher. How many of us have sung along to *The Sound of Music* (1965), a film that continues to captivate audiences with its romanticized images of Austria, catchy tunes, and picturesque children? *The Sound of Music* seems like a reasonable place to start as it raises a number of issues that inspired us to bring together this collection of essays: (1) The pervasiveness of images of Nazism and how they have changed over time, (2) the roles these images have played in the introduction of successive generations to the mythologies of Nazism and the ways in which they feed into the perpetual fascination with, and often fetishization of, Hitler, Nazism, and the Holocaust, (3) the apparent disconnect between many popular representations of Nazism and the ultimate genocide that resulted from Nazi racial politics. While Nazism continues to exert potent currency in popular culture, synonymous with monsters in well-tailored uniforms and symbolized as literal and allegorical monsters from vampires to cannibalistic demons and aliens, material that contextualizes these representations is scattered. Our mixed reactions to the events and personalities of the Nazi period are succinctly portrayed in Alan Bennett's *The History Boys,* when the relief teacher, Tom Irwin, explains that

> this is history. Distance yourselves. Our perspective of the past alters. Looking back, immediately in front of us is dead ground. We don't see it and because we don't see it this means that there is no period so remote as the recent past and one of the historian's jobs is to anticipate what our perspective of that period will be . . . even on the Holocaust.[3]

We hope with this collection to provide some perspective on the manner in which the Nazi part of that recent past is portrayed outside of the discipline of history.

In August 2008, James Cullinane, in reviewing the computer console game *Wolfenstein,* asked a related question: "Where would popular culture be without Nazis?" *Wolfenstein* is a game "conduit," in Cullinane's words, "to our bottomless appetite for scything down satanic Nazi henchmen." It is, so we are told, "all about indulging in simple pleasures."[4] *Wolfenstein* is only one of countless examples of how Nazism is invoked in popular culture as a symbol for inexplicable evil, which, at the same time, is readily and easily consumed. Western society seems to have an unending appetite for all things Nazi, if programming on the Discovery Channel and History Channel (also commonly known as the "Hitler Channel") are any guide. It is a rare week if something to do with the Second World War, Adolf Hitler, the Holocaust, or the Nazi past does not feature somewhere on any one of the western world's leading newspaper web sites. In popular films, pulp fiction, comic books, advertising, television programming, and Youtube videos, the Third Reich is prominently featured and represented. If we are not applauding Indiana Jones for killing a host of nasty Nazis,[5] we secretly indulge in and are horrified by *Ilsa, She-Wolf of the SS* (1974), we witness Huey, Dewey, and Louie finding a copy of *Mein Kampf* on a garbage heap,[6] we take affront at Hitler telling us that AIDS is a mass murderer,[7] we laugh at Hitler offering us even more comic relief on *Family Guy,*[8] we grin at clever remediations of a famous scene in the movie *Downfall* (2004), in which Hitler gets angry at his generals for losing the war, but this time he is upset at someone having stolen his car, changing the name of the yeast-spread Vegemite, and banning him from Xbox Live.[9] Hitler needs no introduction; his voice and inflection are enough for audiences to draw immediate conclusions. It really does not matter what he says, only that he is saying it.[10] In so many ways, Nazism has become part of our everyday wallpaper, that which is always there, needs no explanation, and seems so terribly obvious we barely notice it. Nazis are bad. Hitler was evil. We invoke symbols of Nazism unthinkingly and uncritically, and almost as comfortably as we would wear an old pair of shoes.

Our engagement with representations of Nazism in leisure and entertainment often has very little to do with the historical realities of the Third Reich. It is this disconnect between the Nazi past, its legacies (most notably the Holocaust), and their popular representations that is at the root of the confusion. Most people in the early twenty-first century absorb Nazism primarily through popular media. Given the swastika saturation

Illustration 1: "Scars on the Heart" display at the Auckland War Memorial Museum showing a cabinet of Nazi medals, a Nazi flag, and the giant swastika mural, in front of which the Auckland Grammar boys photographed themselves saluting. (Photograph by Shaun Higgins. Photograph courtesy of the Auckland War Memorial Museum, Auckland, New Zealand)

surrounding us, it should not surprise anyone that the Auckland Grammar boys acted out as they did at the Auckland museum. Similarly, the furor surrounding Prince Harry wearing an Afrika Korps uniform in 2005 was more outstanding because of the media storm it created than the fact that someone was seen dressed in a Nazi uniform at an undergraduate party.[11] Prince Harry and the Auckland Grammar students are a part of a culture that mobilizes images of Nazism to various ends, many of them trivial and trivializing. It is not that these boys know nothing about the Nazi past and its horrors, but what they do know is confused, confounded, and, in part, glorified, by popular culture.

Hannah Arendt, in her now famous report on the Adolf Eichmann trial of 1961, suggests that as one of the orchestrators of the Holocaust, Eichmann was not extraordinary.[12] She posits that he was an ordinary person

Illustration 2: Another part of the "Scars on the Heart" exhibition at the Auckland War Memorial Museum showing a cabinet with a captured Nazi flag, mannequins dressed as Allied soldiers, and information about the military campaigns in Europe during the Second World War. (Photograph by Shaun Higgins. Photograph courtesy of the Auckland War Memorial Museum, Auckland, New Zealand)

who accepted the morality of his state and acted in a manner that was acceptable, permissible, and desirable from the point of view of that state. In this way, he did what all normal law-abiding bureaucrats do, namely, abide by the rules and adapt to the environment. While a modern audience views Eichmann's actions as abhorrent, at the time and from the point of view of the Nazi regime, Eichmann was no more repulsive than any other bureaucrat doing his or her job. From Arendt's perspective, Eichmann demonstrates how the proliferation of evil can become everyday. Arendt's phrase "the banality of evil" summarizes the possibility that all ordinary humans may succumb to the activities of a regime like the Third Reich. Arendt's premise remains controversial. Still, the phrase "banality of evil" has become an accepted part of western popular culture. The purpose of this collection is not to engage with Arendt's argument or to investigate the notion of evilness as it applied to Hitler and the National Socialist German Workers' Party (NSDAP, Nazi Party).[13] What we do suggest here, however, is that if the NSDAP has become an uncritical signifier of evil in western popular culture, then it is imperative to critically engage with the implications of the ways in which the Third Reich, Nazism, and the Holocaust are pedestrianized in that culture. The Nazi past, as it is popularly represented, is not only banal, but has also become mundane.

Nazism in Post-War Popular Culture

Surprisingly, there has been little concerted academic attention given to the appropriation of Nazism in everyday life. While studies on the Holocaust and Holocaust memory in popular culture abound, few scholars have picked up where Susan Sontag famously left off in her 1975 *New York Review of Books* article to investigate further the impact of what she called "fascinating fascism" on our culture, or to critique what Saul Friedländer in 1982 refers to as our preoccupation with "kitsch and death."[14] While most vampire-lore dictates that vampires cast no reflection, Nina Auerbach astutely claimed the contrary when she asserted that: our vampires are indeed ourselves.[15] Can the same declaration be made with respect to the monsters that have represented Nazism to us since 1945?

   The archetypal Nazi is easy to pick out: he is male (or if female, then usually a woman brutalized by Nazi men or the Nazi regime in some way);[16] he is aesthetically pleasing, well-dressed, and uniformed; he is a racist with the utmost contempt for human life; he is linked either to the cold and rational (often depicted as a super scientist) or the dark and mystical; if not a cold and calculating bureaucrat, he is brutal, sadistic, and beyond redemption; he is usually sexually charged (or when comically inverted bereft of all sexual energy, even camp), seductive yet repellent; and he represents all that is sinister and evil. The archetype underpins most references to Nazism in popular culture and brings out the most prominent function of Nazism in that culture, namely as a signifier of secular evil, which is all the more powerful as a signifier because it is rooted in an understanding of something real and historical, as something that really happened. The archetype is also utilized as a signifier of difference because what fascinates us about the Nazis, even as monsters, is that they are so familiar.[17] The familiarity is alarming and, as a result, we feel the need, as Linda Mizejewski pointed out, to "posit *our* difference . . . our horror at and moral superiority to what we would like to think of as a historical aberration and a nightmare."[18]

Obviously, the notion of the Nazi past as evil feeds off the idea that the Second World War was a good war fought by the western Allies against the baddies, both Hitler's Germany and Hirohito's Japan. Of course, the inexplicability of the Holocaust underpins the understanding that the Third Reich was a depraved place, worthy of destruction, and the Second World War was at its heart a heroic battle in which the forces arrayed on the side of good ultimately defeated those aligned with evil. In such depictions, Hitler is often invoked as the Devil incarnate, and the Second World War as the twentieth century's version of a Manichean struggle between light and darkness. Of course, narratives reduced to uncomplicated binaries pitting good versus bad, with due focus on violence and fantasy, are the backbone of the entertainment industry. As the historian Richard Evans explained, "[h]istory as a simple story of heroes and villains has always played a major role in American popular culture, whether in depictions of shoot-outs in the Wild West or fantasy conflict set in the intergalactic future. Moreover, . . . victimhood has now become a major source of legitimacy in American society."[19] The Nazi past is easily absorbed into this trope and attracts us to it, in part because of its origins in the real historical Second World War. In this sense, as Friedländer observed, our attention "has gradually shifted from the re-evocation of Nazism as such, from the horror and the pain— even if muted by time and transformed into subdued grief and endless meditation—to voluptuous anguish and ravishing images, images one would like to see going on forever."[20] The Nazi past, with all its aesthetics, has become endlessly engrossing.

Apparently, the idea that Nazism is evil is a concept that needs no explanation. It is universally understood and (almost completely) uncritically accepted. From a young age, we are exposed to it in all manner of ways, as Sarah Winters's chapter on Nazism in children's literature in this collection reminds us. As a result, it is easy for popular representations to take artistic license with Nazism because the idea of Nazism as evil is an uncontested one. To this end, it almost does not matter *how* Nazism is invoked in a myriad of cultural artifacts, merely that it *is.* We do not question the appropriateness of shooting legions of undead Nazi henchmen on our computer consoles, as we do not ask questions about why a family of Austrian nationalists would need to escape the Nazis during *Anschluss* in 1938 in *The Sound of Music.* Amid listening to the characters sing "Edelweiss," "I Am Sixteen Going on Seventeen," and "Do-Re-Mi," few would perceive a need to contextualize the Nazi takeover of Austria or to answer young Marta's question as to why "the flag with the black spider on it makes everyone nervous?"[21] That the von Trapp family needed to flee Austria seems obvious to a modern audience well versed in the "Nazis are evil" trope. And if this is your first introduction to ideas about Nazism, then the overlap with other simplistic ideas about evil and the fear that causes a wealthy family to flee comes to symbolize Nazism itself. As Joerg Steinitz, assistant director of *The Sound of Music,* exclaimed at the time: "It contains everything that makes a good film for Americans—it is a migration film, there are children, there's music, the landscape, and Nazis. All you need."[22] In a culture that maintains its white hats for good and black hats for evil, it is inevitable that the complexities of Nazi Germany and the *Anschluss* are reduced to a simple binary. Otherwise we might need to question the actions and inactions of the good in the good war, and place under the spotlight the monsters of which we all catch glimpses in the mirror.

In many respects, it is because of the universal acceptance of Nazism as evil that we do not ask questions about the appropriateness of the representations or historicize those representations properly. It is also because of this general understanding that we can and do laugh heartily at Hitler and the NSDAP, and allow all manner of ways in which to ridicule, belittle, dehumanize, and caricature them and the Third Reich. We do not offend anyone by doing so. At the same time, Nazism is a powerful and emotive force in the popular imagination, primarily because it is linked to our understanding of what is right and wrong. Its use in popular culture can have wider political or ideological motivations, as the chapters by Ahmed Al-Rawi, Lynn Rapaport, and Emily Turner-Graham in this collection illustrate. One does not need to look far to see how Nazism is invoked to push all manner of political agendas to an uncritical public. For example, the political enemies of both the Republican George W. Bush and his Democratic presidential successor, Barrack Obama, have used likenesses of Adolf Hitler and the Third Reich to make their point and attempt to undermine the United States public's confidence in their president.[23]

Perhaps one of the reasons that Nazism's role in popular culture has escaped critical attention is because the field of popular entertainment is supposedly apolitical. As William Collins Donahue explains with regard to the pulp fiction category of detective novels, they sit "squarely within that undemanding cultural strata . . . that is, pure entertainment with no obligation to instruct, ennoble, edify, disrupt, subvert, or—least of all—defy commodification."[24] Donahue suggests that when it comes to Nazism in mass entertainment, notions of social responsibility do not hold. Yet he also stresses the seeming paradox of what he calls the "popular culture alibi," as popular culture is precisely the field that critics have lauded for its potential to raise public awareness of the Holocaust.[25]

What Donahue fails to differentiate, however, is that representations of Nazism are not the same as representations of the Holocaust. While Nazis are inevitably present in the latter, the Holocaust is frequently absent (or only indirectly referenced) in the former. Marc Hieronimus's chapter "Hitler is Fun: Sixty Years of Nazism in Humorous Comics" in this collection introduces us to Terrence Des Pres's idea of "Holocaust etiquette," namely that the Holocaust rarely features in popular culture other than as a serious event with due reverence given to its victims (hereby fulfilling its memorialization function very well). Holocaust etiquette dictates that popular culture is not allowed to deal seriously with the Holocaust and Nazism and, therefore, leaves that function to high culture. Accordingly, much of popular culture takes liberty with Nazi themes but removes them almost completely from their Holocaust context for fear of what Lynn Rapaport has labeled, "profaning the sacred."[26]

To this end, popular representations of the Holocaust give primacy to its victims.[27] It is the experiences of Holocaust victims and the need to take due care with the memory of the millions who died in the Holocaust that form the basis of most popular Holocaust narratives. Their stories are sacred and are treated with the utmost consideration. In contrast, popular representations of Nazis focus on agency, power, and perpetration, as those who are capable of the basest of human acts. Even the good Germans in such narratives, characters such as Xavier March in Robert Harris's *Fatherland* or Gerhard Selb in Bernhard Schlink's (of *The Reader* fame) detective novels, stand out as the exceptions that prove the rule that the Nazi regime was nothing other than evil.[28] But because the Nazi part of the Nazi past is not deemed sacred by any stretch of the imagination, almost no care is taken with these representations at all, other than that Holocaust etiquette should be observed. The disturbing consequence of this artificial divide is that not only is the Holocaust often removed from its specific Nazi context but so are Nazi representations divided from their most significant historical legacy. By implication, if we disengage the Nazi agents from their victims in our representations of Nazism, are we not alleviating them from their responsibility for the Holocaust? Disturbingly, it is the public's sensitivities that can be held most responsible for sustaining the artificiality of the divide, because when popular productions overstep the rules of Holocaust etiquette—for example by humanizing the Nazis or representing the Holocaust for the true horror it was—they are widely criticized and lambasted for their insensitivity to the memory of the Third Reich's many victims.[29]

The most disquieting outcome of all this is that Nazism, at least how it is represented in many popular cultural forms, has been removed almost completely from its historical context. In general terms it references indiscriminate evil but in specific terms it fails to give any real shape or form to that evil. In this way, Nazism has become a free-floating signifier that could mean almost anything and, frighteningly therefore, nothing at all. Gavriel Rosenfeld argues that this process is part of a wider "creeping 'normalization'"[30] of the Nazi past in popular consciousness—removing a sense of abnormality or special status to the history of the Third Reich and thereby allowing all manner of treatments of that past. At one level, Rosenfeld's normalization thesis helps to explain why in 2007, Thai students at Thewphaingarm School could put on a Nazi-themed parade, replete with uniforms, swastika flags and a replica of a Nazi eagle with the word "RIP" emblazoned above it;[31] students at Shinchon university in Seoul could down drinks named "Adolf Hitler" and "dead" and admire the aesthetics of Nazi flags and uniforms at the popular Fifth Reich bar;[32] in 2009, the all-girl Korean pop group Girls' Generation could dress in military uniforms pinned with Nazi medals;[33] and why, in that same year, a mayor of a Romanian town and his son could prance around in Wehrmacht uniforms at a local fashion show after being inspired by the film *Valkyrie* (2008).[34] However, in all four instances, as with our Auckland Grammar boys and Prince Harry, the media heavily criticized these events for their participants' seeming insensitivity to the past. Apparently, going for a drink at the Fifth Reich is not (yet) the same as eating at a Genghis Khan Mongolian restaurant, however normalized the Nazi past has become.

Furthermore, the normalization of the Nazi past assumes a degree of public indifference to that past, although it also romanticizes and fetishizes that past in all manner of ways: from Hitler smiley faces and the ubiquitous presence of SS uniforms in costume shops to Kitlers (also known as "cats who look like Hitler").[35] The mere existence of an entire genre of allohistorical works itself begs the question as to why we are so fascinated and so absorbed. Perhaps Donald McKale, in his analysis of Hitler survival narratives, explains it best: we need Hitler as "proof of something nearly inhuman and godlike."[36] The Nazi past offers a set of easily identifiable moral tropes, clearly identifying right from wrong even (or particularly) in a secular world. That past is also compelling because of its mythical elements, particularly its symbology and its links to the inexplicable. To this end, McKale asserts that we need Hitler "for the perverse entertainment that thinking about and seeing him can give us" and that "[o]ur imaginations insist on bringing him back to life" in all manner of ways "so that we may condemn and kill him again and again, the pleasure he so fiendishly deprived the world in 1945."[37]

Above all, if we take seriously what James E. Young posits about Holocaust memory, namely that what is remembered about the past depends on how it is remembered, and how things are remembered depend on the texts that exist to give that memory form,[38] we endanger ever attaining a proper historically informed understanding of the Third Reich and Holocaust. Furthermore, we are at risk of silencing the real voices of this terrible past and replacing them with imaginary and mythical heroes and villains that bedevil our present. In turn, we risk that the real monsters, and monstrosities, of the past and the present remain unrecognized and their subtleties unrecognizable.

Chapter Outline

By no means intended to be exhaustive, this collection hopes to offer a catalyst to some much-needed academic discussions on the role and place of Nazism in post-war popular culture. In it, we bring together established and emerging scholars from different disciplines, who analyze some aspect of the role Nazism plays in their field of the study of popular media. Most pressingly, the collection comes out of a need we have seen in teaching the history and legacies of Nazi Germany and the Holocaust. Our students come to our classroom armed with assumed knowledge about this subject (as Claire Hall's chapter reiterates for secondary school students in Britain as well). They think they understand the Nazis before we even open our mouths and expect us not only to reinforce their existing ideas but also to offer them more material to consume in the same manner. We want to show them that the history of the Third Reich is much more complex and cannot be reduced to binaries of good and evil and explain to them how their perceptions of this past have been shaped by their present, by the culture that they live and breathe. Despite lengthy searches we were unable to unearth a specific and comprehensive text in this area to support our teaching. This collection is, therefore, an attempt to address this important lacuna in scholarship and teaching materials. Perhaps of even greater importance, we hope that *Monsters in the Mirror* will provide the incentive for much more in-depth and critical research in the area.

The collection consists of 11 chapters, most of which thematically interconnect. Some of the recurring ideas that are prominent throughout are: the normalization of Hitler and the Nazi past, the representation of Nazism as secularized evil, the possibilities and problems of humor relating to Nazism, the gendering of representations of Nazism, and the problems of decontextualized Nazism. Many of the chapters herein trace change over time across the decades since the end of the Second World War. All of them seek to problematize a culture that has failed to critically examine some of its most omnipresent representations.

In the opening chapter, Gavriel Rosenfeld picks up where he left off in the exploration of the allohistorical in his book *The World Hitler Never Made* (2005).[39] Alternative worlds where the Second World War never ended or Hitler did not die abound in fiction, both serious and humorous. Rosenfeld asserts that references to Nazism have become so normalized in contemporary discourse that they are no longer viewed through a moral lens. Indeed they have become universalized, and modern audiences fail to connect them to actual historical events. Rosenfeld's discussion of such normalization is extremely important but also opens up to questioning how, if Nazism has been normalized, can it also be simultaneously fetishized as only the taboo can be? His chapter in this collection focuses on allohistorical fiction written in the early twenty-first century. Some of the works utilize alternative worlds to explore issues of contemporary morality, such as the atrocities committed by United States soldiers at Abu Graibh prison in Iraq in 2004 and the participation in unjust contemporary wars. Others use the tool of normalizing Hitler in order to destabilize the triumphalist ideas that have dominated Anglo-American rhetoric surrounding the Second World War. Rosenfeld also explores the differences between authors from various cultures and comes to the conclusion that German authors have typically followed the narrative trajectory that suggests removing Hitler from history altogether would have made for a better world in general. French authors continue to explore their embarrassment at France's capitulation in 1940, while Anglo-American authors continue to claim fictional as well as factual victories in the good war.

Rosenfeld notes that speculative histories tend not to be taken seriously by critics or those outside the communities that read and produce them, a point that Marc Hieronimus's chapter on comics and Ahmed Al-Rawi's chapter on the Nazi-demonization of Arabs in pulp fiction also pick up. The sorts of speculative and sensationalist texts that are regularly produced for mass audiences are precisely the kinds of works often ignored by serious academic scholars. Yet, as Al-Rawi reiterates throughout his chapter, these are precisely the kinds of works in which political ideas are pushed to extremes. Judging by the ongoing success of this formulaic publishing, the popularity of these works, and the often extremist views presented in them, make them particularly important texts for understanding the ways in which Nazism is understood and popularized in western culture more widely.

Since 1945, allohistorical work has persisted as much as have the sensationalized rumors of Hitler's survival.[40] The mythologies surrounding Hitler's death have been so pervasive that even as late as 1969, Hitler look-alikes were arrested around the world.[41] It is not merely fiction that has perpetuated these myths and sightings. In our second chapter, Eva Kingsepp explores documentaries that use their own truth effect—repeating ideas frequently enough to seem true—to cast doubt on the manner and actuality of Adolf Hitler's demise. Kingsepp's and Rosenfeld's work, like many of the chapters in this book, beg numerous questions relating to the morbid fascination with the minutiae of Hitler's life (particularly his sexual prowess) and the artifacts of the Nazi past on which popular culture seems to thrive.[42] Donald McKale worries about the implications of this general fascination by asserting that it elevates Hitler to the plane of the "inhuman" and "godlike,"[43] as does Ron Rosenbaum in his book *Explaining Hitler:* "It might come as a surprise to many that the very notion of attempting to explain Hitler should seem not merely difficult itself but dangerous, forbidden, a transgression of near-biblical proportions."[44] In many respects, all scholars in this field are forced to walk a precipitous tightrope strung between ongoing fascination with all things jackbooted and swastika'd and scholarship. We do so without a net.

Eva Kingsepp's chapter "Hitler as Our Devil?" introduces the idea not only of secularized evil but also of the specific responses of particular audiences to the tsunami-proportioned amount of material relating to Nazi Germany that is available in mainstream media. Kingsepp offers a handy categorization placing some of this material into five main thematic types: apocalypse, mystery, hubris, scientific aberration, and exoticism. In some texts, more than one of these key themes is present, but there is always at least one. It is not only fictional texts that employ these thematic elements; documentaries and docudramas also make ample use of them. She also shows how the Nazi documentary industry has become self-perpetuating, with its own internal logic and internal engines driving it on, even when most of the material presented to audiences is largely repetitive and offers no real insights. The disturbing implication of Kingsepp's analysis is that the ongoing market for these repetitively themed and framed documentaries is precisely that—their ongoing market. Such texts are endlessly recyclable because the themes to which Nazism is attached are so attractive and because the great Nazi evil is unexplainable. The mystery remains mysterious and it is the inexplicability of the mystery that we buy into, over and over again. Nazism, in this sense, is the perfect consumer product.

Kingsepp is one of a very few scholars who has undertaken an audience study of the reception of Nazi representations in mainstream culture. Significantly, as she herself acknowledges, there is much more scholarly work available on neo-Nazism and radical right-wing politics than on popular representations of Nazism.[45] Because of many neo-Nazis' overt connections to and approbations of Hitler and the Third Reich, this collection does not focus on neo-Nazism as such. Of course neo-Nazis tend to glorify the reality of the Nazi past: its racism, violence, genocidal tendencies, and political messages. In contrast, what mainstream representations of Nazism tend to glorify are the aesthetic trappings of Nazism, devoid of a proper historical context, the reality of genocide, and total war. Kingsepp uses the evidence she collected from interviews including a group of, admittedly self-selected, Swedish Second World War enthusiasts to disagree in part with Rosenfeld's ideas on the normalization of Nazism in western society, by showing that there are groups and individuals who disparage what they scathingly refer to as mainstream media representations of the Nazi past.[46] What Kingsepp does not critique in her chapter is how her audience is critical precisely because of their fascination with the Third Reich and its history. Her group meets all the criteria of the fascination with Nazism that is so integral to this collection, but they remain under the radar to many studies because of their interest in pulp productions rather than in replicating Nazi politics. Rather ironically, these enthusiasts, while questioning the accuracy of mainstream depictions and expressing frustration at certain kind of narratives, still seem to keep going back for more.

Sarah Winters's chapter on the ways in which Nazism has become the secular equivalent of religious evil in literature and related film intended for young audiences overlaps with Kingsepp's chapter. If, 50 years after its original publication, we take God out of C. S. Lewis's intended Christian allegory *The Lion, the Witch and the Wardrobe* for a much more secular young audience, then how do we indicate the ultimate evil incarnate in the White Witch? We give her a Nazi salute. Winters argues that contemporary young adult fantasy writers have moved away from ideas of religious evil to evil that is historical. Yet the problem still remains that this historical evil is removed from its historical context and carries with it the same mythic signification as any kind of biblical analogy. The issues of empty signification, thereby, remain. As Winters so neatly puts it: "Indeed, the genre of fantasy seems to demand some sort of Dualist vision of evil not only because it so often constructs its narrative around the battle between good and evil but also because any attempt to imagine evil as nothing results in a linguistically constructed *something*." It is not a great leap, therefore, to consider how the evil we all consider to be unimaginable and yet historical can have been so prolifically imagined and constantly referred to throughout popular literature and film for adults and children alike.

In chapter 4, Marc Hieronimus explores the guilty and not-so-guilty pleasure of laughing at Hitler and asks the question of whether or not this is (or ever will be) really acceptable. Hieronimus traces comic book humor that is both aimed at Nazism and uses Nazism as tropes for dictatorship and evil from the immediate post-war period through to the present. Like a number of our contributors, Hieronimus pinpoints the 1960s and the Eichmann trial as the turning point for both analysis and representation—even in the fantastic realms of comic book authors and artists. The representation of Eichmann's evil as ordinary or banal through Hannah Arendt's work opened up the subject of Nazism for much more humorous treatment, as horrifying as that may sound given the genocidal implications of the "banality of evil." Hieronimus also deals directly with one of the main problems this collection seeks to address—the separation of the Holocaust from Hitler and the Nazis—and cites Terrence Des Pres's "Holocaust etiquette" as a key motivation for that development.

Comic book artists do, on the whole, still treat the Holocaust as sacred, and the sacred rarely features in the comic world. The Nazis, on the other hand, are profane. Since profanity is a big part of humor, and has been since the time of Aristotle, it is entirely unsurprising that Nazism features in comic book representations. The separation of Nazism from the Holocaust and the profane from the sacred are useful devices in the ongoing belittlement of Hitler and the Nazis. What better weapon against the forces of evil from the past is there than to ridicule them in the present, thus enhancing the feelings of superiority to which the victors in any supposedly just war feel themselves entitled? What better means of elevating present generations over the actions and heroes, who turn out to be the villains, of the past by using laughter and humor? Hieronimus shows us how such humorous representations can lead to absurd ends and wonders whether there is a troubling conclusion to the increasing decontextualization of the Nazi past, where we can in one instance "turn the leadership circle of the Third Reich into a clique of likeable homeboys" and, in another, push the boundaries of what is acceptably funny by invoking the violence and horror of the Nazi concentration camps.

Lynn Rapaport's chapter on the eroticization of Nazism in popular culture works with a number of liminal boundaries, including the line between the sacred and profane that Hieronimus discusses and the blurred boundaries between pornography and mainstream cinema. It should come as no surprise that *Ilsa, She-Wolf of the SS* is a favorite of film director

Quentin Tarantino. The sexual elements of this sexploitation film pale in comparison to its uses of violence and its claims to be based on a true story. Rapaport's chapter, originally published in 2003 by the journal *Shofar,* broke new ground in the discussion of the sexual theater of Nazism. As early as the 1940s, Jean Genet typified fascism (and by implication Nazism) as sexual theater, as drama that allures because it is taboo and forbidden.[47] In the early 1970s, Sontag developed this idea further by suggesting that people purposely invoke the Nazi past in the theatricalization of sexuality. In staging sex in this way (particularly in sado-masochism), participants hope the ideas that Nazism stands for—power, violence, aesthetic beauty—offer them a "reserve of sexual energy [that] can be tapped."[48] Nazism has been fetishized in mainstream and not-so-mainstream sexual narratives since the Eichmann trial in particular, as the work by Amit Pinchevsky and Roy Brandt on Israeli stalag fiction of the 1960s and 1970s and Ahmed Al-Rawi's chapter in this volume also reiterate.[49] So while themes of domination and Nazism were linked in erotic texts before 1961 (particularly in United States men's magazines), after the Eichmann trial, they proliferated.[50]

Lynn Rapaport's chapter discusses how sado-masochism and its iconography have long used Nazi symbols because they are accessible tropes about power and violence. She explains that sexploitation films like *Love Camp 7* (1967) and its spin-offs, most notably *Ilsa, She-Wolf of the SS,* profane what is deemed sacred, namely the Holocaust. Yet they are incredibly popular—*Ilsa* was a huge box office success and is still on Amazon's top DVD sales lists today—because they link the traditional narrative of good versus evil with sexual pleasure and voyeurism. Furthermore, since popular culture has deemed that the most accessible expression of evil is Nazism, by inverting the traditional beast in the boudoir sexual relationship (excessive male, victimized female), sado-masochistic narratives reinforce (rather than invert) the traditional stereotype of women who control their sexual lives as evil. Yet Ilsa has inspired her own fan base and erotic subculture, including a California bar that suggests patrons dress in pseudo-military garb and *Ilsa* chic. She is also used to describe all manner of militaristic dominating female characters in popular culture today.[51] In this respect, Ilsa is unique, as one of the few female Nazis we encounter in popular culture, although she exhibits common traits with the archetypes mentioned earlier. She is the ultimate female Nazi—an all-powerful female villain and highly sexualized being, at once dominating men and representing their ideal fantasy. But Ilsa has much in common with a number of female characters who appear in the pulp fiction that Al-Rawi analyzes: she has been abused and is ultimately sexually degraded. She is both presented and defeated in a sexualized way that is unique to the portrayal of women in this kind of material.

Rapaport's work opens up new fields of inquiry in terms of the sexualization of Nazism and the ways in which Nazism is gendered. Ruth McLelland-Nugent takes a different approach to the analysis of Nazi representations and gender, through the examination of the character Wonder Woman, who first wore her star-spangled costume in a comic book that was published in 1941. Since then, like many of her superhero counterparts, she has often been engaged in battles with Nazis. But where other superheroes battle the dastardly deeds of Nazis and seek to combat their megalomania, Wonder Woman seeks to overcome their misogyny. Interestingly, the implicit misogyny inherent in many of the good all-American superheroes is never questioned—evil deeds against women must be overt and horrific and, therefore, are the province only of the ultimate enemy, the Nazis. Similarly, the holes in the historiography about women under the Nazi regime, which reflect a view that there were no women Nazis has a parallel in superhero comic book culture. The villainous Nazis that Wonder Woman faces are all male, and it is their hyper masculinity that underlies their aggression and brutality. They seek to wipe out the feminine, ergo the weak, and the power of love. The gender blindness of history naturally has its reflection in the mirror of popular culture, just as do the stereotypical portraits of monocled male monsters in shiny black boots.

Ahmed Al-Rawi also deals with caricatures of comic-like proportions in his fascinating work on the ways in which Arabs have been cast as Nazis in pulp fiction published from the immediate post-war period to the present. Strongly reflecting western perceptions of Arab politics and their quest for self-determination, these books are published on cheap paper for a mass audience and are available at any train station or airport newsstand. Different authors follow formulas that link Arabs to Nazis in ways that seek to diminish the legitimacy of Arab claims for independence and independent territory by rendering them evil by association. Al-Rawi takes a dual approach in his analysis. He begins by examining the history of Arab quests for independence and the relationships between some groups and Germany in their desire to free themselves from the yokes of British and French imperialism. He then traces the changes in depictions of these relationships through time. Some of the works he examines come under the allohistorical label as examined by Rosenfeld; many depict Arabs as anti-Semitic; and all portray Arabs as tarred with the same evil brush as the Nazis in their desire to wipe the Jewish state of Israel off the map. None of these popular books convey any real understanding of the politics of the Middle East. Instead, they project extreme versions of the pro-Zionist stances of post-war Britain and the United States. Pulp they may be, but they simultaneously reflect and feed off popular perceptions of Nazi evil and Middle East politics.[52]

Cynthea Masson explores the interplay between real and allegorical monsters in her chapter on Nazism in Joss Whedon's creations *Buffy the Vampire Slayer* and *Angel*. In both television series, Whedon toys with numerous references to Nazism and its remediations and, in the process, inverts the clear-cut binaries of good versus evil that we usually associate with Nazism.[53] He not only gives us a slayer who loves a vampire but also offers us a vampire with a soul, as mythically potent as the good German trope. Rarely is evil in a Whedon text of the "straight up black-hat-tie-you-to-the-train-tracks-soon-my-electro-ray-will-destroy-Metropolis-bad" variety.[54] Rather it is nuanced and often seductive, and it is always about power. The episode in season 5 of *Angel* titled "Why We Fight" depicts vampires fighting vampires, but to what end and for whose benefit? The Nazis, it seems, have been recruiting vampires and other demons to breed their own monstrous army, but their demons are proving to be too unpredictable to control. As a criticism of the United States' reliance on military might as a solution to world problems, this episode also depicts the Americans engaged in a similar endeavor—they employ Angel, whom they know to be a vampire, to rescue a submarine carrying vital Nazi intelligence. Significantly, this episode draws on the history of visual association of vampirism with Nazism as well as histories of German cinema. The character the Prince of Lies resembles F. W. Murnau's *Nosferatu, A Symphonie of Horror* (1922), which was remade in 1979 by Werner Herzog and remediated again in *In the Shadow of the Vampire* (2000), where monsters and the myths of film become indistinguishable. The fact that "Why We Fight" takes place on a submarine is also reminiscent of the 1981 German film *Das Boot*, which in many ways distances the submariners from the Nazis, depicting them as honorable military men in much the same way as members of the Wehrmacht have often been portrayed as being different from other Nazis.

In many ways, what Masson's chapter alludes to is that popular representations of Nazism are not without their own critics from within. Through his use of clever remediations and nuanced referencing of the Nazi past, Whedon asks important questions of how popular culture generally fails to be critical of itself or of the past, which it so easily typifies as good versus evil. Another popular text that critiques its audience's conceptualizations of the Nazi past, but one that is not studied in this collection, is Mel Brooks's *The Producers* (1968, 2001, and 2005).[55] In Brooks's text, an unsuccessful musical producer and his accountant come up with a fail-safe way of making vast amounts of money by seeking funds to finance a neo-Nazi musical romp titled *Springtime for Hitler,* which they are sure will be forcibly closed after opening night. In the end, *Springtime for Hitler,* with its gloriously uniformed dancing SS officers, a gorgeous blonde bombshell wearing little more than a swastika, and an over-the-top camp and singing Adolf Hitler, is a raging success, not only with the audience of the musical in the film, but also with the actual audience of the film/show (us). While we laugh uproariously at "Der Guten Tag Hop-Clop" and the many inversions of Nazi evil (from the camp to the downright ridiculous), we must also be aware that Brooks is asking us—his audience—a very important question: why are we laughing with such abandon at something that his producer characters rightly assume should (given the historical context of the Nazi past) abhor us? What Brooks and Whedon have both done is turn the mirrors that we think we have trained on the Nazi monsters of the past on ourselves. The reflections from their mirrors at least should make us think.

Another surprisingly critical reflection of the Nazi past in popular culture comes from the complex subculture of the Neofolk movement. In chapter 9, Emily Turner-Graham skillfully analyzes and isolates the bands Von Thronstahl and Ostara for some of the Nazi imagery they use and the messages they have about what they feel is lacking in contemporary Europe. Whereas Adam Leigh argues that Neofolk groups use Nazism as emotionless if evocative props (as the empty signifiers that we witness elsewhere in popular culture), Turner-Graham argues that both groups have a very good idea of the Nazi past, its meaning, and its relevance for today's world, as they view it. Above all, they use Nazi symbols as means to protest what they perceive as the homogenization of Europe and to, among other things, critique what they perceive as a lack of freedom of speech and a lack of critical reflection in European society more broadly. This protest is best evoked by the words of Richard Leviathan, singer-songwriter of Ostara, when he states that "[t]o play devil's advocate for the most demonic movement in history is still heresy."[56] The groups use Nazism not because they believe in the aesthetics, political messages, power or violence of the Nazi past, but as a way to question the present.

Of course, one need not look far to see that popular music groups—from David Bowie and the Sex Pistols in the 1970s and 1980s to Ministry in the 1990s and Yugoslavian band Laibach in the early 2000s—have used Nazism as means to shock and protest. As Jason Hanley explained in his 2004 article "The Land of Rape and Honey," despite the stated shock value of all these groups—among which he would include Von Thronstahl and Ostara—the audience reception of Nazi (and fascist) imagery is often of the acceptance or promotion of hate politics.[57] As a result, the satirical or think-for-yourself element of the music is lost in the aesthetic appeal and overwhelming imagery of the symbols utilized. That thousands of fans of Croatian rock group Thompson's concerts around the world readily engage in Ustashe war cries, Nazi salutes, and violent behavior, suggests more than ever that Nazi symbology has become part of a much wider mainstream musical culture that evades any real understanding of the recent past.[58]

Where all these elements of popular culture converge, of course, is in the classrooms of history teachers, who face the daunting task of teaching the Third Reich and Holocaust to an audience already well versed in the myths, legends, and symbolic emptiness of Nazi evil. Claire Hall's chapter asks the question that inspired us to begin this collection in the first place: "Where does evil sit in the classroom?" She charts the difficulties of teaching about Nazism and the Holocaust in British secondary schools and urges her colleagues not to look to popular culture to help them make the Nazi past accessible to their students, nor to embrace the limitations of the national curriculum. Instead, she advises teachers to return to a disciplinary approach to this complicated past. Read real history written by real historians and fight your students' misconceptions with historical questioning and contextualization. She admits this is a difficult and often overwhelming task but that it is also too important for us (as teachers) to refuse.

In the final chapter of the collection, Brigitte Sion discusses various post-war remediations of the Nazi Wehrmacht propaganda magazine *Signal:* first in an art exhibition by French artist Christian Boltanski and, second, in an exhibition of French *Signal* photographer André Zucca's work on Paris under Nazi occupation. Boltanski's exposition brings out the propagandistic nature of the content of the original magazine by juxtaposing photographs and heightening awareness of what was not shown in them: the suffering, violence, and horror of Nazi-occupied Europe. In direct contrast, the photo exhibition on Paris during the Second World War deals uncritically with the nature of the *Signal* photographs, the rationale for why they were taken, or the context in which the photographer took them (he was in the paid employ of the Wehrmacht and, in effect, a collaborator of the occupiers). The free-floating signifiers of the photographs have become so far removed from their original anchorage within Nazi propaganda that they have been used in a display that might as well be used in a tourist brochure on Paris. The photographs do not depict the difficulties of life under the German regime during the war, they do not reference poverty or anti-Semitism, and the Historical Library of Paris seems to have done much to obscure the collaborationist activities of Zucca himself. What Sion's chapter argues is that above all else, and this is a highly appropriate place to finish this collection, when we do not offer proper context to the imagery and ideas that represent the past, we are allowing the propaganda of that past to flourish and, even more disturbingly, we are enabling almost anything at all to represent that past to us.

Conclusion

As historians, what is most striking to us is that the western world's fascination with Nazism seems to have clear historical antecedents in the Nazi era itself. The historian Ian Kershaw has written extensively about the prevalence of the Hitler myth in the Third Reich.[59] Between 1933 and 1945, this myth was carefully, cleverly, and universally propagated within and outside Germany and occupied Europe and received widespread popular acceptance. It certainly continued to hold currency through to the 1970s, as the *Was ich über Adolf Hitler gehört habe* (What I know of Adolf Hitler) questionnaires in West Germany attest to.[60] It continues to have popular currency even today. A question we ask all our students before we start our "Nazi Germany and Its Legacies" course at the University of Auckland is: "What is your opinion of Adolf Hitler and the NSDAP?" Their responses tellingly illustrate the allure of Hitler as an evil madman, who was also a remarkable leader who pulled Germany out of the Great Depression, a charismatic public speaker who mesmerized the German public, and a political genius who nevertheless brought Germany and the world to rack and ruin in the Second World War. When, in a subsequent lecture, we explain Kershaw's perspective on the Hitler myth, I specifically ask them: "Who thinks the Hitler myth is still alive today?" I then read out their own words, with the hope that they may themselves become aware of how deep-seated their own fascination is with the appeal of Hitler and the aesthetics of Nazism.

Notes

With grateful thanks to Assoc. Prof. Gordon Morrell for his helpful comments and edit of this introduction.

1. For examples, see "Nazi Incident Seen as Bullying," "Schoolboys Agree to Tell People of Nazi Horrors," *New Zealand Herald,* available at http://www.nzherald.co.nz/nz/news/article.cfm?c_id=1&objectid=10605295 (accessed October 2009); "Grammar Boys Will Apologise for Bowing to Nazi Flag," *New Zealand Herald,* available at http://www.nzherald.co.nz/nz/news/article.cfm?c_id=1&objectid=10604135 (accessed October 2009); "Students' Nazi Facebook Photos 'Ignorant,'" *New Zealand Herald,* available at http://www.nzherald.co.nz/nz/news/article.cfm?c_id=1&objectid=10604135 (October 2009); "Students to Apologise for Nazi regalia Stunt," available at http://www.stuff.co.nz/national/education/2978756/Students-to-apologise-for-Nazi-regalia-stunt (accessed October 2009). The incident featured prominently on all New Zealand news networks at the time.

2. "Students Ordered to Pay Fine, Visit Museum," available at http://www.stuff.co.nz/national/education/2950094/Students-ordered-to-pay-fine-visit-museum (accessed October 2009).

3. Alan Bennett, *The History Boys* (New York, Faber and Faber, 2004), p. 74.

4. James Cullinane, "Review: Wolfenstein," *gameplanet.co.nz,* available at http://www.stuff.co.nz/technology/games/2812534/Review-Wolfenstein (accessed September 2009).

5. *Indiana Jones and the Raiders of the Lost Ark* (1981).

6. "Huey, Dewey and Louie and 'Mein Kampf,'" *Der Spiegel* web site, available at http://www.spiegel.de/international/0,1518,350927,00.html (accessed November 2009); "Donald Fights the Nazis," *Deutsche Welle* web site, available at http://www.dw-world.de/dw/article/0,1549079,00.html (accessed November 2009).

7. Susan Donaldson James, "German AIDS Charity in Bed with Hitler, Stalin," *ABC News,* available at http://abcnews.go.com/Health/AIDS/german-hitler-ad-shocks-aids-charities-us-uk/Story?id=8516276 (accessed October 2009); "Protest against 'Hitler' AIDS Video," available at http://stuff.co.nz/world/europe/2843676/Protest-against-Hitler-Aids-video (accessed September 2009).

8. *Family Guy* (1999–today).

9. All clips available on Youtube.com http://www.youtube.com/watch?v=T8dl4faCpJE&feature=related; http://www.youtube.com/watch?v=V7aM-VH9eS0; http://www.youtube.com/watch?v=sfkDxF2kn1I&feature=related (accessed October 2009). For other popular representations of Nazism, see Adam Shreve, "'Buenos Noches, Mein Fuhrer': A Look at Nazism in Popular Culture," *Journal of Popular Culture,* Vol. 35, No. 4 (2002), pp. 103–112.

10. See Eva Kingsepp's chapter in this collection for more on the intradiagetic use of Hitler's voice and image.

11. "Harry Says Sorry for Nazi Costume," *bbc.co.uk,* available at http://news.bbc.co.uk/2/hi/uk_news/4170083.stm (accessed October 2009).

12. Hannah Arendt, *Eichmann in Jerusalem: A Report on the Banality of Evil* (New York, Viking Press, 1963).

13. Ron Rosenbaum has written an excellent book on this subject—*Explaining Hitler: The Search for the Origins of His Evil* (New York, Random House, 1998)—in which, among many other things, he quotes the historian Alan Bullock, "if he [Hitler] isn't evil, who is?" (p. xxi).

14. Susan Sontag, "Fascinating Fascism," *New York Review of Books,* February 6, 1975, reprinted in Susan Sontag, *Under the Sign of Saturn* (New York, Farrar, Straus and Giroux, 1980), pp. 73–105; Saul Friedländer, *Reflections of Nazism: An Essay on Kitsch and Death* (New York, Harper & Row, 1982). There is a growing literature on the eroticization of fascism in twentieth-century popular culture, for which see Laura Frost, *Sex Drives: Fantasies of Fascism in Literary Modernism* (Ithaca, NY, Cornell University Press, 2002); Dagmar Herzog, *Sex after Fascism: Memory and Morality in Twentieth-Century Germany* (Princeton, NJ, Princeton University Press, 2005). In a recent article, James Page attempts to deconstruct the attraction of the Third Reich by addressing four continuing appeals of Nazism, namely: the Nazi aesthetic, the militaristic nature of Nazi society, the historical idiosyncrasy of the Third Reich, and the discourse of tragedy that surrounds Nazi Germany. Page's analysis is rather cursory and unconvincing in parts, and he also does not engage with what we find most striking about the ongoing appeal of Nazism in popular culture, namely the association between Nazism and evil: "Deconstructing the Enduring Appeal of the Third Reich," *Journal of Intercultural Studies,* Vol. 29, No. 2 (May 2008), pp. 189–196.

15. Nina Auerbach, *Our Vampires, Ourselves* (Chicago, Chicago University Press, 1995).

16. For a useful dichotomy between the good chaste woman in Holocaust representations and the bad sexualized Nazi collaborator, see Sara R. Horowitz, "The Gender of Good and Evil: Women and Holocaust Memory," in Jonathan Petropoulus and John K. Roth, eds., *Gray Zones: Ambiguity and Compromise in the Holocaust and Its Aftermath* (New York, Berghahn Books, 2005), pp. 170–173.

17. Alvin H. Rosenfeld, *Imagining Hitler* (Bloomington, Indiana University Press, 1985); Linda Mizejewski, *Divine Decadence: Fascism, Female Spectacle, and the Makings of Sally Bowles* (Princeton, NJ, Princeton University Press, 1992), p. 5.

18. Mizejewski, *Divine Decadence,* p. 5.

19. Richard J. Evans, *Rereading German History, 1800–1996: From Unification to Reunification* (London, Routledge, 1997), p. 168.

20. Friedländer, *Reflections of Nazism,* p. 21.

21. *The Sound of Music* (1965). See also Robert von Dassanowsky, "An Unclaimed Country: The Austrian Image in American Film and the Sociopolitics of *The Sound of Music,*" *Bright Lights Film Journal,* Vol. 41 (2003), available at http://www.brightlightsfilm.com/41/soundofmusic.htm (accessed November 2009); Johannes von Moltke, "Trapped in America: The Americanization of the Trapp-Familie, or 'Papas Kino' Revisited," *German Studies Review,* Vol. 19, No. 3 (1996), pp. 455–478.

22. As quoted in Finlo Rohrer, "The Cult of The Sound of Music," *BBC News Magazine,* available at http://news.bbc.co.uk/go/pr/fr/-/2/hi/uk_news/magazine/5262588.stm (accessed August 2009).

23. For example, see "German Nazification Phase 1 Seizure of Power 1933: January 30/American Nazification Phase 1 Seizure of Power 2000: November," available at http://www.hermes-press.com/nazification_step3.htm (accessed November 2003); "We Are Respectable Negroes Blog" (Monday October 19, 2009), available at http://wearerespectablenegroes.blogspot.com/2009/10/gop-is-like-pookie-in-new-jack-city.html (accessed October 2009); "Limbaugh Compares Obama to Hitler Again (and Again), Young Turks Episode," available at http://www.youtube.com/watch?v=X8w-Ll0JXSU (accessed October 2009). Thanks to Ruth McClelland-Nugent for providing us with the last two references.

24. William Collins Donahue, "The Popular Culture Alibi: Bernhard Schlink's Detective Novels and the Culture of Politically Correct Holocaust Literature," *German Quarterly,* Vol. 77, No. 4 (Fall 2004), p. 463.

25. Donahue, "The Popular Culture Alibi," p. 463.

26. See Lynn Rapaport's chapter in this collection.

27. Hannes Heer, for example, worried that the focus on victimhood in Holocaust memorialization has resulted in the "perpetrators [having] disappeared" from German public consciousness, as noted by Laurel Cohen-Pfister and Dagmar Wienroeder-Skinner, "History and the Memory of Suffering: Rethinking 1933–1945," in Laurel Cohen-Pfister and Dagmar Wienroeder-Skinner, eds., *Victims and Perpetrators:*

1933–1945: (Re)Presenting the Past in Post-Unification Culture (Berlin, Germany, Walter de Gruyter, 2006), p. 6.

28. Robert Harris, *Fatherland* (London, Arrow, 1992); Donahue, "The Popular Culture Alibi"; Bernhard Schlink and Walter Propp's *Selb's Justiz* (published in English as *Self Punishment*) was originally published in 1987. A number of other Gerhard Selb novels followed authored solely by Schlink.

29. See Marc Hieronimus's chapter in this collection.

30. Gavriel Rosenfeld, *The World Hitler Never Made: Alternate History and the Memory of Nazism* (Cambridge, Cambridge University Press, 2005), p. 15; Gavriel D. Rosenfeld, "Alternate Holocausts and the Mistrust of Memory," in Petropoulos and Roth, *Gray Zones,* pp. 147–164. See also his chapter in this collection.

31. "Sweet Nazi Chic: It Could Only Have Happened in Thailand," available at http://absolutelybangkok.com/sweet-nazi-chic-it-could-only-have-happened-in-thailand/ (accessed November 2009).

32. "They Dressed Well," *Time Asia,* Vol. 156, No. 22 (June 5, 2000), available at http://www.time.com/time/asia/magazine/2000/0605/southkorea.trouble.html (accessed January 2009).

33. "Girls Generation Accused of War Crimes," Pop Seoul web site, available at http://popseoul.com/2009/06/23/girls-generation-accused-of-war-crimes/ (accessed September 2009).

34. "Romanian Mayor Sorry about Nazi Uniform," *CBC News,* available at http://www.cbc.ca/gfx/images/news/photos/2009/07/23/constantia-radu-mazare-cp-RT.jpg (accessed September 2009); "Calls for Romanian Mayor to Resign Over Nazi Uniform," *FoxNews.com,* available at http://www.origin.foxnews.com/printer_friendly_story/0,3566,534340,00.html (accessed September 2009).

35. See Cats Who Look Like Hitler web site available at www.catsthatlooklikehitler.com (accessed November 2009); Smile, Hitler! Hitler Smiley Faces web site available at http://www.cobracountry.com/articles-cobra/humordept-cobra/hitler.html (accessed November 2009); Desiree Costume Shop (Auckland) available at http://www.desiree.co.nz/uniforms.php (accessed November 2009).

36. Donald M. McKale, *Hitler: The Survival Myth* (New York, Stein and Day, 1981), p. 200.

37. McKale, *Hitler,* pp. 207–208.

38. James E. Young, *The Texture of Memory: Holocaust Memorials and Meaning* (New Haven, CT, Yale University Press, 1993).

39. Rosenfeld, *The World Hitler Never Made.*

40. See Rosenfeld, *The World Hitler Never Made;* McKale, *Hitler;* Donald M. McKale, "Hitler's Children: A Study of Postwar Mythology," *Journal of Popular Culture,* Vol. 15 (1981), pp. 46–55. For an example of the persistence of the myth today, see: "Skull Thought to Be Hitler's Is from Woman," available at http://www.stuff.co.nz/oddstuff/2916466/Skull-thought-to-be-Hitlers-is-from-woman (accessed November 2009).

41. McKale, *Hitler,* p. 198.

42. For more, see McKale, *Hitler,* pp. 145–158.

43. See note 36.

44. Rosenbaum, *Explaining Hitler,* p. xv.

45. For example, see Nicholas Goodrick-Clarke, *Black Sun: Aryan Cults, Esoteric Nazism, and the Politics of Identity* (New York, New York University Press, 2002); Angelica Fenner and Eric D. Weitz, eds., *Fascism and Neofascism: Critical Writings on the Radical Right in Europe* (New York, Palgrave Macmillan, 2004).

46. For another of Eva Kingsepp's studies on Second World War fans, see " 'Nazi Fans' but Not Neo-Nazis: The Cultural Community of 'WWII fanatics,'" in Stefan Herbrechter and Michael Higgins, eds., *Returning (to) Communities: Theory, Culture and Political Practice of the Communal* (Amsterdam, Rodopi, 2006), pp. 223–240.

47. See Sontag, "Fascinating Fascism," pp. 104–105.

48. Sontag, "Fascinating Fascism," p. 105.

49. Amit Pinchevsky and Roy Brand, "Holocaust Perversions: The Stalags Pulp Fiction and the Eichmann Trial," *Critical Studies in Media Communication,* Vol. 24, No. 5 (December 2007), pp. 387–388.

50. Pinchevsky et al., p. 393.

51. Andrea Slane discusses the connections between Ilsa, Marlene Dietrich's Lola Lola, and the sexualization of women in politics in the chapter "Sexualized Nazis and Contemporary Popular Political Culture" in her book *A Not So Foreign Affair: Fascism, Sexuality, and the Cultural Rhetoric of American Democracy* (Durham, NC, Duke University Press, 2001), pp. 248–286.

52. For an excellent overview of Arab responses to the Holocaust and NSDAP see Meir Litvak and Esther Webman, *From Empathy to Denial: Arab Responses to the Holocaust* (New York, Columbia University Press, 2009).

53. For example, in season 1 of *Buffy the Vampire Slayer,* Whedon's main evil character, the leather-clad vampire, the Master, presents an ultimate vision of industrialized killings. The Master makes a major reappearance in season 3 in an alternate universe where Buffy never existed. Nazism is also referenced by book burnings ("Gingerbread," episode 11, season 3, *Buffy the Vampire Slayer,* 1999). In *Angel,* Nazism is referenced by the remediation of *Schindler's List* (1993) in the season 1 episode titled "Hero" to a direct engagement with actual Nazis and other assorted vampires in the season 5 episode "Why We Fight," which is the main reference point for Masson's chapter.

54. "Pangs," *Buffy the Vampire Slayer,* episode 8, season 4, 2000.

55. Mel Brooks directed the original film, *The Producers,* in 1968. Brooks subsequently turned it into a Broadway musical in 2001, and the musical was filmed in 2005, starring the original members of the Broadway cast, Nathan Lane and Matthew Broderick, and was directed by Susan Stroman. For more, see http://www.imdb.com/title/tt0395251/ (accessed November 2009).

56. As quoted in Emily Turner-Graham's chapter in this collection.

57. Jason J. Hanley, "'The Land of Rape and Honey': The Use of World War II Propaganda in the Music Videos of Ministry and Laibach," *American Music,* Vol. 22, No. 1 (Spring 2004), pp. 158–159.

58. Simon Wiesenthal Center Snider Social Action Institute, *Response: World Report,* Vol. 29, No. 2 (Fall/Winter 2007), p. 6, also available at http://www.wiesenthal.com/site/apps/s/content.asp?c=lsKWLbPJLnF&b=4442915&ct=5848709 (accessed November 2009).

59. Ian Kershaw, *The "Hitler Myth": Image and Reality in the Third Reich* (Oxford, Oxford University Press, 1987).

60. Dieter Bossmann, *Was ich über Adolf Hitler gehört habe...: Folgen eines Tabus: Auszüge aus Schüle—Aufsätzen von heute* (Frankfurt am Main, Germany, Fisher Taschenbuch Verlag, 1977). See also McKale, *Hitler,* pp. 200–201.

I

The "What Ifs?" of Nazism: Recent Alternate Histories of the Third Reich

Gavriel D. Rosenfeld

In an episode of the popular FOX animated television series, *Family Guy,* from the year 2000, the main character, Peter Griffin, sits in an airplane while talking on the phone with the grim reaper. The hooded figure tells him: "Peter, listen; without death, the world would be a terrible place. Imagine a world where Hitler was still alive!" The scene then dissolves to a mock television talk show titled *Hitler.* An enthusiastic announcer's voice intones: "Today on *Hitler,* we'll be talking with Hollywood hunk, Christian Slater!" The camera pans over to a smiling Adolf Hitler sitting behind a desk preparing to interview his guest. The notorious Nazi opens his questioning by suggestively remarking, "Now...they tell me in your next movie vee get to see your butt....Can vee see it right now?" As the audience roars in approval, the clip concludes with the announcer inform- ing viewers sitting at home: "If you're going to be in the Los Angeles area und would like tickets to *Hitler,* call '(213) DU WERDEST [*sic*] EINE KRANKENSCHWESTER BRAUCHEN!'"

Family Guy's portrayal of Hitler as a lewd talk show host can easily be dismissed as infantile drivel, but it is a notable example of an increas- ingly popular approach to representing the Nazi legacy in western popular culture. The clip is an example of alternate history (allohistory), a counter- factual mode of narrative representation that has been applied to the topic of the Third Reich with growing frequency in recent years. As I discussed in my book, *The World Hitler Never Made: Alternate History and the Memory of Nazism* (2005), the history of Nazi Germany has provided un- ending material for counterfactual speculation in the years since the end of the Second World War.[1] In Great Britain, the United States, Germany, and elsewhere, hundreds of alternate histories have appeared in the form of novels, short stories, films, television broadcasts, plays, comic books, and historical essays. These diverse works have explored an equally diverse range of questions: What if the Nazis had won the Second World War? What if Adolf Hitler had escaped from Nazi Germany in 1945 and become an international fugitive? What if Hitler had been assassinated or had never been born? What if the Holocaust had been completed or could somehow be undone? Since the publication of *The World Hitler Never Made,* major new works of alternate history have appeared on many of the aforementioned questions. This chapter intends to discover what they reveal about the evolving place of the Third Reich in western memory.

In *The World Hitler Never Made,* I argued that alternate histories of Nazism reflect the emergence of an increasingly normalized view of the Nazi era. By normalization, I mean the process whereby an unusually sensitive historical legacy, such as that of the Third Reich, ceases to be viewed from a wholly moralistic perspective and gradually becomes seen as a past like any other. This process can unfold organically over the course of time, with the passing of eyewitnesses to specific historical events, or it can be advanced intentionally via strategies of *relativization* (wherein the past's uniqueness is minimized through comparisons to other historical events), *universalization* (wherein the past's singularity is reduced in the process of explaining it as merely an outgrowth of timeless forces continuing into the present), or *aestheticization* (wherein the past's moral dimensions are neutralized via different narrative modes of representation).[2]

Whatever the method, since 1945 the moralistic perspective has visibly declined in the shifting portrayal of the nightmare and fantasy scenarios that underpin all alternate histories.[3] For example, while early post-war accounts of a Nazi victory in the Second World War bleakly portrayed a Nazi-ruled world as a dystopian hell on earth, later narratives have depicted it less harshly as a relatively tolerable place. Similarly, while early accounts of the world without Hitler showed it to be far better in his absence, later works have portrayed the world as being no better, if not worse. Finally, while early narratives of Hitler's survival depicted the fugitive *Führer* being brought to justice, later ones have shown him eluding justice's grasp, with a growing number—such as the recent *Family Guy* episode—playing his survival for laughs.[4] These diverging portrayals have reflected various motives, mostly having to do with the generational identities and political agendas of their creators, as well as the shifting social, economic, and political conditions in their respective countries.[5]

On balance, however, these works' representations reveal that the emotional impact of Nazism—especially the fears and fantasies it originally spawned—has begun to fade in western consciousness.

How do recent alternate histories of Nazism compare? No unifying trend links the major narratives of the last several years, but many have exhibited a tendency to universalize the significance of the Nazi era. Produced, for the most part, by younger writers of left-liberal backgrounds, these accounts have explored allohistorical scenarios related to the Third Reich in order to comment on, and usually critique, contemporary political trends, especially the growing turmoil in the Middle East in the wake of 9/11. In hitching their allohistorical narratives to present-day agendas, however, these accounts have diminished the Nazi era's singularity and have contributed to the larger process of normalization.

The Nazis Win the Second World War

Tne most popular allohistorical topic related to the Third Reich remains the nightmare scenario of the Nazis winning the Second World War. This premise remains especially popular among Anglophone writers, several of whom have recently published novels exploring what life would have been like in England had the Nazis triumphed in the war.[6] The most prominent example is the Welsh-born Canadian novelist Jo Walton's trilogy of numismatically titled books, *Farthing* (2006), *Ha'Penny* (2007), and *Half a Crown* (2008).[7] The series features a hard-boiled British detective named Peter Carmichael who becomes progressively enmeshed in his country's descent into fascism after its leaders forge a separate peace with the Nazis. As described in *Farthing,* the allohistorical point of divergence is Rudolf Hess's flight to England in May of 1941, which succeeds in convincing British leaders to sign a negotiated peace agreement one month later.[8] The novel is set nearly a decade later in 1949 and focuses on the murder of one of the agreement's main negotiators, Sir James Thirkie, a former MP and prospective candidate for prime minister who belongs to England's ruling aristocratic elite, the "Farthing Set" (named after their headquarters, Castle Farthing, in Hampshire). At the novel's opening, Thirkie is found stabbed to death in his bedroom with a yellow Star of David pinned to his chest. Suspicion immediately falls upon a Jewish guest staying at the estate, David Kahn, a banker and fierce anti-Nazi who is married to the daughter of the Farthing Estate's owner and government minister, Lord Eversley. Most of the novel follows Detective Carmichael in his effort to unravel the crime and determine whether Kahn is guilty or is being framed for political motives. He increasingly comes to suspect the latter after Thirkie's brother-in-law, Mark Normanby, is named prime minister and proceeds to seize near-dictatorial powers using the pretext of the growing "Bolshevik Jewish menace" facing the country.[9] Eventually Carmichael discovers that the killers are, in fact, Normanby and his wife, Angela, who want to eliminate Thirkie because of his opposition to Normanby's power grab. Yet when Carmichael informs his boss at Scotland Yard, Inspector Penn-Barkis, that he has cracked the case, he is told to drop it and charge Kahn with the crime instead. Carmichael protests, but Penn-Barkis coldly reveals that he knows of the detective's homosexual identity and forces him to go along with the frame-up for the sake of political expediency. As the novel concludes, Carmichael reluctantly recognizes that his silence has turned him into a collaborator with his country's fascist government.

The sequel, *Ha'Penny,* picks up the story in 1949 with England sliding deeper into fascism. The plot focuses mostly on Carmichael's effort to prevent the assassination of Prime Minister Normanby and a visiting dignitary, the *Führer* of Nazi Germany, Adolf Hitler. The novel's central plot of killing Hitler is discussed in more detail later in this chapter, but *Ha'Penny's* main subplot provides a further glimpse of a British propensity for collaboration. The novel's main character, a politically apathetic actress named Viola Larkin, resists the effort of her politically engaged friends to enlist her in the assassination plot, which is supposed to take place during a theatrical performance attended by the two leaders. As she tells one of the plotters, Uncle Phil, "You say Normanby had a bloodless coup. What's the difference between that and the bloody coup you're suggesting? I think you're exaggerating how awful they are.... [P]olitics is politics. Mr Churchill...wouldn't...do anything differently from...Normanby. As for Hitler, what happens in the Reich isn't any of our business."[10] Larkin goes so far as to tell Uncle Phil that ordinary Britons actually "like the idea of our having a proper leader, a fuhrer to sort us out."[11] Finally, Larkin's stance is shown to be representative of that of many Britons. When she tells another of the plotters, an Irishman named Devlin, that she does not "think Stalin's any better than Hitler," he responds by saying: "England is like a country of sleepwalkers, walking over the edge of a cliff, and has been these last eight years. You're prosperous, you're content and you don't care what's going on the other side of the Channel as long as you can keep on having boat races and horse shows."[12] In the face of such apathy, the efforts of the patriotic plotters—including the still somewhat ambivalent Viola Larkin—predictably fail. At the novel's conclusion, Carmichael succeeds in alerting Normanby and Hitler to the bomb's presence in the theater and the two dictators end up surviving the ensuing blast.

The trilogy's final installment, *Half a Crown,* is set a decade later in 1960, and portrays England as having fully embraced fascist rule. By this time, the Nazis have defeated the Soviets—they nuke Moscow—and the Japanese have defeated the United States. In England, domestic anti-Semitism has reached a fever pitch as Normanby's government decides to deport the country's Jews to a new death camp located near the southeastern English town of Gravesend. Most Britons are comfortable in this new dystopian world. As the novel's protagonist, an 18-year-old girl under Carmichael's guardianship, Elvira Royston, declares to one of her teenage friends, "fascism ... [is] fun!"[13] By contrast, Detective Carmichael, has developed moral qualms about his complicity with the new order. Although he has been named director of an organization known as "The Watch" (a British version of the Gestapo), he works behind the scenes to smuggle British Jews to freedom. This activity helps him to maintain his dignity. Or as a colleague encouragingly puts it: "You failed a test, yes, ... but you have never surrendered your soul. And I believe it's the same for the whole country."[14]

This remark serves as a hopeful beacon that allows the novel to end on a redemptive note. *Half a Crown* goes on to portray the emergence of domestic political upheaval in England after Normanby's government orders the deportation to Gravesend of a group of British right-wing extremists belonging to the ultra-nationalist Ironsides organization who are hoping to install the Duke of Windsor on the throne as Edward VIII and establish a more dictatorial fascist government. Most ordinary Britons do not support the radical nationalists, but they believe that Normanby's government has exceeded its authority in indiscriminately deporting British citizens without confirming whether or not they belong to the group. As critical media reports and popular demonstrations erupt, the British people rediscover their democratic values. This trend culminates with the political awakening of the otherwise philo-fascist Elvira. After she naively betrays Carmichael for his clandestine activity on behalf of British Jews, she makes an about-face after being told the truth about Normanby's role in murdering

Thirkie 20 years earlier by Carmichael's confidante, the foreign minister, Sir Guy Braithewaite. The novel concludes with Elvira disclosing the explosive news to Queen Elizabeth at a debutante's ball held at the royal palace, and the Queen thereupon going on national television to announce Normanby's arrest and new national elections. As the novel ends, the message is clear: "England was taking her first tottering steps towards being free again."[15]

Whatever Walton's trilogy might lack in plausibility, it offers a clear perspective on the Nazi era. Throughout the post-war period, British alternate histories of a German victory in the Second World War have varied considerably in portraying the British people's behavior in a Nazi-ruled world. While early post-war accounts, like Noel Coward's 1947 play, *Peace in Our Time,* patriotically identified British collaboration as exceptionally rare, later works in the 1960s and 1970s, such as Kevin Brownlow and Andrew Mollo's 1964 film, *It Happened Here,* and Len Deighton's 1978 novel, *SS-GB,* portrayed collaboration as commonplace. Walton's novels resemble these latter works in pessimistically affirming Britain's potential to embrace fascism. Moreover, like the works of the 1960s, which were inspired by a leftist critique of post-war British decline, her nightmare scenario reflects a critical view of the present informed by left-liberal political views. An award-winning fantasy and science fiction writer born in Wales in 1964 (and currently a Canadian citizen), Walton was influenced by the post-9/11 political climate in writing her trilogy. As she put it in a recent interview,

> watching the US and the UK defy the UN and invade Iraq on a trumped up excuse was just too much like Hitler's invasion of Czechoslovakia and Poland for me. I'd been furious, and there hadn't been anything I could...do about it. Then there...[were the violations of] civil liberties....I started writing *Farthing* just after the Abu Ghraib revelations. I didn't set out to write something to draw explicit parallels. But it would be disingenuous to say I wasn't thoroughly aware of the implicit ones.[16]

Like left-leaning writers of an earlier generation, Walton essentially universalizes the significance of Nazism, sensing the presence of Nazi-style ideas even within democratic societies. To be sure, Walton's critique of her own present-day world is not as strident as those of the 1960s and 1970s, thanks to her trilogy's happy ending. By affirming the British people's capacity to revive their democratic values and reject fascism, she essentially endorses the post-war notion that the nation's struggle against the Nazis represented its "finest hour."[17] Yet, by instrumentally using the Nazi past for larger purposes, she diminishes its specificity and contributes to its normalization.

It is difficult to say whether Walton's novels have any representative significance for the British memory of the Nazi period. As they appeared with a United States publisher and had less exposure in the British market, most of the reviews appeared in North America. The trilogy's reception was largely positive, with reviewers praising it as "terrific," "convincing," and "one of the best speculative works produced in years."[18] Significantly, many reviewers commented on the books' presentist aspects. While one noted that "the analogies of this alternate history to our own world today are there to be drawn," another explicitly wrote that *Farthing* was "as much about Bush and Blair as...about World War II."[19] That these reviews noted Walton's universalization of the Nazi legacy without critiquing it suggests a willingness to accept her views of the past. Equally significant is the fact that her novels' themes were echoed in similar alternate histories that appeared at the same time. Murray Davies's novel, *Collaborator* (2003), also portrayed ordinary British people working with their German occupiers and compromising their morals in myriad ways until finally liberating themselves.[20] And Owen Sheers's novel, *Resistance* (2007), empathetically explored the circumstances that prompt the women of a Welsh farming village to collaborate with their German occupiers following the Nazi invasion of Britain in 1944.[21] These works, as well as their positive critical reception, suggest that British writers and readers have become more comfortable de-heroizing their own likely behavior under Nazi rule, a trend that may reflect the emergence of a more self-critical streak in the nation's identity in the years since 9/11.[22] Whatever the case may be, British alternate histories of a Nazi victory in the Second World War point to the ongoing normalization of memory.

The World without Hitler: Better or Worse?

Another popular counterfactual premise related to the Third Reich is the fantasy scenario of Hitler being eliminated from history. One of the more prominent works to tackle this theme in recent years is French writer Eric-Emmanuel Schmitt's novel, *Adolf H.: Zwei Leben (The Two Lives of Adolf H.)*.[23] Originally published in French in 2001 as *La Part de l'autre,* the novel juxtaposes two parallel narratives: one, a dramatic retelling of Hitler's real historical life story; the other, a speculative portrayal of how it would have been different had he been granted admission to (and not, as in real history, rejected from) the Academy of Fine Arts in Vienna in 1907. Schmitt's answer is that this lucky break would have been decisive in keeping the young man from embarking upon a life of political extremism. Thanks to his admission to art school, Hitler is able to undergo a profound psychological makeover, one that allows him to "experience joy" for the first time, arrive at a deeper sense of self-realization, and finally "become a man."[24] Hitler's transformation begins after he suffers a series of fainting spells in the presence of nude models during his first studio sketching classes. In attempting to unravel their cause, Hitler contacts his family doctor, Eduard Bloch, who recommends that he consult with the famed Vienna psychoanalyst Sigmund Freud. After several tense sessions with his reluctant and defensive patient, Freud determines that Hitler suffers from an unresolved Oedipal complex that can only be cured by losing his virginity. Before long, Hitler has several sexual relationships and comes to know a deeper set of human emotions that will eventually find expression in his art.

An even more important influence on Hitler's art is his alternate experience of the First World War. Unlike the real historical loner who finds a sense of purpose in combat, the young artist, after being drafted and serving at the front, turns into a pacifist. He is particularly traumatized by the death of his best friend from art school, Bernstein (who is both Jewish and gay), and after returning to Vienna in 1918, channels his feelings of anger into artistic creativity instead of political activism. In the post-war period, Hitler becomes an iconoclastic modernist, breaking with academic tradition "in a rage of destruction" and developing a unique brand of "Freudian painting."[25] Building upon this creative momentum, he moves to Paris, where he meets André Breton and joins up with the surrealist movement. Soon enough, Hitler meets with critical success and becomes rich, buying himself a Bugatti sports car and conducting amorous relationships with numerous women. His fame ends up being short-lived, however, and he eventually settles into a job as an art professor in Berlin, longing to recapture the creative energy of his early career. By the 1950s, he slowly falls into obscurity (abstraction is all the rage) and he eventually immigrates to the United States in the 1960s, settling in Santa Monica, where he spends his twilight years before dying in his sleep in 1970.

It is not just Hitler's personal life but the course of world history that takes a turn for the better as a result of his acceptance to art school. Without the existence of Hitler and the Nazi party, Germany's development is much more benign. Although the country remains plagued by crisis and witnesses the toppling of the Weimar Republic in the early 1930s, the forces responsible for the political upheaval are not the radical Nazis but the comparatively moderate German army. The new government is thus "authoritarian not totalitarian, conservative, not revolutionary."[26] Moreover, while the new government moves to overturn the Versailles Treaty, it does so in more limited fashion, foreswearing a racial-imperialist drive for *Lebensraum* in favor of a targeted campaign against Poland to recover lost German territories. The ensuing German-Polish war of 1939 is comparatively short in duration (it lasts a mere three months) and mild in its destruction (with around 10,000 German dead).[27] More importantly, it allows Germany to regain its self-respect and satiates the ambitions of its military rulers. There is thus no Second World War. In the decades that follow, Germany's government gradually evolves into a "genuine democracy" and goes on to become a world power, being the first country to develop nuclear weapons and put a man on the moon.[28] In this world, there is no cold war, as the United States remains a provincial backwater and the Soviet Union collapses in the 1960s in the face of popular discontent.[29] In short, thanks to Hitler's acceptance to art school, the world averts the main disasters of the twentieth century.

At first glance, Schmitt's novel appears to be an extreme exercise in normalizing Hitler's evil. The novel's alternate narrative humanizes Hitler to an extraordinary degree. It explains his evil as inherently circumstantial—the result of sexual dysfunction—and thus implies that it is easily treatable. Thanks to psychotherapy and a few healthy relationships, he is cured of his deviant tendencies, or, as Schmitt writes, "[a] ghost disappeared that could have been Adolf Hitler."[30] Moreover, Schmitt successfully convinces readers to root for Hitler's redemption. As he loses his off-putting traits, indeed, Hitler becomes a sympathetic figure. This is epitomized by Hitler's transformation from a Jew-hater into a philo-Semite. The ground for this transformation is prepared by Hitler's friendship with his art school chum, Bernstein, but it is cemented by the hostile attacks against Hitler's radical paintings, which right-wing German critics deride as "Jewish" (later art collectors even believe Hitler to be of Jewish background).[31] These attacks help Hitler to identify with the oppressed, and before long, he has an affair with a Jewish woman, whom he ends up marrying (they later have two children). Indeed, Hitler even becomes a Zionist in order to needle his highly assimilated German Jewish father-in-law.[32] Thanks to these developments, Hitler's evil disappears entirely. By the novel's end, most readers have probably come to share its underlying fantasy: if only Hitler had been granted a lucky career break, the course of history would have been vastly improved.

Schmitt's normalization of Hitler is undeniable, yet his novel shrewdly avoids the charge of ethical relativism thanks to its clever narrative structure. Befitting its title, *The Two Lives of Adolf H.* interweaves its portrayal of Hitler's allohistorical development with a loosely fictionalized account of his life as it occurred in real history. This juxtaposition of historical fiction with alternate history prevents readers from sympathizing too much with Hitler by reminding them of his real historical crimes. Schmitt, for example, makes sure to chart the evolution of Hitler's anti-Semitism and his involvement in the Holocaust, portraying him instructing Himmler: "It is time to find a final solution for the [Jewish] problem," and then thinking to himself, "*A radical final genocide. . . . Shoot them, gas them, and burn them, do with them what you want, the main thing is that it is effective.*"[33] By the time Schmitt gets around to depicting Hitler and Eva Braun's suicide in the *Führer*'s bunker, the author's views of the dictator's real historical evil are clear. Indeed, in the novel's postscript, Schmitt says as much, writing that he views Hitler as "an unforgivable criminal," whom he "hates and scorns."[34]

That said, Schmitt subtly normalizes the Nazi past by universalizing its significance for present-day purposes. Born in 1960, Schmitt is a prize-winning playwright and novelist who has produced numerous celebrated works, including the novella *Monsieur Ibrahim and the Flowers of the Koran* (which was made into a film starring Omar Sharif in 2003). Much of his writing revolves around issues of ethics and religion, a fact that reflects his academic background (he received a doctorate in philosophy from the elite École Normale Supérieur before becoming a full-time writer).[35] These concerns partly explain his intentions in writing the novel, which he says was meant to counteract the tendency of people to view

Hitler as a demonic aberration and ignore the evil that lies in themselves. As he put it,

> The common error with respect to Hitler is that he is seen as an incomprehensible monster.... Yet he was a normal person,... banal like you and I.... Who knows if tomorrow you or I could be the same? Who can be sure to be immune?...
>
> Today people caricature Hitler in order to whitewash themselves. The accusation is inversely proportional to the desire for self-exoneration—that is, the more "other" he is, the less similar he is to one's self.[36]

Schmitt is vague about the reasons for this whitewashing tendency, saying merely that "evil recurs today and will recur tomorrow."[37] But in the novel's postscript, he shows himself to have been influenced by left-wing political notions in declaring that it was only "through the revelations of the slaughter [of the Holocaust] that the... state of Israel was created.... Hitler was the creator of Zionism.... Without Hitler... one would not have built up Israel so hastily, and with such scorn for the indigenous population of Palestine."[38] Schmitt's additional claim that "without Hitler, America... never would have become the world's policeman" further suggests his sympathy to anti-imperialist ideas of left-wing provenance.[39] Although Schmitt claims to "keep... his distance from the world of... politics," his universalization of Hitler's evil follows the familiar pattern of other leftist writers who have applied the lessons of the Third Reich to present-day events.[40]

Schmitt's universalization of Hitler's evil also challenges the triumphalistic Anglo-American memory of the Nazi era. Ever since 1945, most British and United States alternate histories of the world without Hitler have confidently asserted that his removal from history would have done little to improve its course. Works such as Norman Spinrad's novel, *The Iron Dream* (1972) and Stephen Fry's novel, *Making History* (1996), among many others, have insisted that the structural realities of German nationalism, militarism, and racism would have produced a disaster even without Hitler.[41] This claim reflects a sense of contentment with the course of real history among Anglo-American writers and a corresponding lack of desire to wish it had unfolded otherwise. By contrast, German accounts have typically adhered to the fantasy scenario that removing Hitler from history would have improved its course. Although their small number makes it difficult to generalize about their underlying agendas, these accounts satisfy the desire of certain Germans to undo the events that led their nation into disaster and diminish their culpability for it by placing blame exclusively on the Nazi dictator. For his part, Schmitt clearly rejects the deterministic Anglo-American belief in the German people's penchant for political extremism and embraces a more universalistic position.[42] Declaring that "Hitler...lives in...every one of us," he asserts: "My novel...[is] a novel of freedom. It's up to us whether we become racist or tolerant, pacifist or warmongering, lovers or destroyers. We are free to choose."[43]

Schmitt's antideterminist stance reflects a French perspective toward the history of the Third Reich. Schmitt suggests as much in the novel's postscript, where he contrasts the self-confidence with which British historians have investigated the Third Reich—a self-confidence rooted in the fact that "the English were forced to resist [Hitler] and defeated him"— with the "embarrass[ment]" that the French continue to display toward the Nazi period.[44] This embarrassment, rooted in France's humiliating defeat of 1940, may explain why Schmitt is inclined to fantasize about improving the course of history by removing Hitler from it. Unlike the British and Americans, whose positive experiences in the Second World War have led them to vindicate history as it really happened (both believe the fight against the Nazis was "their finest hour" and the "good war," respectively), the French, like the Germans, have been inclined by their wartime suffering to fantasize about preventing the war from happening in the first place.[45] Schmitt's novel may thus be seen as an effort to restore France's national ego. By showing how real history could have easily been different—thanks to the contingent, rather than absolute, nature of Hitler's evil—his novel challenges the whiggish Anglo-American view that their wartime success was somehow foreordained.

This subtext is partly confirmed by the response to Schmitt's book. French reviewers largely praised it and explicitly endorsed many of Schmitt's claims. One reviewer agreed that the novel skillfully validated the fact that "fate...is nothing...but an illusion" and confirmed "the simple and tragic lesson [about] making the wrong choice" in life.[46] Another wrote that the book "forces the readers to ask themselves questions, quite disturbing ones, on the dark side which lays sleeping in them, in us."[47]

Surprisingly, even though Schmitt's book implicitly exonerates the German people of collective responsibility for the Nazi experience, German reviewers were far more critical of it. One objected to the book's allohistorical premise, writing that it was facile to think that "a bit of timely sex would have spared Germany all evil."[48] Another found it "scandalous" that Schmitt had made Hitler the "scapegoat for the Holocaust and the Second World War" and had "exonerated Germany and the collaborating powers of the majority of their guilt."[49] Most significantly, one German reviewer confirmed the suspicion that Schmitt's analysis provided the French with a way to "escape" their lack of pride in "their nation's wartime behavior" by declaring that all people could become Hitler.[50] In short, the review confirms that Schmitt may have universalized Hitler's evil to compensate for a French difficulty in coming to grips with the Third Reich's legacy. If these reviews are representative, then Schmitt's novel can in fact be seen as advancing the process of normalization.[51] The German response to it, however, confirms that, at least among German intellectuals, resisting the process of normalization and accepting historical responsibility for the lessons of the Nazi period has become an important part of the nation's postunification identity.[52]

Schmitt's novel may ultimately be exceptional, however, for other recent alternate histories have cast doubt on the value of removing Hitler from history. A good example is Jo Walton's novel *Ha'Penny,* whose plot, as noted earlier, focuses on the failure of a group of British conspirators to assassinate Hitler while on a state visit to England in 1949. The man who foils the plot, Detective Carmichael, faces the consequences of his actions at the novel's conclusion and significantly consoles himself with the belief that Hitler's death would have made little difference to the course of world events:

> Carmichael...simply stood there, trying to catch his breath. He had saved...Hitler and Normanby, when if he had simply sat still in his box, he could have rid the world of them....
>
> Then, as he stood there...he realized it didn't matter in the least....Hitler and Normanby were evil men, and there was a time when killing them would have changed everything, but that time had gone. If they had been killed tonight, it would only have been more ammunition for their side....[F]ascism wasn't something that could be killed with a bomb.[53]

This claim is further echoed when a co-conspirator, Viola Larkin, is told by an elderly aristocrat at a dinner party that the "Great Man theory of history" is nonsense. "No, nothing would be different. . . . Normanby's just doing his job. . . . Whoever else had his job would . . . do exactly what he's doing. This is what the people want, and we can't have communists and Jews going around murdering people."[54] Walton's skepticism about the efficacy of killing Hitler dovetails with most other Anglo-American alternate histories, though for different reasons. While Anglo-American skepticism mostly reflects the belief that killing Hitler would do little to mitigate the deep-seated political extremism of the German people, Walton's tale—set in a collaborationist, right-wing England—doubted the efficacy of killing the *Führer* because of her left-wing conviction that fascist tendencies lay within the British people as well. Unlike Schmitt, whose universalization of Nazism reflects the desire to lessen the weight of France's historical burdens, Walton is more self-critically inclined and has little time for escapist fantasies.

The diminishing appeal of such fantasies is further visible in the 2007 graphic novel *I Killed Adolf Hitler,* by the Norwegian cartoonist Jason (the pen name of John Arne Sæterøy).[55] This short but celebrated work is set in present-day Germany and features one of the artist's trademark dog-faced characters, an unnamed professional assassin, who is visited one day by an elderly scientist who hires him to use a time machine to return to the year 1938 and kill the Nazi dictator. The assassin agrees and goes back in time to fulfill his mission, but before he can shoot Hitler with his pistol, he is knocked out cold by one of the *Führer*'s bodyguards. Hitler then sees the time machine, enters it, and presses a button that brings him to the assassin's now-altered present. As Hitler exits the machine, however, he is shot by the now-elderly assassin who, in the meantime, has had to wait 70-odd years to carry out his assigned task. The assassin then leaves the scene to enlist the help of his former girlfriend in disposing of the *Führer*'s corpse, but when they return, it is gone (a copy of *Mein Kampf* in Hitler's breast pocket has deflected the bullet's path and allowed him to survive).

The rest of the story features the couple's attempt to track down Hitler in the present-day world. They soon decide that the Nazi dictator has probably gone to a library to learn what happened to the world ever since his disappearance in 1938. Little of dramatic import happens in the pages that follow, but a significant, if subtle, exchange occurs when the assassin's girlfriend, while making tea in her kitchen, hears a shot fired down the

Illustration 3: Extract from Jason, *I Killed Adolf Hitler*. (Courtesy of Fantagraphics Books)

street and looks out the window to see a crow-faced killer having just killed a rabbit-eared man. She then turns to her boyfriend and sadly remarks: "Hitler disappeared in 1938. World War II never happened. Shouldn't the world be a better place?" This remark is the first to cast doubt on the utility of removing the Nazi dictator from history. But the main one takes place at the narrative's conclusion. After failing to locate the fugitive *Führer*, the assassin and his girlfriend are sitting in a bar one day when they witness a violent struggle between two men, one of whom errantly shoots the assassin in the head, killing him. His girlfriend, bereft, now resolves to wait 50 years (the amount of time before the time machine can be recharged for another journey) and return to the point where the assassin shot, but failed to kill, Hitler. This time she is there to tell him to fire a second shot in the dictator's head and he fulfills his mission. Rather than celebrating the reversal of history's disastrous course, however, the couple—both of whom are now advanced in years—are content merely to enjoy one another's company after decades of tragic separation. The story thus ends on a note of romance instead of historical redemption.

It is unclear what the author's motives were in crafting his allohistorical narrative. Born in 1965, Jason is an internationally acclaimed graphic novelist whose books have appeared in numerous countries. What drew him to the premise of killing Hitler is unknown, but his unconventional portrayal of the topic likely reflects his generational identity as someone with a more distanced relationship to the Nazi era. The lack of emotional affect in his story is typical of much of his minimalist work, but it also suggests the fading appeal of the fantasy of killing Hitler. In the story, the desire to kill Hitler is reduced to a simple business transaction, not a matter of existential urgency. Its origins lie in the dreams of an elderly scientist—presumably desperate to undo the past because of his personal experiences—but is carried out by a young person, the assassin, for whom the past means little but a paycheck. The story's representation of Hitler is also significant, for like Schmitt's novel, it depicts the *Führer* as an unthreatening figure. The tale makes no references to the Nazi dictator's historical evil. He commits no new crimes. Indeed, he never utters a word in the few frames in which he actually appears. The result is that the text neglects to make a compelling case for why Hitler should be eliminated from history in the first place. The core allohistorical premise is thus drained of its moral power. In the end, the Nazi past ends up being both universalized and aestheticized. By subordinating the story's allohistorical premise to a universal one of unrequited love and by reducing Hitler to an artistic exclamation point in its visually stylish narrative, *I Killed Hitler* robs the past of its emotional affect.[56] Some reviewers of the book picked up on this fact, commenting, as one did, that the "characters show nearly no emotion," and singling out the text's "deadpan" style.[57] The clincher is the fact that the book denies readers any cathartic release by refraining from revealing whether Hitler's elimination ends up improving history for humanity. In undermining its underlying premise, the narrative suggests that the notion of killing Hitler may be losing its intuitive appeal.

Alternate Holocausts

Alternate histories on the subject of the Holocaust have traditionally been few in number, but several important texts have appeared in recent years. They have focused on a previously unexplored question—how would history have been different had the Holocaust never occurred? The most prominent exploration of this scenario is United States writer Michael Chabon's 2007 novel, *The Yiddish Policemen's Union.*[58] As is true of many other literary alternate histories, the novel's allohistorical elements unfold on the margins of its main plot, which is a noir-ish, detective-drama-cum-political-thriller about the murder of a Hasidic Jewish chess prodigy. Nevertheless, the narrative is based upon a clear point of divergence—the decision of the United States government in 1940 to establish a territorial home for European Jewish refugees in Alaska. This decision ends up changing history in numerous ways. Thanks to President Roosevelt's passing of the Alaska Resettlement Act, two million Jews are able to escape from war-torn Europe to the United States territory (Alaska is not yet a state) and establish a vibrant community, full of social, cultural, and religious diversity. The Holocaust, as we know it in real history, never occurs. Although two million Jews fall victim to what is called the Nazi "Destruction," the lives of four million others in Europe are spared.[59] The novel thus seems to endorse the fantasy that averting the Holocaust—or at least dramatically mitigating its magnitude—would have made history turn out for the better.

In reality, however, *The Yiddish Policemen's Union* casts doubt on whether the course of alternate history would really have been superior to that of real history. On the one hand, far more European Jews survive the Nazi onslaught and many are privileged to partake in the creation of a

Yiddish-speaking homeland in Alaska. Moreover, the defeat of the Soviet Union by the Nazis (which takes place in 1942) means that there is no cold war, a conclusion suggested by Chabon's passing references to a "Third Russian Republic" and a "Polish Free State."[60] On the other hand, however, the state of Israel is never created, as the Jews lose the 1948 War of Independence and are "driven into the sea" by the Arabs.[61] Moreover, the Jews of Alaska are themselves in a precarious situation. The Roosevelt administration's original granting of independence to the Alaskan Jewish settlement is only intended to last for 60 years, at which point it is supposed to be reconsidered. At the time the action of the novel takes place—our present—the president of the United States is inclined to have the territory return back to the United States (a process called "Reversion"), thereby ending the Jews' dreams of political autonomy. Against this backdrop, Chabon spins out his main plot, a complicated conspiracy of religiously fundamentalist Jews and American evangelical Christian Zionists—including the president himself—to destroy the Dome of the Rock in Jerusalem and prepare the groundwork for a massive, messianic-inspired Jewish return to Palestine. At the novel's conclusion, the main characters, detectives Meyer Landsman and Berko Shemets, discover the reason for the murder of the chess prodigy—he is killed because he is unwilling to play the role of the messiah in the conspiracy—and learn the distressing news that the Dome of the Rock has, in fact, just been bombed. Even without the occurrence of the Holocaust, in short, the future looks bleak, with international strife on the horizon between Jews and Arabs. In short, alternate history is little better than real history.

Chabon's decision to explore the fantasy of the Holocaust's nonoccurrence partly reflects his political views.[62] A writer who has long associated himself with the moderate left, Chabon crafted his narrative to critique developments in the Middle East in the wake of 9/11.[63] His book's unflattering portrayal of extremist Zionism and fundamentalist Christianity is a transparent critique of the relationship between Israel and the United States under the administrations of Ariel Sharon and George W. Bush.[64] His novel's suggestion that without the Holocaust there would have been no Israel also echoes leftist critiques of the Jewish national project.[65] That such ideas influenced the novel was suggested by many of its critics. Deriding Chabon as a "Leftwing atheistic Yiddishist...[from] Berkeley," James Lewis described the book as an expression of "Jewish self-hatred" sure to appeal to "paranoid anti-Semite[s]."[66] In a similar vein, Samuel Freedman asserted that Chabon was "apparently imbued with the belief that Israel is a colonial, imperialistic oppressor... [and] has found joy in, at least on paper, making it cease to exist."[67]

These criticisms notwithstanding, Chabon is no rabid anti-Zionist. Indeed, he is sympathetic to the plight of the Jews in the modern world. Explaining his goals in writing the novel, he observes:

> This story... is about the status quo of the Jews, who are always on the verge of being thrown out, of being shown the door....
>
> [B]ecause of the absence of Israel in the world of my book, the Jews are in... [the] position of being guests... I felt I... had to confront... the very real... possibility of expulsion—of Reversion, as it's called in this book. And I realized... it's still the status quo for us today. We may feel secure, with Israel having the fifth-largest military force in the world. But I guess that sense of fragility, of always being on the verge of being expelled—at best—is something I think we're still living with even if we prefer not to think about it.[68]

Chabon's narrative aims to underscore the tragic elements of the modern Jewish historical experience, especially those surrounding the Zionist movement. By portraying Jewish life as precarious even in the absence of the Holocaust, he shows how the effort to establish a Jewish national home was destined to cause problems wherever it was created, whether in Alaska or Palestine. Of course, in making this point, Chabon does not so much explore the Holocaust's ramifications for their own sake as use them to comment on the challenges facing the State of Israel. In other words, he universalizes the Holocaust's significance for larger purposes. In so doing, he advances the larger process of normalization.

By contrast, a very different perspective is offered by historian Walter Laqueur's 2008 essay, "Disraelia: A Counterfactual History, 1848–2008."[69] This analytical alternate history also focuses on the nonoccurrence of the Holocaust, an event that never happens thanks to the creation of a Jewish homeland in the Ottoman Empire in the year 1848. Motivated by the desire to stem the rising tide of anti-Semitism and prop up the declining Turkish regime (which is facing an increasingly assertive Russia), a coalition of interested parties led by Benjamin Disraeli and a group of wealthy Jewish families, headed up by the Rothschilds, convinces the Turkish Grand Vizier that it will be in his empire's financial interest to accept a massive wave of Jewish immigration to Palestine. Jewish doubts about the scheme disappear because of the flare-up of anti-Jewish violence in parts of central and eastern Europe during the revolutions of 1848. And so, between the years 1849 and 1855, some two million European Jews migrate to the Ottoman Empire, settling in "eight cantons…from Jaffa to Kirkuk."[70] This influx of immigrants has far-reaching historical consequences. The region of Jewish settlement, which comes to be known as "Disraelia," begins to industrialize intensively by the 1860s and becomes "the richest and most powerful region" of the Ottoman Empire.[71] It gains outright independence following the empire's collapse in the First World War and proceeds to increase its strength in the years that follow. Perhaps the key development is Disraelia's development of nuclear technology in the 1930s, which allows its government to force Adolf Hitler to cease his anti-Semitic agitation against Germany's 200,000 Jews. As a result, there is no Second World War and no Holocaust. History's course is thus vastly improved. To cap the fantasy, Laqueur concludes by noting that Disraelia

> would have some sixty million inhabitants at the beginning of the 21st century. It would have advanced industries, leading the world in fields such as nuclear and computer technologies. It would be the fifth-largest oil producer in the world, economically reasonably healthy with a growth rate of 6–8 percent, competitive with Europe, America and even Asia. It would have powerful armed forces, living in peace with its neighbors. . . . No one would dare to question its right to exist, and those who did would not be taken seriously.[72]

This concluding section makes clear that Laqueur's narrative, like Chabon's, was influenced by the contemporary political realities of the Middle East. Unlike Chabon, Laqueur stands more on the center-right of the political spectrum.[73] But his essay nonetheless bears surprising signs of a left-wing sensibility. This is made clear by his essay's suggestion that history could have turned out better if the quest for a Jewish homeland had proceeded in a less particularistic direction and unfolded in a way envisioned by the (mostly left-wing) supporters of binationalism. Disraelia is established not as a Jewish, but rather a multi-ethnic state, in which Jews, Arabs, Kurds, and others all have "absolute equality in the administration of the region."[74] The country has two capitals, Tel Aviv and Mosul, and there is a "principle of alternation" in the presidency "by which a Jew is invariably followed by a Kurd or an Arab." Jerusalem is turned into an "internationalized city" out of respect to the "world's leading religions."[75] And "Hebrew, Turkish, and Arabic are official languages." Most importantly, separatist efforts by "Jewish fanatics" to divide the country and expel all non-Jews are mercilessly crushed, following the 1929 assassination of the country's Jewish president.[76] In short, Laqueur implies that had Jewish nationalism developed within a multi-ethnic framework, history would have turned out for the better.

Compared to Chabon's narrative, Laqueur's portrayal of the Holocaust's nonoccurrence is much more of a utopian fantasy. Indeed, his references to Disraelia becoming "a model of friendly coexistence between the Muslim world and the people of the book"—not to mention a haven for "distinguished political refugees," such as Ayatollah Khomeini and "the Saudi entrepreneur Osama bin Laden"—makes clear that his counterfactual narrative was inspired to avoid many of Israel's real historical problems.[77] Laqueur suggests as much in the conclusion, where he argues that Israel's tragedy was to have been born 80 years too late, after the tragedy of the Holocaust and the awakening of Arab nationalism. This gap in time made all the difference between the Jewish homeland being "a strong and rich state, universally respected, and a small and relatively weak country, isolated, without important natural resources." Laqueur adds that the contemporary moral condemnation of Israel is largely due to its small size, writing, "What is considered normal behavior in...a state counting sixty million is a moral outrage when done by a small country [of six million]."[78] By exposing the criticism of Israel as contingent upon its small size, Laqueur essentially defends the Jewish state. Yet this effort did not convince certain critics, such as historian Martin Kramer, who accused Laqueur of having "de-Israelized" the country with a fantasy that is patently unrealistic given the realities of the Middle East.[79] The utopian aspects of his piece notwithstanding, Laqueur ultimately resembles Chabon in the sense that his essay subordinates the Holocaust's legacy to a larger topic—the contemporary fate of Zionism—and thus subtly universalizes its significance.

Conclusion

Recent alternate histories of Nazism reveal a presentist tendency to universalize the significance of the Third Reich in order to comment on contemporary events. This agenda is subtle in some works and more explicit in others, but it is never far from the surface. Given that all works of alternate history reflect the circumstances in which they are written—with writers' views of the present influencing whether they envision the alternate past as better or worse than the real past—it is no surprise that the works of the last decade reflect the complex realities of the post-9/11 world. The rise of Al Qaeda, the United States invasion of Iraq, the ongoing Israeli-Palestinian conflict, and the threat of a nuclear Iran—in short, the tumult of the contemporary Middle East—have directly influenced the portrayal of the Nazi past in alternate history. Given the fact that these crises can largely be traced back to the policies of the Bush administration (or became more acute on his watch), left-leaning writers have been especially active in producing the era's alternate histories. Their allohistorical nightmares and fantasies, in turn, have clearly reflected present-day concerns. Jo Walton's nightmare scenario of the British collaborating with Hitler's victorious Nazi Reich is a critique of present-day British foreign policy; Eric-Emmanuel Schmitt's fantasy scenario of a philo-Semitic Hitler, by underscoring the contingency of evil, draws attention to the capacity of all peoples in the past and present to perpetrate it; and Michael Chabon's fantasy of the Holocaust's nonoccurrence highlights the crisis of contemporary Zionism. All of these writers use the Nazi past in critical fashion in order to call attention to present-day crises, thereby universalizing its significance.[80]

It is difficult in the limited space of a short chapter to assess the representativeness of this trend. But at least in one respect, the universalization of the Nazi legacy diverges from another aspect of its ongoing normalization—namely, its intensifying relativization. Since the turn of the millennium, a flood of revisionist studies has diminished the Nazis' aura of evil in the process of challenging the status of the Second World War as the good war. These books have emanated from both the right and the left: by longstanding critics of Anglo-American interventionism in Nazi Germany, such as Pat Buchanan, and by left-leaning pacifists, such as Nicholson Baker.[81] The foreign policy disasters of the post-9/11 world have shaped both groups' views on the Second World War, reinforcing their respective isolationist and pacifist tendencies. Significantly, in questioning the wisdom of the United States and England entering the Second World War to fight Nazi Germany, both camps relativize the Nazis' crimes: the right by describing them as no worse than those committed by the Soviet

Union, and the left by seeing them as little different from those of the western democracies. In the process, the memory of the Nazi regime's singular criminality has become attenuated. By contrast, recent alternate histories have resisted this trend and retained a stronger sense of Nazism's evil. To be sure, they have done so in order to universalize its significance and call attention to the persistence of evil in the present, but while they may be implicated in the ongoing normalization of memory, recent alternate histories have stopped short of its most extreme forms.

Notes

1. Gavriel D. Rosenfeld, *The World Hitler Never Made: Alternate History and the Memory of Nazism* (Cambridge, Cambridge University Press, 2005).
2. Rosenfeld, *The World Hitler Never Made,* pp. 17–18.
3. Fantasy scenarios envision the alternate past as superior to the real past and thereby typically express a sense of dissatisfaction with the way things are today. Nightmare scenarios, by contrast, depict the alternate past as inferior to the real past and thus usually articulate a sense of contentment with the contemporary status quo. Allohistorical fantasies and nightmares, moreover, each have different political implications. Fantasies tend to be liberal, for by imagining a better alternate past, they see the present as wanting and thus implicitly support changing it. Nightmares, by contrast, tend to be conservative, for by portraying the alternate past in negative terms, they ratify the present as the best of all possible worlds and thereby discourage the need for change. To be sure, exceptions can frequently be found. Nightmare scenarios, by showing how the past could have easily been worse, can function as liberal cautionary tales that challenge the conservative belief that the present-day world was inevitable, that it continues to be virtuous, and that it is destined to be permanent. Fantasy scenarios, meanwhile, can be used in conservative fashion to construct escapist alternatives to the present that evade the liberal injunction to confront its problems.
4. This trend has been particularly visible videos available on the web. See, for example, the "What if Hitler Lived?" video, showing the *Führer* surviving to become a salesman for Subway sandwiches, available at http://www.clipal.com/video/what_if_hitler_lived (accessed June 2009). See also the "Hitler Rap" by the Whitest Kids U'Know comedy troupe, available at http://www.youtube.com/watch?v=gewdaLQ31lo (accessed June 2009).
5. To note simply one example, while liberal-leaning writers who lived through the war years portray the scenario of a Nazi victory in nightmarish terms, later writers of a more conservative bent relativize its horror, believing that it would have

been preferable to the Soviet Union's real historical triumph. These writers, pre-dictably, are motivated by anticommunist sentiments and wrote their pieces dur-ing spikes in cold war tensions between the United States and Soviet Union in the late 1970s.

6. Not all accounts of the Nazis winning the Second World War have come from the British realm. German writers have also entered the field in recent years. Siegfried Langer's novel, *Alles bleibt Anders* (Stolberg, Germany, Atlantis Verlag, 2008), portrays the horror of a Nazi-ruled world, while Volkmar Weiss's novel, *Das Reich Artam* (Leipzig, Germany, Engelsdorfer Verlag, 2007), depicts a Nazi victory from a far right-wing perspective.

7. Jo Walton, *Farthing* (New York, Tor Books, 2006); Jo Walton, *Ha'Penny* (New York, Tor Books, 2007); Jo Walton, *Half a Crown* (New York, Tor Books, 2008).

8. The agreement takes place without the support of Churchill, who says it is not worth "a farthing." England's willingness to pursue negotiations is enhanced by President Franklin Roosevelt's unwillingness to support its British ally in 1940 (Walton, *Ha'Penny,* p. 17).

9. Walton, *Ha'Penny,* pp. 228, 244.

10. Walton, *Ha'Penny,* pp. 84–85.

11. Walton, *Ha'Penny,* p. 209.

12. Walton, *Ha'Penny,* pp. 174–175.

13. Walton, *Half a Crown,* p. 19.

14. Walton, *Half a Crown,* p. 92.

15. Walton, *Half a Crown,* p. 316.

16. Lyda Morehouse, "Subversive Pixel-Stained Technopeasant: An Interview with Jo Walton," *The Internet Review of Science Fiction,* available at http://www.irosf.com/q/zine/article/10407 (accessed April 2009).

17. Walton thereby rejects the more nightmarish conclusions of the alternate histories of the 1960s and 1970s—which portrayed England remaining mired in collabora-tion—as well as more recent fantasies advanced by such alternate histories as John Charmley's work of history, *Churchill: The End of Glory* (Geneva, IL, Houghton Mifflin, 1993), and Christopher Priest's novel, *The Separation* (United Kingdom, Scribner, 2002), both of which suggest that collaborating with the Nazis by nego-tiating a separate peace might have allowed Britain to keep its empire (Rosenfeld, *The World Hitler Never Made,* chapter 1).

18. Douglas Barbour, "Government by Fear," *The Gazette* (Montreal), (October 28, 2008), p. 113; Frida Murray, Review of *Farthing* in *Booklist,* Vol. 104, No. 3 (Oc-tober 1, 2007), p. 40; Kelly Mcmanus, "Ghosts of SF Past," *The Globe and Mail* (March 31, 2007), p. D27. See also Brian Bethue, "A Very Unpleasant Kind of 'Cozy,'" *Maclean's* (September 29, 2008), p. 64; Saul Austerlitz, "Reshuffling His-tory's Deck," *The Forward* (March 9, 2007), p. B6.

19. Barbour, "Government," p. 113; Adrienne Martini, "Heil Britannia," *Baltimore City Paper* (December 12, 2007), available at http://www.citypaper.com/arts/story.asp?id=14955 (accessed June 2009). Another reviewer opined that the book "reads as if it was written just this morning." Lisa Goldstein, Review of *Farthing, Locus* (May, 2006), available at http://www.brazenhussies.net/Goldstein/Review-Farthing.html (accessed June 2009).

20. Murray Davies, *Collaborator* (London, MacMillan, 2003).

21. Owen Sheers, *Resistance* (New York, Faber and Faber, 2008). Sheers humanizes his main German characters, especially Albrecht Wolfram, but includes numerous reminders of German brutality in occupied England to preempt charges of normalizing Nazi evil.

22. Davies's novel won the 2003 Sidewise Award for Alternate History (http://www.uchronia.net/sidewise/complete.html#2003). "The Germans Are Coming," *The Washington Post* (April 27, 2008), np; Paul Binding, Review of *Resistance, The Independent,* (June 15, 2007) available at http://www.independent.co.uk/arts-entertainment/books/reviews/resistance-by-owen-sheers-453137.html (accessed June 2009); Jan Morris, "The Hills Have Eyes," *The Guardian,* (June 2, 2007) available at http://www.guardian.co.uk/books/2007/jun/02/featuresreviews.guardianreview30 (accessed June 2009).

23. Eric-Emmanuel Schmitt, *Adolf H.: Zwei Leben* (Zurich, Ammann, 2008).

24. Schmitt, *Adolf H.,* p. 11.

25. Schmitt, *Adolf H.,* p. 247.

26. Schmitt, *Adolf H.,* p. 397.

27. Schmitt, *Adolf H.,* p. 405.

28. Schmitt, *Adolf H.,* pp. 473–478.

29. Schmitt, *Adolf H.,* p. 472.

30. Schmitt, *Adolf H.,* p. 80.

31. Schmitt, *Adolf H.,* pp. 321–322, 438.

32. Schmitt, *Adolf H.,* p. 415.

33. Schmitt, *Adolf H.,* p. 423.

34. Schmitt, *Adolf H.,* p. 84.

35. In his words: "novels only interest me if they have philosophical implications" ("The Alternate Hypothesis—Comments," Eric Emmanuel Schmitt: The Official Web Site, http://www.eric-emmanuel-schmitt.com/en/work_details_en.php?oesec_id=4&oeit_id=27&oecat_id=2&section_id=2&table=comments&pict=&pict2=) (accessed June 2009).

36. Schmitt, *Adolf H.,* p. 483.

37. Schmitt, *Adolf H.,* p. 486.

38. Schmitt, *Adolf H.,* p. 503.

39. Schmitt, *Adolf H.,* p. 503.

40. "Portrait," Eric Emmanuel Schmitt: The Official Web Site, http://www.eric-emmanuel-schmitt.com/en/portrait_details_en.php?oesec_id=2&portrait_id=4 (accessed June 2009).

41. Rosenfeld, *The World Hitler Never Made,* chapter 5.

42. This is further shown by Schmitt's dedication of the novel to a famous German who did try and act to change history, Georg Elser.

43. Schmitt adds: "It wasn't just the jury of the Fine Arts Academy exam who were responsible for what he became: it was just as much Hitler's interpretation of this rejection" (Eric Emmanuel Schmitt: The Official Web Site, http://www.eric-emmanuel-schmitt.com/en/work_details_en.php?oesec_id=4&oeit_id=27&oecat_id=2&section_id=2&table=comments&pict=&pict2= [accessed June 2009]).

44. Schmitt, *Adolf H.,* p. 485.

45. In the end, Schmitt's narrative is underpinned by a fundamental contradiction. By claiming that history would have been better without Hitler, Schmitt endorses a familiar apologetic cliché of German conservatives, who have long deflected the German people's culpability in the Nazi disaster by concentrating their attention on the uniquely evil figure of Hitler. Schmitt suggests as much in asserting that the Nazi quest for *Lebensraum* "originated in Hitler's psyche, not that of the Germans" and insisting that "the Holocaust...has its origins only in him." Schmitt, *Adolf H.,* pp. 502–503. Yet Schmitt's focus on Hitler's evil undermines his claim that all human beings have the capacity to commit comparably evil acts.

46. *Magazine Littéraire* available at http://www.eric-emmanuel-schmitt.com/en/work_details_en.php?oesec_id=4&oeit_id=27&cri_id=173&section_id=4&table=oeuvre_item&oecat_id=2 (accessed June 2009).

47. *Le Figaro Littéraire* available at http://www.eric-emmanuel-schmitt.com/en/work_details_en.php?oesec_id=4&oeit_id=27&cri_id=170&section_id=4&table=oeuvre_item&oecat_id=2 (accessed June 2009).

48. Jens Mühling, "Die Hohlgesinnten," *Der Tagesspiegel* (April 3, 2008), p. 27.

49. Stephan Maus, "Guter Hitler, böser Hitler," *Stern* (January 31, 2008), p. 130.

50. Andreas Platthaus, "Der menschliche Hitler," *FAZ* (May 8, 2008) available at http://www.faz.net/s/Rub79A33397BE834406A5D2BFA87FD12913/Doc~EF79D1EC78EAF45B09BA86CB176711C48~ATpl~Ecommon~Scontent.html (accessed June 2009).

51. British reviewers found the novel somewhat forced, with the *Economist* calling it "a strange book" that was "forced" and ultimately "unconvincing." "Men of Faction," *The Economist* (November 10, 2001).

52. This is the view of many scholars today. See, for example, Bill Niven, *Facing the Nazi Past: United Germany and the Legacy of the Third Reich* (London, Taylor and Francis, 2002) and Helmut Dubiel, *Niemand ist frei von der Geschichte: Die*

Nationalsozialistische Herrschaft in den Debatten des Deutschen Bundestages (Munich, Hanser Verlag, 1999).

53. Walton, *Ha'Penny,* pp. 318–319.

54. Walton, *Ha'Penny,* p. 250.

55. Jason, *I Killed Adolf Hitler* (New York, Fantagraphics Books, 2007).

56. The book's aestheticization of violence is also unmistakable.

57. Ray Olson, Review of *I Killed Adolf Hitler,* Booklist, (September 15, 2007), p. 56; Review of *I Killed Adolf Hitler,* Publisher's Weekly, (October 29, 2007), p. 37. See also the review in the *New York Times* (December 2, 2007), p. 27.

58. Michael Chabon, *The Yiddish Policemen's Union* (New York, HarperCollins, 2007).

59. Chabon never explains the cooling of the Nazis' genocidal ardor—though it probably has something to do with their early defeat of the Soviet Union's and Germany's own ensuing defeat, capped by the nuclear destruction of Berlin, in 1946.

60. Chabon, *The Yiddish Policemen's Union,* pp. 88, 109.

61. Chabon, *The Yiddish Policemen's Union,* p. 29.

62. In a March 13, 2008 interview, Chabon said "I tried to use my imagination to undo some of the effects of the Holocaust," but ultimately declared that it was a "childish" and "futile" wish to undo the past (Michael Chabon, "Voices on Anti-Semitism—A Podcast Series," available at the United States Holocaust Memorial Museum, http://www.ushmm.org/museum/exhibit/focus/antisemitism/voices/transcript/?content=20080313 [accessed June 2009]).

63. In 2003, Chabon signed a petition to bring back Israeli settlers from the West Bank to Israel's pre-1967 borders (Jewish Alliance for Justice and Peace Web site, http://www.btvshalom.org/pressrelease/041404.shtml [accessed June 2009]). Chabon's marriage to Ayelet Waldman, an Israeli-American writer who has been critical of Israeli policies, has no doubt contributed to his views.

64. In a 2007 interview, Chabon expressed a liberal fear of ultra-orthodox yearnings to build a third temple in Jerusalem and United States evangelical support for breeding a red heifer, a precondition for the messiah's return. "Arctic Jews: An Interview with Michael Chabon," April 14, 2007, available at http://www.dissentmagazine.org/online.php?id=10 (accessed June 2009).

65. This belief is shared by many on the left, whereas many Jews (especially, though not exclusively) on the conservative end of the spectrum, argue that the state's creation would have occurred without the Holocaust, due to the Zionist movement's longstanding engagement on behalf of a Jewish state in Palestine.

66. James Lewis, Review of *The Yiddish Policemen's Union, The American Thinker,* (July 5, 2008), available at http://www.americanthinker.com/2008/07/the_ultimate_pc_novel.html (accessed June 2009).

67. Samuel Freedman, "In the Diaspora: Chabon's Choice," *The Jerusalem Post,* (July 12, 2007), available at http://www.jpost.com/servlet/Satellite?cid=1184168549208&pagename=JPost%2FJPArticle%2FShowFull (accessed June 2009). See also "Novelist's Ugly View of Jews," *The New York Post* (April 22, 2007), available at http://www.nypost.com/seven/04222007/gossip/pagesix/pagesix.html (accessed June 2009).

68. Quoted in Sarah Goldstein, "Jews on Ice," Salon.com (May 4, 2007), available at http://www.salon.com/books/int/2007/05/04/chabon/index.html (accessed June 2009).

69. Walter Laqueur, "Disraelia: A Counterfactual History, 1848–2008," *Middle East Papers: Middle East Strategy at Harvard* (April 1, 2008), pp. 1–21. I would like to thank Eugene Sheppard for sending me a copy of this essay.

70. Laqueur, "Disraelia," p. 14.

71. Laqueur, "Disraelia," p. 16.

72. Laqueur, "Disraelia," p. 20.

73. See, for example, his recent brooding book, *The Last Days of Europe: Epitaph for an Old Continent* (New York, Thomas Dunne, 2007). See also http://www.laqueur.net.

74. Laqueur, "Disraelia," p. 16.

75. Laqueur, "Disraelia," p. 9.

76. Laqueur, "Disraelia," p. 16.

77. Laqueur, "Disraelia," p. 17.

78. Laqueur, "Disraelia," p. 20.

79. This was the claim of Martin Kramer, "Disraelia" (April 1, 2008), available at http://sandbox.blog-city.com/disraelia.htm (accessed June 2009).

80. Their relative youth (Walton, Schmitt, and Chabon were all born in the 1960s) and personal distance from the events of the Nazi era partly also explain their willingness to view it instrumentally instead of for its own sake.

81. See Patrick Buchanan, *Churchill, Hitler and the Unnecessary War* (New York, Crown, 2008), which expands upon points raised in his earlier book, *A Republic, Not an Empire: Reclaiming America's Destiny* (Washington, DC, Regnery, 1999); Nicholson Baker, *Human Smoke: The Beginnings of World War II, The End of Civilization* (New York, Simon and Schuster, 2008). See also Norman Davies, *No Simple Victory: World War II in Europe, 1939–1945* (New York, Penguin, 2006); Michael Bess, *Choices under Fire: Moral Dimensions of World War II* (New York, Vintage, 2006).

2

Hitler as Our Devil?: Nazi Germany in Mainstream Media

Eva Kingsepp

Who needs the four horsemen when we have Hitler and the SS? Over the last 60 years, the history of Nazi Germany and the Second World War has attained mythical proportions in large parts of popular, especially mainstream, media.[1] In numerous factual and fictional representations, Hitler's rise to power, the Second World War, the Holocaust, and the fall of the Thousand Year Reich, are often dramatically described, by producers and audiences alike, as an epic battle between good and evil. It is hard to find any other conflict that can compete with the Second World War in our historical consciousness and, not the least, in the number of mediated representations available about it. It seems that this war has something that makes it outstanding and especially attractive. In this chapter, which is based on my PhD research, I will show how a prevailing mythical image of Nazi Germany, with Hitler as the modern-day devil and the Nazis as his demonlike henchmen, is constructed in mainstream media, and how Swedish viewers with interests in the Second World War respond to these representations.[2] My main interest here lies in how the mythical imagery related to Nazi Germany fits into a rational and secular context. Importantly, while the good-versus-evil trope remains the dominant way in which the Nazi past is represented in popular culture, the manner in which audiences respond to these representations is diverse and suggests a much more complex response to the Nazi past than the good/evil binary would suggest.

Because certain themes, symbols, and stereotypes constantly reoccur in texts from different genres, including digital games, popular history, (pulp) fiction, and comic strips, they create both a model narrative for how to tell the story about Nazi Germany as well as a popular paradigm of basic signifying elements for how to illustrate this story. Often, elements from fictional genres—including visual and sound effects and music—are mixed together with historical facts, resulting in more than a blurring of boundaries; it is rather what film scholar Vivian Sobchack calls a palimpsest of historical consciousness, basically creating a world of its own.[3] And this world is in many ways both easier to understand and more entertaining than the ordinary one we inhabit. Media researcher Nicholas Mirzoeff offers a good example in his comment on the television series *The Sopranos:*

> To retreat from this world, Tony goes to watch the History Channel on TV, the all-Hitler-all-the-time history-as-entertainment channel. In this televisual retreat, Tony finds watching documentaries about the Second World War to be a place where good and evil are clearly defined and distinguished, literally in black and white, unlike the chaos of his own life.[4]

The dichotomy between good and evil that eases Tony Soprano's conscience has become a familiar model for representing the Third Reich in mainstream media.

The idea of Nazi Germany as a struggle to the death between goodies and baddies is a myth that seems to defy conquest. Increasingly, however, within audiences interested in Nazi Germany and the Second World War, many viewers I encountered are critical of such a simplified narrative. As these viewers usually consume a broad range of different media texts dealing with this topic, they develop a high level of media literacy and evaluate the content according to their level of credibility. It is obvious that the transformation of the historical Hitler into a mythical, larger-than-life character—an image already created during his years in power[5]—functions well in fictional genres but becomes problematic in factual representations such as documentaries. References to Hitler as "the evil king" connote myth and fiction, and the critical viewer easily rejects this as implausible. However, as the image is usually presented in an authoritative way and is widely promoted by both commercial and public service media, in many cases, he (or she)[6] also draws the conclusion that there is another real truth behind the simplified narrative. This has important implications not only for historical and political education but also more widely, as some viewers even express the opinion that the dominant political interests in the western world actively promote the myth of Nazism to sustain social stability.[7] In other words, what these viewers argue is that the simplified good/evil dichotomy helps to enforce myths about the moral supremacy of the western liberal democracies and their status as role models for the rest of the world, using emotional means of argumentation that deny intellectual reflection.[8] As a result, these audience members seem to replace one type of myth about the Nazi past (the Nazis as pure evil) with another (that the evil character of the Nazis is useful to political interests today). The idea that the Nazi past is purposely being mythologized in a certain way has obvious ramifications for the public's understanding of Nazism as well as the memorialization of the Second World War, not only in Sweden but also more widely.

Scholars have shown how general interest in history has increased in the last two decades, a trend that is reflected in an increase in history programming on television.[9] The fact that history has become a part of mass culture is discussed by the historian Ludmila Jordanova, who uses the term "public history" to describe this phenomenon: "Among other things, public history is *popular* history—it is seen or read by large numbers of people and has mostly been designed for a mass audience."[10] But public history is also a historical consciousness created and upheld by people and communities outside the establishment—in this regard the Internet functions as an especially vast resource for historical knowledge. Providing space for social connections, for discussions, and for information dispersion, the Internet is an important element in the formation of a grassroots collective intelligence,[11] in this case dealing with Nazi Germany and the Second World War. Today, public history is not only formed through mass media, the publication of academic texts, museums, and heritage sites, but also through these electronic practices, which engage with the past and help to bring about "a diffused awareness of that past that varies from person to person, group to group, country to country."[12] This awareness is part of what is often called popular, cultural, or collective memory.[13] There can, therefore, also be a tension between the construction of a mainstream version of popular history and other constructions.

I contend that when the past is being represented in a fictionalized way through the use of mythical connotations, formulaic narratives, and stereotypes, this might make it more attractive and thus memorable, but at the same time it loses the credibility that is important for that past to be perceived as *real*. The mainstream version of the history of Nazi

Germany—namely that it was an evil regime ruled by an evil ruler—has largely turned into a well-propagated and readily available myth. The myth operates in a similar way as other popular legends, which can induce skepticism in audiences and lead to their reluctance to accept parts of the Nazi past as historical fact. Certainly, not all consumers of the myth as it is presented in popular culture accept it blindly.

In my interviews with Swedish Second World War enthusiasts, for example, their critique of the myth and of the society that promulgates it is scathing. The concept of mainstream repeatedly turned up in the ethnographic part of my study. The word was commonly used as a depreciative label for certain kinds of simplified, fictionalized, good-versus-evil representations that my subjects perceived as the dominant way of presenting Nazi Germany today. In order to find out the basic characteristics in popular media representations of Nazi Germany on the whole, I gathered a large sample of fiction and documentary films currently available on the market or shown on Swedish television, as well as Second World War computer games of the first-person-shooter type. The film study involved two parts: one focused on the visual representation, one on the narrative. An overview of 70 *fictional films* made between 1940 and 2006 (of which almost half originate in the United States; the others come mainly from the United Kingdom and Germany)[14] shows that 78 percent of these can be classified as formulaic, according to literary theorist John Cawelti's definition.[15] In other words, these films reproduce a goodies-versus-baddies formula, in which the Nazis and Hitler are represented as the baddies who are overcome by a series of heroic acts on behalf of the goodies. Cawelti argues that the function of formulaic narratives is the modern equivalent of religious myths, namely to tell morally loaded stories about what it is to be a good human being. Universally shared symbols and archetypes are frequent in such representations and the clear us/them divide can be regarded as a tool for shaping communities, legitimizing them, and holding them together.[16]

The Visual Construction

Many of the films in this study repeatedly invoke symbols and signs connected to the Nazis and use them to signify the presence of the other, namely that which is unfamiliar and remote to the audience. Most prominent of these are, unsurprisingly, the swastika, the Nazi eagle, the Cross of Iron, SS death's heads, SS runes, Hitler's image and voice, and the black SS uniform. Although the broad purpose behind the use of the symbols is to create an atmosphere of another time and place—usually Europe during the Second World War—in some cases the symbols are clearly employed to generally, rather than historically, signify evil. This is most evident in films of an outspoken formulaic character, especially melodramas and adventures. But other signs are also utilized as distinctly Nazi (and evil), despite not being authentically or specifically Nazi: black gloves, a long dark (black) coat, and round, metal-rimmed spectacles (as worn by SS-leader Heinrich Himmler). The use of such general signs to connote Nazism create symbolic bridges between genres, inviting familiar signs from fiction to enter a historical context and through this adding even more power to the connotations of evil. Accordingly, black gloves and black clothes are common signs for baddies in popular films, and Himmler-style glasses have carried over to popular cinematic stereotypes of the mad scientist and cold bureaucrat. The universalism of the symbology is key. Digital games use exactly the same signs and symbols to connote the same ideas.

Some Nazi symbols have attained significance well beyond their historical context and have become signs to represent all things sinister, evil, calculating, and murderous beyond Nazi-related media as well. Of course, signs are constituted by signifier and signified. Signifiers—for example the graphic figure of the swastika—are in themselves pure, while what is being signified depends on the context.[17] Accordingly, the sign of the swastika becomes a sign of Nazism specifically through the context of Nazism. However, in the fiction films and digital games I studied there are two ways of using the swastika: first, it is a sign for Naziness,[18] providing an anchor in time and space, and, second, it carries more or less obvious connotations to the supernatural and the spectacular. A tiny swastika pin on a character's collar can well create a massive sinister effect. The symbol is so powerful it connotes far more than a historical reality; it is anchored in a dramatic idea.

In formulaic melodrama and adventure films, it is noticeable that signs of Naziness are both more frequently used and exposed in a more manifest way, often connected to producing an emotional effect, than in nonformulaic films. In many documentaries, on the other hand, the symbolism of metaphysical evil is usually added to the specific Nazi iconography, often enhanced by references to the Aryan race and Eastern mysticism.[19]

Linking traits of orientalism—that is, of the east as something irrational, undeveloped, even barbaric—with Nazism enhances the idea that Nazism is a counter-image of what westerners consider themselves to be. In this way, Nazism is most identifiably othered and western society is heightened as righteous. In some contexts, where it is obvious that a documentary's contempt for the Nazis is built upon their rejection of the Christian religion, the relationship offered between Nazism and Hinduism or Buddhism through the use of the swastika even imply that these religions could be perceived as evil.[20]

However, sometimes the orientalist connection is disregarded, as in *The Occult History of the Third Reich: The Enigma of the Swastika* (1991):

> The swastika was adopted by the Nazi Party in 1920. But it was neither the Party's invention, nor its discovery. Since the end of the 19th century, the swastika had been spreading amongst the peoples of Europe. And everywhere, it was a sign of a new and powerful force, a deepening fascination with the arcane, the esoteric, and the occult.[21]

Here, Nazism as a spiritual force is promoted and seems to imply that the western obsession with the occult has helped to bring the National Socialist German Workers' Party (NSDAP) into being, almost like a punishment for diverging from the path of secular modernization. A good example of how the signification of the swastika has been westernized into a symbol of metaphysic evil is found in the Canadian docudrama *Hitler: The Rise of Evil* (2003), where the swastika—in a suggestive scene where the young Hitler shows a sketch of the Nazi flag to his stunned friends—is said to possess hypnotic powers.

Importantly, the use of these Nazi symbols across a variety of genres, media types, year of production, and place of origin suggest that some of them—especially the swastika—have become stereotypical stand-ins for representing not only Nazi Germany but also evil more generally. In this way, the symbols have come to constitute the mainstream image of Nazi Germany as evil. Still, there are others that defy such precise categorization, as for example the eagle. Although the *Reichsadler* was one of the most common symbols for the Third Reich, as is particularly evident in archival footage, it has not become a symbol of evil in post-war popular media. A possible explanation might be that the eagle is also a national symbol frequently used by the United States and the Federal Republic of Germany, among other countries.

The Narrative Construction

In order to investigate the popular narrative construction of Nazi Germany, I undertook two case studies: the first on the narrative construction of Hitler's last days and death, the second on Nazi occultism. These narrative frames were chosen as they frequently recur within popular media products dealing with Nazi Germany. The material consisted of 17 documentaries made between 1974 and 2005, 14 fiction films (from 1963 to 2004), and 4 digital games (2000–2006) of the first-person-shooter type.[22] The case studies showed how narrative structures, modes of address, themes, and characters reaffirmed the connections with mythical imagery, using a model of critical discourse analysis to make the case.[23] Five basic themes emerged out of the examination of these media, of which two were predominant regardless of media type, namely the concepts of *apocalypse* and *mystery.* In addition, three other themes were especially common in the texts combining Nazism with the occult, namely, *hubris, scientific aberration,* and *exoticism.*

The theme of apocalypse comes out repeatedly in the films, documentaries, and games. Here the uses of biblical language and a Manichean division of the world into good and evil, light and darkness, is very frequent and evokes a mythical aura. Numerous parallels are drawn between the Nazi past and the religious imagery of the end of the world.[24] Of course, the Second World War offers scenarios well suited to the staging of the end of the world in epic proportions. In films about Hitler's last days, it is the final battle between the forces of good and evil that comes to the fore. The *Führer*-bunker in the burning ruins of Berlin is the last stronghold of a malevolent ruler, a subterranean refuge where he and his last followers have hidden, doomed, and awaiting their gruesome destiny. The voice-over from the initial sequence of *The Last Days of Adolf Hitler* (2005), part of the documentary series *Unsolved Mysteries of the Second World War,* serves as a good illustration. The footage shows images from the battle of Berlin:

[sounds of bombardment in the background] Berlin 1945. Somewhere amongst the ruins of the Reich's last and most formidable citadel, Adolf Hitler contemplates the destruction of all his hopes and dreams. Few of those who shelter with him, beneath the blazing heart of the city, will survive to tell the story of these final terrible days. When the last pockets of resistance are liquidated, and the smoke and smell of death clear from the shattered capital, [eerie music in the background] all that will remain of the dark and revengeful spirit of Adolf Hitler will be a document bearing his name, and reaffirming his message of hatred and annihilation. For Hitler, Berlin will serve as both epitaph and funeral pyre. No trace of him will ever be seen again. And the manner and circumstances of his death will never be fully established.[25]

The theme of mystery goes hand-in-hand with that of apocalypse. The documentaries especially focus on the mysterious elements of the Nazi past and highlight shrouded secrets, unanswered questions, and doubts. In this respect, the differences between the media categories are important. In the majority of fiction films and games a resolution of sorts is reached at the end, the mystery or problem is solved, and the mission accomplished. This is also in accordance with the formulaic pattern of many popular narratives.[26] However, most documentaries remove such certainties and focus on the unanswered elements of the past. In this way, any certainties we may have over the ultimate triumph of evil are undermined. This is particularly true in the numerous documentaries that focus on the possibility of Hitler having survived the war or the possibility that the Russians did something inappropriate with his remains. In the swirling murkiness about Hitler's death, such documentaries—of which both *Secrets of World War II: Adolf Hitler's Last Days* (2001) and *Unsolved Mysteries of the Second World War: The Last Days of Adolf Hitler* (2005) are good examples—heighten the sense of suspense and expectation.

Myths around Hitler's survival have circulated ever since his disappearance in 1945, as well as a fixation with details about his death. Stalin was possessed with the fear of his main enemy slipping away—he did not believe that Hitler was dead, and ordered further investigations.[27] In the western press, sightings of the German ex-*Führer* in different parts of the world were published, and as Soviet soldiers had actually found a Hitler-looking corpse in the Chancellery garden, the idea of the real Hitler faking his suicide, leaving a doppelganger and escaping to some faraway hideout achieved even more credibility.[28] The idea of Hitler surviving has been exploited in fiction particularly (the film *They Saved Hitler's Brain* [1963] is one of the more bizarre examples), and also recurs in Miguel Serrano's esoteric Hitlerism, a current within neo-Nazi mythology.[29] It is better for us to be left guessing, and the macabre implications of the guesswork leave the possibility of unresolved evil open. In this way, such documentaries heighten our sense of wanting more—more investigation, more research, more time spent watching even more documentaries on the Nazis. Nazism has become a marketing tool for documentary makers with its own internal rationale.

The three other themes—hubris, scientific aberration, and exoticism—are often subordinate to the primary themes of apocalypse and mystery. Hubris is represented by the arrogance of the Nazis, who profess superiority in all things and proclaim the right to rule in all matters racial, social, military, and political. It is closely connected to the theme of scientific aberration that is represented by Nazi scientists transgressing all ethical and scientific boundaries in their reckless endeavors for progress and racial domination. Both subthemes are particularly prevalent in the gaming world. *Return to Castle Wolfenstein* (2001), for example, depicts Nazis creating an army of bloodthirsty zombie soldiers. Experimentation with the undead indirectly references the horrific human experiments in the concentration camps, framed within popular stereotypes and legends like those of Dr. Frankenstein and the Golem.[30] Above all, connecting Nazis with the grotesque and underworld helps to distance audiences from the Nazi past and to promote Nazism as something other-worldly and inhuman. In this way, the bizarre figure of the Nazi zombie functions as a way of metaphorically representing some of the horrors of the Third Reich and distancing audiences from that past. It creates an easily accessible moral framework in which Nazism is clearly evil and needs no further investigation or explanation. Distance is also central within the last theme, exoticism, which is visible in the depictions of Nazi Germany and its inhabitants as alien and other-worldly. Nazis are not of this world and need not be treated as such. This represents another type of othering the Nazi past than what was mentioned earlier with regards to the symbology of Nazism, but this type of othering is also common in media representations that can be classified as formulaic.[31] Here again, Nazism is presented as something inhuman and, as result, as something that need not worry the audience.

However repellent and other-worldly they may be, though, Nazis are also endlessly fascinating to modern audiences. There is an apparent fetishism in much of the material presented in the documentaries, films, and games studied here, both in the frequent exposure of visual signs connected to Nazi Germany and in certain specifically Nazi-sounding words and phrases, like "Achtung!," "Schnell!," and "Jawohl!" When connected with the fact that there are many groups in western society that continue to admire the aesthetics of the Nazis,[32] without placing those aesthetics within a contextual framework that includes an acknowledgment of the Holocaust or other elements of the history of the Third Reich, the frequent uncritical representation of the Nazi past in popular media shows a tendency to admire the Nazis, albeit from a distance. This may be the most troubling consequence of distancing Nazism from a real past that was created by human beings. By othering the Nazis and Nazism, we can remove ourselves from culpability for the crimes committed during the Third Reich and, at the same time, admire the achievements of that same regime and not feel morally culpable for doing so.

The Meaning of Hitler

The character of Hitler is crucial and needs special attention. Significantly, unless he is one of the main protagonists, in most of the fiction films studied here, he is usually symbolically rather than physically present, for example as background on paintings or as a bust in some Nazi building. Hitler is a prop in the world of Nazi representations. In some cases his voice is heard, either intradiegetically, as a voice on the radio, or as a sound effect—what he actually says is not important (accordingly, there is usually no translation), but the sound of his voice is key.[33] In this sense, the symbol of Hitler invokes if not outright evil, at least something sinister. In the documentaries, on the other hand, Hitler is usually the central character and often the only real subject, or agent, as all the other Nazi leaders are depicted as his followers. Culpability for the Third Reich and the Holocaust is thus removed from many to one. In this way, it is still Hitler as a lone person that is invoked as the representation of evil, as the modern world's equivalent of the Devil.

To this end, it should be noted that Hitler does not receive an introduction in many documentaries, which indicates the assumption of a level of public knowledge about him. When he is introduced, however, it is usually in extreme terms. In *Secrets of World War II: Adolf Hitler's Last Days* (2001), for example, he is described as "the most evil genius of the 20th century, warlord and war criminal" and "the evil king," and in *The History of Nazism* (year unknown) he is, additionally, a sexual pervert, abuser of children and young women, coprophagist, and Devil worshipper. However, when we consider audience receptions of this imagery, it is vital to consider that multiple images of Hitler do exist in popular consciousness. For example, while some critics lambasted Bruno Ganz's interpretation of the *Führer* in the film *Downfall* (2004) for humanizing Hitler, other critics and many of my Swedish interviewees welcomed this multifaceted and human interpretation.[34] It seems that when the typically Hitlerish aspects of Hitler are downplayed, audiences interpret this as a more authentic representation than the media Hitler that is hyped on the *History Channel.*

According to Gavriel D. Rosenfeld, there is an ongoing naturalization and diminishing of Hitler and Nazi deeds in post-war popular culture, which, he fears, will eventually lead to indifference within our society toward the crimes of the Nazi era.[35] I do not entirely agree with Rosenfeld, as the ethnographic material collected from my Swedish audience study clearly illustrates that any indifference shown toward the Nazis is not disinterest in their crimes or the relevance of those crimes, but rather toward the simplified, often spectacular way of depicting them. There is a significant gap between much of the content in media representations and how viewers receive them. Although some of the media texts might rightly be considered to naturalize Hitler and the Nazis, this does not automatically lead to indifference within the audience nor an acceptance of the good/evil binary on which much of the Nazi imagery in popular culture rests. On the contrary: it is clear that some modern audiences appreciate the opportunity to de-demonize the Nazi past and Hitler in particular and, in doing so, identify the typical Nazi as a fellow human being, a process that is crucial for learning about the Nazis and simultaneously learning about oneself.[36]

Using Popular History: An Audience's View

Audience studies in this field are rare, although parallels can be made to research on factual television, such as media scholar Annette Hill's analysis of viewers in the United Kingdom and Sweden.[37] Another interesting study is ethnographer Jenny Thompson's research on Second World War re-enactors in the United States.[38] Both show significant similarities to my findings and illustrate how audiences "use pre-existing distinctions between public and popular factual genres, and formal and informal knowledge and learning" to come up with complex responses to the Nazi past.[39]

It is important to note that when comparing these studies, and examining my own, the attitudes of communities of people who share an intense interest in Nazi Germany and the Second World War are of a general kind and not necessarily dependent on nationality. The focus of my study has been on Sweden, one of the few countries in Europe that managed to remain neutral in the Second World War. The Swedish background is important, however, in that the country's lack of participation in the war as a belligerent probably changes the way in which the Swedish audience perceives the cultural significance of this conflict. Where large parts of American audiences are likely to accept representations of the Second World War as the good war, most people in my study reacted negatively and skeptically to such expressions of nationalism and patriotism (values that in Sweden are generally considered to be politically incorrect).[40] Nevertheless, despite the cultural specificity of my Swedish study, the linkages with Hill's work on British and Swedish audiences, and Thompson's work on the United States, are numerous and suggest that, at least to some extent, the representation and reception of Nazism in popular culture has transcended national boundaries.

In the selection of interviewees and informants for the study I wanted people who professed an existing interest in either the Second World War or Nazi Germany, as gamers, avid readers, or viewers of Nazi-related media, without being positive to National Socialism as an ideology. Simply put, I did not look for neo-Nazis, mainly as this category has already been the subject of research.[41] As a result of my previous MA study, I knew that there are a number of different (sub)cultural practices connected to an interest in this topic, expressed in gaming, role-playing, alternative popular music, model building, collecting, esotericism, and so on.[42] Accordingly, I was not only looking for individuals who expressed an interest in the topic, but also people who could tell me more about the different cultural practices connected to this.

The study was not designed in order to get an image of the Swedish audience in general, or to gain sociological data that could be used to generalize across the entire Swedish population. Rather, I wanted to explore that part of the audience where Nazi Germany or the Second World War had become part of a cultural practice, or even a hobby, for example by those who collect literature or films on the topic, who participate in different kinds of gaming activities, or who like to build model tanks or planes. I was also interested in musical subcultures using Nazi symbols: how do they look upon the factual historical background of the past they invoke? However, as such an inquiry would certainly risk being considered a study of extremists, nerds, or even freaks, I also wanted some people with more moderate views on the topic and who expressed a more general interest in it. A snowball sample was used: friends of friends and acquaintances, colleagues, students in my classes who expressed an interest in the area, people I met at conferences, and so forth. Out of these I then selected 11 individuals for in-depth interviews. These were all people who were engaged in cultural practices connected to their interest. In order to get a wider perspective, I also undertook more informal interviews with another 40 people (whom I classify here as informants). The informants can roughly be divided into three categories: people with a profound interest in Nazi Germany or the Second World War and engaged in related cultural practices (16), people mainly engaged in cultural practices related to Nazi Germany or the Second World War (such as gaming, music, and esoterics) but with a comparatively lesser degree of interest in the historical topic itself (14), and people with only a general interest in the topic and with no engagement in cultural practices related to it (10). Finally, I undertook several spontaneous chats and short interviews during fieldwork, for example at gaming gatherings, alternative music festivals, and collectors' fairs. Altogether, the number of people involved in this study reached 100. It should be said that almost all of them were male—only one of the interviewees and seven of the informants were female.

There was not one participant in the study who was not critical of mainstream media representations of the Third Reich or war period, mainly because they found it stupid. Mainstream is here to be understood as simplified, highly formulaic entertainment, perceived as being directed at a mass audience. Often, the expression "mainstream" was used together with, or synonymous to, "American" or "Hollywood," which indicates that the cultural difference between the Swedish and American audiences is important. However, as similar views are also expressed in Thompson's study of American war re-enactors,[43] it might be that the antipathy does not only depend on the Swedish perspective, although it is most probably facilitated by it. The ire of my audience was not directed at the subjectivity of media representations of the Nazi past, but rather at the simplification, sensationalism, and, not the least, repetition involved. As one of the interviewees put it, "[I] usually don't find them [fiction films about the Second World War] all that exciting to watch, as it's usually the same story they're telling, although in a slightly different way...Like this: American farmer boys who go to Europe and become men."[44] Another: "Honestly, I'm really tired of all Hollywood productions. So I prefer not to watch them. Because, it's such a counterfeit...eh...glorification that the US won the war, and...instead of all the others. So, I just can't stand that."[45] "American" in this context is used as an adjective to reflect on inferior standards. Several of the participants were actively searching for different fictional representations of the war. The German films *Das Boot* (1981)*, Stalingrad* (1993), and *Downfall* (2004) were generally appreciated, as they were considered to be objective, that is, in the sense that they neither glorified the Germans nor anyone else. For the same reason, Finnish films, like *Winter War* (1989), were held in high regard.

The transmediality of my subjects' experiences is important.[46] The participants make use of different media forms and genres, and while doing this they encounter expressions of the same basic themes, narrative structures, and stereotypes reoccurring in all kinds of representations. As in the symbolic construction, this produces discursive bridges connecting different media texts and genres with each other, thus giving the viewer/gamer/reader the impression of one dominant way of representing Nazi Germany, namely that which many of my subjects called mainstream. Interestingly enough, on a closer analysis it becomes clear that when it came to films and digital games, only a relatively small part actually fits into the interviewees' description of a typical mainstream representation of Nazi Germany and the Second World War. Thus, it seems that the combination of certain well-known signs for Naziness in a stereotypical, formulaic narrative frame produces an emotional impact so efficient that this image is perceived as quantitatively dominant.

The vast majority of the participants in the study were not sympathetic to National Socialism or fascism as ideologies; they were not anti-Semitic, nor were they deniers of the Holocaust.[47] They were critical of mainstream images of Nazi Germany because the representations are not usually subject to any kind of rigorous questioning. Those historically most knowledgeable were annoyed at misrepresentations of facts or misuse of archival footage, but generally the objections were based on the experience that mainstream images are over-simplified, black-and-white, and propagandistic.[48] In this sense, they stress the formulaic, mythical, and ideological elements of the texts. Of the 11 interviewees, 10 also felt insulted as viewers by the didactic methods used by mainstream media to present the Nazi past. Eight of them expressed ethical objections to the reduction of the suffering and death of millions of real people to serve the purposes of entertainment. All of them were critical of what they perceived as hypocrisy: the Nazis are generally condemned in mainstream representations, but an undertone of ill-hidden admiration is also often present:

> I saw some documentary on Discovery [smile] about the SS...that, eh, was peculiarly...little condemning. Where it was coming through quite a lot that they were...tough warriors, and we started making jokes about it being SS-like to do something cool. Eh...And then, then the interest began, I guess, to turn in that direction. [EK asks about the title:] It was surely called *Waffen-SS* or *Hitler's Elite Force,* or something like that. Eh, and it contained these dashing expressions; I think I can still remember one:..."Often, individual men would refuse to give ground even to approaching tanks, and would die making futile resistance." And such things sounded cool.[49]

This quote is an example of how viewers can look back and analyze not only the media texts in a critical way but also analyze their own reception thereof. Most of the participants—especially those having had this interest for several years—expressed an awareness of personal development: having at first been uncritical and naïve and then becoming more critical and reflexive as their media literacy increased. All of the 11 interviewees described their personal development in these terms, although one of them did express a high confidence in documentaries in general, because of his expectations of this genre as being realistic. However, he did not differ from the others concerning the skeptical opinion about fiction films. Every one of the 100 persons in the study expressed their distaste of mythical expressions and spectacular ways of representing Hitler as a Devil-like figure and the Nazis as one-dimensionally evil. All found the media Hitler exaggerated, a caricature, and ridiculous. They criticized this image of Hitler in terms of historical accuracy and with regard to the possible effects on an unaware audience:

> This screaming maniac, he's a kind of leadership figure, as well. In a bizarre way. So I think it can be counterproductive if you try to show someone as a screaming maniac. As some people are *attracted* by screaming maniacs.[50]

Another interviewee made similar connections:

> I believe that both Hitler and Himmler have some kind of...*appeal* to
> people who can in some way be classified as nerds....Hitler's life is
> actually about the same thing as for these guys in Columbine. That:
> how you feel you're an outsider, and a failure, and then you get your
> revenge. And, but in an immensely more grandiose way: you can es-
> sentially destroy the world.[51]

Importantly, what my interviewees (and the majority of the informants) were indicating was that they deemed themselves intellectually
more active than "the mainstream audience."[52] The second of the interviewees also admitted to some of the nerdy qualities within the group of
Nazi-fascinated people. As a nerd is often regarded as someone with an
intense interest in, and knowledge about, a topic that most people consider
odd, this fits very well into the division between those who think for themselves and those who do not, which all of the participants seemed to believe in. In this, they construct an image of a mainstream audience as the
other, as passive media consumers who not only enjoy history reduced to
entertainment but also believe that these representations somehow present
the truth. Here parallels can be made to Hill's study, in which the division
between entertainment and learning as two opposite poles is important:
audiences consider themselves intelligent and able to distinguish between
fact and fiction, which is especially important when fiction is being presented as fact (as in mockumentaries, for example).[53]

The reference to the 1999 Columbine High School massacre exem-
plifies how the participants could make use of a moral compass through
which they thought about Hitler and the Nazi era. The same interviewee
who here referred to Columbine High also confessed he is more interested
in the media image of Nazi Germany than in authenticity. He is attracted
to, in his words, "the apocalyptic Third Reich," as this, being close to the
fantastic and to science fiction, is more exciting than "ordinary" reality.[54]
This, however, did not keep him from applying his moral reflections on
real reality. Several participants also acknowledged that Nazi Germany
is a useful subject to bring up in discussions about examples of absolute
evil precisely because the idea is so common in western society. But they
do also like to problematize the notion of evil. As one of the interviewees
explained,

The problem is if people only relate it [the Nazi past] to something ghastly, and are unable to see that it could reasonably not have been *only* something ghastly, as then it would hardly have been functional. Then I think it becomes problematic, that people don't realize that such things don't just pop up. "Hi, now we're about to do evil things."[55]

None of the participants questioned or doubted the horrors of the Nazi past and Holocaust. They did, however, question how this past is represented in simplistic terms. All of the interviewees found it more credible that the Germans in the 1930s were no different to other people and thus more attracted to the opportunities Nazism offered to create a good life for themselves and their families than to a presumed opportunity of doing evil. They concluded that there must have been aspects of the Nazi regime that Germans (and others) found positive—but these aspects are seldom mentioned in mainstream culture. As many of the participants on the whole—especially those who have been interested in the topic for several years—use both popular history, academic history, and in some cases their own research as sources for their reflections, the difference especially between academic history and mainstream representations adds to their skeptical attitude toward the latter. It also justifies their idea about two versions of history: several of them used the labels "serious" (objective, real) and "unserious" (simplistic, black-and-white, history as entertainment). All of the 11 interviewees also equated the horrors of Nazi Germany with other murderous and genocidal events such as Stalin's Soviet Union, the terror regime of the Khmer Rouge, or the slaughters in Rwanda, and they connected that to a general discussion on the effects of utopian ideologies and totalitarianism. This view was also common among the rest of the participants. Again, they usually reflected that such in-depth discussions do not take part in mainstream media.

What was most illuminating about this group of people was that regardless of level of interest in the historical background, not only were they aware of the over-simplification of the past in mainstream media, they were also asking questions about the relevance and content of various media presented to them. Among the 11 interviewees, all except 1 told the same story about how their interest in the topic began: through watching popular Second World War adventure films, playing war games with toy soldiers, or—for those under 35—through computer gaming. This initial playful phase was followed by a wish to learn more about the reality behind the game or film, which led to the watching of documentary films and the reading of literature. For those who were also building models of tanks and planes, and so forth, the accuracy as compared to the historical originals was of course important. Inevitably, they all became more critical of the limited representations popular culture in general offered them. This description constantly reoccurred when talking to the rest of the people involved in the study. For many of those in the group of self-proclaimed Second World War fanatics, the process of gathering and processing knowledge also resulted in an increased amount of self-reflection and self-questioning: Why am I so fascinated by this topic? Does my interest in some way make me equivalent to a Nazi? What kind of person would I have been if I had been living in Nazi Germany? Of the 11 interviewees, 7 clearly expressed such problematizing thoughts. Without trying to make a psychological analysis, it seems probable that at least some of these people have attempted to work through these difficult questions in a sincere way. Hence, it is clear that attaining a more critical reflection of the Nazi past is possible but that you need to look beyond popular cultural productions about Nazi Germany to do it.

Conclusion

From the examination of a range of different media material it is clear that there is a mainstream popular image of Nazi Germany, namely that of a society ruled by a secular devil—or even the Judeo-Christian Devil incarnate—who inspires evil. The narrative of the Nazi past in these representations is clearly formulaic, with symbolic content based on identifiable archetypes, stereotypes, and tropes. The overtly moral message is simple and contains no demand for intellectual reflection. The fact that the Nazi past *really happened* is also strangely comforting in these representations as they seem to confirm that good does ultimately overcome evil. Simultaneously, there is an element of re-enchantment with all things Nazi, in which links to the fantastical make the real world more exciting.

Among viewers with a broader knowledge or interest in the field, however, this overly simplified good/evil dichotomy causes negative reactions and leads many on a personal quest for the real truth, which often develops into a deeper interest, a hobby, or even a way of life. A common denominator among the people partaking in this negative interpretative community is the idea of a creating a multifaceted image of history and being a person who thinks for him or herself as a reflective individual. Participants in the study valued their own critical reflection abilities even more because of the seriousness of the material they were reflecting on. As one of the interviewees put it: "They [the producers] imagine that the audience doesn't understand. So it [their programs] should be made into some kind of war entertainment instead." Another reiterated:

> It becomes like some MTV music video...There's nothing like...no reflecting activity set going....But I'm a fool for getting stuck on Discovery, they can run the most silly documentary on Nazism and I sit there watching anyway, I mean, because it's...the images are really great looking. Because it's usually old propaganda imagery they're using, so of course they look good! [laughter][56]

As a commercial product, Nazi Germany sells. And it sells better when it is packaged in simple binaries than in complex ideas, with primacy given to images over words, surface over content.

The attitudes expressed throughout this survey also offer further clues to significant changes in the concept of collective memory. Considering that these critical viewers' position on the Nazi past is part of a more general phenomenon, as described by Hill, it may illustrate how the dominant mediated image of this history—or, better, the mainstream image—can be questioned and remediated. Jean-François Lyotard's description of how the character of knowledge building in the postmodern world is changing from metanarratives into a number of smaller, independent, narratives reproduced in information networks, such as the Internet, may illustrate a different future for the collective memory of Nazi Germany.[57] What impact this might have on the established discourse is difficult to say, but it may go some way to unseating the four horsemen.

Notes

1. The simplest definition of *mainstream* is inherent in the word itself: something that is following the main current. Mainstream media content fits several of the basic characteristics of the *popular* and *mass culture:* it is widely broadcast and/or for sale on the media market, it is consumed and appreciated by large audiences, and it is

associated with entertainment and pleasure. There are close connections to literary theorist John G. Cawelti's concept of *formula,* which will be explained further on in the chapter. However, it is important to keep in mind that all formulaic texts are not mainstream, and that everything that is popular is not necessarily mainstream either. In this article, I will use the term *mainstream* for media content that is explicitly formulaic to its character and fits into the preceding definition of mass culture.

2. Eva Kingsepp, *Nazityskland i populärkulturen: Minne, myt, medier* [*The Third Reich in Popular Culture: Memory, Myth, Media*] (Stockholm, Stockholm University, JMK, 2008). The study examines the representation and reception of Nazi Germany in today's popular culture, and was conducted in Sweden between 2001 and 2007. It is mainly based on visual media—altogether more than 200 documentary and fiction films and digital games—but also includes literature, comics, role-playing and table-top games, militaria collecting, and alternative music (especially synth, industrial, and Neofolk). The ethnographic part includes 100 participants and is described in more detail later in this chapter.

3. Vivian Sobchack, "The Insistent Fringe: Moving Images and Historical Consciousness," *History and Theory,* Vol. 36, No. 4 (1997).

4. Nicholas Mirzoeff, *Watching Babylon: The War in Iraq and Global Visual Culture* (New York, Routledge, 2005), pp. 35–36.

5. See Ian Kershaw, *The "Hitler Myth": Image and Reality in the Third Reich* (Oxford, Oxford University Press, 1987). This image was also common in the discourse of the Allied states of the time. An example that has been highly influential, especially concerning the image of Hitler as a black magician (an idea that is still common in many popular representations of Nazi Germany), is Hermann Rauschning's book *Hitler Speaks* (London, 1939).

6. Viewer statistics from *Mediamätning i Skandinavien* (MMS, the Swedish company for television ratings) on documentaries about Nazi Germany and the Second World War broadcasted by Swedish television during the 1990s indicate that this topic especially attracts male viewers, regardless of age, while films about the Holocaust mainly have a female audience. Although the figures are 10 years old, I doubt there has been any significant change. Eva Kingsepp, "Man sitter ju inte där och frossar i nazism: En receptionsstudie av nazidokumentärer" (unpublished MA thesis, Stockholm University, JMK, 2001), p. 7.

7. Interviews conducted by Kingsepp 2002–2007 (recordings, transcripts, and field notes in the author's possession).

8. Kingsepp, *Nazityskland,* p. 212. It turned out that among the 11 interviewees the whole political spectrum from extreme left (anarchism, communism; 3 persons) to extreme right (national socialism, 1 person) was represented, including libertarian, liberal, and conservative. Two persons did not express any political preferences. However, the individuals in this small sample cannot be considered representative for others sharing the same political views.

9. Vivian Sobchack, *The Persistence of History: Cinema, Television, and the Modern Event* (New York, Routledge, 1996), p. 4. See also Erin Bell, "Televising History: The Past(s) on the Small Screen," *European Journal of Cultural Studies,* Vol. 10, No. 1 (2007), pp. 5–12.

10. Ludmila Jordanova, *History in Practice* (London, Oxford University Press, 2000), p. 141.

11. On collective intelligence, see, for example, Henry Jenkins, *Convergence Culture: Where Old and New Media Collide* (New York, New York University Press, 2006).

12. Jordanova, *History in Practice,* p. 142.

13. Kerwin Lee Klein, "On the Emergence of Memory in Historical Discourse," *Representations,* No. 69 (Winter 2000), pp. 127–150; Jordanova, *History in Practice,* pp. 7–8; Barbie Zelizer, "Reading the Past against the Grain: The Shape of Memory Studies," *Critical Studies in Mass Communication,* Vol. 12, No. 2 (1995).

14. The choice aimed at including three categories: films mentioned in literature on Nazi Germany/the Second World War and by the participants in the study; films currently available on the Swedish market (for rent and for sale, including on international web stores like Amazon.com); and films broadcasted on Swedish television between 2001 and 2007.

15. John G. Cawelti, *Adventure, Mystery, and Romance: Formula Stories as Art and Popular Culture* (Chicago, University of Chicago Press, 1976). Although there are some weak points in Cawelti's discussion—especially through his division between formulaic as mass culture and nonformula as high-brow, serious culture—the very concept of formula is valuable. See also Fredric Jameson, "Ideology, Narrative Analysis, and Popular Culture," *Theory and Society,* Vol. 4, No. 4 (Winter 1977), p. 543.

16. See also Stuart Hall, "The Spectacle of the Other," in Stuart Hall, ed., *Representation: Cultural Representations and Signifying Practices* (London, Sage, 1997).

17. Roland Barthes, *Elements of Semiology* (New York, Hill and Wang, 1968).

18. See Roland Barthes, "Rhetoric of the Image," in Stephen Heath, ed., *Image, Music, Text* (London, Fontana, 1977).

19. This is especially evident in documentaries like *Nazis: The Occult Conspiracy* (1998).

20. For example, the Italian documentary *The History of Nazism* (year unknown).

21. *The Occult History of the Third Reich: The Enigma of the Swastika* (1991).

22. The documentaries were produced in the United Kingdom, United States, (West) Germany, and Italy and include *Secrets of World War II: Adolf Hitler's Last Days* (2001) and *The Occult History of the Third Reich.* Ten of the fiction films used came from the United States, one was coproduced in the United States and United Kingdom, and the other three came from the United Kingdom, Germany,

France/Spain, and South Africa. They include *Downfall* (2004) and *Raiders of the Lost Ark* (1981). The games all connect Nazi Germany with the fantastic and the occult: *Return to Castle Wolfenstein* (United States, 2001), *Medal of Honor: Underground* (United States, 2000), *BloodRayne* (United States, 2002), and *Über-Soldier* (Russia/Germany, 2006).

23. Siegfried Jäger, "Discourse and Knowledge: Theoretical and Methodological Aspects of a Critical Discourse and Dispositive Analysis," in Ruth Wodak and Michael Meyer, eds., *Methods of Critical Discourse Analysis* (London, Sage, 2001), p. 32.

24. Good examples are offered in the titles of successful popular history books, such as Max Hastings *Armageddon: The Battle for Germany 1944–45* (New York, Knopf, 2004).

25. *The Last Days of Adolf Hitler* (2005).

26. Cawelti, *Adventure, Mystery, and Romance.*

27. Wolfdieter Bihl, *Der Tod Adolf Hitlers: Fakten und Überlebenslegenden* (Wien, Köln, and Weimar, Böhlau Verlag, 2000), pp. 137 ff; Henrik Eberle and Matthias Uhl, *Das Buch Hitler,* Swedish ed. *Hitler: Stalins hemliga dossier* (Stockholm, Prisma, 2006), pp. 23–25.

28. Bihl, *Der Tod,* pp. 137, 171; Eberle and Uhl, *Das Buch,* p. 23; Joscelyn Godwin, *Arktos: The Polar Myth in Science, Symbolism, and Nazi Survival* (Kempton, IL, Adventures Unlimited Press, 1996), p. 73. The speculations continue. See, for example, "Hitler's Skull Is a Woman's, Say DNA Tests," *Sky News* (September 28, 2009), where Gerrard Williams claims that "[t]here is no forensic evidence whatsoever that Hitler died in the bunker," and indicates that Hitler escaped to South America, available at http://news.sky.com/skynews/Home/World-News/Adolf-Hitler-Skull-Not-His-But-A-Womans-Says-US-Bone-Specialist-Nick-Bellantoni/Article/200909415393951?f=rss (accessed October 2009).

29. Nicholas Goodrick-Clarke, *Black Sun: Aryan Cults, Esoteric Nazism and the Politics of Identity* (New York, New York University Press, 2003), pp. 173–192.

30. See Kelly Hurley, "Abject and Grotesque," in Catherine Spooner and Emma McEvoy, eds., *The Routledge Companion to Gothic* (London, Routledge, 2007), pp. 137–139; Sidney Perkowitz, *Hollywood Science: Movies, Science, and the End of the World* (New York, Columbia University Press, 2007), pp. 142–143.

31. See Hall, "The Spectacle."

32. Kingsepp, *Nazityskland,* pp. 243–247. The themes were chosen as they are easy to demarcate and quantitatively belong to the most exploited in popular media, which might well be a result of their inherent mythical qualities. Other such themes could have been, for example, the battle of Stalingrad, the D-Day invasion, or the Holocaust.

33. See Charles P. Mitchell, *The Hitler Filmography: Worldwide Feature Film and Television Miniseries Portrayals, 1940 through 2000* (Jefferson, NC, McFarland, 2002), p. 2.

34. Kingsepp, *Nazityskland,* p. 151. See also, for example, "'Human' Hitler Disturbs Germans," BBC News, http://news.bbc.co.uk/2/hi/europe/3663044.stm; "Back in the Bunker," *The New Yorker,* http://www.newyorker.com/archive/2005/02/14/050214crci_cinema?currentPage=all (both accessed October 2009).

35. Gavriel D. Rosenfeld, *The World Hitler Never Made: Alternate History and the Memory of Nazism* (Cambridge, Cambridge University Press, 2005).

36. Kingsepp, *Nazityskland,* p. 200.

37. Annette Hill, *Restyling Factual TV: Audiences and News, Documentary and Reality Genres* (London, Routledge, 2007).

38. Jenny Thompson, *War Games: Inside the World of 20th-Century War Reenactors* (Washington, DC, Smithsonian Books, 2004).

39. Hill, *Restyling Factual TV,* p. 168.

40. Kingsepp, *Nazityskland,* pp. 213–217.

41. Extensive ethnographic research on the white supremacy movement in Sweden has been made, especially by Heléne Lööw. See, for example, her *Nazismen i Sverige 1980–1999: Den rasistiska undergroundrörelsen: musiken, myterna, riterna* (Stockholm, Ordfront, 2000). Although I did not look for pro-Nazi participants, it turned out that one of the individuals with whom I conducted in-depth interviews was a National Socialist. However, I decided not to exclude him from the selected group of interviewees, as I would not have excluded anyone else because of his or her political opinion.

42. Kingsepp, "Man sitter."

43. Thompson, *War Games.*

44. In Kingsepp, *Nazityskland,* p. 213. All quotations translated by the author.

45. Kingsepp, *Nazityskland,* p. 213.

46. For more on transmediality, see Jenkins, *Convergence Culture.*

47. As finding out the political preferences of the participants was not part of the study, it would be misleading (and also unethical) to afterwards present any statements about these. However, among the 100 participants, only three expressed doubts about the reality of the Holocaust.

48. It should be said that this view was not only expressed concerning representations of Nazi Germany but of mainstream representations of war and conflicts generally.

49. In Kingsepp, *Nazityskland,* p. 235.

50. Kingsepp, *Nazityskland,* p. 219.

51. Kingsepp, *Nazityskland,* p. 234.

52. Kingsepp, *Nazityskland,* pp. 202–203.

53. Hill, *Restyling Factual TV.*

54. Hill, *Restyling Factual TV,* pp. 237–238.

55. Hill, *Restyling Factual TV,* p. 207.

56. Both in Kingsepp, *Nazityskland,* p. 231.

57. Jean-François Lyotard, *The Postmodern Condition: A Report on Knowledge* (Manchester, Manchester University Press, 1979).

3

From Satan to Hitler: Theological and Historical Evil in C. S. Lewis, Philip Pullman, and J. K. Rowling

Sarah Fiona Winters

The novel *The Lion, the Witch and the Wardrobe* begins "Once there were four children whose names were Peter, Susan, Edmund, and Lucy. This story is about something that happened to them when they were sent away from London during the war because of the air-raids."[1] The cinematic adaptation of *The Lion, the Witch and the Wardrobe* takes these two sentences and transforms them into a six-minute sequence that dramatizes the Pevensie family's experience of those air-raids. In so doing, Disney changes the story from a Christian allegory into a Second World War allegory: instead of battling Satan, the children battle Hitler.

Fifty-five years separate the novel (1950) from the film (2005). In those 55 years, fantasy for children increasingly incarnates evil as the Nazi rather than as the Devil. Writers who were children during the Second World War, including Susan Cooper (b. 1935), Diana Wynne Jones (b. 1934), and Alan Garner (b. 1934), grew up believing in Nazi Germany as the great force for evil in the world. Cooper, for example, writes

> My generation, especially in Britain and Europe, was given a strong image of good and bad at an impressionable age. We were the children of World War II. Our insecurities may not have differed in kind from those of the modern child, but they were more concrete. That something that might be lurking in the shadow behind the bedroom door at night wasn't, for us, a terrible formless bogeyman; it was specific—a Nazi paratrooper with a bayonet.[2]

As a result, the work of Philip Pullman (b. 1946) and J. K. Rowling (b. 1965) show the influence of this representation of evil as the Nazi, and in turn pave the way for the explicit parallels drawn by the film. Where Lewis's evil, while inflected by history, is theological, Pullman's, Rowling's, and Disney's evil, while inflected by theology, is undeniably historical.

As a consequence of the changing *representation* of evil, the texts in question also change the type of *response* to evil. In Lewis's text, the best, indeed only, way for the children to vanquish the White Witch is by not trying to do so; instead, they must simply be obedient to the will of Aslan. However, obedience as a virtue underwent a serious challenge in the popular imagination in the 1960s because of the work the work of Hannah Arendt and Stanley Milgram. In 1963, the year of C. S. Lewis's death, Arendt's *Eichmann in Jerusalem: A Report on the Banality of Evil* argued that it was not fanaticism or hatred that led Adolf Eichmann to the crime of genocide but rather conscientious obedience to the requirements of his job.[3] That same year, the media reported on Stanley Milgram's experiments that showed that in a random group of people, about two-thirds would administer electric shocks to the point of agony and possibly death to another human being when instructed to by an authority figure.[4] David Cesarini has argued that Arendt and Milgram became associated with each other in the public psyche: "From the 1960s on, a synergy developed between the symbol of Arendt's Eichmann and the symbol of Milgram's subjects, involved in discussing everything from the Vietnam war to the tobacco industry, and, of course, reflecting back on the Holocaust."[5] Whereas for Lewis evil lay in rebellion and good in obedience to authority, as a result of Arendt's and Milgram's work, the scale of value for later writers was often reversed.

The Lion, the Witch and the Wardrobe (1950)

In *Mere Christianity,* C. S. Lewis, in his role as Christian apologist, outlines two views of the nature of evil: "One is the Christian view that this is a good world that has gone wrong, but still retains the memory of what it ought to have been. . . . Goodness is, so to speak, itself: badness is only spoiled goodness . . . evil is a parasite, not an original thing."[6] Although Lewis does not use the term, this understanding of evil is Boethian. The other view of evil is Dualist, the belief that "there are two equal and independent powers at the back of everything, one of them good and the other bad, and that this universe is the battlefield in which they fight out an endless war." Lewis, while intellectually rejecting this view of evil, is nevertheless imaginatively drawn to it.

"I personally think that next to Christianity, Dualism is the manliest and most sensible creed on the market."[7] Indeed, the genre of fantasy seems to demand some sort of Dualist vision of evil not only because it so often constructs its narrative around the battle between good and evil but also because any attempt to imagine evil as nothing results in a linguistically constructed *something*.

The first appearance of the White Witch in the text embodies both modes of evil. When Edmund first encounters the White Witch, the text describes her as

A great lady, taller than any woman that Edmund had ever seen. She . . . was covered in white fur up to her throat and held a long straight golden wand in her right hand and wore a golden crown on her head. Her face was white—not merely pale, but white like snow or paper or icing-sugar, except for her very red mouth. It was a beautiful face in other respects, but proud and cold and stern.[8]

The color white functions in this passage as a metaphor for evil as nothingness: white equals blankness and absence. But the text complicates this Boethian metaphor by claiming that the witch's face is "not merely pale," that is, it is not just lacking in color. Indeed, the whiteness of her face is substantial enough to be awarded the compliment of three similes, suggesting that the whiteness is something that exists in its own right, something with substance. The first of these similes is "like snow," an image that connects the witch to the landscape surrounding her, a world of snow that she herself has brought about. In Narnia under the witch's rule it is "always winter and never Christmas."[9] Of course, this state of affairs sounds dreadful and evil, yet when Lucy first walks through the wardrobe into Narnia, the snowy night she finds there is enchanted, beautiful, and an object of desire to generations of readers. The second simile is "like paper" and although white or blank paper does suggest absence, that absence is one of potential, of the blank slate on which beauty can be created; moreover, paper is not usually an evil thing for writers or readers. The final simile, "like icing-sugar," represents evil as insubstantial since icing-sugar is powdery, and as perverted good since sweetness is good but too much of it is an evil and makes one sick. For the child reader, what better metaphor could there be than sugar for the seductiveness of evil?[10] The icing-sugar image is, therefore, Boethian, but it is followed by the image of the witch's "very red mouth." The juxtaposition of icing-sugar and a red mouth evokes the gingerbread house and the hungry witch of *Hansel and Gretel,* her mouth red with the blood of her child victims. So where the icing-sugar whiteness of the Witch's face suggests Boethian evil as the perversion of good, the red of her mouth evokes Dualist evil as force and substance, as something alive. The coloring of the Witch embodies Lewis's imaginative reconciliation of two mutually exclusive theologies of evil.

Only obedience to Aslan can save Edmund and his siblings from the Witch. Questions of obedience are raised very early in the text; Edmund's propensity to evil is established when he challenges Susan: "And who are you to say when I'm to go to bed?"[11] His redemption is achieved partly through his learning to be obedient: "Edmund was on the other side of Aslan, looking all the time at Aslan's face. He felt a choking feeling and wondered if he ought to say something; but a moment later he felt that he was not expected to do anything except to wait, and to do what he was told."[12] Obedience and passivity saves not only Edmund, but also the good children, who are informed by Mrs. Beaver, when they want to rescue their brother from the White Witch, that "the only chance of saving either him or yourselves is to keep away from her"[13] and get themselves to Aslan as quickly as they can. While this emphasis on obedience might be read as didacticism directed toward children, it also corresponds with Lewis's theological message for adults. In *The Screwtape Letters,* published in 1942, Lewis's experienced devil, Screwtape, admonishes his novice nephew, Wormwood, for his excitement over the Second World War in these words: "Let us think rather how to use, than how to enjoy, this European war. For it has certain tendencies inherent in it which are, in themselves, by no means in our favor. We may hope for a good deal of cruelty and unchastity. But, if we are not careful, we shall see thousands turning in this tribulation to the Enemy."[14] The Christian's response to evil, suggests Lewis, should not be to attack it directly, but to turn to God. The historical war is as nothing to the great theological war.

His Dark Materials (1995–2000)

The vision of evil in Pullman's *His Dark Materials* is ostensibly Dualist. In the words of John Parry:

> There are two great powers . . . and they've been fighting since time began. Every advance in human life, every scrap of knowledge and wisdom and decency we have has been torn by one side from the teeth of the other. Every little increase in human freedom has been fought over ferociously between those who want us to know more and be wiser and stronger, and those who want us to obey and be humble and submit.[15]

While Lewis would agree with the first two sentences here, merely assigning, in complete opposition to Pullman, good to the Authority and evil to the Rebels, he would not recognize the dichotomy Pullman constructs in the third sentence. For Lewis, to obey, be humble, and to submit *is* to know more, and be wiser and stronger. Pullman constructs these oppositions not just because of his Blakean reading of Milton, but because he historicizes obedience and submission to Authority as passive acceptance of a fascist regime.

The preeminent incarnation of evil in *His Dark Materials* is Mrs. Coulter. Much of Pullman's trilogy is a rewriting of Lewis's *Chronicles of Narnia,* and Mrs. Coulter is his version of the White Witch. But unlike Lewis's Witch, Mrs. Coulter represents not Satan, but Hitler. Lord Asriel and Mary Malone both function as Satan figures in the series: the former a Blakean and Byronic rewriting of Milton's Satan, a Promethean hero-rebel; the latter a similar rewriting of Milton's Serpent, a tempter who opens minds through the combination of science and the art of storytelling. With the Devil transformed, in the first case into an ambiguous character and in the second into a good one, Mrs. Coulter must take on the role of the evil figure, and partly because Satan is already rewritten she evokes not him but Hitler. In a universe parallel to our own, she serves and represents the Church in the series, a Church that resembles in many ways the Nazi Party during its years of power in Europe. The evil the Church does in the series is modern rather than medieval in its character, more Gestapo than Spanish Inquisition.

While there are many examples in the trilogy to draw from, three narrative sequences must suffice here to indicate Pullman's vision of the

Church as a quasi-Nazi organization. The first is, of course, Bolvangar. The very location of this facility, in the north, alludes to the mystical underpinnings of the Nazis' Aryan myth, since the theory (at least in the twentieth century) was that the Aryans came originally from the North Pole.[16] The scientific patina of the facility, with its "shiny white surfaces" and "faint perpetual hospital-medical smell," its men in "white coats," and (literally) soulless nurses with their "brisk, blank, sensible air,"[17] evokes the efficiency and scientific pretensions of the child tortures carried out by Josef Mengele at Auschwitz. The initial treatment of Lyra upon her arrival echoes the treatment of Jewish arrivals at Nazi concentration camps: "When she was washed and dry, the nurse took her temperature and looked into her eyes and throat, and then measured her height and put her on some scales before writing a note on a clipboard. Then she gave Lyra some pyjamas and a dressing gown. They were clean, and of good quality . . . but again there was a secondhand air about them. Lyra felt very uneasy."[18] "It was hard to tell the difference between these people: all the men looked similar in their white coats and with their clipboards and pencils, and the women resembled one another too, the uniforms and their strange bland calm manner making them all look like sisters."[19] Everything is cleaner and colder in Bolvangar than in Auschwitz, as befits the cold, clean Arctic, but the sinister significance of the measurement taking and the secondhand clothing must be clear to many readers of the text.

Bolvangar is the shiny scientific face of the Nazi concentration camps. The grey and dirty face appears in the World of the Dead. Although the Church does not run the prison, it was established by the Authority that the Church serves, and they perpetuate lies about it. The souls of the dead undergo an experience here that draws upon several different mythological sources, including Sheol, Hades, and Limbo, but that also evokes in several images the evil and despair of Nazi Europe. The newly dead "trudg[e] in silence under a sky that had finally darkened to a dull iron grey" toward a town that "looks like a refugee camp" where "there are hundreds of people arriving every minute," and where visible on the horizon is "a dirty-coloured smoke . . . rising slowly to add its darkness to the dismal air," an air which, in addition to being "heavy and full of smoke" is also redolent of "acrid chemicals, decaying vegetable matter, sewage."[20] This landscape is Hell as imagined by the Moderns, not the Medievals.

The third example from the text of the equation of the forces of the Authority with the Nazi party is the Consistorial Court of Discipline. Fra

Pavel tells the Court that "I had not seen torture before . . . and it made me feel faint and sick."[21] In this sentiment Fra Pavel echoes the Bolvangar scientist who tells Mrs. Coulter with regards to the improvements in the intercision process, "But simply *tearing* was the only option for some time . . . however distressing that was to the adult operators. If you remember, we had to discharge quite a number for reasons of stress-related anxiety."[22] Both statements recall Nazis such as Eichmann who complained of the Jewish genocide that "I was horrified. My nerves aren't strong enough . . . I can't listen to such things . . . such things without their affecting me. Even today, if I see someone with a deep cut, I have to look away. I could never have been a doctor. I still remember how I visualized the scene and began to tremble, as if I'd been through something, some terrible experience."[23] Arendt wrote of this attitude:

> Hence the problem was how to overcome not so much their conscience as the animal pity by which all normal men are affected in the presence of physical suffering. The trick used by Himmler—who apparently was rather strongly afflicted with these instinctive reactions himself—was very simple and probably very effective; it consisted in turning these instincts around, as it were, in directing them towards the self. So that instead of saying: What horrible things I did to people!, the murderers would be able to say: What horrible things I had to watch in the pursuance of my duties, how heavily the task weighed upon my shoulders![24]

Fra Pavel appears to be using the same trick as Eichmann and Himmler. The Court of which he is a part also alludes to the ascetic streak of the Nazi party, embodied most famously by the vegetarian Hitler himself, whose counterpart in the text is Father McPhail, who "drank only water and ate only bread and fruit."[25] Moreover, McPhail couches the decision to embark on a final solution to the problem of Dust in language that deliberately recalls another Final Solution: "The Oblation Board sought to understand the effects of Dust; we must destroy it altogether. Nothing less than that . . . Better a world with no Church and no Dust than a world where every day we have to struggle under the hideous burden of sin. Better a world purged of all that!"[26] Although no one of these details can be reduced to an allusion to Nazi Europe on its own, the cumulative effect is of a regime in Lyra's universe resembling one that existed not in hers, but in our parallel universe, the regime ruled over by Adolf Hitler.

Of course the Church in Lyra's universe is not exactly ruled over by Mrs. Coulter, but she resembles Hitler in other aspects of his role within the Nazi Party. An intensely feminine and feminized figure in the text, she displays in the private and personal realm the same degree of hypnotic charisma that characterized Hitler's performances in the public arena. Almost everyone in the series is deeply afraid of her. Most significantly, she is able to command an astonishing degree of obedience to her will, even from the Specters themselves: "Even in her sickened distress, Lena Feldt could see that Mrs. Coulter had more force in her soul than anyone she had ever seen. It didn't surprise her to see that the Specter was under Mrs. Coulter's power; no one could resist that authority."[27] "Authority" is more than just a dirty word in Pullman's trilogy; it is a synonym for evil. That Mrs. Coulter possesses as much of it as did Hitler makes her a true *Führer* figure.

Obedience is usually a mistake in *His Dark Materials:* unlike the Pevensies, Lyra and Will are disobedient, stubborn, independent children who battle evil directly and, often, alone. The Master of Jordan tells Lyra that her disobedience not does detract from her essential goodness: "You haven't found it easy to obey us, but we are very fond of you, and you've never been a bad child."[28] Lyra must use her own initiative to rescue Iorek, and whereas Susan and Lucy have a fine and easy time riding on Aslan, Lyra finds riding the armored bear decidedly more challenging: "She found she couldn't just sit; she had to ride actively."[29] Like Lyra, Will grows up without owing obedience to his parents, since his father is absent and he has had to parent his ill mother. Although the angel Balthamos initially tells Will "You could do with some sense . . . Some faculty to enable you to recognize wisdom and incline you to respect and obey it,"[30] he is the one who eventually recognizes the importance of Will's mission and tenders the boy *his* respect.

Obedience freely chosen, however, can be a force for good in the series. Naomi Wood argues that "although Lyra begins her quest believing, childlike, in moral clarity, she quickly learns that many adults do not obey the rules. In the first book of the series, Lyra is more successful when she disobeys than when she submits, when she lies rather than tells the truth."[31] In the second book, the issue of obedience becomes more complicated: once Lyra throws her lot in with Will, she starts to obey him just as she learns to obey the alethiometer. This change suggests that Pullman believes disobedience should precede obedience in the process of moral development, in contrast to the conventional thinking that children should be obedient while adults question authority. It is an adult, Lee Scorseby, who experiences the joy of obedience when he shares the visions of the shaman Dr. Grumman: "Lee felt whatever bird nature he was sharing respond with joy to the eagle queen, and whatever humanness he had left felt the strangest of pleasures: that of offering eager obedience to a stronger power that was wholly right."[32] Obedience, therefore, is not a vice in itself; immature and unthinking obedience is. Characters must choose freely whether or not to offer their obedience. The key word in the passage above is "strangest"; Lewis would not find obedience a "strange" pleasure but a natural one, and the fact that Pullman calls it "strange" illustrates just how much disobedience has become the default virtue in his world view. While Wood suggests, rightly, that "Lewis is Augustinian on obedience and the Fall, while Pullman is closer to gnostic theology,"[33] I would add that Lewis is pre–Second World War on obedience while Pullman is closer to Arendt and Milgram.

Harry Potter (1997–2007)

During Harry's first journey on the Hogwarts Express, Ron Weasley gives him a Chocolate Frog card detailing the career in brief of Albus Dumbledore, a career that includes the information that "Dumbledore is particularly famous for his defeat of the dark wizard Grindelwald in 1945."[34] The date sets the wizarding world's battle against evil firmly in Muggle history. Although readers do not learn until *Deathly Hallows* that Dumbledore's defeat of the Germanic-named Grindelwald is not actually an event *in* the Second World War, but fought parallel to it, the date sets the tone for the developing characterization of first Dumbledore, and then Harry and his allies, as fighters against Nazi evil.

J. K. Rowling has stated that she deliberately historicized her evil characters as Nazis in the series. On her web site she characterizes the Death Eaters' obsession with purebloods and mudbloods as identical to that of the Nazis: "If you think this is far-fetched, look at some of the real charts the Nazis used to show what constituted 'Aryan' or 'Jewish' blood. I saw one in the Holocaust museum in Washington when I had already devised the 'pure-blood,' 'half-blood' and 'Muggle-born' definitions, and was chilled to see that the Nazis used precisely the same warped logic as the Death Eaters."[35] In a public interview after *Deathly Hallows* was published (the famous "Dumbledore is gay" interview) she was asked to elaborate on her use of Nazi parallels and replied:

> It was conscious. I think that if you're, I think most of us if you were asked to name a very evil regime we would think Nazi Germany. There were parallels in the ideology. I wanted Harry to leave our world and find exactly the same problems in the wizarding world. So you have the intent to impose a hierarchy, you have bigotry, and this notion of purity, which is this great fallacy, but it crops up all over the world. People like to think themselves superior and that if they can pride themselves in nothing else they can pride themselves on perceived purity. So yeah that follows a parallel. It wasn't really exclusively that. I think you can see in the Ministry even before it's taken over, there are parallels to regimes we all know and love.[36]

Rowling makes the point that institutional evil in her series is not "exclusively" Nazi; the Ministry embodies the lesser evil of the British response to terrorism, a more contemporary historical parallel and one that needs a separate essay to develop.[37] But the Death Eaters are certainly Nazis, as has been frequently argued by fans posting on the Internet. An essay posted on the fan site *The Leaky Cauldron* in 2007 by Wagga Wagga Werewolf, for example, points out some of the Second World War allegory: "[S]ome of the second-guessing of the leader's reactions or wishes, plus jockeying for position, and inability to tolerate dissent, seem alike in both organisations [Death Eaters and the Nazi Party]. . . . The denial by the Minister of Magic, Cornelius Fudge, that Voldemort had arisen echoes Neville Chamberlain's 'peace in our time' statements which preceded the inevitable declaration of World War Two."[38] However, the essay concludes that the Death Eaters are modeled on totalitarian regimes in general rather than the Nazi regime in particular. This argument was persuasive when it was made, but has been superseded by the blatant, deliberate allegory in *Deathly Hallows* of the institutionalism of anti-Semitism after Hitler's rise to power. The parallels are so clear they hardly need delineating here, but they include the Muggle-born Registration Commission, the propaganda leaflet "MUDBLOODS and the Dangers They Pose to a Peaceful

Pure-Blood Society,"[39] and the sculpture, engraved with the slogan Magic Is Might, of a witch and wizard enthroned on "mounds of carved humans . . . with rather stupid, ugly faces."[40]

Whereas *The Lion, the Witch and the Wardrobe* constructs theological evil, and *His Dark Materials* transforms theological into historical evil, *Harry Potter* splits theological and historical, pre-Nazi and post-Nazi ideas of evil both within Voldemort and between Voldemort and other characters. The preeminent incarnation of evil in *Harry Potter* has two names: Tom Riddle, the name belonging to history, and Voldemort, the name belonging to theology. Voldemort is certainly Satanic, with his serpentine features and his snake, Nagini. Yet the deadly whiteness of his skin functions both as the (theological) Boethian evil that characterizes the White Witch and as a signifier for his (historical) racism. His evil lies both in his metaphysical rebellion against his own mortality and in his desire to murder and enslave Muggles and Muggle-borns. The former, however, predominates: Voldemort would never, like Hitler, commit suicide over the failure of his political aims. His priorities are clear in his statement (as Tom Riddle) to Harry at the end of *Chamber of Secrets:* "Haven't I already told you . . . that killing Mudbloods doesn't matter to me any more? For many months now, my new target has been—*you.*"[41] His death, too, is both theological and historical: "Tom Riddle hit the floor with a mundane finality, his body feeble and shrunken, the white hands empty, the snake-like face vacant and unknowing."[42] The text assigns the dead man his human, historical name, since his flight from death (*vol de mort*) is now over. The use of the adjective "mundane" seems highly deliberate here, designed to evoke the post-Arendt understanding of evil as banal; its proximity to the noun "finality" also gestures toward the evil of the Final Solution. Yet the adjectives "empty" and "vacant" characterize evil as Boethian; the triumph over evil reveals that evil is nothingness.

The historical evil in the series resides less with Voldemort than with his followers. The Death Eaters resemble the Nazi colleagues and followers of Hitler to a large degree. The defendants at Nuremberg, for example, can be categorized as the following:

The Thugs: Julius Streicher and Ernst Kaltenbrunner
The Weaklings: Joachim von Ribbentrop and Constantine Neurath
The Power-Hungry: Hermann Göring and Martin Bormann

The Loyalists: Alfred Rosenberg
The Idealists: Rudolf Hess, Fritz Saukel, Baldur von Schirarch
The Obedient Soldiers: Wilhelm Frick, Wilhelm Keitel[43]

Rowling's Death Eaters can be grouped into similar categories.

The Thugs: Fenrir Greyback; Crabbe Snr. and Goyle Snr.
The Weakling: Peter Pettigrew
The Power-Hungry: Lucius Malfoy
The Loyalists: Barty Crouch Jr. and Bellatrix Lestrange

The idealist and the obedient soldier do not appear in the Death Eater ranks, but the former does correspond partly with Grindelwald, who inspires the youthful Dumbledore with the power of his ideas and then spends decades in solitary prison as did Rudolf Hess.

This list of Death Eaters is similar to the way in which Dumbledore, in *Half-Blood Prince,* characterizes Tom Riddle's hangers-on at Hogwarts, some of whom became the first Death Eaters: "they were a motley collection; a mixture of the weak seeking protection, the ambitious seeking some shared glory, and the thuggish, gravitating towards a leader who could show them more refined forms of cruelty."[44] But this passage also partly characterizes the banal evil found on the side of Voldemort's opponents in the Ministry of Magic, namely the ambitious Barty Crouch Sr. and Percy Weasley, and the cruel Dolores Umbridge, all of whom possess some Nazi qualities.

Barty Crouch Sr., Sirius informs Harry, made his career by "ordering very harsh measures against Voldemort's supporters," authorizing use of the Unforgivable Curses against suspects, and becoming "as ruthless and cruel as many on the Dark Side."[45] He places his own son under the Imperius Curse (the forced obedience spell), only to suffer the same fate from that rebellious son. Crouch's error is to use Voldemort's tactics against him, in contrast to Harry who, when faced with the Avada Kedavra Curse (the killing spell) from the Dark Lord, responds with Expelliarmus (the disarming spell). Caught between ruthlessness and family loyalty, Crouch goes mad under the pressure of the Imperius Curse. His rigidity is reflected in his appearance, which includes a (surely deliberate) Hitleresque "toothbrush moustache."[46]

Crouch's biggest fan is Percy Weasley, whose pomposity, rigidity, and ambition lead him to sacrifice his family for the state until his eventual redemption in *Deathly Hallows.* The series begins by not taking Percy at all seriously and only gradually revealing that his faults are not merely ridiculous but evil. Like Eichmann, Percy proves, in Hannah Arendt's words, "that the horrible can be not only ludicrous but outright funny."[47] Percy's biggest critics are his brothers Fred and George; their function in the text is to suggest that while evil can be silly and banal and outright funny, good can be exciting, inventive, and deliberately rather than unintentionally funny: the outlaw twins are superior to their prefect and civil servant brother.

A study from 1966, which examined public perceptions of the Eichmann trial in a Californian neighborhood, concluded:

The evidence presented at the trial, and the way this evidence was reported and interpreted in the responsible mass media, offered three images of Eichmann's complicity. One image was that he was a monster—a sadist, a moral degenerate who had personally murdered. A second image was that he was a zealot, probably not personally engaging in murder, but carrying out his assignment with enthusiasm and zeal. A third image was that he was a bureaucrat, an acquiescent cog in the Nazi machine, acting primarily out of obedience and performing his tasks with impersonal efficiency.[48]

Dolores Umbridge fits all three of these images. She is a morally degenerate sadist who delights in publicly humiliating Sybil Trelawny and Hagrid, and in causing Harry physical pain through the writing of lines in his own flesh, and in her willingness to break the law by performing the Cruciatus Curse. She is certainly a zealot with a fervent enthusiasm for her task of spying on and interfering with Hogwarts. And her endless ordinances and insistence on her title of Senior Undersecretary to the Minister cast her as an efficient bureaucrat. Moreover, she is racist (she hates part-humans), a devotee of a banal aesthetic (pink ribbons and frolicking kittens), and the founder and leader of the Hitler Youth-like Inquisitorial Squad. In *Deathly Hallows,* she reappears as persecuting the Muggle-born and lying about her own pure-blood status. Arguably the most despicable figure in the series, it is likely many readers are more repulsed by her than they are by the Satanic Voldemort himself.

In the previously cited interview, Rowling goes on to answer the second part of the question, about what lessons she wanted readers to learn from her parallels with the Nazi regime:

> So you ask what lessons, I suppose. The Potter books in general are a prolonged argument for tolerance, a prolonged plea for an end to bigotry, and I think [it's] one of the reasons that some people don't like the books, but I think that's [*sic*] it's a very healthy message to pass on to younger people that you should question authority and you should not assume that the establishment or the press tells you all of the truth.[49]

Harry's maturation in the series is characterized partly as his learning when and how to disobey. One of his greatest strengths as the hero is revealed halfway through the series, in *Goblet of Fire,* when he is the only student in his class able to resist the Imperius Curse. All three of the Unforgivable Curses—Imperius, Cruciatus, and Avada Kedavra—correspond with Nazi techniques for domination and control, but only the Imperius Curse can be resisted by its victim once it has actually hit that victim: no one can refuse to be tortured or killed, but anyone can refuse to obey. The operation of the curse resembles hypnosis for entertainment: "Harry watched as, one by one, his classmates did the most extraordinary things under its influence. Dean Thomas hopped three times around the room, singing the national anthem. Lavendar Brown imitated a squirrel. Neville performed a series of quite astonishing gymnastics he would certainly not have been capable of in his normal state."[50] The anthem and gymnastics performed by people hypnotized into obedience in a mass spectacle form a fascinating parallel to the Nuremberg Rallies. Harry's resistance to this curse sets him apart from most other members of the wizarding world.

Harry spends his six years at school questioning authority and learning when to obey and when to disobey it;[51] he then spends his seventh year out of school asking the same questions of the authority of Albus Dumbledore himself. This questioning forms much of Harry's inner conflict in *The Deathly Hallows* when Dumbledore's troubled past is revealed to him (and to the reader). Grindelwald is another Hitler figure: he turns the mystical symbol of the Deathly Hallows into a sign feared and hated by Victor Krum in a process that recalls the history of the swastika; he establishes a feared prison at Nurmengard, where he is ironically imprisoned himself, with the slogan "For the Greater Good" written over the doors (any historically literate reader will think immediately of both Nuremberg and Auschwitz);[52] and he is defeated in 1945. He is Dumbledore's shadowself, his monster in the mirror. Harry, however, chooses to follow the mission that Dumbledore assigned him, and even tells McGonagall that he is at Hogwarts "acting on Dumbledore's orders."[53] However, his obedience is not blind; he *chooses,* after serious soul-searching over Dobby's grave, to seek out Horcruxes rather than Hallows; this decision is his triumph in the realm of the historical allegory.

Harry's decision to obey Dumbledore's orders about the Horcruxes characterizes him as a thinking soldier fighting against Nazi evil; his immediate decision to follow Dumbledore's plan that he allow Voldemort to kill him takes him away from the historical world and into the eternal one: in his walk through the forest to his death, a walk that echoes Aslan's approach to the Stone Table in *The Lion, the Witch and the Wardrobe,* he is no longer a resistance fighter or Allied soldier obeying his leader's orders, but Jesus submitting himself to the will of the God the Father in the Garden of Gethsemane. Because the evil in the series is both historical and theological, the struggle against that evil requires *both* disobedience and obedience. Farah Mendlesohn has argued that "Rowling has no real problem with authoritarian figures and how they are constructed . . . The debate between good and evil in these books has little to do with arguments for egalitarianism."[54] While Mendlesohn's second point here may be valid, the first (made before *Deathly Hallows* was published) is not: the debate between good and evil in the series is structured largely around problems of authority because the series treats authority as both a theological and historical concept.

The Lion, the Witch and the Wardrobe (2005)

The film *The Lion, the Witch and the Wardrobe* announces in its first scenes that it is moving evil from the theological to the historical. The first images we see are clouds in a night sky. The camera dips below the clouds and for an instant we see searching beams of light. These 16 short seconds showing light in the form of searchlights beaming up from London suggests the cosmic battle between the forces of light and dark that structures

Susan Cooper's *Dark Is Rising* series. But then the soundtrack begins with the air-raid siren and martial drums, and the German bombers enter the screen.[55] In the production team's commentary on the DVD, Mark Johnson, the producer, says that the film begins this way partly because "it is where Peter presumably gets the idea of having the griffins drop the . . . ah, the rocks or bombs on the White Witch's army."[56] That it would be acceptable for Peter to adopt an enemy's tactic for use against another enemy supports the filmmakers' vision of the evil in the text as historical rather than theological; Lewis would never condone using the Devil's tactics against him or any other antagonist.

The next image of evil in the film is the White Witch herself. She is as pale as Lewis's Witch, but this paleness is envisaged by the actress playing her, Tilda Swinton, as historically rather than theologically significant: "I thought that if anything she should look Arian [*sic*] because apart from being a fantasy film, it's also a historical film; they're Second World War children and their father's away fighting fascism in Europe, and I thought that if anything she should look Nazi, and I actually do throw a Nazi salute when I'm on the stone table."[57] The film achieves this representation of the Witch as Nazi through both the appearance of the Witch and the allegory of Narnia as occupied Europe.

Tilda Swinton's appearance and acting characterize her as, progressively, an Aryan, a Nazi, and a Hitler-figure. Although Lewis's text never specifies the color of the Witch's hair, Pauline Baynes's illustrations give her long dark hair. In the film, the Witch is blonde.[58] Her war chariot is drawn by polar bears, an invention of the film, and one which resembles *His Dark Materials* in alluding to the Nazi myth surrounding the Arctic origins of the Aryan warrior. The Nazi salute Swinton refers to in her interview is subtle: during the sacrifice of Aslan the Witch throws out her arm in a gesture to halt the noise her followers are making; in the shot that follows she lowers her arm slowly in a movement that looks like the end of a "Heil Hitler!" salute. Moreover, Swinton plays the Witch as emotionally cold and inaccessible. The director, Andrew Adamson, declares "I really wanted the White Witch to be more sophisticated, more . . . more sort of a cold, sophisticated type of evil." Johnson adds, "She has decided to be cold and indifferent which is something that probably scares children more than anything else, an adult who seemingly is emotionless."[59] In this frigidity she embodies not just the frozen world she has created, but also the "icy coldness" Hitler repeatedly claimed to have in the face of his enemies and victims.[60] Swinton's Witch's coldness and impersonality suggest the mechanical efficiency of the Nazi machine.[61]

If the Witch is Hitler, then Narnia is occupied Europe. Adamson makes this connection explicit in the director's commentary when he explains the function of the character of the Fox, who is not in the novel: "It set up the idea of Narnia having almost an Underground, an Allied Resistance."[62] Lewis argues that Christianity believes that the war between good and evil "is a civil war, a rebellion, and that we are living in a part of the universe occupied by the rebel."[63] After the Second World War and after Arendt and Milgram, the popular imagination conceived of rebel as a rebel *against* evil. It is difficult for today's reader of fantasy to conceive of an occupation *by* the rebel; the occupation must be by the tyrant, the military dictator, the *Führer;* the rebel must be, therefore, the fighter for good, not evil. Thus, whereas Lewis's novel characterizes the struggle against the Witch as a submission to the returning King, Aslan, the film based on that novel characterizes that struggle against the Witch as a rebellion.[64]

Rebellion and disobedience are privileged in the film as the appropriate response for the children to the Witch's evil. Whereas the novel's first two sentences characterize the children as passive—the story "happens to them" when they are "sent away"—the film's opening sequence makes the children, particularly Edmund, much more active. The sequence ends with Peter demanding of Edmund, "Why can't you just do as you're told?" This question is both complex and resonant in terms of what follows: Edmund's disobedience has nearly resulted in his and Peter's death, but that disobedience is an act of familial loyalty, prompted by love for his absent soldier father. In the novel, Edmund's independence and defiance is unambiguously evil; in the film it foreshadows the defiance of the Narnian Resistance, disobedient to the White Witch as their European counterparts were disobedient to Hitler. While Edmund comes in the film to submit to Peter's leadership, he disobeys him again at the crucial moment when Peter tells him to flee the battlefield and Edmund instead attacks and destroys the Witch's wand. In the film, it is Edmund's disobedience to authority, even though the authority is benign, that contributes to the defeat of evil. Lewis demands obedience; Pullman and Rowling suggest that both obedience and disobedience can be effective strategies against evil; Disney, by changing the narrative from a Christian allegory to a Second World War allegory, uncharacteristically celebrates disobedience.

Conclusion

If the major fantasy marketed to and consumed by children (and their parents) today does indeed transform the Devil into Hitler, then consequences arise that have implications for the way our culture thinks about evil. One is that by historicizing the theological, fantasy risks theologizing the historical. For example, Jason Isaacs, who plays Lucius Malfoy in the *Harry Potter* films, makes the comment: "If you're someone like me who finds work enjoyably tortured—I'm constantly niggling away trying to make it better and realer and more three-dimensional—it's nice to leave all that at home and turn up at Harry Potter and just be unalloyed Nazi evil."[65] In this statement Isaacs (who is Jewish) characterizes Nazi evil as too pure, too "unalloyed" to be quite real. Belief in the actual historical Nazi, then, may take on the same quality as belief in the Devil: both will become figures not of history but of myth. But once fantastic evil evokes Nazi Germany, then readers born in generations after 1945 may, instead of studying and learning from the variety of specific responses to Nazi evil in the 1930s and 1940s, imagine Hitler and his henchmen as fantastic creatures of supernatural evil, inevitably vanquished by the conventions of the genre. For example, if evil is represented by the Nazi, then good consists primarily of disobedience, and that which was once a virtue inculcated in children, obedience, becomes a sin; but this construction of obedience obscures the fact that historical opposition to the Nazis consisted not only of the disobedience of civilians, but also of the obedience of hundreds of thousands of Allied soldiers to their commanding officers. This complexity of response is certainly not present in the film of *The Lion, the Witch and the Wardrobe,* where Edmund destroys the Witch's wand only when he *disobeys* Peter, his commanding officer, at the climactic moment of the battle. Fantasy uses history for its own purposes; it does not serve history: the *omnipresence* of Nazis as the archetype of evil in contemporary fantasy leads to their construction as monsters of the timeless *present* rather than as humans of a specific past.

Notes

1. C. S. Lewis, *The Lion, the Witch and the Wardrobe* (New York, HarperTrophy, 1994), p. 3.
2. Susan Cooper, "Seeing around Corners: A Talk Accepting the Newberry Medal for *The Grey King,* Given at the American Library Association Convention in

Chicago, August 1976," *Dreams and Wishes: Essays on Writing for Children* (New York, Margaret K. McElderry, 1996), pp. 9–10.

3. Hannah Arendt, *Eichmann in Jerusalem: A Report on the Banality of Evil* (New York, Penguin, 1977).

4. Thomas Blass, *The Man Who Shocked the World: The Life and Legacy of Stanley Milgram* (New York, Basic Books, 2004).

5. David Cesarini, *Becoming Eichmann: Rethinking the Life, Crimes, and Trial of a "Desk Murderer"* (Cambridge, MA, Da Capo Press, 2006), p. 354.

6. C. S. Lewis, *Mere Christianity* (Glasgow, Collins, 1977), pp. 44–47.

7. Lewis, *Mere Christianity,* p. 44.

8. Lewis, *The Lion, the Witch and the Wardrobe,* p. 31.

9. Lewis, *The Lion, the Witch and the Wardrobe,* p. 19.

10. The seduction by sugar is completed when the Witch gives Edmund the enchanted Turkish Delight, surely one of the most memorable moments in the entire canon of children's literature. As a child of war-time rationing, Edmund is even more susceptible to this seduction than most of the children who read about him.

11. Lewis, *The Lion, the Witch and the Wardrobe,* p. 4.

12. Lewis, *The Lion, the Witch and the Wardrobe,* p. 143.

13. Lewis, *The Lion, the Witch and the Wardrobe,* p. 85.

14. C. S. Lewis, *The Screwtape Letters* (London, G Bles/The Centenary Press, 1943), p. 31.

15. Phillip Pullman, *The Subtle Knife* (New York, Alfred A. Knopf, 1997), p. 320.

16. See Joscelyn Godwin, *Arktos: The Polar Myth in Science, Symbolism, and Nazi Survival* (Keptmon, IL, Adventures Unlimited Press, 1996).

17. Phillip Pullman, *The Golden Compass* (New York, Alfred A. Knopf, 1995), pp. 237–238.

18. Pullman, *The Golden Compass,* p. 240.

19. Pullman, *The Golden Compass,* p. 254.

20. Phillip Pullman, *The Amber Spyglass* (New York, Alfred A. Knopf, 2000), pp. 251–252.

21. Pullman, *The Amber Spyglass,* p. 66.

22. Pullman, *The Golden Compass,* p. 272.

23. Jochen von Lang and Claus Sibyll, eds., and Ralph Manheim, trans., *Eichmann Interrogated: Transcripts from the Archives of the Israeli Police* (Toronto, Farrar, Straus and Giroux, 1983), p. 76, ellipses in original.

24. Arendt, *Eichmann,* p. 106. These passages may also allude to the stress undergone by those subjects in Milgram's experiments who, intimated by the scientist in the white coat, did not feel able to put a stop to the torture they believed they were inflicting on the man in the electric chair.

25. Pullman, *The Amber Spyglass,* p. 70.

26. Pullman, *The Amber Spyglass,* p. 71.

27. Pullman, *The Subtle Knife,* p. 313.

28. Pullman, *The Golden Compass,* p. 69.

29. Pullman, *The Golden Compass,* p. 209.

30. Pullman, *The Amber Spyglass,* p. 16.

31. Naomi Wood, "Paradise Lost and Found: Obedience, Disobedience, and Story-telling in C. S. Lewis and Philip Pullman," *Children's Literature in Education,* Vol. 32, No. 4 (December 2001), p. 249.

32. Pullman, *The Subtle Knife,* p. 294.

33. Wood, "Paradise Lost and Found," p. 239.

34. J. K. Rowling, *Harry Potter and the Philosopher's Stone* (Vancouver, Raincoast, 1997), p. 77.

35. J. K. Rowling, "FAQ Question: Why Are Some People in the Wizarding World Called 'Half-Blood' Even Though Both Their Parents Were Magical?" *JK Rowling Official Site,* December 30, 2005, available at http://www.jkrowling.com/text only/en/faq_view.cfm?id=58 (accessed July 2009).

36. J. K. Rowling, "J. K. Rowling at Carnegie Hall Reveals Dumbledore Is Gay; Neville Marries Hannah Abbott, and Much More," *TheLeakyCauldron* (October 20, 2007), available at http://www.the-leaky-cauldron.org/2007/10/20/j-k-rowling-at-carnegie-hall-reveals-dumbledore-is-gay-neville-marries-hannah-abbott-and-scores-more (accessed July 2009).

37. Suman Gupta, for example, has argued that the Death Eaters are fascist, without ever claiming that they are specifically Nazi. Suman Gupta, *Re-Reading Harry Potter* (New York, Palgrave, 2003).

38. Wagga Wagga Werewolf, "Harry Potter and the Third Reich," *TheLeakyCauldron* (March 2006), available at http://www.the-leaky-cauldron.org/features/essays/issue1/ThirdReich (accessed July 2009).

39. J. K. Rowling, *Harry Potter and the Deathly Hallows* (Vancouver, Raincoast, 2007), p. 205.

40. Rowling, *Harry Potter and the Deathly Hallows,* pp. 198–99.

41. J. K. Rowling, *Harry Potter and the Chamber of Secrets* (Vancouver, Raincoast, 1998), p. 230.

42. Rowling, *Harry Potter and the Deathly Hallows,* p. 596.

43. This categorization is my own, based on my reading around the Nuremberg Trials, in particular Eugene Davidson, *Trial of the Germans: An Account of the Twenty-Two Defendants before the International Military Tribunal* (New York, Macmillan, 1966), published the same decade as Arendt's work on Eichmann and the media reports of Milgram's experiments.

44. J. K. Rowling, *Harry Potter and the Half-Blood Prince* (Vancouver, Raincoast, 2005), pp. 338–339.

45. J. K. Rowling, *Harry Potter and the Goblet of Fire* (Vancouver, Raincoast, 2000), p. 457.

46. Rowling, *Harry Potter and the Goblet of Fire,* p. 83.

47. Arendt, *Eichmann,* p. 48.

48. Charles Y. Glock, Gertrude J. Seltznick, and Joe L. Spaeth, *The Apathetic Majority: A Study Based on Public Responses to the Eichmann Trial* (New York, Harper & Row, 1966), p. 59.

49. Rowling, "J. K. Rowling at Carnegie Hall."

50. Rowling, *Harry Potter and the Goblet of Fire,* p. 203.

51. His fifth year in particular involves serious political disobedience; to neutralize the threat that the Death Eaters might accrue some of the glamour belonging to the rebel, Rowling creates not one but *two* movements of resistance on the side of the good, to make sure the good retains some of that glamour: the Order of the Phoenix, in opposition to the evil of rebellion, and Dumbledore's Army, in opposition to the evil of authority. Harry, longing to be in the former, becomes the leader of the latter.

52. Rowling, *Harry Potter and the Deathly Hallows,* p. 294.

53. Rowling, *Harry Potter and the Deathly Hallows,* p. 479.

54. Farah Mendlesohn, "Crowning the King: Harry Potter and the Construction of Authority," *Journal of the Fantastic in the Arts,* Vol. 12, No. 3 (2001), p. 302.

55. In the "Discover Narnia Fun Facts" extra on the DVD, we are informed that "The Nazi aerial bombing attacks on London began in September of 1940 and ended in May of 1941." *The Chronicles of Narnia: The Lion, the Witch and the Wardrobe* (2005). Note the choice of the word "Nazi" rather than "German" or "Luftwaffe."

56. "Production Team Audio Commentary," *The Chronicles of Narnia: The Lion, the Witch and the Wardrobe* (2005).

57. Tilda Swinton, "Aslan and the King of Kings—Disney's 'The Chronicles of Narnia: The Lion, the Witch and the Wardrobe,'" interview by Chris Monroe, *ChristianAnswers.Net,* December 2, 2005, available at http://www.christian answers.net/spotlight/movies/2005/thechroniclesofnarnia2005-interview.html (accessed July 2009). The novel never tells us that the children's father is fighting in the war.

58. Similarly, Pullman's Mrs. Coulter has dark hair while in the film of *The Golden Compass* she is played by the blonde Nicole Kidman, glamorously dressed in the fashion of the 1930s.

59. "Production Team Audio Commentary," *The Chronicles of Narnia: The Lion, the Witch and the Wardrobe* (2005).

60. One of Hitler's favorite expressions according to Joachim C. Fest, *The Face of the Third Reich: Portraits of the Nazi Leadership* (New York, Pantheon, 1970), p. 62.

61. Contrast Barbara Kellerman's passionately angry and reactive, even histrionic, White Witch in the BBC television adaptation of the novel from 1988. Kellerman, who seems to be basing her performance partly on the portrayal of the Witch as Jadis in *The Magician's Nephew,* hisses a great deal in her line delivery, suggesting the Witch as Satan rather than Hitler. *The Chronicles of Narnia: The Lion, the Witch and the Wardrobe* (2005).

62. "Production Team Audio Commentary," *The Chronicles of Narnia: The Lion, the Witch and the Wardrobe* (2005).

63. Lewis, *Mere Christianity,* p. 47.

64. Aslan's sacrifice at the Stone Table makes sense within the Christian allegory of the novel but becomes a problem in the Second World War allegory of the film because it is submission, rather than resistance, to Hitler.

65. Jason Isaacs, "The Big Interview," *The Official London Theatre Guide,* February 14, 2007, available at http://officiallondontheatre.uk/news/interviews/view/item74741/Jason-Isaacs/ (accessed July 2009).

4

Hitler Is Fun: Sixty Years of Nazism in Humorous Comics

Marc Hieronimus

Imagine: a depressed time-traveling Hitler has sexual intercourse with a transvestite Hermann Göring, kills President Kennedy and Arch-Duke Franz Ferdinand by mistake, inspires Nietzsche and Hemingway, and catches Monica Lewinsky (who is in fact Josef Mengele) in the act with President Bill Clinton.[1] Or consider: two prisoners manage to escape a concentration camp in a cow costume patched up out of human skin; a bull jumps the prisoners-come-cow wanting to copulate and they are driven along with other cattle to the abattoir, are slaughtered and put into cans. The Germans at the front do not appreciate them: "they really take us for animals?"[2] Is this funny? Is it permissible to laugh about the Nazi past in such ways—or at all? And if so, under what conditions? It is imperative to analyze the use of humor in comics about Nazism because prima facie there is nothing very humorous about either the Second World War or the Holocaust, and because the function of humor and laughter in society are such difficult concepts to access and explain. Yet humor and the Nazi era are inextricably entwined in popular culture and have become even more so over the last few decades. This chapter examines how we laugh at the Nazis in comics and comes to the conclusion that the Nazi past plays a complex and problematic role in comic media.

Some years ago, the comedian Jimmy Carr "tried to count all the different theories of humor [he] came across, but gave up somewhere north of 100." Carr and his colleague, Lucy Greeves, realized "to their great relief," that there are really only four main principles that help to explain why we laugh, namely: superiority theory, which makes jokes a product of pure emotion and instinct: aggressive, masculine, competitive; incongruity and ambivalence theories, which see jokes as products of reason, crediting us all with perhaps too much cognitive clarity; and the release theory that tries to mirror the physical pleasure of laughter with a similar psychological response.[3]

Applied to the special case of comics examined in this chapter, it is evident that laughter about Hitler and his "willing executioners"[4] is a layered and complex response. In part, we laugh because we feel a certain virile or intellectual and moral superiority over the Nazis, stemming from the military, ideological, and, not least, moral defeat of the Nazi regime. In part, we laugh at good jokes, even when they are positioned within a Nazi background. We also laugh as a release of energy from suffered pains and fears, which in many ways reminds us of the exultation celebrated after wars and epidemics. Much laughter stems from the breaking of sexual, excremental, and other social taboos. Paradoxically, even the death camps can become a matter of humor *simply because* one is not allowed to laugh about them. "Each of the theories is useful," say Carr and Greeves, "but it's crazy to attempt to analyze all jokes using just one of them."[5] To this end, it is important to recognize that some people do and have laughed at the comics about Nazis presented in this chapter. The crucial point, however, is that many people do not find them funny. As the French comedian, Pierre Desproges, pointed out in 1986, you can laugh about anything, but not with everyone.[6] And not at any time, he could have added.

Because of their limited readership, comics tend to mirror rather than influence historical discourses and imageries. Everyone knows Donald Duck's or Charlie Brown's silhouette and some of their sayings, but except for *Asterix* and Gaul 50 BC, there are very few well-known print-comic characters with historical period actually directly built into their characters and storylines.[7] As an art form in their own right, comics share certain qualities with literature in that they usually contain words, characters, and a plot. They have much in common with films—especially the way stories are told and visualized via cut, perspective, zoom, light, and color. Today, many comic artists paint rather than draw their works and use exactly the same materials and tools as other paint artists, including computers and scanners. When related to theater, comics can be regarded as no less than the achievement of the actor's art insofar as not even mime or silent film artists manage to perform the grotesque faces and contortions of many of the most ordinary comic characters. Like any other art form, the comic is unique—artists, public, topics, contexts, contracts, distribution, legislation, market, accessibility, number of artists necessary for a piece of art, and so forth differ between any two of the fine arts—and is thus worthy of its own historical and aesthetic consideration.

In contrast to more established art forms, however, comics have had a short and accelerated development since their emergence in the nineteenth century.[8] Much of the neglect and disdain for comics originates from the misconception that they are largely drawn for, and read by, children and adolescents. Despite their denomination, comics are not limited to the humorous, but are open to literally any content, and graphic artists have only recently begun to explore the endless possibilities of this medium.[9] Many comics aimed at adults depict Nazism in one way or another, with countless comic adventures, comic epics, comic (auto)biographies and comic uchronies[10] that utilize Nazi connotations or backgrounds. Only in the last two decades, and mainly due to Art Spiegelman's prizewinning *Maus,* has the medium gained a certain respectable reputation—the broad discussion in the humanities around *Maus* alone can be measured in bookshelf-feet.[11]

The way we laugh about the Nazi past has changed over time. In the 1950s, war crimes and war-crimes trials were too raw and near, and comics, at that time mainly addressed to younger people, only made the most careful allusions to Nazism. After the 1960s' changes in comic readership and Nazi representation in popular media, it became possible to overtly depict Nazis even in humorous comics, as long as their most atrocious crimes were left out. Today artists know the varieties and perils of Nazi humor and play with them in a much more relaxed manner. Even though not (yet?) considered a subject like any other, Nazism has nonetheless attained a degree of normalization or trivialization, insofar as today the majority of comic readers do not feel offended by the grotesque humor of comic authors such as Walter Moers, Grégor Jarry or Otto T.

From War to the 1960s: The Time of Allusion

Apart from newspaper caricatures in the 1920s and 1930s, superhero comics were the first drawings to really mock Nazis. A recent traveling exposition on comics as a medium of Jewish commemoration tells the familiar story: "The creators of the best known superheroes were Jewish."[12] It is arguable whether all these Hitler-bashing and world-saving "supermen"—a translation of *Übermensch,* from the works of Nietzsche, who was so dear to the Nazis—took revenge on the Nazis for their anti-Semitism and for the repression in the Third Reich. Contemporary audiences may laugh at the stereotypes and predictability of plots in which Captain America's sole aim is to defeat Hitler and his brutish scoundrels. But it is highly unlikely they were intended to be humorous at the time of their creation just before, in the case of *Superman,* or shortly after, for *Captain America,* the outbreak of the Second World War.[13]

In 1945, the world discovered the true extent of the persecution of Jews, Sinti and Romanies, homosexuals, communists, and the mentally disabled under the Nazi regime. A decade later, Bernard Krigstein's grave *Master Race* was the first, and for a long time only, graphic art work about Nazi concentration camps.[14] In the 1950s, nobody wanted to read about such horrors in comics. If humorous comics in the United States and Europe wanted to make allusions to German militarism and Germanness in general, the easiest way was to block out the atrocities of the recent past. In *Asterix and the Goths* (1963), for example, the latter are unmistakably German with a strong twentieth-century touch: the Goths wear spiked helmets, walk in line, and dream of conquering the world. They have barbarian customs such as quartering, and when they are angry, their cuss words are replaced by swastikas. They are still depicted as human, but in an allusion to well-known stories about SS-officers growing flowers in the death camps, one Goth, enraptured by a splendid bouquet, says "So what? One can be barbarian and like flowers, no?"[15] René Goscinny and Albert Uderzo did not want to send their heroes to a land of poets and thinkers or of technical and scientific genius either—their German neighbors had been their enemy in three consecutive wars, after all.

In a similar way to the attempts at under-the-radar allusions to Germany's more recent past in *Asterix,* in volume 18 of André Franquin's Belgian all-age comic book series *Spirou,* published in the 1960s, the protagonists are sent to a fictional land named Bretzelburg. The spike-helmeted policemen of this military state are "the only ones in the world who can shout 'alarm' and blow into a whistle at the same time."[16] The soldiers wear helmets from the First World War and drive tanks from the Second. The authors here have taken evasive action: Greg, who wrote the storyline, apparently wanted some funny German-bashing for the older part of his target group and created a weird totalitarian pseudo-Germany without the SS or the Holocaust, but with policemen and soldiers all over the place.[17] The worst kind of torture conducted in this comic is forcing a victim to listen to nails screeching on a chalkboard and, after the putsch at the end of the adventure, all the villains are forgiven. Once more, slapstick jokes and harmless scuffles amuse the younger readership, while puns and unexpected innuendoes address the older ones. The humor used is innocent, the allusions almost too subtle. There is no direct engagement with the recent past in this volume.

Carl Barks exhibited no such timidity in making much more direct references to Nazism in the Duckburg cosmos he created between 1943 and 1966, which inspired generations of northwest European children and adults alike. Nor did his prizewinning German translator, Dr. Erika Fuchs. Fuchs attempted to liberate the original text from its regional and capitalist background and relocated Donald's hometown for the German release to somewhere in post-war Germany.[18] Now the connections to Nazism are abundant, as German intellectual and Donaldist president-of-honor, Andreas Platthaus, has shown: In "Entenhausen," Donald listens to "The Guard on the Rhine," a patriotic anthem he would have sung when he was engaged in the romantic German *Wandervogel* youth movement; a demolition contractor is named Alfons Blitzkrieg; V2 rockets are tested on a military site; a falconer quotes almost word-for-word Hitler's famous speech about the qualities of the future German boy who would be "slim and fit, lithe as greyhounds, tough as leather and hard as Krupp steel"; the Beagle Boys Inc., dubbed "Panzerknacker" after an anti-tank missile, sing a slightly modified Horst Wessel Lied: "For today the cabbage isle is ours / and tomorrow, the whole world."[19]

Such references are not limited to the text. Research done on *Donald Duck* points out dozens of Hitler salutes among scouts, policemen, and members of the Duck family: "When Huey, Dewey, and Louie have come through a critical situation they show their poise by a corresponding habit. [. . .] Is this the banality of evil or the evil of banality? It is a matter of fact that Hitler found followers in Duckburg."[20] In 2005, a reprint of one of Carl Barks's original 1948 stories, named *April Foolers,* caused a stir in the German media as it showed a copy of *Mein Kampf* on a garbage dump. In Germany (other than in the original context and unlike the more sophisticated allusions just mentioned) even 60 years after the war's end the reference to Hitler's famous book is objectionable. In earlier German releases the title had been retouched.[21]

In these early examples the comical use of Nazism arises mainly from the unexpectedness of the allusions and from the fact that the reader invariably feels superior to allegedly German peculiarities or Germanness (but certainly Nazism) in general. The Russian scientist, Igor Krichtafovitch, claimed to have found that "A person's reaction to a joke or anecdote is determined . . . only by the elevation of his social status within the group in which the joke is told."[22] On the level of national consciousness, jokes and art forms like caricature, propaganda comedies, or satirical songs can do something similar, particularly in time of war. As Simon Critchley points out, "the French laugh at the Belgians, the Belgians at the Dutch, and the Dutch laugh right back. . . . The Scots laugh at the English, the English laugh at the Irish, and the Irish laugh right back. The Germans laugh at the Ostfrieslanders and everyone else laughs rather nervously at the Germans."[23] Given that Germany has been held responsible for so many wars since the Wars of Unification of the 1860s, the persistent image of the proud, bellicose, cruel, and narcissistic German remains in many European countries, and laughing, albeit nervously, at the archetypal German has appeal even in peacetime. But in the context of the early post-war years, Europeans did not laugh at direct references to the Nazi past. Their Nazi-directed humor was muted.

After 1968: Comics Come of Age

As a discrete art form, comics are not isolated but tend to follow more general developments in film and literature. Hitler sells, even if he appears in name only. In his "Essay on Kitsch and Death," Saul Friedländer discusses new discourses on the Nazi era that emerged at the end of the 1960s. After a period of dark and grave representations, writers and film directors began to depict the mythical, apocalyptic, mundane, kitsch, or otherwise seductive elements of Nazism; the very amalgam of kitsch and death so typical and peculiar for Nazi ideology, where discourses and representations of family luck and tradition went together with those of purity, health, power, and invincibility on the one hand and of downfall, ruin, and death on the other.[24] The reproach against the generation of culprits whose acts were tried in the Auschwitz Trials and discussed broadly in public, a smoldering generational conflict, and the 1968 atmosphere of departure spurred filmmakers like Alexander Kluge, Hans Jürgen Syberberg, Helma Sanders-Brahms, and Rainer Werner Fassbinder to try new ways of dealing with the Nazi past.[25]

A similar caesura can be identified in comics, but for different reasons: the cultural explosion of 1968 did much to emancipate comics from their childish image, and with the growing number of adult publications available, serious matters became more prominent in the art form. Entertainment aimed at adults used Nazism more prominently as well—for example, the slightly ironic American adventure and horror comics about "blood, sweat, and tits" with scarred mavericks saving magnificent beauties from wild animals, or the Italian gore and porn material of the 1960s edited by Elvipress/Elvifrance, frequently featured Nazi characters, including Nazi zombies, female concentration camp guards, and sadistic SS researchers.[26]

This is not to suggest that the old stylistic allusions to Nazism disappeared during the 1960s. Marijac's slapstick comic *Les Trois Musquetaires du Maquis* (1968), for example, about three underground musketeers quarreling with the occupation forces, was a republication of a comic originally drawn for the resistance paper *Le Corbeau Déchainé* during the war. It features a lot of fights between soldiers and resistance fighters, rabid pigs, and SS officers on dung heaps—but no one dies.[27] In the same year, Franco Bonvicini (alias Bonvi) created his first *Sturmtruppen* strips and continued drawing them until his death in 1995.[28] These antiwar comic books have been translated into many languages and spawned two films and a videogame adaptation.[29] They are about the adventures of an anonymous German army corps in what appears more like a First than a Second World War theater, replete with sandbags and no enemy contact. The superiors are morons, and allusions to atrocities beyond the combat zone are rare. For example, only one victim in all of the countless volumes is obviously Jewish and wears a Star of David that has been deleted for the German release. In this story, the camp commandant suffers a nervous breakdown. Apart from this lone event, however, Bonvi's silly gags could take place in any war whatsoever, and, apart from the general German-mocking, the comical element in these comics lies in slapstick and scuffle. What Bonvi and Marijac's slapstick seems to suggest is that both authors did not find Nazism that extraordinary or humorous and did not believe their readers would either.

However, the role of Nazism in more mainstream comic art was changing and becoming more prominent, despite remaining far from obvious. The comic artist, François Thomas, for example, overtly fancied Nazi chic. His "world's most chauvinist comic" from the 1980s featuring "the hero with the green tail" is about the snotty art forger Stan Caïman and his adventures with sex.[30] Stan wears the black armband of a political party that is never clearly defined. However, the names ("Büchendorf" and "Tannenbaum"), the architecture, the banners, and the marching troops of blond half-naked male and female soldiers are unmistakable hints of Nazism. In spite of the trappings of fascism, this macho is surprisingly lovable. A clear swastika would perhaps have altered the reader's sympathy for him, however successful, funny, and cool he may be. The ideological ambiguities make the green rascal's sadistic debaucheries easy to forgive: he's just too cool. For the same reason, Büchendorf's fascists are not that daunting either. Actually they are rather smart and dashingly dressed. Like his predecessors, Thomas plays with Nazi allusions. He does not take them seriously, however, nor does he laugh at them to make the reader feel superior. This is not a remonstrative kind of humor. Instead, he seduces us with Nazism in ways of which Friedländer warned us.

Two Comics That Went Too Far

It is no coincidence that a few years after Thomas's green-tailed hero appeared, other comic artists also discovered Nazi chic and made links between its sadism, (homo)sexuality, and style.[31] In the 1980s, this fetishization of Nazism was particularly in vogue. Popular artists of all disciplines explored how far they could go in their casual play with Nazism. Merely alluding to the Nazis was no longer taboo enough. Instead they played with the trope and tried to cause a sensation, without evoking too much of a backlash.

What most of the humorous films about the Nazi past, and the lion's share of the comics analyzed in this chapter, have in common is that they willingly omit the Holocaust and do so for a simple reason: "Perversely it is precisely . . . [the] . . . severing of an overt link between Hitler and the Holocaust that allows them [the artist or filmmaker] to escape criticism."[32] In other words, mention extermination camps in a humorous film or comic and people will be offended. Terrence Des Pres described three principles of the more or less established Holocaust etiquette for popular art that any artist has to abide by: The Holocaust has to be shown as an event of its own, isolated of all history before and after; its representation has to be as exact as possible, and there is no room and no legitimation for artistic manipulations; the Holocaust has to be approached as an almost religious event and with the utmost seriousness. Two more principles can be added: representations of the Holocaust must be embedded in high culture: "popular products are automatically suspicious and in any case less important. Comedies [and, by implication, comics] address in general a less educated audience and therefore have difficulties in being labeled high culture." And finally: "the artist is supposed to have the right attitude and the right motivation . . . Even if the product is funny, the artist has to show the appropriate sincerity."[33]

When artists breach these basic principles, their work becomes offensive and, more often than not, causes controversy. Two comic series that illustrate this well are Yann and Hardy's *La patrouille des libellules*[34] and Jean-Marie Gourio and Philippe Vuillemin's *Hitler = SS,* both of which appeared in the 1980s.[35] The former series was never completed as the controversy about *Hitler = SS* raged in France. Both sets of authors represent extreme archetypes of Nazism, the Holocaust, and Holocaust victims. Yann and Hardy, for example, introduce a caricature of a Jew in prisoner's clothes moaning less about the persecutions than the fact that he had prepared for a long war, like in 1914, and was now holding big stocks of shovels and spades he would never sell.[36] In volume 3 of the series, a group of deported Jews arrives in a concentration camp and are summoned: "the ugly to the left!" Everyone goes to the left, and the commander says: "bloody Jewish masochism!"[37] At another point, the Nazis are looking for a particular Jew who was once Hitler's teacher and is now haunting his nightmares with the math riddle: "If you have a train with 3.000 Jews in two wagons starting at Paris at a speed of . . . " In the same volume, an infantilized Hitler sucks his thumb, and a trainer of the Hitler youth is depicted in bed with a *Hitler boy.*[38]

Gourio and Vuillemin took such crass depictions to a new level in *Hitler = SS.* In the two-pager "Berlin 1933," one of the first stories of the black-and-white charcoal album that was to become *Hitler = SS,* a person of Jewish appearance walks along a dull street when a limousine stops and Hitler gets out. The *Führer* draws a gun and makes the Jew eat dog's excrement. When the Jew seizes the gun, it is Hitler's turn to taste. At the end, the Jew comes home and says to his wife: "You won't guess who I had dinner with."[39]

The majority of the Auschwitz comics in *Hitler = SS* are of an even cruder kind. One is about camp guard Otto and his habit of raping female inmates. His subordinates choose them for him and share the rest; the ugly ones are gassed. One girl considers herself a "beauty from inside." They send her to the hospital where she is to be "opened," "to be sure." Otto is caught by his superior while he is having sex with another girl. She has to be killed but Otto is stuck: he waits in front of the gas chamber's door with his penis still inside his victim. But it is no use, he stays locked in her dead body. Finally he cuts off her arms and legs and paints the rest like a penis—seeing his enormous organ, his superior forgives him.[40]

Much more than Yann and Hardy, who focused on sexual explicitness, reduced Hitler to a caricature, and augmented anti-Semitic Jewish stereotypes, like greed and self-hatred, Vuillemin and Gourio willingly exceeded all boundaries of good taste in *Hitler* = *SS*. Never before and never since has a comic represented Nazi death camps in this manner. In an interview, the comic book author and editor Marcel Gotlib, who lost a large part of his family in the Holocaust, defended their work "insofar as it helps to avoid that a monster like Hitler becomes a myth," but appreciated that people might find the violence offensive.[41] Vuillemin and Gourio also remain unapologetic. They hold that Holocaust survivors and their relatives should be more offended by a TV series like *Holocaust* (1978) "with the good who are crying and the bad who are shouting and a train leaving into a somber light . . . all these romantic clichés that banalize the thing and even make it beautiful."[42] Vuillemin and Gourio purposely transgressed Holocaust etiquette and did so for the best of reasons: they wanted to show the camps as the violent depraved places they were. In so doing they utilized "humor" as "an aggression that does not bear any limits."[43]

Importantly, in spite of having set out its parameters, Des Pres also disagrees with the prescription of Holocaust etiquette. Referring to several comic works, he argues that humor is helpful and important at times. A tragic response tries to stay as truthful as possible to the historical events, whereas a comical one makes no attempt at truthful representation and refuses to take the Holocaust on its own terms. The comic mode, therefore, has a potential that the tragic lacks: it allows for distance, self-possession, evaluation, and protest toward the finality and brutality of the events. Des Pres writes: "In the realm of art, a comic response is more resilient, more effectively in revolt against terror and the sources of terror than a response that is solemn or tragic."[44] The implication of this is key to our understanding of the role of Nazi tropes and the Holocaust in popular culture.

Abiding by Holocaust etiquette prevents the events, however unique in history they may be, from being historicized within the context they occurred. Instead the rules of this etiquette turn the Holocaust into the sacred and forbid any laughter. Psychology suggests that humorous representations are especially helpful in reconciling and coming to terms with the harrowing past that has been so long smothered through the German *Vergangenheitsbewältigung.*[45] Importantly, many readers of *Hitler = SS* and at least two courts of justice did not share this view: in France the sale of *Hitler = SS* has been forbidden since 1989 and in Spain it has been outlawed since 1995. It almost goes without saying the work has not been translated into German.

1990s to Date: It's So Trivial

The last one and a half decades have been marked by a broad trivialization of (or normalization in the handling of) Nazi history, including the Holocaust, in comics. Since the publication of Spiegelman's pioneering *Maus,* an entire genre of Nazi graphic novels has appeared, including Jason Lutes' *Berlin* and Jean Pierre Gibrat's masterpieces *Le sursis* and *Le vol du corbeau,* uchronic fiction like *Das Reich,* and even explicit Holocaust representations such as Pascal Crocy's *Auschwitz,* Joe Kubert's *Yossel,* or *Judenhass* by Dave Sim.[46] Importantly, almost all these graphic novels target an adult—and not a young adult or child—audience.[47] It would seem that graphic art, children, and the Holocaust are not yet integrated.[48]

A new generation of comic artists also use Nazism to have fun. Walli and Michel de Bom, for example, send their two protagonists, Gil Sinclair and Flint Bottleneck, straight to Berchtesgarden on the Adlerhorst, Hitler's mountain hut, where they meet Heydrich, Goebbels, Göring, Speer, Bormann, Hitler's personal physician Morell, and the "sinister Dr. Mengele." The intruders' mission is to replace the *Führer*'s she-dog Blondie with a doppelganger in order to get the ultra-secret war plans hidden in her necklace. While hostile to most Germans, Gil eventually succumbs to Hitler's charms: "He smiled at me, he smiled at me, Heil Hitler!" On a walk with the *Führer,* Gil kills him just the same, furious about a kiss Hitler has given Blondie: "Infamous pervert! To kiss by force an animal! All you deserve is death!" In the end, the plans hidden in the necklace are useless fakes and the murdered Hitler was a look-alike. The real one then says: "Aaah! Everybody wants to kill me! Perfect! Now I will kill everybody! Hey, look, I will concoct you one of these little genocides, hm, Blondie?"[49] In Gil Sinclair's world, it is not anti-Semitism, the insane logic of total war, the Nazis' hatred of communism or liberalism, or anything of this kind that led to the Holocaust. Rather, it was Hitler's personal vendetta. Furthermore, the worst thing Gil, the secret service agent, pins on Hitler is a peck on the nose of a dog. In one fell swoop, Walli and de Bom have turned the Nazi past into an inconsequential event and Hitler into a foolish nonentity. They mention the Holocaust but never actually show it.

The caricature representation of Hitler and the Nazi leadership in *Gil Sinclair* and similar recent comic books, such as *Operation Odin,* seems to serve complex ends.[50] The German scholar Bernd Dolle-Weinkauff, for example, holds that "the scope of humorizations like this is limited, they elude insistently any rational or educational constraint. Their advantage is undoubtfully the banalization of the pathos of the Third Reich."[51] Michael D. Richardson adds to this when he argues that "by reducing Hitler to an easily defeated caricature, subjecting him to physical and psychic humiliations, these [comic] portrayals substituted real violence with humor in order to offer audiences symbolic victories over a thoroughly de-auraticized and disempowered Hitler." And he continues:

> The persistence of representations that disempower the Nazis by turning them into evil or bumbling and inept clowns demonstrates both a desire to construct a morally good, strong, and intelligent identity as completely distinct from this image of the Germans as Nazis and an unconscious wish to enact a fascist fantasy of control whereby disavowed negative characteristics are given free reign.[52]

In this way, these funny and uncritical representations of Hitler are therapeutic for the authors and readers alike. They enable the creation of a nonthreatening image of what is worthy rather than what is not (the reality of the Nazi past and its personages). Still, this begs the question of misrepresentation. What are we doing to ourselves and to the Nazi past, if we turn the leadership circle of the Third Reich into a clique of likeable homeboys?

This question becomes all the more troubling when Nazism becomes entwined with increasingly more humorous and decontextualized comic content. Walter Moers's *Adolf* is arguably the funniest and certainly the craziest comic about Hitler to appear in recent years.[53] After decades of hiding in a sewage system, Adolf Hitler is still haunted by his "unfortunate" anti-Semitic instincts. A "Doktor Furunkel" prescribes him a "proper fuck." At Hamburg's Reeperbahn he meets the transvestite Hermine *aka* Hermann Göring and does what Furunkel advised him to do. Hooked on crack, he prostitutes himself but gets bashed by skinheads who do not recognize their idol. Now the doc prescribes him cold turkey and a trip to Paris where he buys back the Eiffel tower from a conman and starts working as a bodyguard. Obliged to help out as a chauffeur, he kills Lady Diana in a famous accident and gets hijacked by aliens who force him to catch up with the historical and cultural events since 1945, but he refuses to fulfill their plan to have him copulate with Mother Theresa. After a short trip to Japan on board Airforce One, Diana, who has actually faked the accident, awaits him to unleash an atomic war. Hitler hesitates. Finally he kicks Diana out of the plane and lands in South America, where he and Hermine open a "brown-bread and sushi art gallery" for elderly Gauleiters. Their love withstands all odds: at the end of the second book, Hitler and Hermine even leave for Russia together. Hitler wants to become Minister of the Interior there, while Göring wants to sell his watercolors on the Red Square. "But the kids," objects the *Führer* with his last words against a romantic sunset, "we cannot abandon them like that." "Of course we can," says Hermine, "we're Nazis after all."[54] And that is exactly what they are, a thing one tends to forget when laughing about Moers's grotesque ideas.

What Moers's version of the Nazi leadership does is remove Hitler and his comrades from their horrid past and place them within an almost completely decontextualized story line. Moers can do this because he knows his readers are all too familiar with the Hitler as evil trope. His allusions to Nazism are unmistakable. Similarly, Grégor Jarry and Otto T.'s *The Conquest of Mars* (2009), a uchronic account of what happened to Hitler after he did not kill himself in his bunker in April 1945, removes cruelty and violence from the past and replaces them with ultra-ridiculous plot lines, like Eva Braun giving birth to Hitler's son on Mars and complaining about Josef Mengele: "Before I met Adolf [who died on board a space craft] he [Mengele] used to court me and drag me to I do not know how many performances of heili-heilo [an apocryphal Nazi song reminiscent of the more contemporary 'Smurf Song']"[55]

Most significantly to all these ridiculous representations of Nazism and the Nazi leadership is that they do the exact opposite of *Hitler = SS*.

Pour fêter ce succès, Hitler me reçut en personne dans son quartier général de Prusse-Orientale. Il fut impressionné par ma jeunesse et me compara à Alexandre le Grand. J'avais peur d'être intimidé par le Führer, mais finalement mon angoisse se dissipa et je pris beaucoup de plaisir à la partie de dominos que nous fîmes ce soir-là.

Illustration 4: Wernher von Braun and Eva Braun playing dominoes at Hitler's in Grégory Jarry and Otto T, *La conquête de Mars*. (Extract courtesy of Grégory Jarry, Otto T, and Thomas Dupuis, Éditions FLBLB)

They avoid representing the Holocaust at all; instead they use well-known tropes of evil (for example, caricatures of Mengele) as devices to allude to the Holocaust without having to show it. Still, it is not out of respect for the Holocaust that it is not represented. Rather than adhere to Holocaust etiquette, it would seem that the Nazis are removed from any real sense of the past. As a result, it is possible to caricature Hitler as a sympathetic and only slightly foolish man. In this way, these authors reproduce the Manichean cliché of the good patriarchic *Führer* (leader) and the machinations of his evil generals and advisers.[56] Rather ironically, the Hitler myth is thereby continued and the Nazi past further trivialized.

This trivialization becomes even more apparent when Nazi plots are set in remote places and times. In part this move away from depicting Nazis in any real historical space must be seen as a response to the reception of *Hitler = SS,* namely as a recognition that Nazi history is not suitable for provocation and crude humor. When popular culture has created an acceptable place for Nazis as humorous sidekicks and nasty antagonists, it

1er janvier 1947. Il vient de se produire un événement extraordinaire. Alors que le petit Adolf Hitler allait rendre l'âme en couinant, l'air de l'étable s'est réchauffé soudainement et Sissi, une chienne qui était du voyage, s'est couchée près du bébé. Personne n'avait remarqué qu'elle avait les mamelles gorgées de lait. Le petit Adolf a tourné la tête et s'est mis à téter.

Illustration 5: The young Adolf Hitler II on his way to Mars in Grégory Jarry and Otto T, *La conquête de Mars*. (Extract courtesy of Grégory Jarry, Otto T, and Thomas Dupuis, Éditions FLBLB)

is only through removing them from the horrors of war and extermination into outer space or elsewhere. By placing Nazis in a historical or space/ time vacuum, they become purified. What remains of the nasty Nazi in these depictions is their simple-mindedness, which is humorous precisely because this is an inversion of the accepted idea of Nazis as ruthless, violent, and evil. It, therefore, becomes imperative to ask to what extent these representations depict Nazis and history at all.

Examples of such inversions are numerous in recent comic work. Pixel Vengeurs's *Phantom in Trevira versus the Doomed Legion of the Fourth Reich,*[57] for example, is about a mad scientist and a squadron of Nazi guards in the Bay of Bengal in the late 1940s who have preserved Hitler's body in order to resurrect him and invoke a legion of Nazi zombies. After a short glitch—Hitler is reanimated but turns out to be cretinous— they metamorphose him into a powerful (but still rather stupid) werewolf and attempt to use him to conquer the world. The plan is foiled by Phantom, his loyal friend Hero, and a female tapir: Werehitler's tank falls off a cliff, and the crying hordes of doomed zombies follow him like lemmings, leaving the scientist and his chief commander petrified. In the epilogue, they are still standing there 20 years later, in a place that has been converted into a Hindu or Jainist sanctuary worshiped for its swastikas.

This is not to suggest that all references to Nazism in recent comic art are fantastical. However, humorous Nazi comics can still be innovative without necessarily all being so fantastic or fictitious. In *Adolf,* Yann, the scenarist of the abandoned *Libellulles* series,[58] sends his monk Odilon Verjus from the Papua jungle to the center of world history, Berlin at the end of 1932, where the reader gets to know the other Germany of that time with its artists (the touring Josephine Baker, Leni Rieffenstahl, George Grosz and some of his famous paintings), and its social minorities such as a group of mutilated war veterans who have lost their limbs in the trenches and "do not want to give the rest serving an illuminated jumping jack."[59] Here the Nazi followers are anonymous masses, whereas the dissidents are drawn as distinct individuals. "The author's exuberant imagination full of allusions and citations," the researcher Joachim Sistig noted, "suggests a thorough examination of the story's characters, events and places with the result that this comic, as far as the underlying image of Germany is concerned, breaks up the classical clichés."[60] Yann's work is refreshing in this respect for acknowledging that there was a world, and especially a Germany, before Hitler and Nazis and asking us to question our understanding of the Nazi past.

It is much more difficult to write a Nazi story line today than it was in the 1980s. Because the readership is spoiled, demanding, and deems itself better informed historically, many plots and clichés are worn out, while others are tabooed. The growing infotainment around Nazism of recent years, and the strong presence of the Holocaust in popular media,[61] make it difficult for comic artists to depict Nazism without referring to historical events, personalities, and the numerous crimes that were committed during the 12 years of the Third Reich. Above all, what has become abundantly clear is that the care with which Nazism was approached in the immediate post-war years has been replaced with a degree of haphazardness and trivialization. Nevertheless, it is possible to have fun with Hitler and his cronies but, it seems, only when the violence and horror of the Holocaust are avoided as topics of representation.

Still, it is a sign of the times that *Hitler = SS* has spawned new, equally crude, comic art humor. Johnny Ryan's *Comic Book Holocaust,* with its front page showing dark smoke coming out of two chimney stacks, is a

Illustration 6: The "Kuntzenjammer Kids" strip by Johnny Ryan.

collection of comic parodies.[62] In a sea of gore, "shit," and porn comic strips one can find a handful of Nazi references and references to other famous comic representations, including Spiegelman's *Maus,* in narratives such as "George Hairyhand's Krazy Kunt" having saved all the bricks Ignatz Mouse threw at him to build a state-of-the-art "Kuntzentration Kamp," or "Fart Spewgelman" discovering that his father made up "the whole fucking thing" about his experiences in Auschwitz and Majdanek—he is not even Jewish and shows his enormous foreskin. The "Kuntzenjammer Kids" slice open "der grössen gütten" of "der Kaptain" in order to "zpray dee shit und dee pissen on it," then they carve "der star uf David" in it and inform the Nazis "that der Kaptain iz hiding a filthy jüden heart in his body." Weeks later they show their mother a lampshade the Nazis gave them—it is made of the Kaptain's head.[63] Undoubtedly, Ryan's depictions offend many. Nevertheless, what is significant is that they exist at all. In this sense, in the arena of certain comics even the Holocaust is losing its sacred aura.

Conclusion

Comic Book Holocaust illustrates the effect of the overload in Nazi infotainment—the one thing that crosses Ryan's mind when he thinks of a Jewish artist is the Holocaust. It also shows the long road comic authors and readership have traveled since Asterix's and Donald's shy allusions to the Nazi past. Obviously, laughter about Hitler and his followers is generationally dependent. Mixed reactions to Benigni's 1997 film *La vita è bella* demonstrated that the immediate post-war generation is much less indulgent when it comes to laughing about Hitler and Auschwitz than later generations.[64] For example, the *New Yorker* film critic David Denby criticized that "Benigni's jokes and games just aren't enough, and you leave the movie thinking that what's touching is not Benigni's ministrations to the little boy but his own need to believe in comedy as salvation." The Nazis "were beyond ridicule for the same reason that they were beyond rationality."[65]

Many people who take offense at a comedy show or a comic do so on behalf of a minority group of which they themselves are not members. Jimmy Carr and Lucy Greeves point out: "A joke about 'cripples' is far more likely to result in walk-outs than wheel-outs."[66] Psychology teaches that there is always a need to laugh, even (or especially) about the worst experiences. But only now that there are very few survivors of Nazi persecution left, and the readership of comics consists mainly of people born many years after the events of the Second World War, are moral thresholds low enough for the less concerned to tune in and laugh without fear of censure.

In quoting stand-up comic Bill Hicks, Carr and Greeves provide some useful insights into context and the signification of the joke teller's identity that are also evident in comics.

> So [the black American comedian] Chris Rock can joke about hiding money in books so that black people do not steal it, because 'books is like Kryptonite to niggers.' Neither that sentiment nor that vocabulary would be available to a white comedian, but in Rock's hands it becomes incisive social comment—and, more importantly, funny.[67]

In the same way, it matters if the graphic artist of a Nazi comic descends from victims or culprits. It is certain that the polemics about *Hitler = SS* would have been much less stormy if Vuillemin's and Gourio's ancestors had suffered or died under Nazi repression. A lot more people would have felt allowed to feel amused, because the victim or his or her descendants are justified to laugh (as a release, out of relief, to become superior, or master the situation), and only their laughter allows others to follow suit. Without this personal connection to the joke or the past, any other person's laughter is an echo of the original crime. That is what makes it so difficult to laugh about the Holocaust and other persecutions during the Third Reich with their very clearly defined culprits and victims: one fears to laugh from the wrong side. In contrast, laughter about Hitler and Nazis is almost without risk and even liberating as long as they are, in Richardson's words, depicted in a "de-auraticized and disempowered" way. It is easy to laugh at something that is so universally accepted as evil and morally corrupt.[68]

Of course, historical representation is subject to constant renegotiation and redefinition. Visual imagery helps to define what the past was and how it is defined. "Strictly speaking, there is no such thing as collective memory," Susan Sontag wrote. "What is called collective memory is not a remembering but a stipulating: that this is important, and this is the story about how it happened, with the pictures that lock the story in our minds."

Today, remembrance is visual: "To remember is, more and more, not to recall a story but to be able to call up a picture."[69] It is worth considering to what extent visualized people of the Nazi period (like the smiling Mengele, Eva Braun, the little boy in Warschau with his hands up) push aside the less or nonvisualized (like the ministers Walther Darré, Robert Ley, or Baldur von Schirach, endlessly more famous at their time than the aforementioned, but little remembered now as they are not attached to iconic photographs). Comics too deliver strong images. The risk persists that younger or less erudite readers perceive the Nazi past as harmless and comical because of how they are exposed to this past in popular culture. The question remains, then: Should comic artists be held responsible to representing the past responsibly? Can, or even should we, really laugh at Hitler at all?

Notes

1. Walter Moers, *Adolf: Äch bin wieder da* and *Adolf: Äch bin schon wieder da* (Frankfurt, Eichborn, 1998/2000).
2. Jean-Marie Gourio and Philippe Vuillemin, *Hitler = SS* (Vitry-sur-Seine, Loempia, 1990). This was the last edition before the interdiction; the first one was released in 1988.
3. Jimmy Carr and Lucy Greeves, *The Naked Jape: Uncovering the Hidden World of Jokes* (London, Penguin, 2006), pp. 88, 101.
4. The term "willing executioners" (to put it bluntly: most and especially Germans) was coined by Daniel J. Goldhagen in *Hitler's Willing Executioners: Ordinary Germans and the Holocaust* (New York, Knopf, 1996).
5. Carr and Greeves, *The Naked Jape,* p. 101.
6. Interview with Yves Riou and Philippe Pouchain in 1986 available at http://www.desproges.fr/accueil/voir/393 (accessed October 2009). Pierre Desproges, *La seule certitude que j'ai c'est d'être dans le doute* (Paris, Seuil, 2001). He also said: "It is better to laugh about Auschwitz with a Jew than to play scrabble with Klaus Barbie" (available at http://www.desproges.fr/citations/index/272 [accessed October 2009]). Pierre Desproges, *Vivons heureux en attendant la mort* (Paris, Seuil, 1997).
7. *The Flintstones* being an animated television sitcom.
8. There is a long academic discussion about which were the first comics ever, the works of Wilhelm Busch and Rodolphe Toepffer, the Bayeux Tapestry, Trajan's Column or the Egyptian Book of the Dead. Only the publication of comics in (United States) newspapers in the late nineteenth century turned them into a mass

medium. For more, see Scott McCloud, *Understanding Comics: The Invisible Art* (Northampton, MA, Kitchen Sink Press, 1993); Stephan Ditschke, Katerina Krouchevam, and Daniel Stein, eds., *Comics. Zur Geschichte und Theorie eines populärkulturellen Mediums* (Bielefeld, Transcript, 2009).

9. See Scott McCloud, *Reinventing Comics: How Imagination and Technology Are Revolutionizing an Art Form* (New York, HarperCollins, 2000).

10. Uchronies or counterfactual histories very often deal with altered wars, especially the Second World War. See Éric B. Henriet and Emmanuel Carrère, *L'uchronie* (Paris, Klincksieck, 2009); Éric B. Henriet, *L'histoire révisitée. Panorama de l'uchronie sous toutes ses formes* (Amiens, Encrage, 2004), and Gavriel D. Rosenfeld's contribution in this book.

11. The misleading name "comics" led to inventions like "graphic novel," "Bildgeschichte," and others in English and German; "bande dessinée" (French), "historieta" (Spanish), and "fumetti" (Italian) are much less delusive. Two introductions into and classifications of historical comics are written in German: Christine Gundermann and Jenseits von Asterix, *Comics im Geschichtsunterricht* (Schwalbach, Wochenschau Verlag, 2007) and René Mounajed's PhD thesis published as *Geschichte in Sequenzen. Über den Einsatz von Geschichtscomics im Geschichtsunterricht* (Frankfurt/Main, Peter Lang, 2009). For a bibliography about Art Spiegelman, *Maus* (2 volumes, New York, Pantheon, 1986 and 1991), see the academic web site http://www.lib.berkeley.edu/MRC/maus.html (accessed October 2009).

12. Danny Fingeroth, "Superheroes, Secret Identities and Jews," in Raphael Grass and Erik Riedel, eds., *Superman und Golem. Der Comic als Medium jüdischer Erinnerung,* (Frankfurt, Jüdisches Museum, 2008).

13. Jerry Siegel's and Joe Shuster's Superman first appeared in *Action Comics* #1 (New York, DC Comics, 1938); Jack Kirby and Joe Simon, *Captain America Comics* #1 (New York, Marvel, 1940).

14. Al Feldstein and Bernard Krigstein, "Master Race," in *Impact* 1 (West Plains, MO, Russ Cochran, 1988).

15. René Goscinny and Albert Uderzo, *Astérix et les Goths* (Paris, Dargaud, 1963), pp. 7, 19.

16. André Franquin and Greg, *Les Aventures de Spirou et Fantasio, vol.18: QRN sur Bretzelburg* (Marcinelle, Dupuis, 1966), p. 23.

17. Franquin and Greg, *Les Aventures de Spirou et Fantasio.*

18. Carl Barks's collected works are being republished in many languages by Egmont, Copenhagen (Filderstadt for the German edition).

19. Andreas Platthaus, "Short Cuts—Kleine Ideen zu großen Themen, Teil 2: Hände Hoch. Nazi-Duck. Eine Polemik," *Der Donaldist,* Vol. 25 (2005), pp. 4–17.

20. Platthaus, "Short Cuts," pp. 8–9. Another scientist discovered an alleged similarity of the scouts and army sport groups: Hartmut Haensel, "Wehrsportgruppe

Fieselschweif," *Der Donaldist,* Vol. 53 (1985), pp. 3–7. The "banality of evil" is a phrase coined by Hannah Arendt in her book on the Eichmann Trial: Hannah Arendt, *Eichmann in Jerusalem: A Report on the Banality of Evil* (New York, Viking Press, 1963).

21. Rafael Heiling, "Vergangenheitsreste in Entenhausen," *Deutsche Welle,* available at http://www.dw-world.de/dw/article/0,2144,1546720,00.html (accessed October 2009). Carsten Laqua has written a very fine book about Disney in and (later) against Germany: Carsten Laqua, *Wie Mickey unter die Nazis fiel. Walt Disney und Deutschland* (Reinbek bei Hamburg, Rowohlt, 1992).

22. Igor Krichtafovitch, *Humor Theory: Formula of Laughter* (Denver, CO, Outskirts Press, 2006), pp. 143–145.

23. Simon Critchley, *On Humor* (New York, Routledge, 2002), p. 69.

24. Saul Friedländer, *Reflets du Nazisme* (Paris, Seuil, 1982); see also Anton Kaes, *From Hitler to Heimat: The Return of History as Film* (Harvard, Harvard University Press, 1989). As Sander S. Gilman has shown, there is a long tradition of anti-Nazi humor in films from Charlie Chaplin's *Great Dictator* (1940) and Ernst Lubitsch's *To Be or Not to Be* (1942) through *Hogan's Heroes* (1965–1971) to the award winning Italian film *La vita è bella* (1997), and, most recently, from Germany, Dany Levy's *Mein Führer* (2007): see Sander L. Gilman, "Is Life Beautiful? Can the Shoah Be Funny? Some Thoughts on Recent and Older Films," *Critical Inquiry,* Vol. 26 (2000), pp. 279–308. See also Rand Holmes, *Hitler's Cocaine* (Northampton, MA, Kitchen Sink Press, 1984). On the psychological background of the Nazi discourses around purity, death, and so forth, see Klaus Theweleit, *Male Fantasies* (Minneapolis, University of Minnesota Press, 1987; first edition in German: *Männerfantasien* [Frankfurt, Roter Stern, 1977/78]), and Wilhelm Reich, *The Mass Psychology of Fascism* (New York, Farrar, Straus and Giroux, 1980; first edition in German, Berlin, 1933; revised version Köln, Kiepenheuer & Witsch, 1971).

25. Kluge: *Die Patriotin* (1979); Syberberg: *Hitler. Ein Film aus Deutschland* (1977); Sanders-Brahms: *Deutschland, bleiche Mutter* (1980); Fassbinder: *Die Ehe der Maria Braun* (1979) and *Lili Marleen* (1980).

26. *Blood, Sweat and Tits* is the title of the men's adventure magazine history in Max Allen Collins and George Haegenauer, *Men's Adventure Magazines* (Cologne, Taschen, 2003). For an impression of the Elvi-universe see the collectors' web sites available at http://poncetd.perso.neuf.fr/Index.htm and http://bdtrash.forum dediscussions.com/index.htm (accessed October 2009). Elvifrance published a series called *Hitler* (Paris, 1978): Hitler fakes his death, escapes Germany, then suffers from amnesia, works for the KGB, and so forth.

27. Marijac, *Les Trois Mousquetaires du Maquis,* (two volumes, Albatros, Paris 1968 and 1969; two more have been published in 1982 and 1989).

28. Bonvi (Franco Bonvicini), *Die Sturmtruppen* (several volumes, Berlin, Beta Verlag, 1980s).

29. Films: *Sturmtruppen* (1977) and *Sturmtruppen II* (1983), directed by Salvatore Samperi; the videogame *Sturmtruppen* (1992) was published by iDea.

30. François Thomas, *Stan Caïman le héros chic à la queue verte; Stan Caïman est épatant; Stan Caïman en Amagonie; Stan Caïman contre les pin-up!* (Paris, Dargaud, 1986–1989).

31. Some other artists: Ricardo Barreiro and Franco Saudelli, *La fille de Wolfland* (Paris, Dargaud, 1985); Alvaro Ortega, *Les Architectes* (Paris, Soleil, 1990); Eric Warnauts and Raives, *L'Innocente* (Paris, Casterman, 1991).

32. Michael D. Richardson, "Heil Myself!: Impersonation and Identity in the Comedic Representation of Hitler," in David Bathrick, Brad Prager, and Michael d. Richardson, eds., *Visualizing the Holocaust: Documents, Aesthetics, Memory,* (Rochester, NY, Camden House, 2008), p. 279. For instance, Bernard Fein's and Albert S. Ruddy's TV series *Hogan's Heroes* stuck to this command and ran for six years (1965–1971); Roberto Benigni's *La vita è bella* (1997) has been a topic of heated discussion.

33. Terrence Des Pres, "Holocaust Laughter?" in Berel Lang, ed., *Writing and the Holocaust* (New York, Holmes & Meier, 1988), p. 217. Two more principles: Kathy Laster and Heinz Steinert, "Eine neue Moral in der Darstellung der Shoah? Zur Rezeption von 'La vita è bella,'" in Margrit Frölich, Hanno Loewy, and Heinz Steinert, eds., *Lachen über Auschwitz – Auschwitz Gelächter? Filmkomödie, Satire und Holocaust* (München, edition text + kritik/Richard Boorberg Verlag, 2003), pp. 186, 189. Breaking of taboos: Yosefa Loshitzky, "Verbotenes Lachen: Politik und Ethik der Holocaust-Filmkomödie," in Frölich et al., eds., *Lachen über Auschwitz,* p. 29.

34. Yann and Hardy, *La patrouille des Libellules,* 3 volumes: *Le chien des Cisterciens; Défaite éclair; Réquiem pour un Pimpf* (Grenoble, Glénat, 1985–1988).

35. Jean-Marie Gourio and Philippe Vuillemin, *Hitler = SS* (Vitry-sur-Seine, Loempia, 1990).

36. Yann and Hardy, *La patrouille des Libellules,* volume 2: *Défaite éclair* (Grenoble, Glénat, 1987), p. 41.

37. Yann and Hardy, *La patrouille des Libellules,* volume 3: *Réquiem pour un Pimpf* (Grenoble, Glénat, 1988), pp. 3, 46; *Hitler boy: La patrouille des Libellules,* volume 2: *Défaite éclair* (Grenoble, Glénat, 1987), p. 3.

38. Yann and Hardy, *La patrouille des Libellules,* volume 3, p. 46; *Hitler boy.* volume 2, p. 43.

39. Vuillemin, "Berlin 1933," *Les Échos des Savannes,* Vol. 7 (1984).

40. Gourio and Vuillemin, *Hitler = SS,* pp. 59–67.

41. Interview between Marcel Gotlib, Jean-Marie Gourio, and Philippe Vuillemin, "Hitler = SS et l'humour sans bornes," *Cahiers de la BD,* Vol. 85 (1989), pp. 54–60, 56.

42. Interview between Marcel Gotlib, Jean-Marie Gourio, and Philippe Vuillemin, "Hitler = SS et l'humour sans bornes," p. 58. In the year of their conversation (1987) the discussion about the ethical and legal limits of the representation of the Holocaust had just begun.

43. Interview between Marcel Gotlib, Jean-Marie Gourio, and Philippe Vuillemin, "Hitler = SS et l'humour sans bornes," p. 60. Likewise, in 2002 Zbigniew Libera's "LEGO Concentration Camp Set" exposed at the "Mirroring Evil" exhibition of the New York Jewish Museum gave much food for discussion. Designing a model of Auschwitz for educational or artistic purposes is quite arguable, but the little Danish manikins just did not fit. One thing Vuillemin and Gourio finally could not bear was working with original photos.

44. Des Pres, "Holocaust Laughter?" p. 220.

45. Torben Fischer and Matthias N. Lorenz, *Lexikon der "Vergangenheitsbewältigung" in Deutschland. Debatten- und Diskursgeschichte des Nationalsozialismus nach 1945* (Bielefeld, Transkript, 2009).

46. Jason Lutes, *Berlin* (2 volumes, Montreal, Drawn & Quarterly, 2000/2008); Jean Pierre Gibrat, *Le sursis* (Marcinelle, Dupuis, 1997/1999) and *Le vol du corbeau* (Marcinelle, Dupuis, 2002/2005), two volumes each; Rodolphe and Claude Plumail, *Das Reich,* (two volumes, Toulon, Soleil, 1997/2002); Pascal Crocy, *Auschwitz* (Paris, Emmanuel Proust Editions, 2002); Joe Kubert, *Yossel* (Paris, Delcourt, 2003); Dave Sim, *Judenhass* (Kitchener/Ontario, Aardvark Vanaheim, 2008).

47. Nazi-comics for the youth: Eric Heuvel, *Die Entdeckung/Die Suche* (Amsterdam, Anne Frank Haus, 2003/2007). See also Bernd Dolle-Weinkauff, "Danach, das Ende und der Anfang: Aktuelle Comic-Schlaglichter auf die Zeit der NS-Herrschaft und des II. Weltkriegs," in Petra Josting and Jan Wirrer, eds., *Festschrift für Norbert Hopster* (Hildesheim, Olms, 1996), p. 174. Pascal Crocy, *Auschwitz* (Paris, Emmanuel Proust Editions, 2002) is used in French schools for 14- and 15-year-olds.

48. This may have commercial reasons: not sure about the commercial success of a Holocaust comic for young people, editors and authors depend on whether the usually rather conservative educational system is interested or not.

49. Walli and Michel de Bom, *Gil Sinclair. 4 volumes: L'île truquée; Le carnet rouge; Mission Nid d'Aigle; Le murmure de Berlin* (Brussels, Éditions du Lombard, 1990–1994), pp. 31, 40, 42, 48.

50. Mike Maurus and Wolfgang Schneider, *Operation Odin* (Hamburg, Carlsen, 1991).

51. Bernd Dolle-Weinkauff, "Das 'Dritte Reich' im Comic: Geschichtsbilder und darstellungsästhetische Strategien einer rekonstruierten Gattung," *Jahrbuch für Antisemitismusforschung,* Vol. 2 (1993), p. 307.

52. Richardson, "Heil Myself!" pp. 278, 280.

53. Moers is a very prolific writer and artist. His grotesque fairy-tale novels are inspired by, among others, Rabelais, Fischart, and the gothic novel. In his artwork he uses a minimalist drawing style to treat a wide range of topics and address a very mixed audience. He has published several books about his teenage character Little Asshole, has illustrated giftware books, and writes episodes of a popular children television series. Despite his sparse drawing style he has become one of Germany's most famous comic authors since he published his series on the return of Hitler to the contemporary world. Some of his novels are available in English: Walter Moers, *The 13/2 Lives of Captain Bluebear* (New York, Overlook Hardcover, 2005); *The City of Dreaming Books* (London, Harvill Secker, 2006); *Rumo and His Miraculous Adventures* (New York, Overlook Hardcover, 2006).

54. Walter Moers, *Adolf: Äch bin wieder da* and *Adolf: Äch bin schon wieder da.*

55. Grégory Jarry and Otto T., *La conquête de Mars, vol. 1: Le premier homme sur la Lune; vol. 2: Germania* (Poitiers, Éditions FLBLB, 2008).

56. "Wenn das der Führer wüsste . . . " ("If the Führer knew that . . . ") was a frequent saying during the Third Reich. Today, revanchists like David Irving try to prove that Hitler did not know about the Holocaust by pointing out that there is no written and signed order on his behalf.

57. Pixel Vengeur, *Fantôme en tergal contre La Légion Damnée du IVe Reich* (Paris, Albin Michel, 2007).

58. Yann and Hardy, *La patrouille des Libellules.*

59. Yann and Laurent Verron, *Odilon Verjus,* volume 4: *Adolf* (Brussels, Éditions du Lombard, 1999), p. 5.

60. Yann and Verron, *Odilon Verjus, Adolf,* p. 40; Joachim Sistig, *Invasion aus der Vergangenheit: Das Deutschlandbild in frankophonen Bandes Dessinées* (Frankfurt/M, et al., 2002), p. 86.

61. Norman G. Finckelstein's *The Holocaust Industry: Reflections on the Exploitation of Jewish Suffering* (London, Verso Books, 2000) started a discussion about the alleged overrepresentation of the Holocaust with regards to other genocides.

62. Johnny Ryan, *The Comic Book Holocaust* (Oakland, CA, Bonaventura Press, 2008).

63. Ryan, *The Comic Book Holocaust* (no pagination).

64. For a psychological explanation of this phenomenon, see Christian Schneider, "Wer lacht wann?" in Frölich et al., eds., *Lachen über Auschwitz,* pp. 135–154.

65. David Denby, "Life Is Beautiful," *New Yorker* (November 23, 1998). He even wrote a second review: David Denby, "In the Eye of the Beholder: Another Look at Roberto Benigni's Holocaust Fantasy," *New Yorker* (March 15, 1999). See also Kathy Laster and Heinz Steinert, "Eine neue Moral in der Darstellung der Shoah? Zur Rezeption von *La vita è bella,*" Frölich et al., eds., *Lachen über Auschwitz,*

pp. 181–198; and Andrea Lauterwein and Colette Strauss-Hiva, eds., *Rire Satire Shoah. L'Humour Et La Catastrophe* (Paris, Éditions de l'éclat, 2009).

66. Carr and Greeves, *The Naked Jape,* p. 181.
67. Carr and Greeves, *The Naked Jape,* p. 189.
68. Richardson, "Heil Myself!" p. 278.
69. Susan Sontag, *Regarding the Pain of Others* (London, Penguin, 2003), pp. 76, 80.

5

Holocaust Pornography: Profaning the Sacred in *Ilsa, She-Wolf of the SS*[1]

Lynn Rapaport

Introduction

The 1974 sexploitation film *Ilsa, She-Wolf of the SS* begins with a voice-over of Adolf Hitler delivering a speech while a titlecard from the producer, listed as Herman Traeger, states the following:

> The film you are about to see is based upon documented fact. The atrocities shown were conducted as 'medical experiments' in special concentration camps throughout Hitler's Third Reich. Although these crimes against humanity are historically accurate, the characters depicted are composites of notorious Nazi personalities, and the events portrayed have been condensed into one locality for dramatic purposes. Because of its shocking subject matter, this film is restricted to adult audiences only. We dedicate this film with the hope that these heinous crimes will never occur again.

> The camera in the opening scene pans slowly to the left across Ilsa's living quarters. Through a mirror on the wall, we catch a glimpse of Ilsa and a prisoner making love. She is on top, moaning, "No, no, no not yet! No please. You should have waited." The male prisoner had already ejaculated.

Originally published as Lynn Rapaport, "Holocaust Pornography: Profaning the Sacred in *Ilsa, She-Wolf of the SS," Shofar: An Interdisciplinary Journal of Jewish Studies,* Vol. 22, No. 1 (2003), pp. 53–79. Copyright © 2003, Purdue University. "This material is used by permission of Purdue University Press." With grateful thanks to Lynn and Purdue University Press for allowing us to republish.

Ilsa satisfies herself in the shower—the downward tilt of the camera reveals that she is moving the showerhead across her naked body, giving the impression that she is masturbating. In the next scene Ilsa and her guards wake the prisoner and carry him away. This is followed by the film's title credits over the backdrop of a montage of new female prisoners being transported into the camp. The film then cuts to a laboratory room where Ilsa and her two guards are leaning over the male prisoner who is on the operating table.

"Once a prisoner has slept with me, he will never sleep with a woman again. If he lives, he will remember only the pain of the knife," Ilsa reports. When the prisoner asks why, Ilsa laughs, "To castrate."

The film is set in Poland in 1945 during the final days of the Second World War. When she is not castrating male prisoners who fail to satisfy her sexually, blond and busty Ilsa, the Nazi commandant of Medical Camp 9, is busy conducting medical experiments on female prisoners. Her goal is to prove that women can withstand pain better than men and should therefore be allowed to serve the military in combat positions. She is so sadistic in her experiments that "even the Nazis fear her," claims the voice-over in the trailer.

What happens to Holocaust memory when the Holocaust is eroticized? Emile Durkheim has written extensively about the distinction between the sacred and the profane. He argues that things collectively held as sacred are always separated from things considered profane.[2] Sado-masochistic iconography has long exploited Nazi imagery by linking sex with power and violence. When victims and perpetrators become sexual partners in Holocaust film narratives—contrary to the Nuremberg racial laws—what does this say about our cultural imagination? What does the popularity of a film like *She-Wolf* reveal about what Nazis "mean" in American culture? What fantasies about society are being expressed by associating Nazi imagery with themes of power and gender, sexuality and violence?

While research is growing on how the Holocaust is represented within popular culture, little exists on pornography employing Nazi themes and imagery.[3] This paper explores how things collectively held as sacred—the Holocaust and its memory, the body, traditional gender roles and sexual relations—are systematically profaned in this film. I also make explicit comparisons between the events and characterizations presented in the film and the well-documented history of the Holocaust. By "reading" this film as a cultural text, I hope to uncover the socio-cultural understandings and appreciation of the moral ramifications of the Holocaust in American culture. I will describe how cultural context, historical trauma, and aesthetic form interplay in *Ilsa, She-Wolf of the SS.* More generally, I will question why Holocaust memory is being eroticized, gendered, and ultimately, profaned.

Research for this paper is based on a close textual analysis of the film, and in-depth interviews I conducted with actress Dyanne Thorne (Ilsa), actor Buck Flowers (Dr. Binz—Ilsa's sidekick), and *She-Wolf* 's director Don Edmunds. I also conducted an analysis of a representative sample of 508 web sites related to the film on the search engine *google.com,* and of newspaper reports and secondary literature.

Holocaust Pornography

Ilsa, She-Wolf of the SS fits two fictional film genres—Women in Prison (WIP) and sexploitation. WIP films began shortly after World War II when "good girls" of the silver screen were replaced with more adventurous role models, reflecting changing gender roles during wartime. Many films were set in prisons, and women characters were hard, mean, and tough. Archetypal roles included the queen bee or dominant female prisoner, the new fish—the lead actress in jail for the first time, the sadistic warden, the prostitute with the heart of gold, and the lesbian guard.[4]

By the mid-1960s the genre was taken over by sexploitation films, and the settings transformed from prisons to slavery rings. Bob Cresse's *Love Camp 7,* released in 1967, was the first soft-core porn film set in a Nazi concentration camp. In the film, women are held captive for the sexual pleasure of Nazi officers and soldiers.

The 1960s and early 1970s was also the golden age of American film violence. Cinematic expressions of the counterculture challenged classical Hollywood genres and their underlying myths, like that of the masculine hero. The film industries of many countries followed a remarkably similar pattern: a "golden age" in the fifties or sixties, a slide into sexploitation in the seventies, and a slow decline through the eighties, followed in the nineties by video and the dominance of Hollywood.[5] Through the exaggeration of formulaic images of aggression, productions increasingly mirrored cultural preoccupations with violence. Filmmakers also tried to expand the bounds of conventional film practice with stylistic and narrative innovations. By doing so, they sought to join in a broader discussion about the nature of human aggression and the impact of violent images.[6]

The Italian film industry developed the Nazi porn concept.[7] Luchino Visconti's *The Damned* (1969), for example, introduced mainstream audiences to cinematic Nazi controversy by linking sexual decadence to Nazism. *The Damned* focused on the demise of powerful German industrialists who supported Hitler's doctrine during the early days of the Third Reich, suggesting incest, homosexuality, and pedophilia. By the mid-1970s the Italian film industry released a spate of sex and swastika films.[8]

Bob Cresse's *Love Camp 7* was the catalyst for making *Ilsa, She-Wolf of the SS*. Producer David Friedman explains:

> What inspired this film, a couple years before, Bob Cresse, Lee Frost and I had made a picture called *Love Camp 7,* which was basically a German stalag where all of the inmates were young ladies who were being used by the officers and it was a soft exploitation picture. But the picture went through the roof in Canada. I mean it killed 'em up there. The distributor of that picture wanted to make another such picture. We're using the device of a Nazi concentration camp full of women, only this time instead of the women being used as sex slaves they were being used as experiments à la Dr. Mengele. They contacted me and I was working on something else. So Don [Edmunds] and my associate Bill Castleman went up and made the deal.[9]

Don Edmunds, *She-Wolf*'s director, describes his motivation for making the film:

> You know, it was a very different world. It was the end of Vietnam, it had a sense of loose morality in that period of time. It was the love generation. It was just a different world. When I was approached to make this picture, I was just starting as a director. There wasn't anybody throwing pictures at me. So when it was offered to me, I said to the man who was the funder/producer, I'd read it. God I was just some kid hustling around Hollywood. I hung out and I needed the money. And I just said, 'this is the worst piece of shit I ever read.' And he started peeling off money. Being the whore that I am, when he got down to $2000, I kept going, 'maybe I can find a socially significant reason.'[10]

She-Wolf was filmed in nine days on the abandoned set of *Hogan's Heroes*. Friedman explains:

> I had just finished a picture on the old Selznick lot, 'The Erotic Adventures of Zorro,' and so I was well known on that lot. The old Hogan's Heroes set was on the back lot there, and I knew that they had sold that property for condominiums. I asked the studio manager if I could burn that thing down, and he said, sure, do anything you want. I hired this young make-up guy named Joe Blasco, and he got into it. He came up with some of the greatest effects I've ever seen. Later on he became head of make-up at ABC and runs a series of schools on make-up. He came up with all of those effects, and they worked like gangbusters. Of course, that was a relatively bigger budget picture, $110,000. It was at the same studio where *Gone with the Wind* was made![11]

Breaking Taboos—Themes within the Film

Fitting within the genre of sexploitation films, *Ilsa, She-Wolf of the SS* was made to make a quick profit by shocking and titillating audiences with sensationalism. Underneath these surfaces lies the concrete and very real presence of history. The film mocks in graphic detail the horrendous tortures of imprisonment in Nazi concentration camps. It touches on the taboo themes of forced prostitution, rape, castration, sterilization, and medical experimentation. Referring to his discussion with the producer, Edmunds recalls why he decided to make the film. "He told me at the time there'd been a lot of research done on the picture and that the atrocities were real, that there was documentation that those [things] had been done in prison camps over the years. . . . And I believe it," he says. He continues:

> There really was a man named Joseph Mengele. There really was a lady named Ilsa Koch . . . Dachaus and Buchenwalds—they really existed. There was a quest to make a super race. The things that are in Ilsa, I told him at the time, 'You wanna see this stuff? Because I can put it on the screen for you. You want to pull back and cut away?' And he said, 'No.' And I said, 'Then I'm going to give it to you, brother' . . . And I did. These things came up, fairly horrific scenes. There's probably half a dozen—seven or eight different scenes in this

picture. The syphilitic woman, putting gangrene pus in the wounds . . . see how cold we can get a human being and not kill 'em. . . . For the amusement of the dinner party they hang a girl from a block of ice, and you know . . .[12]

While the film is characterized as "porno" and "sexploitation," I counted only five specifically sexual scenes, and 44 torture scenes, although some torture scenes included topless women or nudity. Indeed, the Internet Movie Database (*imdb.com*) lists more keywords associated with torture than sex in describing the plot: boiling-alive, Nazi-exploitation, breast-electrodes, lesbianism, sexual-exploitation, maggot, vaginal-electrodes, depressurization-chamber, perversity, prison-camp, gang-rape, violence, torture, war-crime, video-nasty, exploitation, sadism, sex, disturbing, uniform, castration, blood, gas-gangrene, medical-experiment, typhus, uranism, women-in-uniform, Nazi, nudity, death, dildo, rape, gore, independent-film, and syphilis.

In some ways, *She-Wolf* appears as more of a horror film than a pornographic one. In Durkheimian terms, horror refers to transgressions against what is sacred. Ilsa, the mad scientist movie monster, is a high ranking Nazi doctor. The film deals with the struggle between "good" and "evil," the collapse of the spiritual and moral order, death, the degradation of the human body, and the impact and effect of the past—typical themes of the horror genre. It also deals with anxieties arising in the modern world—women gaining power and the fear of science gone mad.

Castration, Sterilization, Prostitution, and Rape

Following the opening castration scene, the film continues with the arrival of new recruits. When Ilsa asks Dr. Binz, her male assistant, how many new prisoners are in the transport, he says fifteen, thus trivializing the Holocaust, where at its peak victims were arriving in much greater numbers. "They expect us to work miracles. Five days," she says. "Someone should tell them it's too many," the assistant responds. "My research is more important than their sterilization. Ours is the most important of any of the camps. Ours is different. It is important," Ilsa says. Ilsa then addresses the new arrivals:

There is no need for you to be afraid. This is no Dachau, no Ravensbrück. We are doctors, we are here to help you. Your stay with us will
be short, but in it you will be helped to serve the Third Reich. That is
your destiny. We welcome you to Camp Nine.

Medical experiments in concentration camps fell into two categories:
those sponsored by the regime for specific ideological and military purposes, and those that were done *ad hoc* out of allegedly scientific interest
on the part of the SS doctor. The first type included sterilization, exposure
to cold or high altitudes, artificially created wounds and gangrene and the
injection of sulfonamides and other "therapeutic" agents, and the effectiveness of various serums for typhus and yellow fever. The second type
referred to experiments individual doctors conducted in their desire to do
"scientific work." The experiments on identical twins performed by Josef
Mengele in Auschwitz or Eduard Wirths on precancerous growths on the
cervix are cases in point.[13]

The next scene depicts a selection process. Ilsa, in a white doctor's
smock, is sitting behind her desk. A large swastika banner hangs on the
wall behind her, reminding us that she is a Nazi. Her assistant is standing
at the door, and the female prisoners are lined up behind it. Ilsa is conducting an inspection. The guard introduces the female recruits by their
"number," and they enter Ilsa's office one by one. Although they have
been given a number, their hair has not been shorn. The first nude prisoner walks into Ilsa's office, covering herself with her clothes bundled in
her arms around her chest. She says she is ashamed, and Ilsa says there
is nothing to be ashamed about, as "we have to see you in order to know
what work to assign you. We are doctors." When the next prisoner enters
and asks what type of work they will do, Ilsa responds that some of the
women will be "re-trained" to serve the soldiers of the Third Reich.

Ilsa is referring to forced prostitution. Indeed, in the summer of 1941,
Heinrich Himmler ordered the establishment of bordellos for the use of
male inmates of concentration camps. About a year later, the SS began
to establish camp bordellos, and by the end of 1944 at least 11 existed in
Buchenwald, Dachau, Mauthausen, Gusen, Auschwitz, Monowitz, Birke-
nau, Flossenbürg, Neuengamme, Sachsenhausen, and Dora-Mittelbau.
Concentration camp bordellos and those established by the Nazi state for
the Wehrmacht, SS officers, and foreign and forced laborers working in

the German Reich, formed part of an extensive system in which a minimum of 34,140 women were forced to work as prostitutes during the Third Reich.[14]

Bordellos were established to prevent homosexual relationships among male inmates, to divert inmates' attention away from resisting or organizing politically, and to provide an incentive for male prisoners to work harder.[15] Himmler ordered the establishment of the bordellos as part of a new incentive system that paid inmates small amounts of "camp money" when they produced at higher rates or fulfilled certain quotas. They could use this money to purchase hard-to-obtain items such as cigarettes or various food products—or they could visit the bordello, which otherwise was only to be had for a price of RM2.[16]

While conditions in the bordellos varied from camp to camp, the female inmates working as prostitutes were forced to fulfill a quota of eight men per day. These men would be subject to a hygienic inspection before and after their visit to the prostitute. According to some accounts they were given shots. The female inmates were also required to wash after each visit. They were not provided birth control, though some women underwent compulsory sterilization prior to their forced prostitution. Christa Paul quotes several accounts of pregnancies and forced abortions, some resulting in death for the women involved.[17]

The film does not refer to forced female prostitution in any other way. On the contrary, in a reversal of traditional gender roles it depicts forced male prostitution. The men must have intercourse with Ilsa, and if they fail to satisfy her, she castrates them. Ilsa is portrayed in a non-traditional manner—a dominatrix, who is on top both in bed and in the camp. She is a female villain, a feminist, and as Rush Limbaugh has coined, a "feminazi." In the opening castration scene, we see three female Nazis in positions of power while the man is victimized. While Ilsa sadistically dominates men and women, she wants to prove that women are stronger, more tolerant of pain, and should be in battle. However, she is not the quintessential feminist, as she is also the object of the viewer's gaze. She conforms to the male fantasy of a blond, blue-eyed bombshell, with larger-than-life breasts and an insatiable sexual appetite—always wanting it, always needing it. She is a femme fatale—a metaphor for transgressions of sexuality and morality. While her Nazi uniform reflects militarism and power, prolonged shots show her breasts threatening to bulge out of her barely buttoned, crisp-white blouse.

When a new recruit of male prisoners arrive, Ilsa inspects them. "Baum will be pleased," Ilsa says to the naked men. "I see no manhood between your legs." While Jews or other non-Aryans are never mentioned throughout the film, Ilsa is referring to Baum's theory that inferior races have smaller genitalia. She takes a special interest in Wolfe, a German-born American, because of his blond hair. "You bastard German, it's clear to see your blood is tainted. This is not the build of a true Aryan," she says referring to his genitals. "Size is not everything, Commandant," he replies. Wolfe finds out the next day that another prisoner, Mario, spent the night with Ilsa and was castrated for not satisfying her. Mario, feeling only half a man, tells Wolfe he lives for revenge.

What anxieties or angst are being symbolized about conventional masculinity in these scenes? Ilsa is portrayed as the all-powerful female villain. She is in a position of power, and the male prisoners must answer to her. The male prisoners are in the passive role of sexually servicing and satisfying Ilsa on command. It is the complete opposite of male-dominated sexual intercourse.

Is this a fear of impotence—a crisis in male identity? Do men feel emasculated by powerful women? Is this emasculation through castration—a man unable to sexually satisfy a woman is not a real man? These scenes are also structured to focus attention on the penis. In general, pornography limits the representation of the penis to the large, ever-present, long-lasting erection—asserting that this is what women want and need. Yet, in *She-Wolf,* the penis is not visualized. On the contrary, during the opening castration scene, Ilsa is standing directly in front of spectators' views of the penis. Also, in the scene where Ilsa is inspecting the genitals of the new male arrivals, the camera shoots the men from behind, showing their naked rear ends. Once again, the spectator is not in the position to see the penis. Indeed, there are no shots of male frontal nudity throughout the film. When a male is shown naked, it is from the waist up.

Film scholar Peter Lehman argues that when the penis is represented or shown or even referred to in popular culture, it is nearly always part of a discourse which attempts to carefully regulate that representation: hard-core porn represents large, mostly erect penises; sexology represents statistically average, "normal" penises; and penis-size jokes usually refer to small inadequate penises.[18]

Perhaps Wolfe is supposed to be a representation for every man, rather than a masculine ideal. Furthermore, men may fear that the representation of the penis gives women a basis for comparison and judgment, even though men have long engaged in such comparisons of women. The lack of male frontal nudity in a film that draws attention to the penis in performance anxieties, castration anxieties, and size, is curious. Even more so for a film marketed for its shock-value, being released when frontal male nudity was part of a larger cultural climate in the Broadway productions of *Hair, Tom Paine,* and *Oh! Calcutta!* of the late 1960s and 1970s.

Perhaps the film embodies the contradictions associated with female power. The monster in the horror film dares to speak the truth of repressed desire. Whether male or female, the monster speaks the unspeakable, defies order and system, flaunts morality and law.[19] Is this masculine anxiety part of a whole backlash in the 1960s and 1970s in popular culture against the women's movement and women reaching positions of power?[20] Why is the Holocaust being eroticized and gendered? In the film there is a mirroring of two conflicts—the Nazis against the prisoners, and women torturing men. These male anxieties are being exaggerated by fantastical instances of female violence. It is the female guards who throughout the film beat or torture male and female prisoners. Ilsa, the main character and movie monster, symbolizes generic evil, Nazism, horror, perverse sexuality, and social malaise. The Holocaust is not just being sexualized, but it is also being gendered—a woman in power is evil, a Nazi, a feminazi.[21]

Human Guinea Pigs in Medical Experiments

When the prisoner in the selection scene asks what she will do, Ilsa responds, "You will serve in a different manner, to help the cause of medical research and thereby save thousands of lives." In a scene taking place in the female prisoners' quarters, we learn that the female prisoners have been infected with bacteria like tetanus, rabies, and syphilis, in the Nazis' attempt to develop experimental drugs. One scene shows a woman with maggots on her leg, and Ilsa explains to the General who is inspecting the medical camp that the prisoner has been infected with a new strain of typhus. When asked whether she uses anesthesia, Ilsa responds, "One does not give caviar to guinea pigs." In another shot, her assistant is infecting a prisoner's exposed wound with gangrene. In an earlier scene, Kala, a female prisoner with a monster-like deformity akin to a burn victim on one side of her face, tells another prisoner she was infected with syphilis. "It is simply a matter of how long it will take me to die," she says. Then echoing testimony from Holocaust survivors, she remarks, "God cannot help you here. He has forgotten this place."

Indeed, on the basis of orders and instructions from pharmaceutical corporations, SS physicians carried out pharmacological experiments in Dachau, Buchenwald, Ravensbrück, Sachsenhausen, Natzweiler, Strutthof, and other concentration camps. As a rule, pharmaceutical studies were tested simultaneously at various camps in order to compare results. The prisoners of these camps were human "guinea pigs." Various pathologies were induced to observe the effect of medicines on the course of the disease, and to establish the proper medical dosage and toxicity. Other prisoners were infected with the disease but not given the medicines, so that they could be observed as a control group. These experiments took place on the initiative of the highest medical authorities of the Third Reich, at the request of pharmaceutical companies, institutes, the Wehrmacht staff, and the SS, with the approval of Himmler and responsible authorities of the Nazi health service. SS camp physicians also carried out these experiments on their own initiative.[22] The people used for these experiments did not agree to them voluntarily. The experiment was forced upon them with the use of pressure, strategies, and deception. The purpose of the experiments was not to benefit the prisoner, but to observe the reaction to the drug, even when it was quite harmful to the prisoner.

Besides the pharmacological experiments, Ilsa was conducting her own private research, trying to test her theory that women can withstand more pain than men and therefore should be allowed to serve in combat positions on the frontline. The most graphic and gory scenes in the film depict women prisoners undergoing horrific tortures to indicate their threshold for pain. For instance, in one scene in the female sterilization room, women prisoners are lined up awaiting treatment. Ilsa enters the room and tells them they will undergo a series of tests. Several naked female prisoners are then examined by members of Ilsa's entourage. Three types of medical experiments are depicted. The first is a sterilization process with an electrical phallus. The second involves placing prisoners in a pressure chamber, and in the third they are in a boiler room.

Compulsory sterilization programs existed in Germany as early as 1933 and, with the establishment of the "euthanasia" program in 1939, became a medical link to the extermination in concentration camps. Indeed,

Himmler actively promoted sterilization experiments, based on doctors' claims that they were on the verge of achieving efficient and economic methods for large-scale sterilization of inferior peoples. These experiments involved injecting caustic substances into the uterine cervix of women, and x-raying the genitals of men and women, and eventually removing the testicles or ovaries surgically to study the effects of the x-rays.[23]

In the first experiment, we are reminded that this is a pornographic film as Ilsa grabs and caresses an electrically charged 12-inch dildo. A female prisoner is strapped to a stretcher in a makeshift operating room. Ilsa pushes the electric phallus up the women's vagina to sterilize her. She does this to the first prisoner, who cries out in pain, and also to the second one, who screams. She uses the electric dildo on Anna, the third prisoner, who is able to withstand the pain. Regarding the film's themes of gender relations and dominance, perhaps the message is that Anna is able to withstand unnaturally intense penetration. Ilsa remarks to her assistant that they have found "the one."

In the second torture experiment, through a small window on the door to a pressure chamber, we see a female prisoner cuffed to the wall inside. The pressure is set at 6,000 meters and Ilsa remarks that the Luftwaffe will have much to thank them for. She instructs her assistant to reduce the pressure by five kilos. The pressure is reduced and the female prisoner's eyes bulge, blood oozes from her mouth, she screams and eventually passes out.

The third torture scene takes place in a boiler room. The prisoner is being burned alive in a tub of scorching water. Ilsa asks what the temperature has been in the water, and for how long, and inquires about the prisoner's vital signs. She tells her assistant to increase the water temperature (which was already at 82 centigrade) by five degrees, and when he resists, she says, "Our soldiers are dying in the inferno of our burning tanks. It's for them we do it, for the Fatherland. Five degrees!"

In a later scene when Ilsa shows the General Anna's tortured body, and claims that "no man could have withstood such pain," the General remarks that Ilsa should not be wasting Germany's time with her own personal project.

Ilsa, the Feminazi

Dyanne Thorne in a voice-over commentary on the DVD release describes the feminist aspect of the film. "She's on top . . . we want to make that very clear. . . . " Thorne's comments refer to the opening sex scene. "This is the first one [film] where they had a female villain. She was like the leader of the feminists, if you will . . . because even with this scene [opening castration scene] the victim was the male and the three females are standing there with total control." Thorne goes on to say that the entire Ilsa series was the pioneer for a new generation of women heroines, like *Charlie's Angels.*

While ten percent of employees at concentration camps were female, women were never in charge of camps. Women served through the SS (not as full members—a category limited to men) in a variety of capacities including SS doctors, nurses, and office personnel. They served as guards in concentration camps with women's divisions, such as Strutthof, Auschwitz (as of March 1942), Majdanek (as of August 1942), Mauthausen, Dachau, and Sachsenhausen. There were also 240,000 women married to SS men, many of whom lived with their husbands at concentration camps.[24]

While women guards always served under male authority and were not directly involved in the decisions to organize and carry out murder, they did participate in selecting inmates for death, and for punishment, which often led to death. Some also committed a wide range of violent abuse of prisoners.

The Ilsa film-series is based on a composite of Nazi medical doctors and commandants.[25] "I understand that it was loosely based on the real Ilsa, Ilsa Koch," says Buck Flowers, the actor who plays Ilsa's assistant in the film, Dr. Binz. Yet, Flowers is mistaken when he says, "she evidently had a camp of her own where she was experimenting on Jewish women, to try to get the superior woman, while old Adolf was hunting for superior men." Ilsa Koch, also known as "The Bitch of Buchenwald," did not have a camp of her own. Her husband, Karl, was the commandant of the Buchenwald concentration camp.[26]

While Karl supervised the camp, Ilsa Koch was earning her own reputation. There are reports that she liked to walk through the camp dressed provocatively, causing prisoners to look at her and demanding they be punished for their presumption. Although she had no formal authority in the camp, she was known to have beaten prisoners with her own hands, and with a riding whip, lashing out at anyone who displeased her. There were reports she took her husband's dog with her, squealing with delight as she let it loose upon pregnant women and women carrying heavy loads. There were accusations that "she spent her evenings making lampshades from the tattooed skins of innocent murdered men."[27]

Ilsa Koch corresponded with the wives of commandants in other concentration camps, giving them instructions on how to turn human skin into a book cover, lampshade, gloves, or a fine table cloth. The talk of lampshades and the whippings had filtered out of the camps through dissatisfied guards, and at the end of 1941 Ilsa Koch and Karl Koch were brought before Court XXII, an SS police court in Kassel, to answer charges of "gross brutality, corruption and dishonor." According to the verdict against her, the suffering of prisoners brought her pleasure, and the psychiatrist who examined her diagnosed sexual aggression.[28]

The role of an overly powerful female character has been a popular staple in independent films. In *She-Wolf,* does Ilsa represent the Nazi ideal? Or, by making Ilsa the villain of the film, are we feminizing Nazi evil? In *Hitler's Willing Executioners* Daniel Goldhagen shows how ordinary German men were willing to murder Jews, even though they could have refused without sanctions.[29] In Christopher Browning's study of the *Einsatzgruppen* entitled *Ordinary Men,* he shows how peer pressure encourages male cruelty.[30] Susannah Heschel takes a gendered approach to this question of evil and cruelty and asks whether female commandants in Nazi prison camps could likewise be considered ordinary women.[31] After reviewing the memoir literature and popular press on female perpetrators, Heschel argues that female Nazis, including Ilsa Koch, are often described as being crueler than men.[32] This cruelty is not a result of the types of atrocities they committed, but based on the "pleasure" they enjoyed—often described as "erotic"—in tormenting prisoners.[33]

Barb Serfozo and Henry Farrell argue that the sexualizing of Nazi images, as mediated through pornography, provides a discourse for the right wing to attack feminists. Rush Limbaugh's term "feminazi" or Newt Gingrich's sexually loaded language to describe right wing fascination with fascism is saturated with popular culture images linking Nazism with sado-masochistic sex.[34]

Moreover, while Dyanne Thorne hails Ilsa as a "superwoman" and the movie as a pioneer for "feminist films," Ilsa falls into traditional gender expectations as she is ultimately tamed by Wolfe's sexual power. We first learn of Wolfe's unusual sexual abilities in an earlier scene when he confides in Mario, another male prisoner, that he is a "freak of nature." He tells Mario that he is a "sort of human machine" because he can hold an erection as long as he wants. He is a "machine that can set its controls to fast, slow, or never," he tells Mario.

Wolfe demonstrates his sexual prowess in his first sex scene with Ilsa. "I need you. I need to feel you inside me," Ilsa says while admiring Wolfe's body. "I will satisfy you until you beg me to stop," he responds. In his next sexual encounter with Ilsa, she affirms his manhood. "No man can perform as you did. No man," she says. Asking whether she thought it was a dream, Ilsa makes Wolfe have sex with her two female guards, so she can watch. Wolfe is engaged in intercourse with one of her guards, while the other one strokes his body. Sitting on a chair stroking her whip, with German music playing on the radio in the background, Ilsa looks like she is falling asleep. A film cut implies that time has elapsed, as Wolfe continues to have sex with the first guard, who is screaming with delight at reaching climax.

About halfway through the film, after proving his manhood, the next time Ilsa and Wolfe meet, he is the one giving her orders as part of their sexual play. "Now, my beautiful commandant, this time will be different," he says. "Take your clothes off. I want you to undress while I sit and watch you. No! Slowly, show me yourself. Slowly. Slowly. You look beautiful, Ilsa." As they awaken early the next morning, Wolfe prepares to leave. "Must go now," he tells Ilsa. "When victory comes, we shall make children. They will be beautiful, strong," Ilsa says and then falls back to sleep.

While Wolfe is American, he has a German name, and is blond-haired and blue-eyed. He is the hero of the film, and Ilsa is the movie monster. While male monsters in horror films (ape, werewolf, vampire) represent the repressed bestial desires of civilized man, the woman is almost always the object of this aggression—the victim of acts of terror unleashed by the werewolf, vampire, alien, "thing." Monsters are frequently initially represented as sympathetic characters with whom spectators are encouraged to identify. This is also the case with female monsters, like Sissy Spacek in *Carrie,* or Linda Blair in *The Exorcist.* Yet, we do not feel sympathetic towards Ilsa, as we initially might to other monsters.

The film raises questions about the interrelationship among gender, sexuality, and power. Horror films in general problematize links between different kinds of desires and between sexuality and violence. The film entails a literal attack upon the masculine. On one level, the film becomes a drama about relinquishing certain heterosexual white male prerogatives, i.e., it is a film about males forced to relinquish power to women, of male trepidation over deference to women required of them as prisoners in Nazi concentration camps. Male fear of women with newly won social power surfaces in the form of an ultimately violent, sexually desirous female aggressor. Ilsa appears as a threat precisely because she has taken on traditional masculine characteristics of the very type that the men in general, and prisoners in particular, were forced to give up. Ilsa wears the pants in this film by occupying a masculine position in terms of broader cultural conventions of action, the gaze, and of voice. Moreover, Ilsa controls a substantial portion of the physical action of the film. By acting on violent and sexual desires in ways that are not open to any of the males in the film, it is Ilsa who is crucial to forwarding the narrative, because she acts and others react.

Resistance and Rebellion

It is only at the end of the film, when the prisoners plan an escape, that they move the narrative forward. When Ilsa calls Wolfe to her quarters for sex, Wolfe takes on a domineering role. He ties Ilsa to the bedposts and gags her. He leaves her lying there while he prepares for an escape. Outside the prisoners have begun fighting off the guards. Shooting ensues, and they get the upper hand over the soldiers. The remaining prisoners gather Ilsa's cohorts in the yard. Although Wolfe pleads to hand them over to the Allies for trial, the prisoners execute them by bullets to the head. More German troops arrive as everyone makes an escape. The disfigured Anna, her body a mass of welts and lacerations, attempts to stab Ilsa, who is tied naked to the bed, but dies as she crawls to the bedside. A Nazi Captain arrives on the scene, shooting dead a hysterical Ilsa. Outside, the Captain informs the General that Camp 9 has been demolished. The Allies will never know the horrific events that occurred there. In the last scene, Wolfe and Rosette, a prisoner with whom he has formed a romantic alliance, have escaped from the camp and look out from a distant hillside.

While horror films consistently exaggerate gender by relying on a monstrous male and a victimized female, Barry Keith Grant writes that probably the most common image in horror films is the "beast in the boudoir."[35] From *Dracula, Psycho,* and *Rosemary's Baby* to the *Nightmare on Elm Street* series, the monstrous appearance of excessive male desire threatens women with subordination, abject surrender, or death.[36]

Yet, in *She-Wolf*, the reversal of gender roles, whereby Ilsa is the female monster, is rectified as Ilsa is sacrificed in a bloody massacre that redeems male masculinity and power. While Ilsa is portrayed as sexually dominant throughout most of the film, ultimately she is unable to control men's bodies. In the opening scene despite being "on top," Ilsa cannot control the prisoner's ejaculation despite her commands that he wait. Her excessive sexual desire and her inability to control Wolfe's body suggests that women can (temporarily) exert control of their sexual lives, but doing so eventually transforms them into something evil, and ultimately destroys them. Moreover, excessive female desire and female domination is a common male fantasy. Thus, films portraying nymphomaniacs and female domination could also be understood as reinforcing conventional masculinity—the women appear to overly crave and dominate men, but since men are receiving what they (secretly) desire, men are at least partly in control.

Although the prisoners began the revolt, Ilsa is killed by a male Nazi, thereby ending the rivalry between male and female power. If Ilsa were killed by the American Wolfe, or by another prisoner, it might represent mythologies of democracy overtaking Nazism, or of American superiority. But by portraying Nazi atrocities as eroticized encounters between men and women, and Ilsa as the female monster-villain, does the film hold women responsible for Nazi evil?

The Film's Reception

In 1974, *Ilsa, She-Wolf of the SS* opened in 17 countries around the world before opening in the United States. It was banned in Germany, refused certification—making it illegal to distribute—in the United Kingdom, and not rated in the United States. Opening in one theater in New York and Washington, DC simultaneously, *She-Wolf* was so successful that it earned a spot in that week's *Variety*'s listing of the 50 top-grossing films. Indeed, Vincent Canby went to the 42nd Street theatre in New York City to review it for the Sunday *New York Times*. He describes it as "possibly the worst soft-core sex-and-violence film of the decade—and the funniest." Canby writes that the film was based on true events, and describes Ilsa as having "a warped mind, as well as breasts so large and unwieldy you suspect that the Nazis pioneered the use of silicone." He describes how the castration scene entertained the largely male audience with whom he saw the film, even though he left after ten minutes.[37]

When Ilsa first appeared on the screen she became a pop cult-icon. Dyanne Thorne, the blond and busty star of the film, today still receives over 200 fan letters monthly. Although Ilsa was killed at the end of her debut in *She-Wolf,* Cinepix realized she was a valuable commodity and cashed in on her notoriety by creating sequels. Cinepix focused on the character of Ilsa, distancing themselves from the Nazi concentration camp setting. Dyanne Thorne reappears in three Ilsa sequels set in various places around the world. In *Ilsa, Harem Keeper of the Oil Sheiks,* also directed by Don Edmunds, Ilsa and her lesbian guards run a slavery ring in the Middle East. In Jess Franco's *Ilsa—The Wicked Warden,* Ilsa is the sadistic ruler of a South American prison for deranged women. And in *Ilsa—Tigress of Siberia,* directed by children's filmmaker Jean Lefleur, she is a commander of a Russian prison camp. There were three more Ilsa films announced for the series, but never made: *Ilsa vs. Bruce Lee in the Devil's Triangle, Ilsa vs. Idi Amin,* and *Ilsa—Nanny to Royalty.*

Ilsa, She-Wolf of the SS has surpassed $10 million at the box office.[38] With its video release the film reached cult status. In 2000 Anchor Bay distributors released a DVD version, complete and uncut, generating a revival. The bookseller *Amazon.com* lists the VHS sales ranking at 1,838, and the DVD ranking as 1,396.[39] According to *Amazon.com* the VHS version is their seventh most popular selling video in Israel, and the fifth most popular in Powell, Tennessee.[40]

Ilsa, She-Wolf of the SS won Adult Video News' (AVN) Best Alternative Video Award. *Trash Compactor Magazine* recommended it as one of its top 10 castration films.[41] And Sean Axmanker's website "On Video: Expert Guide to Video and DVDs" chose the Anchor Bay DVD Ilsa series in his "Classic Film Picks" for July 10, 2000, along with Stephen Spielberg's *Jaws: Anniversary Collector's Edition.*

Besides video and DVD rentals and purchases, the film is still being shown in theaters around the world. Indeed, in January 2001, the Royal Cinema in Toronto played an Ilsa double feature, presenting *Ilsa, She-Wolf of the SS* at 9:15, and *Ilsa, Harem Keeper of the Oil Sheiks* at its 11:30 PM show. Paradise Cinema in Toronto also showed the double feature. It has also been shown on college campuses. For instance, Associated Students of UC Davis advertised it ironically as "the heart-warming, inspirational

World War II epic" for a free-screening, Lewis and Clark College played it during its "alternative movie night," and Rochester Institute of Technology showed it for "fucked up movie night."

The film is studied in UCLA film classes, is a favorite of Quentin Tarantino's, and appears as a question in the game Trivial Pursuit. In an October 28, 1999, *New Times Los Angeles* article on things to do on Halloween, they suggest dressing in costumes from *Ilsa, She-Wolf of the SS* for the Variety Arts Center's Halloween Masquerade Ball. Das Bunker, a nightclub within the lesbian bar Que Sera in Long Beach, California that is open the first and third Fridays of every month, became infamous for making a video advertisement using Nazi imagery. It has been described as a place "where patrons dress in pseudo-military garb and *Ilsa, She-Wolf of the SS* chic."[42] One can buy *Ilsa, She-Wolf of the SS* movie posters in English, Italian, and Japanese on the web.

Several musical bands have songs based on the film and Ilsa character. For instance, the heavy metal band At War released a CD called *Ordered to Kill* with a song entitled "Ilsa, She Wolf of the SS." The group Diabolos Rising also has a CD, *Blood Vampirism and Sadism,* with a song called "Ilsa, She Wolf of the SS." In rock band Murphy Law's CD *Back with a Bong!,* they have a song titled "Ilsa." And alternative jungle house band Journeyman has a song titled "Ilsa" on its CD *New Idol Son.*

Ilsa is also a popular reference for film and theater critics. For example, in a 1989 review of the Broadway musical *Starmites,* drama critic Michael Kuchwara mockingly describes Susan Hirschfeld's costumes designs as making the women in the play "look like extras out of *Ilsa, the She-Wolf of the SS.*"[43] In a 1990 review of the premiere of *Sweetie* at the Cannes Film Festival, Peter Goddard of *The Toronto Star* describes the main character (Sweetie) as "Baby Jane, Baby Doll, Mother Courage, Joan Jett and *Ilsa, She-Wolf of the SS* all rolled into one."[44]

In 1987 film critics Gene Siskel and Roger Ebert devoted the last half of one of their nationally syndicated weekend TV programs, *Siskel and Ebert at the Movies,* to the horror films available at video stores. From talking to video store operators Ebert found that *She-Wolf* was popular among teenagers. Referring to them as "splatter films," Ebert says that parents hearing their kids screaming in the family room may think they are looking at horror films like they saw 20 years ago. "These movies are really in a different category," Ebert says. "One of the things they often have in common is the mutilation and sadistic torture of women."[45]

Sometimes Ilsa's name is invoked regarding her role as the commandant of a prison camp. For example, in a 1994 Gannett News Service video review of the Steve McQueen film *The Great Escape,* done as a dialogue between the two reviewers, Sue Kelly and Steve Jones, Jones brings up the Ilsa series. "I was recently in the video store and stumbled over a series of titles that I thought you might like—*Ilsa, Harem Keeper of the Oil Shieks, Ilsa, She-Wolf of the SS, Ilsa, Tigress of Siberia,* and *Ilsa, the Wicked Warden.* With this naughty torturer in charge of the prison camp, maybe McQueen, Garner, Bronson, et al [in *The Great Escape*] did seem uniquely unsuited to the task, so maybe Ilsa would have been a better choice."[46]

Other times her name is invoked as a metaphor for evil. For instance, the *Gazette* movie critic, John Griffin describes a character played by Sam Phillips in the film, *Die Hard with a Vengeance,* "as a Teutonic Ilsa: *She-Wolf* of the SS type, played with Dietrichian cold-bloodedness."[47] In a 1995 review of the film *Judge Dredd* Anne Billson describes Ilsa, an evil scientist played by Joan Chen, as a "not-so distant cousin, presumably, to *Ilsa—She Wolf of the SS.*"[48]

She is also used as a reference for associating sexuality with violence. For example, in a 1993 *Toronto Star* review of the play *Bob's Kingdom,* the character of Dr. Hertogenbosch, a hermaphroditic "queen and king of darkness" played by Patricia Collins, is described as a "sternly verbose mix of Ilsa, *She-Wolf* of the SS, Count Dracula and a deadly praying mantis . . ."[49] In a review of *Basic Instinct* Kenneth Turan of the *LA Times* describes Sharon Stone's character, Catherine: "beautiful, seriously uninhibited, with the looks of a Grace Kelly ice princess and the wicked, blistering tongue of *Ilsa, She-Wolf of the SS,* Catherine intimidates men without half trying."[50]

Even film critics reviewing children's programs and family entertainment have invoked her name. For example, a reviewer of the new game show *The Weakest Link,* compares Anne Robinson, the show's host, to Ilsa.[51] Furthermore, in a 1997 review of *Home Alone 3,* Anne Billson describes how a gang of international criminals in search of a "mistle-chip" stolen from the American air force and concealed in a toy car, are electrocuted, squashed, dunked, clobbered in the testicles and dropped from great heights. Their sadistic slapstick would make '*Ilsa, She-Wolf of the SS*' look like the Teletubbies.[52] Moreover, in *Mr. Headmistress,* Carole Horst describes Katey Sagal as "stomping around like *Ilsa the She-Wolf of the SS* in her clichéd character," and goes on to state that the production succeeds in being family entertainment.[53]

Ilsa on the Web[54]

According to the web search engine *Google.com,* approximately 1390 sites reference *Ilsa, She Wolf of the SS.* Of these 1390 sites, Google provides links for a representative sample of 656 sites.[55] Of the 656, 111 sites are in foreign languages (Japanese, French, German, Italian, Russian, Swiss, and Dutch), some sites are repetitive, and a few were unrelated to either the film or the character Ilsa. After eliminating these sites, I conducted a content analysis of 508 remaining web sites related to the film. Table 1 summarizes this distribution.

Over a third of the web sites are reviews of the film or related sales sites. Almost a fifth of the web sites (n = 99) were movie reviews. Of these reviews, 21 are on video sales sites serving to market the movie. Of the 78 that were not written explicitly to sell the video, 51 were unrelated to a sales site, and 27 had a link on the web page that directed one to a sales site.[56] Table 2 summarizes the type of review on web sites listing the video for sale, and the type of review on non-sales sites.[57]

The film was described as "probably the most famous Women in Prison flick," "unusual and sometimes disturbing," "should be THE definitive cult film," "one of the most notorious and reviled films of our time," "this trend-setting trash epic created a new low in guts 'n gore prison cinema garnering $10 million worldwide box office, and made Dyanne Thorne a household closet name." The review sites were more likely to have a definitive opinion on *She Wolf,* with 46.2% giving it a positive review, 26.9% giving it a negative review, and only 26.9% giving a neutral review. There were no negative reviews on sales-sites. Overall, the sales sites were more likely to maintain a neutral standpoint (61.9%) to the film, while admitting to the film's gore as a warning for the faint of heart.

Every sales site characterized Ilsa as cruel, sadistic, and brutal, whereas only 62.8% of the review sites did. Also, nearly twice as many sales sites as review sites noted Ilsa as being dominant and fearsome (81% on sales sites vs. 43.6% on review sites). She was described as "one mean bitch," "ball-busting commandant," "SS whore," "the ultimate feminist warrior," "the female Hitler," "a woman to be feared," and the like.

Review sites covered more details regarding Ilsa's insatiable sexual desire. Ilsa was described as sexually insatiable by 57.1% of sales sites and only 46.2% of review sites. She was then described as eventually tamed by 38.1% of the sales sites and merely 29.5% of review sites. One web

TABLE 1
Contents of 508 representative web pages for *Ilsa, She-Wolf of the SS*

	# of Sites (out of 508)	% of Sites
Movie Reviews	99	19.5
Lists of videos for rent, sale, or trade	84	16.5
Lists of favorite movies or of a film genre	60	11.8
Descriptions of dominating people or sadistic actions as Ilsa or Ilsa-like	47	9.3
Sites on films in a similar genre	41	8.1
Sites with a photo, link, or title but no text	33	6.5
Sites about a member of the film's cast or crew	31	6.1
Academic papers, articles, or books	27	5.3
Reference in a personal webpage or email post-board	17	3.3
Sites mentioning songs, pets, nicknames, or venues named after Ilsa	14	2.8
Brief film recommendation	10	2
Movie Trivia	10	2
List of TV or Movie show times for public viewing	9	1.8
"Other" sites	9	1.8
Credit *Ilsa, She-Wolf of the SS* as one of the Worst Movies of all time	6	1.2
Site selling movie posters	6	1.2
Stories involving or based on Ilsa	5	1

site described the film as "the rather sexist cliché of the cruel and sexually insatiable woman in power who is ultimately tamed by a man and whose lust proves her undoing." Another placed it in the "female submissive category."

While sales and review sites were equally likely to describe the film's violence and torture as disturbing, review sites were more likely to describe the violence and torture as appealing (48.7% of review sites versus 38.1% of sales sites). Typical comments include "the basic appeal of [the film] is a parade of tortures," "a gleefully nasty 'roughie' that doesn't

TABLE 2

Content of *Ilsa, She-Wolf of the SS* movie reviews on web sites with and without video sales

	% of Video Sale Reviews	# of Video Sale Reviews (out of 21)
Positive Review	38.1	8
Negative Review	0	0
Neutral Review	61.9	13
Ilsa as cruel, sadistic, brutal	100	21
Ilsa as dominant, fearsome	81	17
Ilsa as sexually insatiable	57.1	12
Ilsa as eventually tamed	38.1	8
Violence, torture as disturbing	47.6	10
Violence, torture as appealing	38.1	8
Holocaust setting as disturbing	0	0
Film as notorious	52.4	11
Graphic photo on site	9.5	2
Discuss quality of audio, image, etc.	38.1	8

	% of Video (No Sale) Reviews	# of Video (No Sale) Reviews (out of 78)
Positive review	46.2	36
Negative review	26.9	21
Neutral review	26.9	21
Ilsa as cruel, sadistic, brutal	62.8	49
Ilsa as dominant, fearsome	43.6	34
Ilsa as sexually insatiable	46.2	36
Ilsa as eventually tamed	29.5	23
Violence, torture as disturbing	50	39
Violence, torture as appealing	48.7	38
Holocaust setting as disturbing	26.9	21
Film as notorious	53.8	42
Graphic photo on site	11.5	9
Discuss quality of audio, image, etc.	28.2	22

skimp on the blood or babes," "it is a truly sick and sleazy movie . . . but well-made and effective." Both types of sites were equally likely to describe the film as notorious (52.4% of sales sites and 53.8% of review sites). Interestingly, no sales site noted the Holocaust setting as a disturbing choice, while over a quarter (26.9%) of review sites did.

Conclusion

One way we know the past is through how it is represented. Popular culture plays an important role in linking words and images that create and sustain certain collective memories. Thus it provides useful cultural artifacts for critical attention that reveal and react to the broader sensibilities of an entire culture. Moreover, American popular culture is a preeminent site of cultural dissemination in the contemporary world. What America collectively and Americans individually think about the Holocaust matters for the way the Holocaust is and will be understood in the world.

Should the character of the Holocaust impose special limitations or demands on its representation? Who has the authority to speak about the Holocaust? What is the role of popular culture in political and social life, and how does it serve the interests of Holocaust education? Moreover, while many popular culture treatments of the Holocaust have been criticized for their anesthetized representation, *Ilsa, She-Wolf of the SS* is just the opposite—lots of sex, grisly murders, and torture. It's part of the sexploitation genre that links Nazi iconography with sex and violence. But, what purpose do such films serve? Is the sexploitation genre an appropriate site for restaging collective trauma? Is it appropriate to capitalize on the Holocaust for entertainment and financial profit?

Gloria Steinem has argued that "pornography is not about sex. It's about an imbalance of male-female power that allows and even requires sex to be used as a form of aggression."[58] Andrea Dworkin argues that "pornography is the graphic, sexually explicit subordination of women that includes a series of scenarios . . . from women being dehumanized—turned into objects and commodities—through women showing pleasure in being raped, through the dismemberment of women."[59]

Films might rely on actual events for legitimacy, but reshape the narratives by rendering characters as all good or all evil. Films also address underlying problems as personal rather than social, thus simplifying the social and historical complexities of the problems presented. According to David Friedman, by putting in a disclaimer like "the film you are about to see is based on actual events," he could bypass censorship codes and air the film.[60] As Dyanne Thorne remarks,

> I never felt that *She-Wolf* was a picture that was out there to perpetuate something. A lot of it was based on ugly fact, there is a lot of ugliness in this world, and it was just presenting that. As for sensationalizing the subject matter, the truth is that many of the things in that film were based on factual records, documents that showed these atrocities really took place, and that doctors used human beings as guinea-pigs. *She-Wolf* presented that and people just thought it was being done for sensationalism—I'm sure that *was* partly in the producer's minds— but as far as the actors and the director were concerned they were just carrying out what the writer had written. It's not my place to be political, it's my place to take the material and work with it.[61]

Moreover, is there a voyeuristic pleasure in watching sex and violence? Is that pleasure derived from mastering in fantasy a situation that is fundamentally dangerous and threatening? While the film makes a conscious effort not to refer to Jews as the only prisoners, is watching the sexual relations between Jews and Germans in concentration camps a pleasurable experience, precisely because the act was forbidden according to the 1935 Nuremberg laws? As voyeurs and spectators in personalizing Nazi evil, are we trespassing between public and private spheres, intimate relations and social relations, as we stage the contradiction as spectacle? How an audience sees a film has been characterized in a variety of ways: through the camera's eye; how characters view an event; and what spectators see. In his discussion of pornography Paul Willemen has named a fourth view, the spectator looking at something that he or she is not supposed to look at.[62] Horror films also include the act of "looking away," in spite of a morbid desire to see as much as possible of graphic horrifying images.[63]

All told, the Holocaust was real, and it was a horror. Thus, characterizing the film as a horror movie is accurate. The film is disturbing for a variety of reasons, and hard to watch. We want to look away, but also peek. While most films portraying the Holocaust white-wash its horrors, *She-Wolf* blatantly exposes them. Although we might want to criticize the representations of Nazi evil in a film like *She-Wolf,* the sad truth is that the real Nazis were much worse.

Notes

1. I am grateful to several students, Hector J. Preciado, Katherine Greeley, and Anna Rooke, for their assistance in data collection and analysis. I also thank Lawrence Baron, Susannah Heschel, Mikel Kovel, Stephen Lebowitz, and Andy Roth for their comments on an earlier draft of this paper.
2. Emile Durkheim, *The Elementary Forms of the Religious Life* (New York, The Free Press, 1915), p. 52.
3. For a more general discussion of issues related to Nazism and pornography see Chapter 3, "Sadistic and Pornographic Touch," in Linda Holler, *Erotic Morality: The Role of Touch in Moral Agency* (New Brunswick, NJ, Rutgers University Press, 2002); and Chapter 2, "Feminizing Fascism," in Kriss Raveto, *The Unmasking of Fascist Aesthetics* (Minneapolis, University of Minnesota Press, 2001). For a good discussion of eroticized expressions of fascism in anti-fascist literature, see Laura Frost, *Sex Drives: Fantasies of Fascism in Literary Modernism* (Ithaca and London, Cornell University Press, 2002).
4. Jim Morton, "Women in Prison Films," in V. Vale and Andrea Juno, eds., *Incredibly Strange Films* (San Francisco, Re/Search Publications, 1986), pp. 151–152.
5. For a good treatment of "fantastic cinema" around the world, see Pete Tombs, *Mondo Macabro* (New York, St. Martin's Griffin, 1997).
6. J. David Slocum, ed., *Violence and American Cinema,* (New York and London, Routledge, 2001), p. 7.
7. In an analysis of Italian sexploitation films from 1975 to 1977, Mikel Kovel argues that many of these films fall into two categories: "Nazi Bordello" and "Love Camp" threads. While "Love Camps" are Nazi bordellos, they privilege the spectacle of rape by featuring a group of captive and imprisoned women forced into prostitution against their will. With Nazi bordello films, the women are presented as more "complicit" in their sexual exploitation (Mikel J. Kovel, "'The Film You are About to see is Based on Documented Fact:' The Curious Case of the Nazi Sexploitation Film," Conference paper, January 25, 2002).
8. Following in the wake of Liliana Cavani's *Night Porter* (1974), which examined the sexual power games played by an ex-Nazi and his former victim, Luigi Batzella incorporated sex and torture scenes in his low-budget war movie *Achtung! The Desert Tigers* (1975), about the evil doings performed on sexy inmates of Nazi camps. In 1977 Batzella produced *Horrifying Experiments of the SS Last Days* (known in the United Kingdom as *The Beast in Heat*). The beast is a sex-crazed midget who rapes female inmates at the hands of a sexy SS doctor. Down

in the torture chamber, one woman is eaten by guinea pigs and another is having her fingernails extracted with pliers. Bruno Mattei completed *SS Girls* (1976), about a brothel where traitors to the Nazi high command are eradicated. To help the brothel succeed, Hitler enlists the aid of a scientist, who enables a prostitute to satisfy any and all perverse needs of Nazi Generals. And in 1977 Mattei made *Women's Camp 119,* about a female inmate in a concentration camp who is forced to assist a crazed Nazi doctor, exposing her to horrifying medical experiments. In 1976 Sergio Garrone made *SS Experiment Camp,* about a Nazi commander who seeks to cure his impotence by having a healthy man's testicles implanted in his scrotum. Simultaneously he made its companion-piece, *SS Camp 5: Women's Hell,* where the Nazis use female inmates for their wild victory orgies, and torture them when they are caught escaping. There were also *Gestapo's Last Orgy, SS Hell Camp, Blue Ice, Stalag 69,Nathalie—Fugitive from Hell, Nazi Love Camp 27, Salon Kitty, SS Cutthroats, She-Devils of the SS, SS Special Section Women, Girls of the Third Reich, Prisoner of Paradise, Kolassal Orgie,* and countless others.

9. Commentary on the DVD version of *Ilsa, She Wolf of the SS* (Anchor Bay, 2000).

10. Personal interview, July 25, 2001.

11. Nathaniel Thompson interview with David F. Friedman, Mondo Digital web site.

12. Personal interview, July 25, 2001.

13. Robert Jay Lifton, "Medicalized Killing in Auschwitz," in *The Nazi Concentration Camps* (Jerusalem, Daf-Chen Press, 1984), p. 218.

14. As quoted in Nanda Herbermann, *The Blessed Abyss,* trans. Hester Baer, ed. Hester Baer and Elizabeth Baer (Detroit, MI, Wayne State University Press, 2000), p. 34.

15. See Christa Schultz, "*Weibliche Häftlinge aus Ravensbrück in Bordellen der Männerkonzentrationslager,*" in Claus Füllberg-Stolberg et al., eds., *Frauen in Konzentrationslagern Bergen-Belsen, Ravensbrück* (Bremen, Edition Temmen, 1994), pp. 135–46. See also, Christa Paul, *Zwangsprostititon: Staatlich errichtete Bordelle im Nationalsozialismus* (Berlin, Edition Hentrich, 1994).

16. Similar to the depiction of the selection process in the Ilsa film, Margaret Buber-Neumann in her memoir describes the use of Ravensbrück inmates as prostitutes for Mauthausen: In 1942 a "Commission" of the SS officers arrived from Mauthausen. They inspected the human flesh available in Block 2 and made a preliminary choice. All the women picked out were then led off to the wash-room, where they had to strip and be examined by the "Commission." Those with firm breasts, sound limbs and general physical attractions were short-listed, so to speak, and from their "re-education" in the camp they were sent to replenish the SS brothel in Mauthausen. After six months of this activity they were promised their freedom—to return to the world of free citizens "re-educated" and cleansed (as quoted in Nanda Herbermann, *The Blessed Abyss,* p. 33).

17. Christa Paul, *Zwansprostititon.*

18. Peter Lehman, "Crying over the Melodramatic Penis," in Peter Lehman, ed., *Masculinity* (New York, Routledge, 2001), p. 33.

19. Barbara Creed, "Dark Desires: Male Masochism in the Horror Film," in Steven Cohen and Ina Rae Hark, eds., *Screening the Male: Exploring Masculinities in Hollywood Cinema* (London, Routledge, 1993), p. 120.

20. For a good overview, see Susan Faludi, *Backlash* (New York, Crown Publishers, 1991), pp. 75–140.

21. Indeed, there is only one scene where male guards are violent against women prisoners. This takes place when a new female recruit protests about having her pubic hair shaved. A female guard plans to teach her a lesson by putting her to work that night in the guard's house. In a segment entitled, "A Night Without Mercy," six male guards douse the female recruit with beer, while fondling and subsequently gang raping her.

22. International Auschwitz Committee, *Nazi Medicine* (New York, Howard Fertig, Inc., 1986), pp. 14–15.

23. Lifton, "Medicalized Killing in Auschwitz," p. 218.

24. Susannah Heschel, "Does Atrocity Have a Gender? Women in the SS," in Jeffrey Diefendorf, ed., *Lessons and Legacies VI: New Currents in Holocaust Research* (Evanston, IL, Northwestern University Press, 2004), forthcoming.

25. I will use the full name Ilsa Koch to refer to the real person, as opposed to the term Ilsa, which refers to the fictional character in the film.

26. Born in 1906 in Saxony to a laborer, Ilsa Koch, a diligent student, popular with village boys, was trained as a librarian. She met and became romantically involved with her husband Karl in 1936, when she was hired as his secretary when he worked at the Sachsenhausen, the first concentration camp, as a Standartenführer (Colonel). They married at the end of 1936 in an SS ceremony, and in 1939 when Karl was sent to form the camp at Buchenwald, he took Ilsa with him (Allan Hall, *Murder and Madness* [Leicester, UK, Bookmart, Ltc, 1993], p. 51).

27. Ilsa Koch became known as the lady of the lampshade, and was particularly interested in male prisoners with tattoos. Reports indicated she used the treated skins of murdered prisoners to make practical home accessories she was proud of. It is said she liked skins of gypsies and Russian prisoners-of-war, men who had swirls of color across their chests and backs. For instance, Albert Grenowski, a Jew who was forced to work in the pathology laboratory at Buchenwald, told Allied judicial authorities after the war, how those with tattoos were given orders to report to the dispensary: "After they were examined by her, those who were deemed to have the most artistically interesting specimens were killed by lethal injection. It was important that the skin of the victims was not damaged. There was one sure way to find yourself in a coffin and that was to damage the skin that the *Hexe* (witch) wanted for her lampshades. The bodies were taken to the

pathology lab where they were treated with alcohol and the skins were removed with painstaking attention to detail so as not to split them or otherwise mark them. Then they were dried, often oiled afterwards, and taken in small packages to Ilsa Koch so they could be made into lampshades or gloves. Once we saw her walking around the compound wearing a brightly patterned pair of summer gloves and just sexy underwear—you know, like she had forgotten to put a dress on. I particularly paid attention to the gloves. The last time I had seen their decoration was on the back of a gypsy prisoner in my block" (Hall, *Murder and Madness,* p. 51).

28. Tom Segev, *Soldiers of Evil* (New York, McGraw-Hill, 1987), p. 143.

29. Daniel Goldhagen, *Hitler's Willing Executioners* (New York, Vintage, 1996).

30. Christopher Browning, *Ordinary Men* (New York, HarperCollins, 1992).

31. Susannah Heschel, "Does Atrocity Have a Gender? Women in the SS." Lecture presented at the Western Jewish Studies Association, University of Oregon, March 24, 2003.

32. For a contrasting view of female camp guards see the memoir by Ruth Kluger, *Still Alive: A Holocaust Childhood Remembered* (New York, Feminist Press, 2001).

33. She also argues that these acts of cruelty were described as colliding with a woman's physical beauty, or were part of her physical ugliness. See Heschel, "Does Atrocity Have a Gender?"

34. See Barb Serfozo and Henry Farrell, "From Sex-Vixens to Senators—Representations in Nazi Porn and the Discourse of the American Right Wing," *Journal of Social and Political Thought,* Vol. 1, No. 1 (1996), pp. 1–23.

35. As cited in J. David Slocum, *Violence and American Cinema* (New York and London, Routledge, 2001), p. 12.

36. Slocum, *Violence and American Cinema,* p. 12.

37. Vincent Canby, "Now for a Look At Some Really Bad Movies," *New York Times,* November 30, 1975, Section D, p. 13.

38. Darrin Venticinque and Tristan Thompson, *The Ilsa Chronicles* (Huntington, England, Midnight Media, 2000), p. 3.

39. Customers who bought the DVD also bought *Ilsa—The Wicked Warden, Cannibal Ferox* (A.K.A. *Make Them Die Slowly*), and *Female Vampire.*

40. This was on June 6, 2001.

41. Susan Devins, *The Toronto Star,* "B Movie Fanatic Pushes his Passion to Outer Limits," November 20, 1988, p. G8.

42. Lisa Derrick, "City of Night," *New Times Los Angeles,* July 10, 1997.

43. Michael Kuchwara, "'Starmites,' A New Musical, Opens on Broadway," *Entertainment News,* April 27, 1989.

44. Peter Goddard, "Cast and Filmmakers combine to make wacky Sweetie a Delight," *The Toronto Star,* March 2, 1990, p. D6.

45. The most popular film was the three-part "Faces of Death" videos, which depict dead people. Other popular titles were "Make Them Die Slowly," "Bloodsucking Freaks," and "2,000 Maniacs." (The Associated Press, June 4, 1987).

46. Sue Kelly and Steve Jones, "Staying Home with the Movies," *Gannett News Service,* May 13, 1994.

47. John Griffin, "Die Hardest; Third in action-packed series starts with a blast—then carries with a vengeance," *The Gazette,* May 19, 1995.

48. Anne Billson, "The Party is Over," *Sunday Telegraph,* July 23, 1995.

49. "Give us This Day our Daily Bread," *The Toronto Star,* January 15, 1993, p. D12.

50. Kenneth Turan, "Movie Reviews; Blood and Lust," *Los Angeles Times,* March 20, 1992, Part F, p. 1.

51. Gary Pettus, "Could the real weak link be to, uh, Satan?," *The Clarion Ledger,* April 27, 2001.

52. Anne Billson, "The Arts: My Inner Child goes on a Festive Rampage Cinema," *Sunday Telegraph,* December 21, 1997.

53. Carol Horst, "Wonderful World of Disney," *Daily Variety,* March 12, 1998.

54. I am grateful to my student, Katherine Greeley, for gathering and analyzing this data.

55. *Google.com* states, "In order to show you the most relevant results, we have omitted some entries very similar to the 656 already displayed."

56. In the analysis, I combined the unaffiliated movie reviews with the movie reviews that had a link to a sales site. It appeared that the reviews with the link on site were written by people who were not directly affiliated with the sales site or any commission from that site.

57. I will use the term "review sites" to refer to reviews without sales information, and "sales sites" to refer to reviews accompanied by sale information.

58. As quoted in Leora Tanenbaum, "Pornography Does Not Always Harm Those Involved in Its Production," in David Bender and Bruno Leone, eds., *Pornography* (San Diego, CA, Greenhaven Press, 1997), p. 58.

59. As quoted in *Pornography,* p. 137.

60. He describes this process in *Mau Mau Sex Sex,* a documentary about the sexploitation industry.

61. Darrin Venticinque and Tristan Thompson, *The Ilsa Chronicles* (Huntingdon, England, Midnight Media, 2000), p. 42.

62. See Paul Willemen, "Letter to John," Screen 21, Vol. 2, (1980), pp. 53–66.

63. Barbara Creed, *The Monstrous Feminine* (London, Routledge, 1993), p. 29.

6

Wonder Woman against the Nazis: Gendering Villainy in DC Comics

Ruth McClelland-Nugent

Encased in gleaming metal, a huge masked man looms over a helpless hero.[1] If the swastika on his gauntlets were not enough to signal to the reader that he is a Nazi, then his words certainly do so: "I am the living embodiment of Aryan purity—the Fuhrer's great ideal . . . none shall defeat me—least of all, a female!" His moment of racial and gender superiority is short lived, however. The hero, a dark-haired woman clad in red, white, and blue, manages to both free herself and unmask the villain, who flees moaning: "can't let anyone . . . see my face . . . my face." The woman muses, "Mysteries of Pluto, he's fled! And all because his mask came off? May I live a thousand years, I'll never understand man's vanity!"[2]

Considering the Nazi villain and classic American super-powered hero, a reader might be forgiven for assuming this is a scene from a comic book produced during the Second World War. In fact, this scenario appears in a 1977 issue of DC Comic's *World's Finest,* and it featured a clash between Wonder Woman and her Nazi foe, Baron Blitzkrieg, in a nostalgic Second World War setting. Between 1973 and 1985, a rogue's gallery of war-time Nazis from Armageddon to the Red Panzer plotted world domination in the pages of DC. The writers and artists of these comic book tales produced a remarkably consistent set of traits that signaled Nazi villainy: sadistic tendencies, a desire to enslave the world, and a virulent, murderous racism. The latter frequently referenced the Holocaust, with Nazis menacing Jews with threats like: "You would be worth less alive than dead! As a corpse, we could at least use your body for soap!"[3]

The adventures of DC's Wonder Woman included all these elements of Nazi villainy, and one more: vicious misogyny. Wonder Woman's foes, as in the preceding scene, often articulated sexism ("Least of all a female!") along with other elements such as racism ("Aryan purity"). Further, the title character's dialogue overtly located Nazi gender prejudice in a wider spectrum of patriarchy: "The arrogance of men constantly astounds me—particularly the arrogance of a Nazi! For the sake of the world—that arrogance must end!"[4]

What made Wonder Woman different from other superheroes who also battled evil Nazis from the 1940s right up to the present? The gendered critique of the 1970s has its roots in the proto-feminism of the original 1940s *Wonder Woman.* Created by psychologist William Moulton Marston to serve as an example of empowered womanhood among the scores of male superheroes, the original character fought Axis villains in the name of Aphrodite, goddess of love and beauty. Her opponents were puppets of hypermasculine Mars, god of war. Marston's framework had made the struggle between Allies and Axis a quest for cosmic gender balance: "Wonder Woman is helping America win the War and if America wins, peace will return—the world will be ruled happily by the love and beauty of Aphrodite!"[5] Yet the gender retrenchment of the cold war in the United States erased both this proto-feminism and the theme of Nazi misogyny from American comics. Thanks to a curious crossover of pop culture feminism and Second World War nostalgia, the idea of fighting Nazism as a symbol of fighting patriarchal misogyny resurfaced in the 1970s, if only in the pages of *Wonder Woman.* The 30-year journey of this gendered critique of Nazi villainy serves as a testament to the power of popular culture to both preserve, and erase, historical memory.

A Strictly Non-Aryan Sock on the Jaw: From the Golden Age to the 1950s

It is not surprising that 1970s comic book editors wished to return to the Second World War, for during that time comics had become almost ubiquitous in American life. The United States' entry into the war doubled comic book sales, from 10 million copies a month in 1941 to a staggering 20 million by 1944.[6] In the pages of these comics, super-powered mystery men reigned supreme, battling the Axis in Europe and gangsters Stateside. Their very names suggested hyperpatriotism: Captain America, Fightin' Yank, Uncle Sam.[7] Americans loved the fantastic adventures of these heroes: 91 percent of girls and 95 percent of boys between the ages of 6 and 11 read more than six comic books a month, choosing from over 150 different titles.[8] Comic books had an adult readership as well. Forty-four percent of men in military training camps read more than six books a month. The increased number of servicemen reading comic books made the 18–30-year-old comic book reading demographic heavily male; in fact, 28 percent more men than women in this age bracket read comics.[9]

Considering the large number of young men reading these comics, it is perhaps not surprising that most comic book superheroes appeared as muscular young men, with male sidekicks, and perhaps a female love interest. Superman, for example, had both young newsboy Jimmy Olsen and the female reporter Lois Lane among his supporting cast, while Batman had the "boy wonder" Robin at his side.[10] Few female characters were stars in their own right. 1940 saw the debut of Claire Voyant, also known as the Black Widow, who used mysterious powers to thwart Nazi plots and send the souls of evil-doers to Satan.[11] Newspaper comic strip hero Miss Fury, created by female writer Tarpe Mills, began appearing in April 1941. This catskin-clad heroine was an undercover agent against the Axis, and frequently battled a one-armed Nazi named General Bruno.[12] The year 1941 also saw the debut of Spider Queen, the Silver Scorpion, and Black Cat, all of whom used martial arts, disguises, and special equipment to battle crime and the Axis.[13]

The most long-lived of these new mystery women was Wonder Woman. Hailing from an all-female Greco-Roman society of Amazons, she was, unlike other female heroes, truly super-powered: "beautiful as Aphrodite, as wise as Athena, as swift as Mercury, [and] as strong as Hercules." In her secret identity as mousy Diana Prince, she worked as an officer in United States military intelligence, giving her a convenient way to track Axis spies and saboteurs. In her role as Wonder Woman, she fought these same baddies, while encouraging women to stand up for themselves, usually by becoming professionally accomplished and physically fit. In one 1942 adventure, she urged a hapless woman to "Get strong! Earn your own living—join the WAACS or the WAVES and fight for your country! Remember the better you can fight, the less you'll have to!"[14] The character's creator, psychologist William Moulton Marston, openly identified the character as a piece of propaganda for a new vision of liberated womanhood, one which would bring a gendered psychological critique to portrayals of both the Axis and United States society.[15]

Marston's fellow writers had already introduced American readers to a Nazi prototype in which "German officers possessed monocles and dueling scars, much as they did in the wartime renditions of Hollywood filmmakers."[16] Exaggerated caricatures of Hitler and other Axis leaders also leered at readers from the covers of comics, frequently being strangled, punched, or otherwise subdued by American superheroes. The ubiquity of the theme suggests how much Americans liked the idea of Superman or Captain Marvel doing away with Hitler once and for all.[17] Explanations of Nazi villainy occasionally referenced racism; in a 1940 Superman story, for example, Superman faced down Hitler, telling the dictator that he would "like to land a strictly non-Aryan sock on your jaw."[18] More commonly, Nazi villainy was linked in the comics to cruelty toward civilians, especially women and children. For example, when an elderly fisherman mercifully tried to save Captain Nazi (the German counterpart of Captain Marvel) from drowning, the villain murdered the old man and tried to kill his young grandson as well.[19] In a 1941 Blackhawk comic, a Nazi bomber dropped a bomb onto a farmhouse, heedless of the family inside.[20] In a Wonder Woman story from 1943, two escaped Nazi POWs kidnapped children, forcing them to steal food and carry it for the Germans soldiers. When one such child becomes exhausted, the German loomed over her and threatens her with a gun: "I gif you a long rest—ve Nazis are always kind—ha! ha!"[21]

The idea that Nazism promoted brutality was already a part of United States popular culture well before the country's entry into the war. Cultural figures like playwright Robert Sherwood sounded the alarm about Nazi actions in occupied Europe, writing in 1940 that "[t]he Nazis have established the world's most thorough despotism, trampling over the decayed body of liberty to achieve authority."[22] Hollywood films like *Beasts of Berlin* (1939) portrayed the brutal suppression of an underground anti-Nazi resistance movement, while *Escape* (1940) showed an American man's desperate attempt to liberate his own mother from a Nazi concentration camp.[23] *The Mortal Storm* (1940) highlighted the changes that Nazism wrought in human behavior, following events in a German university town before and after Hitler came to power. Before, children respected elders, university students learned attentively from wise professors, and citizens debated political controversies without rancor. Afterward, Nazi thugs beat up an elderly teacher, a non-Aryan professor goes to a concentration camp for his research into human genetics, and books are burned in the village square.[24]

These film and comic book portrayals of Nazis signaled their brutishness by showing cruelty to women and children, but United States propaganda seldom touched directly on specific Nazi laws or statements relating to women or family policy. This propaganda paid no attention, for example, to the exclusion of German women from political office after 1933, nor to the disbarring of female judges and public prosecutors after 1936. One would be hard pressed to find an American source covering the plight of female physicians under the Reich, even as they lost the right to payments from the state health system, and as married female physicians lost their right to practice altogether.[25] A few Allied films did focus on specific policies related to women and children under fascism. The short *Education for Death* (1943), for example, outlined the way Nazi schooling twisted children into fascists; the feature *Hitler's Children* (1943) showed women in a *Lebensborn* home, forced to breed children out-of-wedlock for the Reich.[26] *So Ends Our Night* (1941), on the other hand, showed viewers the fate of women legally determined unfit to breed; they are sterilized, for reasons the film lists as ranging from "hereditary color blindness to dangerous political thinking."[27]

These expressions of Nazi sexism, both in reality and in propaganda, were perfect fodder for the pen of Marston. Educated at Harvard during the height of the United States' Progressive era, Marston was an ardent supporter of women's participation in politics, the professions, and all aspects of life. He had told the *New York Times* in 1937 that in the next 100 years, "women would take over the rule of the country, politically and economically."[28] In *Wonder Woman,* he proposed a framework for Axis evil that posed Nazism as a toy of Mars, the god of masculinity and brutality. Opposed to Mars stood Aphrodite, goddess of feminine love and compassion. The two of them had been locked in a cosmic battle for eons; in the war-time world of the 1940s, Mars and the war-mongering men he dominates gained the upper hand. But Aphrodite warned Mars, "Your rule will end when America wins! And America WILL win! I'll send an Amazon to help her!"[29] This framework for the struggle against Nazism was simultaneously cosmic, psychological, and gendered; in a Nazi world dominated by Mars's masculine force, people become corrupt, heartless, and brutal. Such masculine power must be balanced by feminine influences, as represented by service to Aphrodite.

Marston was not, strictly speaking, a gender essentialist; he held that both men and women could exhibit masculine and feminine qualities. In his view, however, the world had tipped too far toward valuing "blood-curdling masculinity," and Nazism was a perfect example of this psychological imbalance run amok.[30] Marston's framework in Wonder Woman was a more poetic version of his psychological theories about women's leadership. As early as 1928, in his book *Emotions of Normal People,* he had suggested that women made better leaders, because they tended to be motivated by acquiring happiness rather than material success. They simply needed encouragement to become self-reliant, while men needed to become restrained and to value "feminine" qualities.[31]

In Marston's stories, there was even hope for individual Nazis to regain the proper balance between assertiveness and compliance. For example, the wicked Nazi spy, Baroness Paula von Gunther, prone to gunning down civilians and running over children with her car, had once been a loving Austrian mother. But the Nazi Party had killed her husband and put her daughter in a concentration camp. Brutalized by this experience, she became hard and unfeeling—the perfect Nazi agent. Fortunately, Wonder Woman correctly diagnosed the Baroness's psychological problems and rescued her daughter from the concentration camp. Wonder Woman then proceeded to cure the Baroness's Nazi-induced beastliness. After several issues, the Baroness came to see that love is a greater power than force. Completely reformed, she embraced the service of Aphrodite, and vowed to fight against the Nazis and the power of the god Mars.[32]

The gendered nature of Marston's critique is perhaps most obvious when compared to another comic that also proposed an otherworldly, cosmic explanation for Nazi evil. In the pages of *Captain Marvel,* Hitler and other Axis powers were also portrayed as servants of a higher power: an ambitious alien named Mister Mind. Mister Mind, a tiny, bespectacled worm of super-genius capacity controlled the Nazis as puppets in his dreams of conquering earth and foiling Captain Marvel. The Nazis were an integral part of his plan.[33] In this satiric view of fascism, the supposedly all-powerful dictators were simply puppets of another power—in this case, a tiny, rather ridiculous, worm. Marston's Wonder Woman stories shared the idea that Nazis were puppets, but of a far more sinister force. In *Wonder Woman,* Hitler was portrayed hearing otherworldly voices on a mental radio directly connected to Mars: "Slave NZ-1 . . . Attend Gestapo Conference in Berlin tonight!" Yet his master was not an absurd little worm, but the brutishly masculine god Mars.[34] Marston's gendered cosmos was a unique interpretation of the differences between Nazi Germany and the United States; no other comic made gender quite so central to its message. The post-war years, however, would not be kind to Marston's radical gender politics. The gender retrenchment of the cold war era would stifle his visions of both feminism and Nazism until the 1970s.

No Better Than the Nazis? From the 1950s to the 1970s

The 1950s brought a harsh gender conservatism to American culture. Political theory and popular culture alike linked feminism, homosexuality, and other threats to heterosexual patriarchy directly to communism. Marston's vision of women's liberation through employment and political engagement ran completely counter to the dominant cultural messages for women in the 1950s. Analyzing women's magazines in the 1950s, feminist Betty Friedan concluded that articles about politics had completely disappeared, in favor of stories that celebrated motherhood and homemaking to the exclusion of other goals. Male magazine editors claimed that women would not read political features: "They are not interested in the broad public issues of the day."[35] Women were dissuaded from pursuing any career other than that of wife and mother. At the 1955 graduation ceremony for elite women's university Smith College, prominent Democratic politician Adlai Stevenson informed the graduates that their most important contribution "in a great historic crisis" would be to assume "the humble role of housewife."[36]

Marston did not live to see this backlash against the feminist ideals he cherished, as he passed away from lung cancer in 1947. Wonder Woman survived the new era and her creator's death, but in drastically altered form. Under the direction of writer-editor Robert Kanigher, her 1950s stories increasingly revolved around love and romance with her boyfriend, Steve Trevor. Although she still fought against threats such as intergalactic spacemen and giant beasts, the gendered critique of good and evil, so central to Marston's war-time stories, disappeared entirely from Wonder Woman stories altogether.[37]

She was lucky to survive at all in an era when superheroes went out of fashion and their book sales fell dramatically.[38] Post-war protests against their influence on children, such as 1948's mass comic book burnings in West Virginia and New York State, attacked comics for promoting homosexuality, occult themes, drugs, and other allegedly communist influences.[39] Just as Hollywood films came under attack for promoting anti-Nazi (and therefore potentially procommunist) themes, so did comic books suffer for their progressive war-time politics. In 1954, psychologist Frederic Wertham, author of many anticomic articles in the 1940s, published his influential book *Seduction of the Innocent,* calling comic books "primers for crime." He specifically criticized the supposed sexual and gender deviance in comics, singling out Batman and Robin as homosexuals, while Wonder Woman, with her Amazons, became "the Lesbian counterpart of Batman."[40] This attention sparked a Congressional investigation into the pernicious influence of comic books; in response, most publishers promised to deemphasize violence, drugs and sexuality, adopting a rigid self-censorship code.[41] In addition, many comic book publishers began cutting superhero titles altogether.[42]

Yet comics were not quite dead. Publishers replaced their superheroes with new features: romance and teen-themed titles for girls, and western or war-themed comics for boys. This gendered segregation of children's comics allowed writers to tailor their messages in what were considered gender-appropriate fashion. Combat war stories were viewed as healthy psychological fare for boys, which is hardly surprising given that the wartime heroics of leaders like John F. Kennedy and Lyndon B. Johnson were key to both their masculinity and their political credibility.[43] By the late 1950s, DC already had several war-themed titles in place: *G.I. Combat, Our Army at War, Our Fighting Forces, All-American Men of War,* and *Star-Spangled War Stories.*[44] Indeed, playing war formed a major part of a wider boys' culture in the 1950s and 1960s, with war-themed movies, television, and toys all serving as important gender signifiers.[45] There was no room in this atmosphere for a critique of Nazism based on its hypermasculinity.

There was, however, still room for Nazi enemies. Although the combat-themed comics were sometimes set in Korea, and, later, Vietnam, the Second World War remained a consistently popular setting in their pages. Historian William W. Savage argues that the Second World War was popular because it was more clearly identifiable as a good war than either Korea or Vietnam: "In the popular mind, ambiguity had not characterized the American response to World War II. An evil enemy had been decisively defeated. . . . If they wanted a war in their entertainments, they could watch the Nazis get it in the neck again."[46]

Why were these Nazis so satisfyingly evil? Initially, DC's 1950s war comics recycled the war-time trope that Nazis were terribly brutal, particularly toward civilians. For example, in a 1950s story from *Our Army at War,* a bald, hulking Nazi commandant viciously punished innocent civilians as a response to the actions of the resistance. He ordered an underling to "[t]ake a dozen hostages from the town in reprisal for Mlle. Marie's actions—and let the townspeople know she is to blame!"[47] By the 1960s and 1970s, racism began to appear as a key part of Nazi villainy. A 1971 story from *Star-Spangled War Stories,* "Totenkanz," took Allied secret agent the Unknown Soldier to a concentration camp. There he was horrified to witness Jews being tortured, hanged, and generally abused by an evil commandant.[48] Writer-editor Robert Kanigher and artist Joe Kubert also linked Nazi racism to the civil rights concerns of the contemporary United States.[49] In a 1965 issue of *Our Army at War,* for example, Nazi paratroopers took prisoner African American GI Jackie Johnson, who happens to be heavyweight fighter. One of his captors, a former boxing foe, forced Johnson to fight again: "It will not be said that I did not give the ex-champion of an inferior races a return match!" The long, vicious fight was interrupted by the Nazis taunting Jackie about his "black" blood. Johnson's comrades arrive just as he wins. Amazingly, he is still willing to donate his own blood to save his enemy's life, and the Nazi gasps: "The color of your blood—is red!" Jackie responds with "You're catching on, buster."[50] The comment on universal manhood challenged the prejudices of the fictional Nazis and, potentially, of American readers; in 1965, after all, many Americans still supported segregation, voting rights were not assured in much of the South, and many states retained bans on interracial marriage.

The theme of universal brotherhood came to be of such importance that, late in the period, some comic book Nazis redeemed themselves by showing fraternal respect for their American peers. Good Nazis expressed professional admiration for American soldiers' daring and ingenuity; in one story, a good Nazi officer even risked his life to prevent the execution of an innocent American soldier.[51] The emphasis on brotherhood in the war comics did not allow much room for sisterhood, but it did include a few implicit questions about masculinity and violence. Historian Andrew Huebner notes that the "public images of soldiers in Vietnam (and in Korea for that matter) indicated that the very terms of masculinity may have been . . . part of an ongoing 'masculinity crisis' that has preoccupied scholars of postwar America."[52] Although there was no overt critique of masculinity in the pages of the war comics (and certainly no Wonder Woman–style female characters to drive such critiques), the figures of Nazi evil frequently appeared as a challenge to the ethical limits of masculine violence in wartime. In other words, were the Americans brothers to the good Nazis, or to the bad ones? In a 1971 Sergeant Rock story, for example, the titular sergeant grew increasingly uneasy with an American GI who gunned down people dressed as civilians, even though they did, in fact, turn out to be disguised Nazi agents. When the young man decided that a group of women being held hostage by Nazis were faking it, Rock halted the action: "Hold it, Johnny! If you're wrong . . . we're no better'n the Nazi Butchers we're fightin' against!"[53]

Comics were not the only medium to complicate the picture of American heroism and Nazi villainy. The popular television comedy *Hogan's Heroes* (1965–1971), for example, featured American heroes outwitting their bumbling yet sympathetic Nazi captors. It may seem strange that these comical, even lovable Nazis could appear just a few years after early Holocaust films *The Diary of a Young Girl* (1959) and *Judgement at Nuremberg* (1961). But Hollywood images of the Second World War were growing increasingly complex. In *Catch-22* (1970), for example, the enemy is not so much the Nazis as the United States' own war machine, while *Kelly's Heroes* (1970) celebrates the frankly criminal exploits of American GIs who steal German gold.[54] Cultural historian Tom Engelhardt suggests that the 1970s desire to both deconstruct and celebrate the Second World War could be related to a wider angst in American culture: "By the 1970s, America's cultural products seemed intent either on critiquing their own mechanics and myths or on staking out even newer frontiers of defensiveness."[55] In light of the United States failure in Vietnam, and the attendant perceived crisis in American masculinity, it is not surprising that the Second World War held nostalgic appeal for those who yearned for simple days. It also demanded deconstruction from those questioning contemporary American militarism. Among the latter were American feminists, who, in the 1970s, were responsible for resurrecting the Second World War's greatest female hero, and, with her, William Moulton Marston's gendered critique of Nazism.

Peace and Justice in '72: Feminism Meets War Nostalgia

In 1972, Gloria Steinem launched *Ms.* magazine, one of the most influential publications of the burgeoning American feminist movement. On its cover, she placed Wonder Woman, drawn in the style of Second World

War art, with the byline: "Wonder Woman for President! Peace and Justice in '72." A child of the war-time period, Steinem revered the original version of the character as a rare example of a strong proto-feminist role model from the 1940s, whose stories were a "version of the truisms that women are rediscovering today . . . in the end, all are brought to their knees and made to recognize women's strength."[56] With her combination of strength and love, the classic Wonder Woman seemed to Steinem a perfect feminist icon for the troubled 1970s. She was appalled to find the comic had become a pseudo-romance book and that, in 1968, the editors had stripped the title character of her costume and superpowers. Steinem lobbied DC comics to return *Wonder Woman* to its feminist roots; beginning in 1973, they did so.[57]

For most of the next decade, the title became at least nominally feminist. It was a muted feminism, to be sure, and in no way compared to underground and independent feminist comics like *It Ain't Me Babe* (the first comic produced entirely by women), *Wimmen's Comix,* or *Tits 'n Clits.* These comics, not limited by the Comics Code and created by committed feminist authors, tackled such controversial topics as abortion, lesbianism, and women's sexual pleasure.[58] *Wonder Woman*'s authors and editors were far more conservative in their story choices, but it became one of the few DC superhero comics to tackle feminist storylines at all; workplace sexism, street harassment, and equality within heterosexual relationships all played key roles in the *Wonder Woman* plots of the 1970s.[59] By 1975, the rejuvenated comic had inspired a live-action television series starring former model Lynda Carter as the titular heroine. The series' first season was set in a semi-comic version of the Second World War; the comic book followed suit and returned to the 1940s, where the comic would retain its commitment to feminist themes.[60]

Many other comic book characters joined Wonder Woman in this 1970s return to war-time nostalgia. Both DC and its major publishing rival, Marvel, revived old super-powered heroes from the Golden Age, and, in some cases, invented new Second World War heroes. Some of the resurrected heroes had formerly been the corporate property of another publisher. For example, the Freedom Fighters, reintroduced in DC comics 1973, were long-defunct Quality Comic characters, now portrayed as living in a 1970s world where the Nazis had won the Second World War. At Marvel, writer and editor Roy Thomas formed a new team (The Invaders) from similar Golden Age roots in 1975.[61] By 1981, DC had wooed him to their publishing house, where he created *All-Star Squadron,* which featured a rotating cast of Golden Age heroes and villains, many of whom had not seen print since the Second World War.[62] A variety of other titles took temporary sojourns into the Second World War era as well, while the short-lived *Steel* introduced an all-new eponymous 1940s era superhero.[63]

As they spun their new war stories, most of the creative teams at DC had little time for historical research. Although specific creative processes differed greatly from team to team, an editor usually set general trends for the title, the writer produced a script with dialogue and suggested visuals, and the penciller drew the initial illustrations. Inkers, colorists, and letterers also contributed to the final product; considering that every member of this team was often working on several titles at once, the creative pace could be quite hectic.[64] Not surprisingly, easily accessible images from popular culture often informed the creative process; a Wonder Woman story titled "Tomorrow Belongs to Me," for example, invoked memories of the 1972 Nazi-themed musical *Cabaret.* Popular histories also influenced the new stories. Author Gerry Conway recalls that "in school I'd read Ellie [sic] Wiesel's 'Night,' and I'd seen Alain Renais' [sic] documentary, 'Night and Fog,' and I'd read Shirer's 'Rise and Fall of the Third Reich,' as well as 'Inside the Third Reich' by Albert Speer."[65] The names of Roy Thomas's Nazi villains, Night and Fog, reflect the influence of these works.[66]

But popular culture accounts of women under Nazism were virtually nonexistent; even if writers had time to search academic sources for information on this topic, they would have found little, in the mid-1970s, to satisfy their curiosity. Writing in 1987, historian Claudia Koontz noted that despite 50,000 books and monographs about the Third Reich, "half of the Germans who made dictatorship, war and genocide possible have largely escaped observation. . . . Historians have dismissed women as part of the timeless backdrop against which Nazi men made history, seeing men as active 'subjects' and women as the passive 'other.'"[67] In the index to William Shirer's best-selling *The Rise and Fall of the Third Reich,* for example, one searches in vain for an entry under "women," while "Communists" get nearly 50 pages. Women's history and gendered historical analysis were still in their infancy in the 1970s, and few English-language studies of women under Nazism were in print. If the writers of comics wanted to include an overtly gendered analysis in their writing of Nazis, they would have to find another source.

Something Truly Twisted and Inhuman:
Fascist Foes against a Feminist Hero

The writers of *Wonder Woman* had just such a source: William Moulton Marston's original scripts. According to Gerry Conway, his own scripts represented a combination of the feel of those Golden Age stories, a 1970s feminist ethos, and his own understanding of women's history under Nazism.[68] The modern writers picked up many of Marston's ideas and themes about gender. Jack Harris, for example, reintroduced Marston's gendered metaphysics in a 1978 script where the goddess Aphrodite announced that, with war's end, "the threat of Nazi slavery is over . . . and Mars licks his wounds!"[69] Wonder Woman and other characters frequently feminized resistance to Nazism; in one story, Wonder Woman even claimed to fight "in the name of Womanhood!"[70] Her super-powered colleague, Dr. Mid-Nite, suggested that it was not Wonder Woman's might, but her feminine caring, that may be "the last hope of our sad, savage world."[71]

Nazis, of course, sneered at this femininity. Nazi henchmen, for example, disputed whether or not she was worth ammunition: "We have our orders—to kill any intruders! But why waste a bullet on a mere female?"[72] In another story, the Red Panzer sneered: "I caution you, *fraulein* . . . there is only one thing more hateful than a woman who attempts to be clever . . . und that is a woman who fails to show respect for her betters."[73] In a very Marston-esque bit of dialogue, Golden Age villain Dr. Psycho explained in a 1978 story that he joined the Nazis for their vision of female slavery: "I escaped from prison and began my vengeance against womankind— vengeance which brought me here, to these noble Nazis, who also understand the true evil of femininity—evil which must be subjugated to the wisdom of man! Under Nazism, the world will be devoid of strife caused by women—and there will be a blessed peace—forever!"[74]

Wonder Woman also experienced sexism from her American colleagues. As she saved General MacArthur's life, for example, he snapped that he did not "need a female . . . to fight [his] battles!"[75] It is notable, however, that the American men in Wonder Woman stories usually get over their sexist attitudes. In one storyline, Wonder Woman's colleagues in the Justice Society fret patronizingly over her ability to handle difficult assignments but eventually see the error of their ways and learn to trust her skills.[76] This is, perhaps the greatest difference between Nazis and Americans in the 1970s stories: Americans may be flawed, but they learn from their mistakes. Nazis never do. Yet if the male superheroes in the pages of *Wonder Woman* displayed an admirable support for feminist goals (eventually), they must have somehow suffered amnesia when participating in other adventures. The issue of sexism disappears almost entirely in the pages of most other 1970s and 1980s DC comic books set in the Second World War.

Nazi villains also suffered from the same amnesia, articulating sexism as part of their villainy almost exclusively in the pages of *Wonder Woman*. Very occasionally, Nazi villains in *All-Star Squadron* made sexist comments about the female heroes they faced. For example, one Nazi-allied assassin faced down Liberty Belle with the comment "Himmel! You are a formidable opponent—for a woman!"[77] But only in the pages of *Wonder Woman* were Nazi villains consistently, predictably, sexist. This is all the more astonishing because, in other respects, DC's 1970s and 1980s Nazi villains varied little from portrayal to portrayal. They were almost always racist; one *All-Star Squadron* story, for example, makes much of the treatment of African American athletes at the 1936 Olympics: "Hell, *Der Fuehrer* wouldn't even shake [Jesse] Owen's hand."[78] Nazis all dabbled with destructive mysticism or super-science. For example, in a 1978 DC special, Adolf Hitler's Earth-2 incarnation wielded a "Spear of Destiny" with which he could call down Valkyries to wreak havoc on the earth and assassinate Franklin Delano Roosevelt.[79] The villain Armageddon was outfitted with boots that cause the energy of an object to turn in on itself, a sort of molecular holocaust.[80] Even the names of Nazi villains were somewhat repetitive and interchangeable, often suggesting weaponry and destruction: Iron Claw, Red Panzer, Zyklon (literally, "Cyclone," but also the name of the poison gas used in death camps).[81] They were usually physically maimed: Red Panzer, for example, was missing an eye, while Iron Claw proudly noted that "I lost my hand in service to the Reich!"[82] They were sadistic, and brutal. When a group of Nazi soldiers captured members of the Freedom Fighters on Earth–X, they looked forward to having "some amusement" with their unconscious prisoners before handing them over to the Gestapo.[83] Readers noticed the interchangeability of DC's Nazi villains. A letter from Randy Prislow of Salem, Oregon, published in *Wonder Woman* 238 complained that Nazis "all have the same, boring personality and motive (world conquest)."[84] In *All-Star Squadron,* writer-editor Roy Thomas concluded that "[r]eaders seem equally divided on whether villains should be Axis-oriented or not."[85] But if the Nazi villains were so interchangeable, why did the trope of Nazi sexism not appear more universally across DC comics?

Some possible explanations can be immediately discarded. It was not that DC's writers and artists were incapable of complexity, or of showing different aspects of Nazi villainy as intersectional. For example, racism easily coexisted with destructive mysticism in an *All-Star Squadron* story arc from 1982. In it, an SS officer plotted to bring back Quetzalcoatl, the Aztec feathered serpent god, in order to command Indian-descended Mexicans to do battle on behalf of the Reich. The Allied heroes noted the hypocrisy of using an "inferior" race's magic, with Hawkman musing: "Pure blooded 'Aryan' and pure-blooded 'Mayan deity' is an alliance that can't last long."[86] *Wonder Woman* laced the trope of Nazi sadism with the misogynistic threat of sexual assault. In a 1977 story, the Red Panzer gloated as Wonder Woman struggles to free herself from captivity: "Ach! Your aggression . . . your ferocity . . . they excite me! So much so, in fact, that your death I will regret . . . ALMOST."[87]

In fact, some of DC's writers were quite gifted at portraying the intersections of Nazi villainy. In a Gerry Conway-penned 1977 tale, racism, sexism, and mass destruction all coexisted in the evil Captain Strung. This Nazi villain kidnapped a Jewish psychic, Friederich, who mysteriously commanded sea animals with his mind. Holding over Friederich the lives of his children, trapped in a concentration camp, Strung forced the helpless psychic to make sharks sink an Allied ship and then devour its survivors. Here, Nazi racism intersected with misogyny; as an Amazon, Wonder Woman was clearly not an Aryan, and Captain Strung gloated over this as he captured her with her own magic lasso: "This is as it should be—the Aryan in control, the inferior in submission."[88] Strung both gendered and racialized his slurs, calling Friederich a "dog," Wonder Woman a "witch" (suggesting an even stronger gender-based slur which the Comics Codes would not allow).[89] In one two-issue story, Captain Strung embodies all the major tropes of the 1970s Nazi villain: racist, capable of mass destruction via mystic means, and deeply sexist.

Another possible explanation for the disappearing nature of Nazi misogyny might simply be differences between villains: some were sexist, while others were not. Yet the very same Nazi character might appear as sexist in *Wonder Woman* but not in another title. Baron Blitzkrieg provides a clear example. The Baron's origin includes the familiar themes of racism, sadism, and super-science run amok. A Prussian aristocrat who enjoyed his work running a concentration camp, he was maimed when a young Jewish chemist threw acid in his face, horribly disfiguring the Baron.[90] Wonder Woman muses of him: "his very body tormented by a secret medical experiment, ordered by Hitler himself . . . Is he a man, anymore? Or has he become something truly twisted—and inhuman?"[91] The sexist Baron boasted to Wonder Woman that "none shall defeat me—least of all, a female!"[92] After defeating the Baron's evil plans, Wonder Woman waxed philosophical about Nazism's wider implication as a form of militarism: "Blitzkrieg was the embodiment of hate—and hate will never end, so long as madmen make war—and soldiers march off—to die."[93] This comment, so in keeping with Marston's vision of the character as one in the service of peace-loving Aphrodite, further places the Baron's Nazism in the old Wonder Woman framework of masculine violence and aggression posed against feminine love.

When Baron Blitzkrieg reappeared in the pages of *All-Star Squadron* in the early 1980s, he was still very much the race-conscious Nazi whose Japanese allies are "Little Yellow Brothers."[94] He called the Americans a "a stupid, mongrel breed."[95] He did not hesitate to use his increasing powers for mass destruction, planning to use a deadly ray from the eyes of his costumes in order to destroy a major United States city.[96] But he articulated no sexism. This is not because of the absence of female heroes as targets for his abuse; he faced a number of women adversaries, including Liberty Belle, Phantom Lady, and Firebrand. Unlike Wonder Woman, none of these women articulate their struggle against the Baron in gendered or feminist terms. Why?

It may be tempting to chalk up this lack of awareness to a pervasive culture of comic book sexism. Feminist critics like Trina Robbins and Lillian Robinson, among others, have expressed frustration with the pervasive misogyny of comic book culture, in which readership is often assumed by editors, writers, and artists to be exclusively male, with female protagonists treated primarily as sex objects.[97] But some DC staff, including Roy Thomas of *All-Star Squadron,* made great efforts to address the problem of historical Golden Age gender discrimination and provide respectful portraits of interesting super-women. Thomas went out of his way to include many female heroes in *All-Star Squadron,* even going so far as to redesign a male Golden Age hero (Firebrand) into a female one.[98] He criticized the lack of feminine leadership in many Golden Age comics, especially the sexism in Wonder Woman's position as secretary of the

Justice Society (despite her powers far outpacing those of most of the male heroes). In the new comic, female hero Liberty Belle was even elected president of the All-Stars.[99]

Roy Thomas's attention to these details suggests that the near-invisibility of Nazi sexism in *All-Star Squadron* did not preclude criticism of American sexism. Such criticisms might have been difficult in the 1950s and early 1960s, when any divergence from conservative American gender values prompted charges of communism. But, as noted already in this chapter, by the 1970s American popular culture could critique its own shortcomings. The difference between Nazis and Americans was often only that American heroes would accept correction of their faults. For example, when a member of the All-Star Squadron expressed a racist hatred for the Japanese, she was corrected: "[O]ur real enemies are the fascist dictators, not the people under their yoke. The day we forget that—the world's really in trouble!"[100]

Still, even if some writers were aware of sexism as a social problem in United States society, it does not negate Robbins's and Robinson's overall point: feminism had a limited role in mainstream American comics of the 1970s and 1980s. Alternative comics provided far more opportunities to explore feminist themes fully; *Wonder Woman* was a feminist title mainly by virtue of being one of the few mainstream superhero titles to acknowledge any feminism at all. A widespread disinterest in overt gender politics may certainly have affected editorial and artistic choices in the portrayal of Nazis, but in this, however, comic book creators were hardly alone. Very few popular films of the 1970s, for example, explored the experiences of women under Nazism, and few of these used gender as a category of analysis. The pornographic film *Ilsa, She-Wolf of the SS* (1975), for example, hardly qualifies as a feminist critique. The 1977 film *Julia* explored the historical experiences of a feminist who opposes Nazism, but its major struggles were personal, and only implicitly political. The Holocaust drama *Playing for Time* (1980) focused largely on women's experiences as Jews, with few references to the way their gender intersected with their Jewishness.[101]

Yet if popular culture could bury the historical memory of Nazism's gender politics, it could also preserve it. The comic book writers of the 1970s who consulted William Moulton Marston's original scripts found in them a rich framework for understanding Nazi oppression in psychologically gendered terms. Marston's stories included few references to specific

Nazi policies or statements about women, but in casting Nazis as slaves of Mars and Wonder Woman as the champion of Aphrodite, he criticized Nazism as a form of dangerous hypermasculinity. When DC revived the wartime setting for *Wonder Woman* stories, its nominal adherence to 1970s feminist themes helped give life to the frameworks found in Marston's old scripts. Ahead of other popular culture, and ahead even of many academic historians, *Wonder Woman*'s writers and artists revived the memory of Nazism as a patriarchal system of oppression in which racism, totalitarianism, and sexism intersected. In this overtly gendered portrayal, resistance to Nazi evil was not merely fighting for the American way; it was fighting "in the name of Womanhood" itself.

Notes

1. I am grateful to Robert S. Haulton for his assistance with this chapter.
2. Gerry Conway (writer), Don Heck (pencil), and Vince Colletta (ink), "Wonder Woman: The Baron's Name is Blitzkrieg," *World's Finest* 246 (New York, DC Comics, August-September 1977), p. 10.
3. Gerry Conway (writer), Don Heck (pencil), and Joe Giella (ink), "And Death My Destiny," *Wonder Woman* 234 (New York, DC Comics, July 1977), p. 14.
4. Gerry Conway (writer), James Sherman (pencil), and Liz Berube (ink), "Wonder Woman: Hell on Skis," *World's Finest* 245 (June-July 1977), p. 11.
5. William Moulton Marston, "The God of War," *Wonder Woman Archives Volume 2* (New York, DC Comics, 2000).
6. Ian Gordon, *Comic Strips and Consumer Culture, 1890–1945* (Washington, DC, Smithsonian Institution Press, 1998), p. 139.
7. William W. Savage Jr., *Comic Books and America, 1945–1954* (Norman, University of Oklahoma Press, 1990), pp. 7–9.
8. William M. Tuttle Jr., *Daddy's Gone to War: the Second World War in the Lives of America's Children* (Oxford, Oxford University Press, 1993), p. 58.
9. Gordon, *Comic Strips and Consumer Culture,* p. 139.
10. Savage, *Comic Books and America,* pp. 7, 78.
11. Maurice Horn, *Women in the Comics* (New York, Chelsea House Publishers, 1977), p. 127.
12. Trina Robbins, *The Great Women Superheroes* (Northampton, MA, Kitchen Sink Press, 1996), pp. 16–21.
13. Robbins, *The Great Women Superheroes,* pp. 26–31.

14. William Moulton Marston (writer) and H. G. Peters (artist), "The Battle for Womanhood," *Wonder Woman* 5 (June-July 1943), in *Wonder Woman Archives Volume 3* (New York, DC Comics, 2002), np.

15. Les Daniels, *Wonder Woman: The Complete History* (San Francisco, Chronicle Books, 2000), pp. 18–23.

16. Savage, *Comic Books and America,* p. 10.

17. Savage, *Comic Books and America,* p. 10.

18. Jerry Siegel (writer) and Joe Shuster (art), "What If Superman Ended the War?" (February 1940), in *Superman: The Greatest Stories Ever Told* (New York, DC Comics, 2004), p. 84.

19. Ed Herron (writer) and Mark Raboy (art), "The Origin of Captain Marvel, Jr.," *Whiz Comics* 25 (New York, Fawcett Comics, December 1941).

20. Will Eisner (writer) and Chuck Cuidera (art), "Blackhawk" (1941), in Michael Uslan, ed., *America at War: The Best of DC War Comics* (New York, Simon and Schuster, 1979).

21. William Moulton Marston (writer) and H. G. Peter (art), "The Story of the Fir Balsam," *Sensation Comics* 14 (February 1943), in *Wonder Woman Archives Volume 2* (New York, DC Comics, 2000), np.

22. Robert Sherwood, "Rush All Possible Aid to Britain," *The Reader's Digest,* (September 1940), pp. 12–17, quoted in Allan M. Winkler, *The Politics of Propaganda: The Office of War Information, 1942–1945* (New Haven, CT, Yale University Press, 1978), p. 16.

23. Robert L. McLaughlin and Sally E. Parry, *We'll Always Have the Movies: American Cinema during World War II* (Lexington, The University Press of Kentucky, 2006), p. 32.

24. *The Mortal Storm* (1940).

25. Claudia Koontz, *Mothers in the Fatherland: Women, the Family and Nazi Politics* (New York, St. Martin's Press, 1987), p. 145.

26. *Hitler's Children* (1943); *Education for Death* (1943).

27. McLaughlin and Parry, *We'll Always Have Movies,* pp. 114–115.

28. William Moulton Marston, "Marston Advises 3 L's for Success: 'Live, Love and Laugh' Offered by Psychologist as Recipe for Required Happiness," *The New York Times* (November 11, 1937), quoted in Daniels, *Wonder Woman,* p. 19.

29. Marston Peters, "The Battle for Womanhood," in *Wonder Woman Archives Volume 3* (New York, DC Comics, 2002), p. 55.

30. William Moulton Marston, "Why 100,000,000 Americans Read Comics," *The American Scholar,* Vol. 13, No. 1 (Winter 1943), quoted in Robbins, *The Great Women Superheroes,* p. 7.

31. Geoffrey C. Bunn, "The Lie Detector, Wonder Woman, and Liberty: The Life and Work of William Moulton Marston," *History of the Human Sciences,* Vol. 10, No. 91 (1997), p. 104.

32. William Moulton Marston (writer) and H. G. Peter (ink), "The Secret of Baroness Paula von Gunther," *Wonder Woman* 3 (February/March 1943), in *Wonder Woman Archives Volume 2.*

33. Otto Binder (writer) and C. C. Beck (art), "The Monster Society of Evil Chapter 2: The Jungle Trap," *Captain Marvel Adventures* 23 (New York, Fawcett Comics, March 1943).

34. William Moulton Marston (writer) and H. G. Peter (ink), "The Earl of Greed," *Wonder Woman* 2 (Fall 1942), in *Wonder Woman Archives Volume 2,* p. 27.

35. Betty Friedan, *The Feminine Mystique* (New York, WW Norton, 1963), p. 37, quoted in Nancy A. Walker, *Shaping Our Mother's World: American Women's Magazines* (Jackson, University Press of Mississippi, 2000), p. 9.

36. Adlai E. Stevenson, "Women, Husbands, and History," speech at Smith College, June 6, 1955, in Walter Johnson, ed., *The Papers of Adlai E. Stevenson,* (Boston, Little, Brown and Company, 1974), quoted in Daniel Horowitz, *Betty Friedan and the Making of the Feminine Mystique* (Amherst, University of Massachusetts Press, 1998), p. 124.

37. Daniels, *Wonder Woman,* pp. 76–102.

38. Savage, *Comic Books and America,* pp. 12–13.

39. David Hajdu, *The Ten-Cent Plague: The Great Comic-Book Scare and How It Changed America* (New York, Farrar, Straus and Giroux, 2008), pp. 114–125.

40. Robbins, *The Great Woman Superheroes,* p. 11.

41. Tom Engelhardt, *The End of Victory Culture: Cold War America and the Disillusioning of a Generation* (Amherst, University of Massachusetts Press, 1995), pp. 134–135.

42. Gordon, *Comic Books and Consumer Culture,* p. 149.

43. Robert D. Dean, *Imperial Brotherhood: Gender and the Making of Cold War Foreign Policy* (Amherst, University of Massachusetts Press, 2001), pp. 37–62.

44. Trina Robbins, *From Girls to Grrrlz: A History of Women's Comics from Teens to Zines* (San Francisco, Chronicle Books, 1999), pp. 15–66.

45. Engelhardt, *The End of Victory Culture,* pp. 81–86.

46. Savage, *Comic Books and America,* p. 59.

47. Robert Kanigher (writer) and Mort Drucker (art), "TNT Spotlight," (1950), in Uslan, ed., *America at War.*

48. Bob Haney (writer) and Joe Kubert (art), "Totentanz," *Star Spangled War Stories* 158 (August-September 1971), in *Showcase Presents: The Unknown Soldier 1* (New York, DC Comics, 2008).

49. Michael Uslan, preface to Uslan, ed., *America at War,* pp. 9–10.

50. Robert Kanigher (writer) and Joe Kubert (art), "What's the Color of Your Blood?" *Our Army At War* (November 1965), in Uslan, ed., *America at War,* p. 154.

51. Bob Haney (writer) and Joe Kubert (art), "Man of War," *Star Spangled War Stories* 159 (October-November 1971) and Bob Haney (writer) and Jack Sparling (art), "Witness for a Coward," *Star Spangled War Stories* 165 (October-November 1972), in *Showcase Presents: The Unknown Soldier Volume 1.*

52. Andrew J. Huebner, *The Warrior Image: Soldiers in American Culture from the Second World War to the Vietnam Era* (Chapel Hill, The University of North Carolina Press, 2008), p. 205.

53. Robert Kanigher (writer) and Mort Drucker (art), "Dead Count," *Our Army at War* (June 1971), in Uslan, ed., *America at War.*

54. Jeanine Basinger, *The World War II Combat Film: Anatomy of a Genre* (Middletown, CT, Wesleyan University Press, 2003), pp. 183, 316.

55. Engelhardt, *The End of Victory Culture,* p. 178.

56. Gloria Steinem, "Introduction," in *Wonder Woman* (New York, Holt, Rhinehart and Winston, 1972), unpaginated.

57. Gloria Steinem, "Introduction."

58. Robbins, *From Girls to Grrlz,* pp. 83–93.

59. Lillian Robinson, among others, argues that *Wonder Woman*'s authors often did not understand feminism well. Nevertheless, *Wonder Woman* remained the most visible comic in the 1970s to accept the mantle of feminism, no matter how imperfectly. Lillian S. Robinson, *Wonder Women: Feminisms and Superheroes* (New York, Routledge, 2004), pp. 86–88. For a discussion of other experiments with feminist themes in 1970s superhero comics, see Robbins, *The Great Woman Superheroes,* pp. 122–138.

60. Daniels, *Wonder Woman,* pp. 136–146.

61. Les Daniels, *Marvel: Five Decades of the World's Greatest Comics* (New York, Harry N. Abrams Publishers), p. 172.

62. The two lines even shared a similar tagline: "The Greatest Heroes of World War Two!" (*All-Star Squadron*) and "The Greatest Super-heroes of World War Two!" (*Invaders*). See Roy Thomas (writer) with various, *Invaders* 1–41 (New York, Timely [Marvel Comics], August 1975-September 1979).

63. Gerry Conway (writer) and Don Heck (art), *Steel* 1–5 (New York, DC Comics, January-February 1978 through October-November 1978).

64. The process and level of collaboration can vary greatly; in the famous Marvel Method, for example, the writer provides a synopsis, the artist draws the story, and the writer fills in specific dialogue based in part on the pictures. Daniels, *Marvel,* p. 87.

65. Gerry Conway, e-mail message to author, May 14, 2009.

66. Roy Thomas (plot), Paul Kupperberg (script), and Arvell Jones and Pablo Marcos (art), "Night and Fog," *All-Star Squadron* 44 (New York, DC Comics, April 1985).

67. Koontz, *Mothers in the Fatherland,* p. 3.

68. Gerry Conway, e-mail message to author, May 14, 2009.

69. Jack C. Harris (writer), Jose Delbo (pencil), and Joe Giella (ink), "Tomorrow's Gods and Demons," *Wonder Woman* 242 (New York, DC Comics, April 1978), p. 9.

70. Gerry Conway (writer), Don Heck (pencil), and Vince Colletta (ink), "Sea Death," *Wonder Woman* 233 (New York, DC Comics, July 1977), p. 12.

71. Gerry Conway (writer), Jose Delbo (pencil), and Vincent Colletta (ink), "Armageddon Day," *Wonder Woman* 236 (New York, DC Comics, October 1977), p. 5.

72. Denny O'Neil (writer), Jose Delbo (pencil), and Vince Colletta (ink), "Wonder Woman: Jeopardy Times Two!" *World's Finest Comics* 244 (New York, DC Comics, April-May 1977), p. 9.

73. Martin Pasko (writer) and Jose Delbo (art), "Retreat to Tomorrow," *Wonder Woman* 228 (New York, DC Comics, February 1977), p. 6.

74. Gerry Conway (writer), Mike Vosberg (pencil), and Bob Smith (ink), "Wonder Woman: A Fire in the Sky," *World's Finest* 249 (New York, DC Comics, February-March 1978), p. 11.

75. Gerry Conway (writer), Jose Delbo (art), and Vince Colletta (art), "The Secret Origin of Wonder Woman," *Wonder Woman* 237 (New York, DC Comics, November 1977).

76. Gerry Conway (writer), Joe Giella (art), and Jose Delbo (art), "Wanted: One Amazon—Dead or Alive!" *Wonder Woman* 240 (New York, DC Comics, February 1978).

77. Roy Thomas (writer), Adrian Gonzales (art), and Jerry Ordway (art), "Afternoon of the Assassins," *All-Star Squadron* 8 (New York, DC Comics, April 1982).

78. Roy Thomas (writer) and Jerry Ordway (art), "Secret Origin of Amazing Man," *All-Star Squadron* 23 (New York, DC Comics, July 1983), p. 3.

79. Paul Levitz (writer), Bob Layton (art), and Joe Staton (art), "The Untold Origin of the Justice Society," *DC Special* 29 (New York, DC Comics, August-September 1977).

80. Conway, Delbo, and Colletta "Armageddon Day," *Wonder Woman* 236.

81. Zyklon B entered popular history fame in William Shirer, *The Rise and Fall of the Third Reich* (New York, MJF Books, 1990), pp. 970–972.

82. Iron Claw quoted in Conway, Sherman, and Wiacek, "Wonder Woman: Hell on Skis." See Red Panzer in Pasko and Delbo, "Retreat to Tomorrow," *Wonder Woman* 228. See also: Gerry Conway (writer), Jose Louis Garcia Lopez (pencil), and Dan Adkins (art), "Superman vs. Wonder Woman," *All New Collector's Edition* C-54 (New York, DC Comics, 1978); Conway, Heck, and Giella, "And Death My Destiny"; Roy Thomas (writer), Pablo Marcos (ink), Arvell Jones (pencil),

"Give Me Liberty, Give Me Death!" *All-Star Squadron* 45 (New York, DC Comics, May 1985).

83. Len Wein (writer), Dick Dillin (pencil), and Dick Giordino (ink), "Crisis on Earth-X," *Justice League of America* 107 (New York, DC Comics, October 1973).

84. Randy Prislow, "Letter to the Editor," *Wonder Woman* 238 (New York, DC Comics, December 1977), np.

85. Roy Thomas, "Editorial," *All-Star Squadron* 5 (New York, DC Comics, January 1982), np.

86. Roy Thomas (writer), Jerry Ordway (ink), Rich Buckler (pencil), "Mayhem in the Mile-High City," *All-Star Squadron* 6 (New York, DC Comics, February 1982), p. 4.

87. O'Neil, Delbo, Vince Colletta, "Wonder Woman: Jeopardy Times Two!"

88. Conway, Heck, Colletta, "Sea Death," p. 15.

89. Conway, Heck, and Giella, "And Death My Destiny," p. 9.

90. Gerry Conway (writer), Jose Luis Garcia Lopez (pencil), and Dan Adkins (ink), "Superman vs. Wonder Woman," *All New Collector's Edition* C-54 (New York, DC Comics, 1978).

91. Gerry Conway (writer), Jose Delbo (art), and Vince Colletta (art), "Wonder Woman: The Man in the Doomsday Mask," *World's Finest* 247 (New York, DC Comics, October-November 1977), p. 7.

92. Conway, Heck, and Colletta, "Wonder Woman: The Baron's Name is Blitzkrieg," p. 12.

93. Conway, Delbo, Colletta, "Wonder Woman: The Man in the Doomsday Mask," p. 8.

94. Roy Thomas (writer), Rick Hoberg (ink), and Bill Collins (pencil), "The Wrath of Tsuanami," *All-Star Squadron* 34 (New York, DC Comics, June 1984); Roy Thomas (writer), Rick Hoberg (ink), and Bill Collins (pencil), "That Earths May Live," *All-Star Squadron* 35 (New York, DC Comics, July 1984).

95. Thomas, Marcos, Jones, "Give Me Liberty, Give Me Death!" p. 10.

96. Roy Thomas (writer), Dann Thomas (writer), Pablo Marcos (ink), Arvell Jones (pencil), "Philadelphia—It Tolls for Thee!" *All-Star Squadron* 46 (New York, DC Comics, June 1985).

97. Robbins, *The Great Woman Superheroes,* pp. 121–137, 166–169; Robinson, *Feminisms and Superheroes,* pp. 83–86.

98. Thomas, "Editorial."

99. Roy Thomas (writer) and Jerry Ordway (art), "A Tale of Three Citadels," *All-Star Squadron* 21 (New York, DC Comics, May 1983).

100. Roy Thomas (writer) and Joe Kubert (art), "One Day, During the War . . . " *All-Star Squadron* 13 (New York, DC Comics, September 1982), p. 9.

101. Caroline Joan Kay Picart, ed., *The Holocaust Film Sourcebook Vol 1, Fiction* (Westport, CT, Greenwood Publishing Group, 2003), pp. 181, 203–205, 296.

7

Conspirator or Collaborator?
Nazi Arab Villainy in Popular Fiction

Ahmed Khalid Al-Rawi

Although the Second World War ended and was superseded by a preoccupation with the cold war in the west, German Nazis have remained staple villains in films, popular fiction, and video games. Nazis have also become associated with the new villains of the western world, the Arabs, who, as a direct result of the Arab-Israeli conflict, have taken on the mantle of being representative of evil. Tens, if not hundreds, of novels and films appeared during and after the Second World War portraying Nazis in minor background roles supporting Arab terrorists in the building of a nuclear bomb, the design of biological weapons, or plotting to destroy Israel and the west. These new images of Nazis and their Arab sidekicks are expressions of a cultural reality that has two implications. The first one is the deliberate political and ideological association made by some writers between Nazis and Arabs in order to suggest that both intend to wipe out the Jews. Ironically, most writers suggest that Arabs have anti-Semitic feelings toward the Jews, even though Arabs themselves are Semites. Second, it is implied that Nazism shares common ground with Islam because both seek to destroy the west in general and Israel in particular, disregarding the core dimension of the Arab-Israeli conflict, which is directly linked to geopolitical ambitions.

This chapter is divided into three sections. The first section provides historical background to the cooperation that existed between Nazis and some Arabs before and during the Second World War and demonstrates the links between representations of Nazism and some constructions of Arab nationalism at that time and subsequently. The second section investigates how some writers of popular fiction have tried to link Nazi and Arab characters in order to vilify the latter through such an association. Though they are in the background playing minor roles, Nazis remain an embodiment of evil whose function is to enhance the appearance of criminality and villainy in Arab characters. Finally, the last section offers a more detailed close discussion of four novels that link Arabs with Nazis, which has a direct effect on the way Arabs have been perceived and treated by the west. As these negative images recur in many entertainment media, they come to resemble undisputed facts complicating the nature of political relations between the west and the Arab world.

Historical Background

Historical links between the Arab world and Nazi Germany are easy to find. Many of these connections emerged from Arab discontent particularly in dealings with France and Great Britain in the aftermath of the Sykes-Picot agreement of 1916, which saw the division of the Arabic-speaking region into separate states. The agreement was the first of many disappointments experienced by the Arabs in their dealings with Britain during the war and inter-war period. Arab nationalist independence movements began to resist British and French control with uprisings such as the 1920 revolution in Iraq. Even when Iraq gained its independence from Britain in 1932, the former colonial ruler continued to exercise close control over the country, in similar ways to how the French controlled other Arab states.[1] The ongoing intervention by European powers was viewed by the Arab masses as ongoing humiliation to their national pride.

One of the nationalist Arab figures in Iraq, Rashid Ali Al-Kaylani, was appointed as prime minister in 1933, representing the Party of National Brotherhood. Al-Kaylani aimed to gain complete independence from Britain following the signing of the Anglo-Iraqi Treaty in 1930. In the same year as the emergence of Al-Kaylani, a pan-Arab committee was created in Baghdad to discuss the unity of the Arab world and the means of gaining independence from foreign domination. The committee asked for assistance from the German ambassador in Baghdad, Fritz Grobba, because the Arab nationalists knew they could not achieve their aims of uniting, and especially gaining independence for Palestine, without foreign military aid.[2] Some Arab nationalists sought an affiliation with Germany because it did not seem to have colonial ambitions in the region, unlike France, Britain, and Italy. What made this potential alliance even more attractive was German opposition to Zionist calls for the establishment of a Jewish homeland in Palestine at the expense of Arab Palestinians. However, Germany rejected any form of cooperation, preferring to stay neutral in this thorny issue that involved a clash of interests with Britain.[3]

At about the same time, several Arab leaders recognized the need to follow a new political system that would lift poor and uneducated Arabs out of centuries of economic and intellectual stagnation. They were particularly taken by German works describing socialism such as A. Rosenberg's *Mythos des Zwanzigsten Jahrhundert,* J. Gottlieb Fichte's *Reden an die Deutsche Nation,* and Hitler's *Mein Kampf.* Arab intellectuals such as Sati' Al-Hussari, Michel 'Aflaq, Antoon Sa'adah, and Pierre Jumayle also traveled to Europe to learn about new political and social movements and wanted to apply them in their own countries.[4] Some of them viewed the ideology of the National Socialist German Workers' Party (NSDAP) with admiration because of its "disciplined, militaristic and intensely nationalistic posture" as well as its explicit opposition to Zionism.[5]

The question of possible large-scale Jewish migration to Palestine in the 1930s made Arab leaders even more wary of the British and French and saw them seek aid from Nazi Germany in their campaign to protect pan-Arabism in the region. In Palestine in 1933, for example, the grand mufti of Jerusalem, Haji Amin Al-Husseini, expressed his willingness to cooperate with the Germans in a telegram sent to Berlin.[6] The mufti had hopes of liberating his nation from the British; however, he remained optimistic that Britain could solve the question of Palestine without the need to involve other foreign powers.[7] However, according to Philip Mattar, a radical change in the mufti's attitudes was prompted in 1936 following the realization that Britain would not keep its promises to the Palestinians and would allow Jewish migrants into Palestine.[8] Other efforts to align with Germany came from Syria with Amir Shakib Arsllan, who was one of the advocates of pan-Arabism based on Islamic ideology. In 1934, he visited Germany in the hope of seeing Hitler and gaining his support in waging a holy war against France. His requests, however, fell on deaf ears.[9]

Although Al-Kaylani did not stay long in office in 1933, he was re-elected as prime minister of Iraq in 1940. At this early stage of the Second World War, the propaganda war between Britain and Nazi Germany was in full swing. It was relatively simple for Germany to promote anti-British feeling in the region, as most Arabs wanted independence from British and French control and looked to Nazi Germany to help them achieve this.

So when rumors abounded that the British had assassinated the national-ist king, Ghazi son of King Faisal I, Iraqis protested in front of the British Embassy in Baghdad.[10] Britain attempted to counter German propaganda with their own efforts, such as Freya Stark's Brotherhood of Freedom or-ganization that opposed Nazism and worked on showing Arabs the Al-lied perspective in the war.[11] Of course, Britain was preoccupied with its economic interests in Iraq, particularly its holdings in the British Pe-troleum Company and Iraqi Petroleum Company, which left Iraqis scant management of their natural resources and provided clear reasons why Al-Kaylani's nationalist government was "willing to align themselves with Nazi Germany, Britain's deadliest enemy" as a way of achieving independence.[12]

Even before the outbreak of the Second World War, British military involvement in the region helped to push some Arabs closer to Nazi Ger-many. For example, as a direct result of British military involvement in Iraq during the 1936–1939 Revolt, the mufti of Jerusalem, Haji Amin Al-Husseini, decided to go to Baghdad in order to help Al-Kaylani with his 1941 revolution. Al-Kaylani courageously "challenged Britain militarily" by refusing to side with the Allied forces during the war and by overtly supporting the Axis Powers,[13] with the result that Britain invaded Iraq in 1941 and supported the execution of four of the military colonels who backed Al-Kaylani. The latter fled to Saudi Arabia, where he was granted political asylum. From Iraq, Britain extended its occupation to Syria, Leb-anon, and Persia. Although some pro-Nazi Arabs "continued to hope for their liberation [from Britain] through an eventual German victor," this was perceived as increasingly unlikely after the Battle of Stalingrad.[14]

As for the mufti, he fled to Germany and worked in Nazi Germany's propaganda ministry through Radio Berlin, which had been broadcasting in the Arab region since the middle of 1938. The Germans wanted to per-suade the Arab peoples of the justness of the Nazi cause through the rheto-ric of recognition of the rights of Palestinian Arabs.[15] Unsurprisingly, the mufti was accused of anti-Semitism because of his anti-Zionist stance and support for Nazi Germany. It is important to note, however, that there is no evidence to indicate he was against the Jews per se, although he was decidedly opposed to mass Jewish settlements that would threaten the pos-sibility of securing a Palestinian homeland similar to many other Arab states that had achieved independence. As Kathleen Christison states, the mufti's nationalist "actions were never very effective, and he never participated in atrocities against the Jews."[16] In fact, he had no connection with the Holocaust other than that he was working for the NSDAP in Germany during the war, but his name was later intentionally linked to it, particularly after the trial and execution in Israel of Adolf Eichmann— "the architect of the Holocaust"—in 1962. At that time, then Israeli Prime Minister Ben-Gurion asserted that the Arabs who were attacking Israel were "actually disciples of the Nazis" and used the example of the mufti in order to strengthen his claim.[17] Ben-Gurion was one of the first Israeli politicians to emphasize the link between Nazis and Arabs, a trend that gained momentum in the following decades not only in political spheres but in popular culture as well.

It is worth noting that the deceased Palestinian leader, Yasser Arafat, was one of the mufti's nephews, with the effect that the mufti was further demonized by western politicians and in the western media in order to demean Arafat's cause and heighten the perception of the threat he posed not only to Israel but to the west as a whole.[18] The mufti had gone to Germany to seek a safe haven from which he could secure the Palestinian interests that Arab governments were too weak to safeguard. Being allied to the devil (as the west interpreted Hitler and the NSDAP) appeared to be his only viable choice for achieving his goals. In the post-war world, it served the cause of the Zionist lobby to spread the myth that the ongoing Arab-Israeli conflict stemmed from Arabs' hatred of Jews.[19] Yet there is much evidence to suggest that Jews had no cultural clashes or differences with Arab Muslims when they lived together. Even after the beginning of the Arab-Israeli conflict, "Arab writings on Palestine and [the] conflict issues generally distinguish carefully between Jews and Zionists in defining the enemy."[20]

Ironically, the western media's preoccupation with the mufti's supposedly Nazi character helped to inflate his personality in such a way that he was seen to represent more than a billion Muslims around the world. In many ways, the incorrect connection of Islam to Nazism has been an ongoing survival technique through which Israeli authorities have justified their assault on Arab Palestinians. Israeli arguments about self-defense have been bolstered by the world's sympathy for the plight of the Jews during the Second World War and have intentionally cast Arab Muslims as unrighteous aggressors. Janice J. Terry argues that "most Westerners' support for Israel and hostility to the Arab world springs solely from a desire to see a people grievously wronged given some measure of retribution."[21]

The tenuous connection between the Arab self-determination movements of the first half of the twentieth century and Nazism through the actions of one man serves to bolster Israeli claims to legitimacy and western sympathy, so much so that there is a display in the Israeli Holocaust Museum showing the mufti and Nazi officers together, which states that Palestinian nationalist aspirations, which Israel regards as unlawful, resemble the Nazi schemes to destroy the Jews.[22]

Another common technique employed by some Israeli politicians and writers is promoting all criticism of Zionism as anti-Semitic attacks on the state of Israel. Any nation or group that is critical of Zionist political activity is presented as anti-Jewish. Robert S. Wistrich, Neuberger Professor of Modern History at the Hebrew University of Jerusalem, reiterates this as follows: "Whoever wants to defame or destroy [Israel], openly or through policies that entail nothing else but such destruction, is in effect practicing the Jew-hatred of yesteryear, whatever their self-proclaimed intentions."[23] Wistrich equates defaming Israel with destroying it. Furthermore, Michael Suleiman argues that Zionists gained much sympathy in the west by associating "anti-Israeli" issues with an "anti-Jewish position."[24] In other words, the Palestinian struggle for independence has been viewed as a means to make another Holocaust. Jewish scholar Marc Ellis asserts that "insofar as Palestinian Arabs and the Arab world in general attempt to thwart Jewish empowerment in Israel, they symbolize to Holocaust theologians the continuity of the Nazi drama."[25] Again, this rhetoric has been used to justify preemptive attacks carried out by Israel on Arabs in Palestine, Lebanon, and Syria.[26] The rhetoric of these Israeli scholars is reminiscent of the language used by some Muslim fundamentalists who view the United States-led war on Iraq and Afghanistan as a war against Islam rather than viewing the political, military, and economic factors behind them.[27] Indeed, the rhetorical invocation of monsters is mirrored on all radical sides of the politics in the Middle East in order to demean and vilify the enemy on each side.

Another connection between Arabs and Nazis made in the west stresses that after the war a number of Nazi scientists sought refuge in Arab countries, particularly in Egypt and Syria, and helped to build up their military power. With the rise of the nationalist Arab leader Gamal Abdul Nasser,[28] and his pan-Arab efforts to unite Egypt with Syria, more fears were articulated in the media claiming that Nazis and Arabs were determined to build an arsenal of atomic, biological, and chemical weapons to be used against Israel.[29] These accusations were enhanced by the fact that some Arab countries like Egypt, Syria, Iraq, and Libya bought weapons and sought technical expertise from the former Soviet Union during the cold war.[30] By introducing Nazi scientists aiding Arabs, this anti-Arab propaganda further implies that Arabs are unable to manage their military projects without foreign aid, indirectly suggesting a deficiency in the Arabs' way of thinking. The supposed links with German scientists underscored the myth of a backward anti-Jewish people bent on ruthless destruction.

The misrepresentation of Arabs as quasi-Nazis has appeared in different western media including "the press, films, radio, television, newspapers, magazines, books, journals . . . , schools and universities, peer groups, churches, [and] places of work."[31] In addition, Hollywood has played a major role in distorting the image of Arabs by linking them with Nazis in all the ways we have already seen. Jack Shaheen reveals that more than 900 films produced in Hollywood since the beginning of the twentieth century present Arab Muslim characters, most of whom are portrayed in a highly negative way.[32] Such films include Albert Herman's *A Yank in Libya* (1942), Léonide Moguy's *Action in Arabia* (1944), and Steven Spielberg's *Indiana Jones and Raiders of the Lost Ark* (1981), which are all set in Second World War locales. Others, such as Menahem Golan's *Trunk to Cairo* (1965) and *Cairo Operations* (1965), Jim Abrahams's *Hot Shots! Part Deux* (1993), and Spike Lee's *Inside Man* (2006), make direct links between Nazi scientists and Arab baddies.[33]

Characterizations of the bad Arab abound in western media, including political cartoons, product advertisements, and television shows.[34] Even school textbooks have been used to enhance the idea that Arabs are vindictive people. Samir A. Jarrar concluded his study of United States school textbooks' treatment of Muslim Arabs by saying that they were shown as "[p]rimitive, backward, desert dwelling, nomadic, war-loving, . . . terrorist. The Arab world is most often depicted as . . . united in its hatred of Israel."[35] As a result of such hammering of the negative ideas of Muslims and Arab Palestinians, the United States public has only seen the Arab-Israeli conflict from the perspective of Israel.[36] Furthermore, and even more worryingly, these representations of Arabs are frequently tainted with direct and indirect allusions to Nazism and the Holocaust.

Literary Background

Perhaps unsurprisingly, political and popular media representations of Arabs are replicated in post-war popular fiction as well. Popular fiction is distinguished by its two defining attributes: its low style and its ready availability to the public. Such fiction employs colloquial expressions, erotic scenes, and vulgar styles. The books are very cheap so as to ensure wide public reach. Reeva S. Simon states that more than 600 novels published in the United States and Britain in 1985 alone had Middle Eastern themes or characters, mostly employing cultural and religious slurs against Islam and Arabs.[37] Kathleen Christison argues that the impact of popular fictional works on readers is higher than that of some other media because the former are "geared to the widest possible audience and because they are dramatic presentations—they tell stories that hold one's interest."[38] Furthermore, some novelists try to employ historical details and real incidents in order to increase credibility and a sense of realism. The problem with this is that when the novelist then introduces a stock of stereotypes, the reader will not necessarily distinguish between fiction and reality, making it "easier for the reader to accept the 'unreal' portrayal of Arabs."[39] Many of the distortions in these novels are based on the assumption that the Arab-Islamic culture is inferior to its western and Israeli counterparts and ignores the literary and scientific contributions of the Arabs to world civilizations.[40] Israel and the west are seen as siding in one block, whereas Arabs are always on the opposite side trying to conspire to bring down the state of Israel.

Importantly, some of the best-selling post-war American writers such as Saul Bellow, Norman Mailer, Irwin Shaw, Bernard Malamud, and Israel Joshua Singer are Jewish and "enthusiastically Zionist."[41] As Janice J. Terry argues, writers with pro-Zionist attitudes "recognized the effectiveness of popular fiction as a vehicle to establish and reinforce sympathy for Israel."[42] Leon Uris (1924–2003), for instance, ardently supported Zionism and made unprecedented distortions to the image of Arabs and Islam in *Exodus* (1958) and *The Haj* (1984). Uris claimed that "[I]f Israel goes down, the West goes down with them. I am thoroughly convinced of this."[43] Of course, popular fiction is often closely linked with the foreign policy ideas of the nations in which the novels are written. In this way, such novels can be used as a means of expressing fears and voicing aspirations in economic, political, and religious spheres.[44]

Much like their depictions in Hollywood films, Arab characters in popular post-war fiction are mostly portrayed as villains whose mental and physical abilities are inferior to those of westerners. They are usually presented as uneducated people who cannot understand the reality of the world around them; hence, they always lose. Their villainy is enhanced by overt linkages to the Nazi past, Nazi personages, and motifs of Arabs as lesser Nazis, for example in James H. Hunter's *The Mystery of Mar Saba* (1940), Charles L. Leonard's *Expert in Murder* (1945),[45] William Copeland's *Five Hours from Isfahan* (1975),[46] and the French writer François Ponthier's *Assignment Basra* (1969).[47] When mentioning historical events, fiction writers unilaterally overstate the historical links between the Arab world and the NSDAP. The Palestinian mufti and Al-Kaylani are constants in such fare and are almost always portrayed as inherently evil. In *Exodus,* for instance, Leon Uris refers to the mufti as the "most vile, underhanded schemer in a part of the world known for vile, underhanded schemers."[48] It is extremely rare to find positive characterizations of Arabs in novels of this genre.

As the Arab-Israeli conflict intensified in the late 1950s, Arab characters were depicted collaborating with Nazi scientists or neo-Nazi groups in order to destroy the state of Israel. The number of novels utilizing postwar settings greatly increased from this point on as well, in comparison to the novels that depict the events of the Second World War.[49] Other novels attempted to connect Arabs with the Holocaust or warned of a future risk of a similar genocidal conflagration.[50] During the 1970s, the Palestinian *fedayeen* were used in popular fiction to project a highly negative image of all the Palestinians as terrorists who conduct assassination attempts and hijacking operations anywhere and anytime. This image was introduced as a reaction to the hijacking attempts made by radical Palestinian groups in order to draw the world's attention to their cause. Writers of popular fiction have blended the Palestinian threat with the neo-Nazi movement in order to enhance the menace they supposedly represent. For example, Charles Robertson in *The Elijah Conspiracy* (1980) describes the Nazis as having "aligned themselves with dangerous men, men who feel they have been betrayed." By implication, the Palestinians have become Nazi allies and collaborators.[51]

Even instant histories—works that deal with the factual documentation of recent wars between Arabs and Israelis—are often written in a way that connects Arabs and Nazis. For instance, Michael Barak in *The Secret List of Heinrich Roehm* (1976) claims to document the 1973 October War. However, his plot is based on the Mossad attempt to capture the Nazi agents mentioned in Heinrich Roehm's list.[52] In Gay Courter's *Code Ezra* (1986), the writer attempts to narrate the history of the creation of the Jewish state in which the mufti of Jerusalem is portrayed as a murderer who is paid by the Egyptian President Sadat "to hire assassins to liquidate British officers."[53] Indeed, there are plenty of other works that tackle Arabs in the most negative manner by relating them to Nazis. Hence, writers of popular fiction and instant histories help to justify reprisal attacks by Israel and the western world against Arabs who are intentionally depicted as born criminals.[54]

In brief, popular fiction is a medium of expressing cultural and political fears and aspirations. In almost all the novels noted, the villains, both Arabs and Nazis, ultimately lose. This poetic justice technique is used to emphasize that Arabs and Nazis are interchangeable villains and that the Arab-Muslim cause is morally corrupted by association with Nazism. The implications of these associations are vital to our understanding of the usage made of Nazism in popular culture and to our understanding of the vilification of Arab society and culture in the western world.

The Novels

Popular fiction is a mirror that reflects the beliefs and cultural realities of its authors. The following novels are representative of a trend to represent Arabs as evil and to embody most of the prevalent stereotypes of Arabs as Nazis before and after the Arab-Israeli conflict. They show how the Arab image has changed from a conspirator with Nazi Germany against Britain during the Second World War to a collaborator with Nazi scientists and other Nazis to destabilize the status quo and achieve the economic destruction of Israel and the west in the post-war period.

Spencer Bayne's *Agent Extraordinary* (1944) is typical of the Arab-as-conspirator genre that was popular in English-language fiction during the Second World War. It follows an Agatha Christie–style plot involving an American detective, Hendrick Van Kill, who tries to decipher the secret of the murder of Robert King, a British archaeologist working in Baalbek. The locale for the novel is in Syria and Lebanon, and its plot describes supposedly real events that occurred in the Middle East during the Second World War. In fact, Bayne replaces Palestine with Syria and changes names in order to conceal the identity of real people and locations. The conflict itself is shown as a fight between the "British lion" and the "Axis jackals,"[55] and Van Kill finds himself caught in a complex web of intrigue and conspiracy after realizing that King was poisoned because he knew too much.[56] After a series of improbable disguises, Van Kill discovers that the mufti of Damascus, Jamal, who stands for the mufti of Jerusalem, is involved in King's death. Jamal is described as the "self-appointed Head of Islam. Spoiled scion of a fabulously wealthy aristocratic Arab family, European in sophistication, Oriental in treachery, red-headed Jamal."[57] The Mufti is characterized as corrupt and deceitful, a person willing to do anything in order to reach his objectives, including selling his soul to the highest bidder. He is a "rascal,"[58] a "suave thug,"[59] and an immoral man. The cause he fights for is defined as "political yelling"[60] that is unlawful and illegal, for he "raised the bogey of Pan-Arabism to mask his gangster-ish ambition," and he does not mind taking "any money he can get....Any money which will hire him more gangsters to make raids south of the border and to make uprisings anywhere."[61]

The depiction of the mufti as a sinister villain is connected to his siding with the Germans: "When he was making his fiery speeches in the mosque, he said he was for a free Syria and exhorted the rabble to rise against all foreigners. Like other fools Jamal thinks he can embrace the Germans and save his ribs."[62] Bayne's tone is both indignant and cynical when he shows that the mufti's national efforts are futile and doomed to fail. The mufti is also presented as dishonest because he "never kept a pledge," unlike the British, who "have certainly kept some."[63] In order to undermine Jamal's national struggle, Van Kill discovers that "son-of-a-bitch Jamal"[64] killed four different people. In an unbelievable turn of events, the author writes that Jamal had renounced his Islamic religion and converted to Christianity, which was all documented, but the papers were destroyed.[65] However, Robert King made copies and hid them. Despite all his efforts to cover up his past, the mufti was pressured to "desert his cause" and was later blackmailed by Van Kill to leave the country, which "would be to Britain's interest."[66] In many ways, *Agent Extraordinary* presents an archetype of Arab struggles against the British and allies during the Second World War. In this way, Bayne uses Nazism to reiterate the ruthlessness of Arab nationalists, willing to go to any lengths to achieve their ends.

By the 1970s, the idea that Arabs were collaborators with Nazism was well established in popular fiction. This is best shown by another novel that mirrors Bayne's treatment of Arabs in *Agent Extraordinary,* namely Geoffrey Household's *Doom's Caravan* (1971). Though the novel was published in the early 1970s, the events take place in Lebanon and

Palestine during the Second World War. The narrator works for I (b), the British counter-espionage agency that is investigating the sudden disappearance of Captain Oliver Enwin, assistant defense security officer. Like Bayne in his murder mystery, Household uses the investigation of Enwin's disappearance from Nazareth as the basis for a plot that involves a great deal of intrigue and conspiracy. The purpose of the novel is to create a suspenseful read. In the process, it depicts the conflict in the Middle East in typical fashion. Arabs are referred to as "wogs" whether they are "poor or well-dressed."[67] Rashid Ali Al-Kaylani is presented as an anti-British rebel hiding in Rome, waiting for the right moment to come and lead the fight.[68] The Nazi connection is ever-present, most notably in the form of a host of minor characters, who influence a series of unpredictable evil schemes. As for the mufti, Household refers to him as the one responsible for all the evil of the time.[69] In the novel, the hero, Enwin, goes to the desert in disguise, pretending to be a famous Arab fictitious rebel called Mokaddem in order to infiltrate the Arab group who is conspiring with the Nazis. The main aim of the group is to achieve "[u]nity and independence of all Moslem lands,"[70] and they have a deep admiration for Hitler. "They are fascinated by him. For the fanatic he is the enemy of the Jews. For the simple he has lots of those oily instruments of death which you all love, and better ones."[71] The first anti-British figure Enwin meets is a Bedouin sheikh who originally "liked the British and tolerated the Jews." But after losing a son during the mufti's revolt against the British in 1936, the sheikh "looked forward to the arrival of German armoured divisions"[72] in order to defeat the British army. The other Arab characters depicted by Household include hypocrites and homosexuals. They are all presented as traitors who are ungrateful toward the British. Above all, the Arabs' inferiority to Europeans is consistently stressed. He describes them as followers rather than leaders. When they rebel against the British, it is because the Germans are behind them. As Enwin proclaims, "I had no faith in Arab organization without a European commander."[73] The novel ends with a Zionist attack on the town where Arab rebels and Nazis are stationed, leading to a total defeat of the pro-Nazi Arab group. Hereby, the villainy of the Arab is debased much further than in Bayne's earlier novel—Household's Arabs do not just collaborate with the Nazis, they are the evil agents of an even larger and more sinister plot to do away with the Jews.

As stated earlier, the other way in which popular novels depicting Arabs utilize Nazi themes is by introducing a variety of Nazi scientists collaborating with Arab nationalists. This is most prevalent in Steve Shagan's *The Formula* (1979), which connects Nazis with Palestinian PLO members and Saudi Arabian princes. Shagan dehumanizes and emasculates the Arab characters in much the same way as Household does by depicting them as ruthless terrorists, homosexuals, and sex maniacs. By stressing Arab co-ordination with Nazis, the writer further manages to enhance the villainy of the Arab characters.

In a flashback, Shagan begins with a scene from the Second World War during which Nazis try to hide secret documents among which are those pertaining to the Genesis project, a secret hydrogenation project initiated in 1939 that aimed at creating a formula to convert coal into different types of synthetic fuel. The project, which employed Jews "recruited from the thirteen 'killing centers' throughout Eastern Europe,"[74] was supervised by Hermann Göring. Later, ex-Nazi scientists in Germany such as Diestel and Obermann try to conceal the formula because of various economic interests.

In the novel, Arabs are connected to Nazis in different ways. For example, PLO members hire a German blond called Lisa Suhrens whose father worked as the "commander of the Ravensbrück concentration camp" that witnessed the extermination of 300,000 women.[75] While Lisa's father is executed after the war, Lisa and her mother managed to escape detection. Lisa's Nazi views cause her immense frustration with the situation in post-war Germany—"I hated the new Germany for building their power structure with no regard for the past."[76] She decides to take action and joins a militant Palestinian group. She is sent to Damascus to be trained by Habash and becomes desensitized to any kind of fear or compassion—"They made me submit to every sexual indignity. With men. With women. With animals. And I didn't care, because for me it was a purge."[77] The writer tries here to distort the Arabs' cause and exaggerate their evil nature by showing their complete disregard for human life and dignity. Lisa takes orders from her leader, Dr. Habash, whose group is funded by the Saudis.[78] The use of a Nazi woman in the novel is particularly relevant as she is manipulated by Arab male terrorists, which reminds the reader of the misconceived idea that all Arab women are ill-treated and used as instruments to serve and please their men. Hence, Lisa—already debased by her Nazi connections—has become further debased by her association with Arabs.

Shagan foregrounds the Arab movement as the cause behind all the world's villainy. For instance, the "Red Brigades and NAP in Italy are trained in Havana and Damascus. The Red Army here in Germany is trained in Tripoli by Habash's group...The PLO is financed by the Saudis and the oil sheikhdoms."[79] In this way, the Nazis (which he still uses as a trope to represent evil, mindless violence, and human destruction) have become subject to an even more insidious movement, namely the Arabs, who are also represented as Nazi clones, having no language but murders and assassinations and the elimination of Jews. As Lisa claims, "I knew that terror and violence were the only means."[80]

Shagan's novel ends with Israel as the sole victor since the document that contains the Genesis formula is taken there. Here Shagan cleverly re-introduces the influence and relevance of Nazism to the modern world, by suggesting that the scientific achievement and malice created by Nazism during the Second World War has not washed away and that the world still suffers from its aftermath. Importantly, there is also an implicit admiration of the Nazis' scientific achievements, which he presents as a means of overturning the 1970s economic recession.

Similar to Shagan's treatment of the Arabs in *The Formula,* Daniel Easterman's *The Last Assassin* (1984) presents a fatal threat to the west caused by an Islamic universal jihad that is supported by Nazi scientists.[81] The author is a British academic whose real name is Denis MacEoin. He studied Islam and particularly Shi'ism at King's College, Cambridge.[82] In his novel, he refers to the Hashashun, a 12th-century Ismaili group.[83] Easterman's use of this fanatic group is intended to show the link between the past and the present as well as to indicate that Islam has been associated with murder for a long time, even though the group completely deviated from the teaching of Islam. Easterman also uses this novel as a means of expressing the western concern over the rise of Ayatollah Khomeini's power in Iran in 1979 and his threatening antiwestern policies.

The novel begins in Iran before the year 1979, when a group of Muslim fanatics called Qolhak are ordered to kill seven world leaders. The group plans to make all Muslims around the world follow a new Mahdi, or Savior, who will appear in Islam's holiest place, Mecca. During the holy pilgrimage, Muhammed ibn Abd Alah Al-Qahtani, an Arab Bedouin from Saudi Arabia, is supposed to help his brother-in-law, Juhaiman ibn Saif al-Otaybi to "proclaim his appearance on earth at the beginning of the fifteenth Islamic century,"[84] as the new Mahdi. Easterman based this part of his story on a real incident that occurred in 1979 in Mecca.[85] The writer suggests that Sunni and Shi'ite Muslims are conspiring against the world by uniting their forces in order to defeat any political or military power that opposes them. In Tehran, the leader of the group urges Husayn Nava'i to go to Saudi Arabia to be trained by the Mahdi group as the first step in the plan to assassinate the then president of the United States, Jimmy Carter.

In Easterman's book, German Nazi scientists find affinity with the new jihadists as they share the same vision of eliminating the Jews. For example, the writer introduces the ex-Nazi scientist, Professor Ernest Kleiber, head of the Deutsche Rakete und Satellit Gesellschaft (DRASAG) that produces V-2 rockets. DRASAG is connected to the neo-Nazi movement in Germany by its association with Deutsche Akiongruppe. Arabs are involved in the plot since DRASAG searches for a place to conduct their experiments, so it negotiates a "move up north to Libya, where Gaddafi plans to give them a home."[86] When the Iranian Revolution erupts, Peter Randall, the CIA operative, heads to Tehran, where he meets there with another Nazi scientist called Dr. Felix Rascher, nicknamed Izra'il, or Angel of Death. Felix is wanted by the Allies because his brother, Dr. Sigmund Rascher, was the one responsible for "the hideous 'freezing experiments' and other acts of medical sadism at Dachau."[87] Felix is suspected of being involved in his brother's criminal experiments. But he fled to Egypt in 1945 because the Egyptian government "welcomed" Nazi scientists who "in later years repaid the favour by working for them on a missile project with the purpose of destroying the Jewish herd that had taken control of Palestine."[88] According to Easterman, Egypt was in dire need of German scientists to develop its military and technological capabilities so as to be able to defend itself against foreign offenses. After three years in Egypt, Felix heads toward Iran because of the Aryan link between the Germans and Persians. Besides, Iranians admired the "inspiring example of Rashid Ali's pro-Nazi régime in Iraq,"[89] which made them yearn to follow the same ideology.

As with all the other novelists discussed, Easterman clearly promotes the Nazi-Arab allegiance as part of a wider conspiracy to eliminate the Jews. But, much like Shagan, Easterman suggests that Muslims by their nature are worse than Nazis. In describing the character of Imam Hasan, he says: "He had a wider vision, something that reminded me of the Füh-rer. He dreamt of conquering not just the Jews, but the world. His aim was to fight a jihad, a holy war, and to establish a sort of Islamic Reich."[90] Felix confesses to Randall that the Muslims he lived with are more crimi-nal than were the Nazis. "I've been with these people a long time now but I still find their ways a little strange. In some aspects they seem to me even harsher, more fanatical than my own people were."[91] The writer uses Na-zism as a touchstone to demonize Islam and Muslims and as a device to reaffirm his opinion that all Arabs are dangerous and bent on initiating a new, even more destructive, Holocaust. Felix aids the fanatical group by giving them advice on how to wage a jihad and by supplying them with nuclear devices that are supposed to be ignited over New York, Jerusalem, Moscow, and London in order to inflict a "widespread holocaust."[92]

The novels discussed in this section demonstrate the evolution and change of Arab stereotypes over time. Spencer Bayne's *Agent Extraordi-nary* and Geoffrey Household's *Doom's Caravan* fall into the same cate-gory since both focus on the Arab-Nazi alliances during the Second World War by presenting the Arab as a conspirator, for he is against the Allied forces. As for the novels written after the start of the Arab-Israeli conflict, like Steve Shagan's *The Formula* and Daniel Easterman's *The Last Assas-sin,* they depict Arabs as collaborators with ex-Nazi scientists or neo-Nazi groups in the efforts to annihilate the Jews. Islam is also linked to Nazism from the beginning by making references to the mufti of Jerusalem, but the connection is further exaggerated after the 1960s in order to discredit the Palestinian cause and its leaders.

Today, Nazism, which is viewed by most people as the embodiment of evil, has become a political cliché used to vilify opponents and justify con-flicts. Instead of being limited to its historical context, Nazism has most recently been used as a means to accuse Arab nations of guilt by associa-tion in order to pressure governments, blackmail politicians, and achieve economic and cultural gains. As Gregory Orfalea says, there is a "unique literary-political convergence" in the west represented in the fact that "crit-icism of the Nazis' heinous crimes came to mean unquestioned support for the new state of Israel,"[93] which includes collaboration between Nazis and Arab nationalists. Unfortunately, a concurrent development viewing any pan-Arab or pan-Islamic movement that called for uniting Muslims and Arabs or securing a Palestinian homeland as worse than Nazism itself also emerged. This has made it easy to paint any Arabs who disagree with the west and Israel as Nazis and provides the moral pretext to vilify and demean them. The politics of fiction and the fictions upon which politics are based closely replicate such themes. When the Bush administration decided to invade Iraq in 2003, it accused the ruling Baath party of being a Nazi regime and applied the "debaathification" system, which is reminiscent of the "denazification" process in post-war Germany. In the future western imagination, the emergence of more Arab Nazis is guaranteed. As long as Arabs continue to challenge the political and economic domination of the west in their countries, and as long as Nazism continues to maintain its jackbooted supremacy in the popular imagination, writers of popular fiction will keep on deploying Arab antagonists, standing for the forces of malice and hate, against western protagonists, representing the forces of humanity and goodness.

Notes

1. Daniel Silverfarb, *Britain's Informal Empire in the Middle East* (New York, Oxford University Press, 1986), p. 105.
2. Francis R. Nicosia, *The Third Reich and the Palestine Question* (New Brunswick, NJ, Transaction Publishers, 2000), pp. 89–90.
3. Nicosia, *The Third Reich.*
4. Stefan Wild, "National Socialism in the Arab near East between 1933 and 1939," *Die Welt des Islams,* New Series, Vol. 1, No. 4 (1985), pp. 126–173.
5. Wild, "National Socialism," p. 87.
6. Nicosia, *The Third Reich,* p. 85.
7. Philip Mattar, *The Mufti of Jerusalem: Al-Hajj Amin al-Husayni and the Palestinian National Movement* (New York, Columbia University Press, 1988), p. 28.
8. Mattar, *The Mufti of Jerusalem,* p. 17.
9. Nicosia, *The Third Reich,* pp. 88–89. Arab nationalist movements in the twentieth century were blended with pan-Arab dreams. During the late Ottoman control of the Arab world, there were some pan-Arab calls to establish an Arab homeland tied by its language and history and sometimes by the religion of Islam, such as the efforts made by Abdul Rahman al-Kawakibi (1854–1902). Later, several thinkers emerged who advocated the idea of pan-Arabism like Aziz Ali Al-Masri, who in 1911 established the Al-I'had Society in Turkey that called for an Arab homeland as a protest against the "Young Turks" movement. Some theorists followed, like Sati' al-Hussari (1879–1968), who was born in Yemen; the Syrian thinker Zaki Al-Arsuzi (1900–1968); the Lebanese intellectual Amin

Al-Raihani (1876–1947); and the Iraqi writers and journalists Ahmed Izzat Al-Adhami (1880–1936), who published a magazine called *Allissan* before 1920, and Abdulrazaq Al-Hassan (1895–1964). These figures struggled in different ways to achieve their dream, but no lasting outcomes were materialized.

10. Khalid Habib Al-Rawi, "Nazi Propaganda in Iraq," *Foreign Propaganda Directed Towards the Arab Homeland with Emphasis on Iraq* [in Arabic] (Amman, Warraq Printing Press, forthcoming).

11. Freya Stark, *Dust in the Lion's Paw: Autobiography 1939–1946* (London, John Murray, 1962), p. 2. Stark mentioned that during the Second World War, she "tried to convince the Middle East...to trust in our eventual victory. We believed in it ourselves, and during the war we succeeded." In Iraq alone, Stark's propaganda efforts persuaded more than 7,000 members to join the Brotherhood of Freedom. See Freya Stark, *East Is West* (London, John Murray, 1947), p. 165.

12. Silverfarb, *Britain's Informal Empire,* p. 105.

13. Silverfarb, *Britain's Informal Empire,* p. 139.

14. Majid Khadduri, *Independent Iraq: A Study in Iraqi Politics since 1932* (London, Oxford University Press, 1951), p. 200.

15. Al-Rawi, "Nazi Propaganda."

16. Kathleen Christison, *Perceptions of Palestine: Their Influence on U.S. Middle East Policy* (Berkeley, University of California Press, 1999), p. 56.

17. Sidney Liskofsky, "The Eichmann Case," *The American Jewish Yearbook 1961,* Vol. 62 (1961), p. 208.

18. Idith Zertal, *Israel's Holocaust and the Politics of Nationhood* (Cambridge, Cambridge University Press, 2005), p. 175.

19. Christison, *Perceptions of Palestine,* p. 112.

20. Christison, *Perceptions of Palestine,* p. 112.

21. Janice J. Terry, "Images of the Middle East in Contemporary Fiction," in Edmund Ghareeb, ed., *Split Vision: The Portrayal of Arabs in the American Media* (Washington, DC, The American-Arab Affairs Council, 1983), p. 316.

22. Christison, *Perceptions of Palestine,* p. 119.

23. Robert S. Wistrich, "The Old-New Anti-Semitism," *The National Interest,* Vol. 72 (Summer 2003), p. 65.

24. Michael Suleiman, "National Stereotypes as Weapons in the Arab-Israeli Conflict," *Journal of Palestine Studies,* Vol. 3, No. 3 (Spring 1974), p. 110.

25. Marc H. Ellis, *Beyond Innocence and Redemption: Confronting the Holocaust and Israeli Power: Creating a Moral Future for the Jewish People* (San Francisco, Harper & Row, 1990), p. 3.

26. When Israel bombed the Iraqi Tamuz nuclear reactor in 1981, some Israeli writers claimed that the attack came as a direct result of the Holocaust: "The Israelis...given their fears...with the ever-present experience of the holocaust, decided

to destroy the Iraqi nuclear reactor." Amos Perlmutter, Michael Handel, and Uri Bar-Joseph, *Two Minutes over Baghdad* (London, Corgi Books, 1982), p. 14.

27. These Muslim fundamentalists also cite quotations from western leaders as proof of their claims. In his War on Terror campaign, President George W. Bush once said: "This crusade, this war on terrorism is going to take a while" (Jonathan Lyons, "Bush Enters Mideast's Rhetorical Minefield," *Reuters,* September 21, 2001).

28. It is noteworthy that Nasser was accused of being a pro-Nazi because he hired some German scientists, though the United States and Britain employed thousands of German scientists after the end of the war.

29. Tom Segev, *The Seventh Million: The Israelis and the Holocaust,* trans. Haim Watzman (New York, Hill & Wang, 1993), p. 192. See also David G. Galin, *The Myth of Hitler's Pope* (Houston, TX, Regency Publishing, 2005), p. 139.

30. Martin A. Lee, *The Beast Reawakens: Fascism's Resurgence from Hitler's Spy-masters to Today's Neo-Nazi and Right Wing Extremists* (London, Taylor & Francis, 1999), p. 126. The United States president Franklin D. Roosevelt approved Operation Paperclip in 1945, after which German Nazi scientists were brought to the United States. See also Linda Hunt, *Secret Agenda: The United States Government, Nazi Scientists, and Project Paperclip, 1945 to 1990* (New York, St. Martin's Press, 1991), pp. 176, 204, 259. This fact was echoed in Steve Shagan's novel, *The Formula,* in which he says: "After the war the Americans, British, French, and Russians took thousands of captured German scientists back to their own countries." Steve Shagan, *The Formula* (New York, Bantam Books), p. 204.

31. Suleiman, "National Stereotypes as Weapons," p. 114. See also Janice J. Terry, *Mistaken Identity: Arab Stereotypes in Popular Writing* (Washington, DC, American-Arab Affairs Council, 1985), p. 93.

32. Jack Shaheen, *Reel Bad Arabs: How Hollywood Vilifies a People* (New York, Olive Branch, 2009), p. 20.

33. For more information on how Saddam Hussein was associated with Nazism before the first Gulf War, in 1991, see Craig LaMay, Martha FitzSimon, and Jeanne Sahadi, *The Media at War: The Press and the Persian Gulf Conflict* (New York, Gannett Foundation, 1991).

34. Gregory Orfalea, "Literary Devolution: The Arab in the Post-World War II Novel in English," *Journal of Palestine Studies,* Vol. 17, No. 2 (Winter 1988), p. 110.

35. Samir Ahmad Jarrar, "Images of the Arabs in United States Secondary School Studies Textbooks: A Content Analysis and a Unit Development" (Unpublished PhD dissertation, Florida State University, 1976), p. 161.

36. Shelley Slade, "The Image of the Arab in America: Analysis of a Poll on American Attitudes," *The Middle East Journal,* Vol. 35, No. 2 (Spring 1981), p. 160.

37. Reeva S. Simon, *The Middle East in Crime Fiction: Mysteries, Spy Novels and Thrillers from 1916 to the 1980s* (New York, Lilian Barber Press Inc., 1989), p. vii.

38. Kathleen Christison, "The Arab in Recent Popular Fiction," *The Middle East Journal,* Vol. 41, No. 3 (1987), p. 398.

39. Suha J. Sabbagh, *Sex, Lies, and Stereotypes: The Image of Arabs in American Popular Fiction,* No. 23 (Washington, DC, ADC Research Institute, n.d.), p. 5.

40. Terry, "Images of the Middle East in Contemporary Fiction," p. 317.

41. Orfalea, "Literary Devolution," p. 125.

42. Terry, "Images of the Middle East in Contemporary Fiction," p. 317.

43. Cited in Elise Salem Manganaro, "Voicing the Arab: Multivocality and Ideology in Leon Uris' The Haj," *MELUS: The Journal for the Study of Multi-Ethnic Literature of the United States,* Vol. 15, No. 4 (Winter 1988), p. 12.

44. See Ahmed K. Al-Rawi, "Foreign Policy and Its Impact on Arab Stereotypes in the 1970s–80s English Popular Fiction," in Christopher Flood, Stephen Hutchings, Henri Nickels, and Galina Miazhevich, eds., *Islam in the Plural: Identities, (Self-) Perceptions and Politic* (Leiden, Brill Publishing, forthcoming).

45. Charles L. Leonard, *Expert in Murder* (New York, Doubleday, 1945).

46. See Wyndham Martyn, *Cairo Crisis* (London, Jenkins, 1945) and William Copeland, *Five Hours from Isfahan* (New York, Bantam, 1975).

47. François Ponthier, *Assignment Basra* (London, Cassell, 1969). The novel was originally published in French in 1966 and deals with a Jew, working during the Second World War for the German Intelligence, who manages to stop a German scheme to destroy Britain's oil resources in Basra, south of Iraq. Other novels of this type include George F. Gibbs, *The Road to Baghdad* (New York, Appleton-Century, 1938).

48. Leon Uris, *Exodus* (New York, Doubleday, 1958), p. 253.

49. Novels of this ilk include Frederick Forsythe's *The Odessa File* (1972), which deals with a reporter who tracks Nazis to Egypt, where the Egyptians are trying to develop weapons with the help of Nazi scientists. Thomas Harris, who wrote the screenplay for *The Silence of the Lambs,* describes in his novel *Black Sunday* (1975) Najeer and Dahlia, Arab Palestinian fighters, as vengeful persons who are probably worse than the Nazis themselves. These two Palestinians would have felt great elation at the "restoration of Palestine to the Arabs," and Najeer "believed in holocaust, the fire that purifies." Thomas Harris, *Black Sunday* (New York, Signet, 2001), p.10. See Frederick Forsyth, *Three Complete Novels, The Day of the Jackal, The Odessa File, The Dogs of War* (Botuar, New York, Avenel, 1981). Also, Uri Dan and Edward Radley's *The Eichmann Syndrome* (New York, Leisure Books, 1977) recalls the incident of the kidnapping of Adolf Eichmann from Argentina in order to emphasize the superior qualities of the Mossad agents. The novel tackles the intrigue of hunting down a Nazi officer, and Arabs are shown as anti-Semites determined to make another Holocaust. Finally, Ken Follett's *Triple*

(London, MacDonald, 1979) presents espionage in which Israelis try to get uranium to build nuclear bombs, claiming that they are intended for the purpose of protecting themselves. In order to stress the Arab-Nazi alliance, Follett introduces the American physicist Schulz, a man of German blood, who is originally hired to build the Qattara Depression project in Egypt. Another character, Cortone, advises a Jewish man, Nat Dickstein, not to go to Palestine: "Arabs are murdering people out there. Jeez, Nat, you only just escaped from the Germans" (p. 9).

50. For instance, E. Howard Hunt's *The Gaza Intercept* (New York, Stein & Day, 1981) deals with an Arab terrorist cell that steals a nuclear weapon and ignites it over Tel Aviv. Fortunately, there are no human casualties, but Arabs are clearly shown to sympathize with Nazis. Also, Jere Maudsley's *Hunter* (New York, Jove Books, 1985) tries to implicate the Libyan leader, Muammar Qadafi, in the efforts to destroy Israel, suggesting that he is extremely anti-Semitic. When the fictional Qadafi hears that the nuclear missiles that he tried to obtain could lead to the complete destruction of the Jewish state, he begins "to laugh, to clap his hand like a child" (p. 4).

51. The plot revolves around an ex-CIA operative called David Hogan who tries to stop the new Arab-Nazi group by foiling their assassination plans during the Geneva Peace Convention. The Palestinians who receive financial and military aid from the new Nazis are shown as ruthless murderers. They are led by Dr. Abdel Haddad, leader of the Patriotic Front for the Liberation of Palestine, whose 150 members are supported by Iraq's Baath Party. Charles Robertson, *The Elijah Conspiracy* (New York, Bantam Books, 1980), pp. 96–97.

52. The writer is obviously writing a propaganda work because he himself is an Israeli author writing under the pseudonym of Michael Barak. He worked as press secretary to General Moshe Dayan during the Six Days War and served in the Israeli army. Although there is an emphasis on the Soviet-Egyptian alliance during the cold war, the author tries to link Nazis, Arabs, and communists together since they all pose a threat to the west—whether real or imagined. For example, the Soviets are shown to be building military bases in Egypt from which they will be able to "threaten any oil-producing Arab country in the Middle East." Michael Barak, *The Secret List of Heinrich Roehm* (New York, A Signet Book, 1977), p. 17.

53. Gay Courter, *Code Ezra* (New York, A Signet Book, 1986), p. 303. Even during the reign of the pro-western King Farouk of Egypt (1920–1965), the writer claims that Nazi scientists went to this country after the war because they found a "congenial atmosphere as well as a regime willing to allow them a free hand in technological development" (p. 310). As for Gamal Abdul Nasser, he is shown as an ambitious Arab and "a man to fear," for he is a "Pan-Arabist." "Israelis had long dreaded the day when an Egyptian leader would put Arab primacy ahead of Egyptian cultural pride to launch a holy war against Israel" (p. 302). Finally, Jews are shown to be on the side of the west and willing to die in order to protect western

interests. For example, the Iraqi Jew, David Raziel, helped the British in 1941 in order "to suppress Rashid Ali el-Khilani's pro-Nazi rebellion" (p. 183).

54. These novels include: Michael Barak's *Double Cross* (1968), Alan Caillou's *Who'll Buy My Evil?* (1966), Nick Carter's *Assignment: Israel* (1967), Beverly Keller's *The Baghdad Defections* (1973), F. van Wyck Mason's *Two Tickets for Tangier* (1955), Abraham Rothberg's *The Heirs of Cain* (1966), and many other titles.

55. Spencer Bayne, *Agent Extraordinary* (London, Eyre & Spottiswoode, 1944), p. 166.

56. Bayne, *Agent Extraordinary,* p. 19.

57. Bayne, *Agent Extraordinary,* p. 30.

58. Bayne, *Agent Extraordinary,* p. 35.

59. Bayne, *Agent Extraordinary,* p. 36

60. Bayne, *Agent Extraordinary,* p. 64.

61. Bayne, *Agent Extraordinary,* p. 35.

62. Bayne, *Agent Extraordinary,* p. 35.

63. Bayne, *Agent Extraordinary,* p. 103.

64. Bayne, *Agent Extraordinary,* p. 201.

65. Bayne, *Agent Extraordinary,* p. 170.

66. Bayne, *Agent Extraordinary,* p. 166.

67. Geoffrey Household, *Doom's Caravan* (London, Michael Joseph, 1971), p. 51. Of course, racial slurs of Arabs were nothing new in the English-speaking world.

68. Household, *Doom's Caravan,* p. 126.

69. Household, *Doom's Caravan,* p. 134.

70. Household, *Doom's Caravan,* p. 136.

71. Household, *Doom's Caravan,* p. 136.

72. Household, *Doom's Caravan,* p. 67.

73. Household, *Doom's Caravan,* p. 159.

74. Shagan, *The Formula,* p. 211.

75. Shagan, *The Formula,* p. 301.

76. Shagan, *The Formula,* p. 301.

77. Shagan, *The Formula,* p. 302.

78. However, Shagan seems to be unaware that Dr. George Habash, the former Christian Palestinian leader of the Popular Front for the Liberation of Palestine, opposed the policies of the PLO. In fact, the two organizations had different political agendas.

79. Shagan, *The Formula,* p. 183.

80. Shagan, *The Formula,* p. 302.

81. This novel should not be confused with Barry Eisler's *The Last Assassin* (2007).

82. See HarperCollinsCanada, "Daniel Easterman," available at http://www.harpercol lins.ca/authors/50000285/Daniel_Easterman/index.aspx?authorID=50000285 (accessed July 2009).

83. This group was known for its fanaticism and its tremendous political influence during its time. It was led from Iran by Hassan Al-Sabah, who trained his followers to assassinate Muslim leaders. The word "assassin" (in English) is derived from this group.

84. Daniel Easterman, *The Last Assassin* (London, Grafton Books, 1990), pp. 81–82.

85. For more details, see Thomas Hegghammer and Stéphane Lacroix, "Rejectionist Islamism in Saudi Arabia: The Story of Juhayman al-Utaybi Revisited," *International Journal of Middle East Studies,* Vol. 39, No. 1 (2007), pp. 103–122.

86. Easterman, *The Last Assassin,* p. 211.

87. Easterman, *The Last Assassin,* p. 365.

88. Easterman, *The Last Assassin,* p. 376.

89. Easterman, *The Last Assassin,* p. 376.

90. Easterman, *The Last Assassin,* p. 377.

91. Easterman, *The Last Assassin,* p. 371.

92. Easterman, *The Last Assassin,* p. 377.

93. Orfalea, "Literary Devolution," p. 125.

8

"Evil's Spreading, Sir—and It's Not Just Over There!": Nazism in *Buffy* and *Angel*

Cynthea Masson

In a fictional world that relentlessly explores the complexities of literal monstrosity, what purpose can figuratively monstrous Nazis serve? The Buffyverse features several references to Nazis, ranging from the occasional off-hand remark to extended war-time storylines of the *Angel* episode "Why We Fight" and the graphic narrative "Sonnenblume."[1] According to Geoffrey Winthrop-Young, "Almost any combination of swastikas, black uniforms, and German accents will ensure instant drama by providing an immediately accessible good-versus-bad set up with little need for further elaboration."[2] The Buffyverse occasionally draws on Nazi stereotypes to connote evil; for example, the *Angel* episode "Hero" (1.9) features uniform-clad, militaristic, pure-breed demons known as The Scourge, who march through the streets hunting half-breed demons to exterminate. However, throughout much of both *Buffy* and *Angel,* categories of good and evil are explicitly and repeatedly dismantled. As Gregory Stevenson explains, though "Buffy operates with a clear moral imperative" and though "it is her duty to fight evil in the service of good," nevertheless, "the boundaries between good and evil are often blurry."[3] Thus, in *Buffy,* when Giles declares, "The good guys are always stalwart and true, the bad guys are easily distinguished by their pointy horns or black hats," Buffy astutely replies, "Liar" ("Lie to Me," 2.7).

Angel himself is a vampire with a soul who "helps the helpless,"[4] and in the *Angel* episode "In the Dark" (1.3) a sadistic torturer reminds Angel, "[y]ou did terrible things when you were bad, didn't you? And now you're trying so hard to do good. But, Angel, there's nothing either bad or good but thinking makes it so." A few seasons later, Angel's son Connor asserts, "[g]ood. Evil. They're just words" ("Inside Out," 4.17). And the seemingly all-powerful but recently defeated Jasmine exclaims, "Angel, there are no absolutes. No right and wrong" ("Peace Out," 4.21). Like so many other bad guys in the Buffyverse, depictions of Nazis upset comfortable assumptions about good and evil. Nazis are not merely caricatures of evil used as an easy reference for viewers; rather, they provide a human point of comparison amid the panoply of literal demons. The Buffyverse blurs distinctions not only among demons and humans but also between bad-guy Nazis and good-guy Americans, thereby exposing the hypocrisy of a government and a nation that claims to be "the land of the free" while simultaneously exercising its military might to maintain its ascendancy.

"Why We Fight"

"We are determined that before the sun sets on this terrible struggle, our flag will be recognized throughout the world as a symbol of *freedom* on the one hand, of *overwhelming power* on the other."[5] These words, attributed to United States Chief of Staff, G. C. Marshall, mark the opening segment of Frank Capra's Second World War propaganda film series *Why We Fight.* In the identically titled episode of Joss Whedon's television series *Angel,* Angel is recruited by the United States military to recover, from "hostile territory," "a T-class German-prototype submarine" and the Americans trapped onboard ("Why We Fight," 5.13).[6] Though "the Krauts...know how to build a boat," Angel learns that its crew was unable to control their cargo: "Sub-Damonen, Genauer Vampire" (sub-demons, more precisely vampires)[7] on whom the Nazis have been "experimenting" in order to create an army. Given that Hitler's "political program" is often seen to have been guided by "the ethic of expediency," and propaganda from both the Allies and the Nazis portrayed Germany as being prepared "to fight 'by all possible means,'"[8] the use of demons by the Nazis to reinforce military supremacy seems a plausible plotline within the fantastical realm of *Angel.*

Describing the films comprising Capra's *Why We Fight,* Claudia Springer writes, "They make sweeping generalizations that dramatize old dichotomies between right and wrong, good and evil, and the 'free world versus the slave world.'"[9] *Angel*'s "Why We Fight" does just the opposite by breaking down these dichotomies—revealing that the actions of the U.S. military parallel rather than oppose those of the Nazis. Whereas, according to the "popular historical memory" explored by David Hoogland Noon, "the Second World War represents the default symbol of national virtue" for Americans,[10] in *Angel* such stereotypical virtue becomes discreditable vice. The episode could well be a response to the glorification of the Second World War perpetuated by the Bush administration in the years immediately preceding the episode (which aired February 11, 2004). Noon investigates this phenomenon, arguing that "our [American] narratives about World War II repeat familiar dualisms that bifurcate the world into mutually exclusive, opposing forces" and that the American "commemorative impulse tends to define the experience of World War II...in ways that emphasize the ideological unity of the nation in the face of 'evil.'"[11] Consequently, as Noon describes the situation, "millions were asked to believe that...a Hitlerian reincarnation had again terrorized the global peace in the form of Osama Bin Laden."[12]

However, within a few years of 9/11 and Bush's extended use of Second World War analogies in support of military decisions regarding Afghanistan and Iraq, the rhetorical tide had begun to turn.[13] Unlike the ways in which the Second World War can be historically reconstructed, neither the War on Terror nor the Iraq War fit into the just war paradigm. Angel's adventures as a United States submariner in the Second World War can be read as part of a mounting wave of protest against the body counts and inadequate explanations of the Bush administration's foreign policies. Such a critique of the United States is evident in yet another film titled *Why We Fight,* which appeared the year after Angel had fought his last good fight on television. Playing on the propagandistic title of Capra's original film, this 2005 documentary by Eugene Jarecki openly questions and criticizes United States military policies and procedures. By 2006, accusations of U.S. tyranny abounded in scholarly works and local and international media. For example, Henry Giroux contended in 2006 that "[w]hile it would be ludicrous to suggest that the United States either represents a mirror image of fascist ideology or mimics the systemic racialized terror of Nazi Germany, it is not unreasonable...to learn to recognize how different elements of fascism crystallize in different historical periods into new forms of authoritarianism."[14] Such elements of fascism in the United States military are evident in *Angel*'s "Why We Fight"—not the least of which is the revelation that the Americans are experimenting with literal demonic evil (that is, vampires) in order to strengthen their own military power against *perceived* human evil. "Why We Fight" reveals that both the Nazis and the Americans are seeking a powerful new weapon, the deployment of which is justified by self-serving propaganda.

A parallel between actions occurring in the present-day (2004) and those that occurred during the Second World War (1943) is made in "Why We Fight" through a series of flashbacks. In present-day Los Angeles, a man named Lawson arrives unexpectedly at the Wolfram and Hart offices, Angel's current place of employment. He takes hostage Angel's closest associates (Gunn, Fred, and Wesley) and then proceeds to discuss wartime events with Angel. As the episode reveals, at the time of Angel's mission, Lawson had been one of the few surviving United States servicemen aboard the submarine. Gradually, through various discussions and flashbacks, a disturbing truth about Lawson is exposed: he was sired (turned into a vampire) by Angel in 1943—an action that Angel believed necessary in order to safely recover the submarine. Lawson initially presents himself to Fred as an acquaintance of Angel's "back when [Angel] was in his patriotic phase." However, as is emphasized during the 1943 flashbacks, Angel was not so much a patriotic volunteer as he was reluctant conscript: United States military men forcibly enter Angel's room, threaten to stake him, and demand he assist in "the war effort." These men identify themselves as representatives of "a relatively new agency—Demon Research Initiative." When the man in charge calls Angel "the solution to our little problem," Angel responds, "I'm not interested." Angel is immediately beaten and told, "We don't particularly care. We figure we strap enough weight to you, you will sink, regardless of your interest." Nikki Stafford aptly describes this situation: "Angel has once again been recruited to do something that he loathes, but he's taken on the job because he has no choice."[15] Angel must "once again" work for a powerful and power-hungry organization that exploits both people and demons to increase its own power. He has no more choice with regard to joining "the war effort" than the millions of Germans who, as Wolfram Wette explains, were "forced to serve"—as, indeed, were United States prisoners "recruited" in the Second World War for special operations.[16] The Demon Research Initiative's forcefully expedient method of securing Angel's assistance to the war effort creates a notable parallel between the stereotype of Nazi coercion and the recruitment techniques of the United States military.

In "Why We Fight," the Nazis are depicted as having lost power to literal demons rather than as managing to harness their power to commit atrocities. By the time Angel arrives on the submarine, most of the

Nazis have been killed by the vampires. The one remaining Nazi poses little threat. Indeed, the Nazis are portrayed both as the victims of demonic barbarism and as the butt of the vampires' jokes. Though Spike (a vampire) initially appears to be a Nazi, sporting a black jacket and swastika-emblazoned armband, he responds to Angel's question "You're a Nazi?" with "Oh, no. I just ate one." The use of Spike's camp aesthetics here is one technique that plays down the association of Nazism with evil.[17] Even Spike's reported capture by the Nazis provides a moment for humor: "Nabbed me in Madrid. Sneaky bastards, the SS. Don't ever go to a 'Free Virgin Blood' party. Turns out it's probably a trap." Likewise, when Angel informs Spike, "We don't kill the humans till we reach land," Spike responds with a two-fingered hand gesture and the phrase "Heil Hitler!"— thus Angel, by virtue of Spike's "up yours" association, is representative of the United States military *and* Nazi dictatorship. Moreover, to the vampires (as stated by the Prince of Lies), the actual Nazis are merely "insignificant maggots." Thus, in "Why We Fight," the Nazis are not the demonic enemy, either figuratively or literally, but rather represent a *human* military force fighting, like the Americans, for what they believe.

Consequently, when Lawson tells Angel "[t]hese monsters butchered my crew," he refers not to the Nazis but to the vampires. Yet the subsequent conversation between Lawson and Angel reveals a different sort of monstrosity—one embedded in a power dynamic that demands blind obedience without the necessity of moral compunction. A good soldier is not supposed to *think* about what he has been ordered to do. In this scene aboard the submarine, Lawson attempts to understand Angel's questionable decision not to destroy the vampires:

LAWSON: They're monsters. And I don't know why we—

ANGEL: You don't need to know why. We gotta bring this sub in. Those are our orders. Isn't that the point? Following orders?

LAWSON: There's a difference between orders and purpose, sir. I didn't sign on 'cause I needed directions. Hell, growing up, I used to make fun of the military boys. Always figured they wouldn't know how to tie their shoes if someone didn't give 'em the go-ahead. Then I saw pictures of what the Krauts were doing. Evil's spreading, sir— and it's not just over there. It was on my ship, it killed my crew, and we gotta stop it! And I've been scared out of my mind since I signed on for this duty, but I can keep it together, I can even handle dying, if I know it's for a greater purpose.

ANGEL: We got a job to do. That job is gonna help us win the war. I don't need you to understand every detail—just know we're fighting on the same side. I need you to trust that I'm gonna get us all through this—safe and sound.

Though the vampires are literal demons who readily and with pleasure destroy human life—and who, in this episode, are seen to be more barbaric in that regard than the Nazis—Angel's intent is to capture rather than destroy the submarine, in the interests of the United States military's efforts to "win the war." The humans, on the other hand—both the Germans and the Americans—are apparently readily dispensable in the war effort.

As Walter E. Eaton explains (in 1947) regarding military rules, "The serviceman...was never persuaded to obey them; he was simply told to do so, and so severe were the penalties for disobedience that he usually complied."[18] Yet it is not the threat of penalties alone that keeps soldiers in line—it is also the propaganda surrounding heroism, patriotism, and the greater good. Lawson claims to have seen "pictures of what the Krauts were doing" (which, given the 1943 setting, may well be a reference to Capra's *Why We Fight*) and, thereby, to have found a purpose. Lawson is not *persuaded* by Angel regarding the specific purpose of the 1943 mission; instead, he merely obeys Angel's higher command. Though, historically, German atrocities did indeed provide Americans with a reason to fight, in Whedon's fiction Lawson is revealed to be naïve—to have found his purpose via propaganda and to be ignorant of his military's intention regarding the demons aboard the submarine. In effect, Lawson is one of the very "military boys" he negatively critiqued in his patriotic speech to Angel. The "evil" that Lawson claims is "not just over there" is, in this episode, part of the United States military's "greater purpose," which is to ensure that both soldiers and citizens avoid questioning the morality of military methodology.

According to Jarecki, Capra's *Why We Fight* "explored America's reasons for entering the war;" in contrast, warns Jarecki, "with our troops engaged in Iraq and elsewhere for reasons far less clear, I think it's crucial to ask the questions: 'Why are we doing what we are doing? What is it doing to others? And what is it doing to us?'"[19] *Angel*'s "Why We Fight" explores this dilemma not only via the 1943 discussion between Angel and Lawson but in the juxtaposed 2004 scene when Lawson repeats Angel's edict verbatim. With Gunn, Fred, and Wesley secured by wire nooses and perilously positioned on chairs, Lawson says to Angel: "I don't need you to understand every detail, but I do need you to trust that I'm gonna get us all through this, safe and sound." The juxtaposition of rhetoric used in 1943 to secure military loyalty during a "just war" with Lawson's clearly *unjust* threat to murder innocent bystanders in 2004 provides a parallel to Bush's appropriation of Second World War rhetoric to justify actions many Americans believed unjustifiable. The echoed dialogue in "Why We Fight" makes the implication clear: the expectation of blind trust or, worse, unquestioning obedience, whoever enforces it, is evil because it preempts any possibility of critiquing prevailing power arrangements.

"Why We Fight" counters what Winthrop-Young observes as a typical representation of Nazis in popular culture, where "it becomes necessary to show that the Nazis were not overcome by better-equipped, better-fed, and better-paid troops, but by better men."[20] Aboard *Angel*'s Nazi submarine, the Americans are not "better men"; they are merely trained to follow orders without the benefit of full disclosure of the military's intentions, much like their Wehrmacht counterparts or, indeed, military personnel of any nationality. When Spike finds German documents involving vampires, he must threaten the Nazi officer to attain information. Lawson, who speaks some German but does not understand the papers, acts as translator. Notably, in the midst of his repeated request for information about the papers, Lawson (speaking German) warns the Nazi about Spike: "I won't be able to stop him." Here, the American and the Nazi are allies against a common enemy, albeit momentarily. The Nazi (speaking German) says that the documents contain research: "intra-brain stimulation and power over sub-demons—more precisely, over vampires." Both Spike and Lawson readily understand the implications. "They're trying to create an army out of things like you," says Lawson or, as Spike phrases it, "an army of vampire slaves." Lawson retorts, "Only you and your fuehrer could come up with something this sick." The error and hypocrisy of this statement is announced by the Nazi, who replies (speaking German) to Lawson, "We are not the only ones doing it, my boy," and to Angel, "Are we?" In other words, what Angel knows and Lawson does not is that the Americans are also building an army of vampire slaves; thus, the United States military is as morally questionable as the German.

The experimentation on and torture of humans by the Nazis have long been cited as evidence of their uniquely evil nature, yet Spike infers from the exchange about sub-demons between Lawson and Angel that "the Yanks are after this stuff too."[21] Spike then proclaims (in regard to Lawson), "I'm not getting experimented on by his government"—yet such experimentation is precisely what happens to Spike during season 4 of *Buffy* when he is captured by the contemporary Initiative. Lawson insists, "We wouldn't do that! You don't win a war by doing whatever it takes. You win by doing what's right." Spike replies, "Yeah? Let me know how that works out for you, Popeye." Lawson is no more informed about his government's intentions than a cartoon sailor fortified with cartoon spinach.[22] In terms of his knowledge of his military's intentions, the Nazi is superior to the American. In its critique of Lawson's ignorance, Whedon's "Why We Fight" reinforces what Dan Rather contends in Jarecki's *Why We Fight:* "limiting information to cover the backsides of those who are in charge of the war is extremely dangerous and cannot and shouldn't be accepted."[23] Lawson, in his progression from innocent human to vengeful vampire, personifies the danger generated by enforced ignorance.

In the 2004 Wolfram and Hart offices, Lawson admits to being a monster; yet, arguably, his true monstrosity is that he feels nothing in response to his acts of human annihilation. He explains to Angel his current predicament—one that contrasts his original humanity with his imposed demonic existence:

> Mom, apple pie, the stars and stripes—that was good enough for me till I met you. Then I had this whole creature-of-the-night thing going for me—the joy of destruction and death—and I embraced it. I did all the terrible things a monster does—murdered women and children, tortured fathers and husbands just to hear 'em scream. And through it all, I felt nothing.

Is detachment such as Lawson's not as much a condition of literal vampirism as it is a condition of war and military indoctrination? Wette describes the results of such indoctrination by the Third Reich, stating, "[s]oldiers' sense of humanity and justice became dramatically deformed."[24] "Germans," Wette explains, "were virtually paralyzed by a military discipline that suppressed all rational reflection."[25] In 2004, just before Angel stakes Lawson, thus ending his existence permanently, Lawson pleads,

"Come on, chief. Give me a mission." This request suggests that he longs again for the "purpose" Angel took away from him at his siring—the one originally imposed upon him by the military and its propaganda and the one taken from him when he came to fully understand his government's intentions and his own role therein. Lawson's predicament is one described by Robert A. Nisbet in a 1945 article about assimilation into civilian society after the war: "[T]he soldier's life is more coherent than the civilian's, and being more coherent is more tranquil. He is spared the agonies of indecision which must torment the man who knows not what ends his life serves."[26] As Angel tells Spike in the final words of the episode regarding Lawson's attack at Wolfram and Hart, what Lawson sought was "a reason." Similarly, as Charles Lewis protests regarding the Iraq war in Jarecki's *Why We Fight,* "[t]he embedded coverage had flags and banners but no one was actually finding out the truth about the reasons, the rationales for going in."[27] "Why We Fight" counters the image of Nazis as stereotypical "theatrical villains."[28] The good-versus-evil dichotomy rendered in Capra's *Why We Fight* breaks down alongside moral certitudes in Whedon's "Why We Fight," thus drawing comparisons between the Second World War and the War on Terror as biased, hypocritical rhetorical posturing.

M. D. Feld describes the "structuring of information" in the military to be "an instrument of authority": "It apportions knowledge to rank and thus enables commanders to maintain control over subordinates.... The assertion of superior knowledge and the assertion of authority are often one and the same act."[29] "Why We Fight" implies that the power structure of the United States military (indeed, any military) turns its servicemen into monsters—a figurative implication made literal by Lawson's transformation from human to vampire. This monstrosity is not only witnessed by Angel during his 1943 mission but perpetuated by him both in 1943 and 2004. As one reviewer of "Why We Fight" suggests, Lawson has "open[ed] Angel's eyes" to his own hypocrisy.[30] At the end of season 4, Angel agrees to become CEO of Wolfram and Hart in return for the guarantee that his son, Connor, will be "safe and sound." To accomplish this, Connor is given an entirely new life; his memories of his previous life are erased. Likewise, all memories about Connor are erased from the minds of all those who knew him. Consequently, throughout most of season 5, the only person who remembers Connor is Angel. Thus Gunn, Fred, Wesley and others are working for Wolfram and Hart in complete ignorance of the reason behind

Angel's decision. When following the orders of the United States military in 1943, Angel resorted to turning someone who was "fighting on the same side" into a literal monster in order to complete his mission; in 2004, Angel must reflect on both his literal (vampiric) and figurative (authoritarian) monstrosity. As the First Evil insists in the final season of *Buffy*, "It's not about right; it's not about wrong; it's about power" ("Lessons," 7.1). Or, as Angel himself contends as part of his "Power Play" (5.21) in the penultimate episode of the series, "Power tips the scale, power sets the course, and until I have real power, global power, I have nothing." This is the predicament critiqued in "Why We Fight." The Nazi uniform alone does not itself *equate* evil. Spike is evil not because he dons a swastika but because he is a literal demon with no respect for human life. In "Why We Fight," audience expectations of a Second World War plotline, elsewhere conditioned by stereotypical Nazi signifiers, are challenged by the placement of a powerless Nazi amid the abuses perpetrated by a power-hungry United States armed force.

"The Initiative"

During the first few seasons of *Buffy*, the Scoobies find themselves battling the monstrosity of repressive ideology alongside literal demons—an ideology repeatedly compared with Nazism.[31] For example, in "Gingerbread" (3.11), Xander compares the new regime created by Principal Snyder and MOO ("Mothers Opposed to the Occult") with "Nazi Germany." This episode involves book burnings and the abuse of innocent people by anti-occult fanatics, culminating in an attempt to burn Buffy and friends at the stake. Elsewhere, Principal Snyder is referred to as "Our new Fuehrer," "a tiny, impotent Nazi," and as "Commandant Snyder."[32] Though *Buffy* is populated by myriad literal demonic enemies, even the early seasons frequently align villainy with the abuse of power, albeit via stereotypical allusions to Nazis. In doing so, *Buffy* implies that the monstrosity of Nazi ideology is not a "historical idiosyncrasy" or "radically other than the present," as James Page discusses in his analysis of the enduring appeal of the Third Reich;[33] instead, parallels to Nazism can be found in the contemporary United States.

Though the first three seasons of *Buffy* feature literal demons as the "big bad," the fourth season illustrates "an increasing move toward a more relativistic and nontraditional approach to the constituency and meaning of villainy."[34] Indeed, there is a general darkening of the series as the stakes become higher and the evil is identified as extending beyond the more adolescent trope of high school as hellmouth.[35] Thus, the demonic monsters of the opening seasons are supplanted by the human Initiative—presumably, the 1943 Demon Research Initiative is the historical forerunner to the contemporary agency. As in *Angel*'s "Why We Fight," *Buffy*'s Initiative locates sources of evil *within* communities (whether local, national, or international) and *within* species (whether human or demonic) rather than in some convenient other. Thus, fascist ideology and praxis, rather than fascists themselves, are critiqued to produce for the viewer a relevancy that is both contemporary and local.

In season 4's opening episode, Buffy refers to the Nuremberg rallies in a conversation with her friend Willow ("The Freshman," 4.1). The Nuremberg allusion is notable given that the Initiative is "a top secret branch of the U.S. Military which does research and experiments on demons and vampires."[36] Even before Buffy officially learns of the Initiative's existence and stated purpose, she and the Scoobies associate its members with a strict military regiment. Its weapon-toting agents are repeatedly spotted wearing "military garb," which Xander describes as "the latest in fall fascism" ("Wild at Heart," 4.6; "The Initiative," 4.7). Similarly, when Spike is first taken prisoner by the Initiative, knowing nothing of the agency beforehand, he wonders aloud whether his captors are the "government" or the "Nazis" ("The Initiative," 4.7). In this moment, the two organizations are indistinguishable—they are both guilty of past abuses and, therefore, equally suspect. As subsequent episodes reveal, the parallels between the Initiative and the Third Reich are extensive.

Most prominent is the Initiative's abuse of power in the realm of technology. Page argues that one of the five primary reasons the Third Reich still captures the popular imagination involves the ongoing obsession with technological achievement: "The technological advances of the Third Reich continue to hold a fascination for twenty-first century societies, perhaps precisely because we too hold technology as autonomous from morality. In this way, we tend to operate within the same discourse as the Nazi regime."[37] The Initiative protocol is comparable to Hitler's ethic of expediency as described by Steven B. Katz, who posits "two kinds of expediency that can be used to supplant an existing morality," one of which is "technological expediency, motivated by technology itself."[38] Indeed, in

Whedon scholarship, the Initiative's technological and experimental practices are referred to as "Nazi-like science."[39] Using "the latest in scientific technology and state-of-the art weaponry" ("A New Man," 4.12), the Initiative performs "xenomorphic behavior modification" for the purposes of "reconditioning the sub-terrestrials—bringing them to a point where they no longer pose a threat" ("The I in Team," 4.13). Similar to their precursors' use of vampires in "Why We Fight," the current Initiative experiments on demons with the aim of creating a new breed of soldier—this time by piecing together human and demon body parts. Adam, the resulting neo-Frankensteinian monster, becomes a destructive and life-threatening menace to humankind. Thus, in season 4, the monstrosities against which Buffy and the Scoobies rebel are those perpetrated or created by a technologically and scientifically driven military whose methodologies lead to the implementation of deadly "final solutions." *Buffy* viewers thus witness in the technological expediency of the Initiative a disturbing parallel to what Robert Skloot calls "the defining paradigm of the perversions of medical science"—that is, the experiments conducted by Josef Mengele during the Holocaust.[40] Like *Angel, Buffy* provides an unsettling reminder that Nazi ideology is "not just over there." Instead, it continues to exist both here and now.

Initiative soldiers, moreover, are trained not to distinguish among demon types—every demon, whether or not it poses a threat to human life, is considered the enemy and portrayed as such. Kristen Williams Backer explains that Nazi propaganda "frequently used the image of a monster to represent nationalities, ideologies, or ethnicities that were considered outside the narrow bounds of acceptability in the totalitarian regime."[41] The information provided to the Initiative soldiers about literal demons is likewise a form of propaganda, given that every demon is portrayed as the evil other. Thus, when Buffy accuses Riley (her boyfriend and an Initiative agent) of "sound[ing] like Mr. Initiative: demons bad, people good," Riley merely replies, "Something wrong with that theorem?" ("New Moon Rising," 4.19). Whereas Buffy believes "It's just different with different demons," Riley classifies all demons as "evil" ("New Moon Rising," 4.19). According to Breton and McMaster, this debate "underlines [Riley's] immersion in a system where a mathematical theorem might well be expected to map morality"; Buffy, on the other hand, recognizes discrimination against demons as "a form of bigotry and elevation of the human a form of Nazism."[42] Whereas "we can summarize Buffy's first moral principle as

Do not harm those who typically do not pose a threat to human beings,"[43]
the Initiative "adopt[s] a policy of maximization,"[44] perpetuating an ethic
of expediency for the capture or extermination of all demons, whether or
not they pose a viable threat.

The soldiers of the Initiative, like Lawson from "Why You Fight,"
enact unquestioning obedience, without moral compunction. Riley exem-
plifies this position when he tells Buffy, "In the military you learn to follow orders. Not ask questions" ("The I in Team," 4.13); "All my life,"
Riley explains, "that's what I've been groomed to do. They say jump, I ask
how high? I get the job done" ("This Year's Girl," 4.15). Though Buffy
questions both Riley and the Initiative—and thereby "distinguishes herself from the other soldiers not only by her dress and gender but especially
by her desire to know"[45]—Riley believes, "I know all I need to know"
("The I in Team," 4.13). Similar to Lawson's conception of his purpose,
Riley believes, "We're doing good here. Protecting the public. Removing
the sub-terrestrial threat. It's work worth doing." However, the plot arc
of season 4 makes it clear that Riley, like Lawson, is ignorant of the Initiative's true intentions. A hallmark of authoritarian regimes is a chain of
command in which a select few are in control of events while the majority
is deliberately kept in ignorance. Thus, when Giles suggests that the Initiative is "secretly . . . working towards some darker purpose—something
that might harm us all," Riley protests, "No! That's—that's not what happens there. . . . I would know" ("Goodbye Iowa," 4.14). Lawson's protest
("We wouldn't do that!") is thus echoed by the similarly uninformed modern Initiative agents. In Riley's case, however, Initiative technology takes
indoctrination one shocking step further—though he insists, "I cannot be
programmed. I'm a man," it turns out Riley has indeed been programmed,
first via a regimen of drugs and second via a computer chip inserted in his
chest. Both human and demon become military experiments in the hands
of the Initiative. As J. Michael Richardson and J. Douglas Rabb aptly describe the situation, "Riley is as much a victim of the Initiative's unethical
Nazi-like modes of experimentation as is Spike."[46] What Riley has, that
Lawson did not have, is Buffy—someone who consistently "undermines
the traditional power structures of rationalist authority."[47] Thus, when
Riley insists, "I'm a soldier. Take that away, what's left?," Buffy sup-
portively responds, "A good man" ("This Year's Girl," 4.15). Riley manu-
ally digs the computer chip out of his chest, in an graphic act of resistance
against "unethical Nazi-like modes of experimentation," thus illustrating

that resistance is possible. In this way, *Buffy* counters the lie that events are inevitable rather than products of ideology.

As further evidence that fascist praxis is embedded in its organizational structures, the Initiative is determined to limit knowledge of its activities just as the Nazis had endeavored to keep the general populace ignorant of its human experiments and genocide. In the final minutes of *Buffy*'s "Primeval" (4.21, the penultimate episode of season 4), the scenes shift rapidly between the apocalyptic battle at the Initiative headquarters and Mr. Ward (an Initiative high official), who is delivering his final orders:

> The Initiative represented the government's interests in not only controlling the otherworldly menace, but harnessing its power for our own military purposes. The considered opinion of this counsel is that this experiment has failed.... The demons cannot be harnessed. Cannot be controlled. It is therefore our recommendation that this project be terminated and all records concerning it expunged. Our soldiers will be debriefed. Standard confidentiality clause.... The Initiative itself will be filled in with concrete. Burn it down, gentlemen. Burn it down, and salt the Earth.

To the bitter end, the Initiative official sees the problem embedded in the other—specifically in the "otherworldly menace"—rather than in the Initiative's own protocols and methodologies. Though the commander admits it was "only through the actions of the deserter [Riley] and a group of civilian insurrectionists [Buffy and company] that our losses were not total," he does not advocate changing the military's course but merely concealing its destructive designs.

"Sonnenblume"

"Sonnenblume" presents a notable though far less nuanced reading of Nazis in comparison to that of *Angel*'s "Why We Fight." The graphic narrative by Rebecca Rand Kirshner (story) and Mira Friedmann (art and colors) focuses on a young slayer named Anni in 1938 Nuremberg. Its depictions of Nazis seem to be drawn straight from Second World War propaganda without benefit of any critical reading of those images. As Daniel Greenfield declares in an online review of *Tales of the Slayers,*

"Sonnenblume" is "the weakest of the tales": "predictable," "painfully obvious," "cliché[d]," and "simplistic."[48] According to Greenfield, "Sonnenblume" "is far less a story of vampires or even slayers, than it is a story of coping with human evil, in which the demonic evil of vampires is if anything secondary to the evil humans perpetuate."[49] This plotline might be commendable if the tale were indeed one of "human evil." However, what Greenfield neglects to acknowledge in his review is that the *graphic* depiction of the Nazis resorts to propaganda-based stereotypes of literal monstrosity—the open-mouthed Nazis reveal vampiric fangs. Literal vampires kill by instinct rather than moral choice or under the influence of military propaganda. Such conflation of human and monster glosses over the moral complexities that form the substance of *Angel*'s "Why We Fight" and *Buffy*'s Initiative. Thus, although "Sonnenblume" illustrates the problem of erasing individuality through military indoctrination, it also decisively (and problematically) erases human agency and free will by conflating the human being with the literal monster.

The indoctrination of Anni as a member of the Hitler Youth is established within the first few pages of the text. The first frame presents a close-up of a hand; the next frame reveals the hand belongs to a young blonde girl, the next that the girl stands among several other girls all wearing uniforms,[50] the next that these girls are marching as part of a larger group, the next that the girls are part of an even larger group, and the last frame (of the first page) that thousands of faceless people are all marching together. Meanwhile, the words "Tromp! Tromp! Tromp!" (which are featured in the final three of the six frames of the page) become progressively larger. The next page has only one large frame titled "Nuremberg, Germany, September 10, 1938." Nazi flags dominate the foreground of the frame, behind which Hitler is addressing thousands of faceless people who are crying "Heil Hitler!" The movement from the close-up of the hand to the faceless masses responding enthusiastically to Hitler emphasizes the loss of individuality, as does the accompanying text of Anni's thoughts: "I was glad to be part of something bigger than myself. I was glad not to be alone" (featured on the sixth frame of the first page). However, Anni's personal experiences outside the Hitler Youth lead her to oppose Nazi indoctrination. Through the course of the story, Anni observes increasingly violent anti-Semitism, culminating with events dated November 9, 1938 (which, though not stated in the text, marks the "November pogrom" known as Kristallnacht).[51] As a result of bearing witness to these horrors,

Anni concludes, "I finally recognize the real evil here. And now I will fight it. Now I will begin. Because I can't be like everyone else."[52] She thus reestablishes her individuality, thus illustrating the possibility of exercising free will even in the face of indoctrination. However, the tale uncritically accepts the Nazis as the source of evil without ever suggesting (as both *Buffy* and *Angel* do) that evil/fascism are reproduced in methodologies and praxis rather than the demonic other.

The Nazis of "Sonnenblume" are depicted as deprived not only of individual free will, but also of humanity itself. As with Anni in the Hitler Youth frames, the Nazis throughout "Sonnenblume" are identifiable by their uniforms; for example, the November 9 attackers are dressed in traditional uniforms: brown jackets, black pants, and a swastika-emblazoned armband.[53] However, unlike historical Nazis, the November 9 attackers also bear fangs. This suggests that the Nazis *are* vampires—which then places their violent acts in the realm of the literally monstrous or demonic rather than the human. Most vampires (as opposed to several other types of demons) on both *Buffy* and *Angel* are portrayed to be evil by nature rather than by choice. Thus "Sonnenblume" suggests that Nazis are naturally evil demons rather than human beings capable of exercising free will against monstrosity. Whether intentional or not, the conflation of vampire and Nazi in this text perpetuates a problematic stereotype that both Anni and the text appear otherwise to fight against: the transformation of human into monster. This transformation is evident in the text's depiction of propaganda against the Jew. One of the Nazis explains to Anni and others, "We are Germans. We are good. We are pure. And our very blood is being threatened."[54] He then points to an old, disfigured person standing behind him and says, "Look carefully at this face. This is the threat to us. This Jew—all Jews—will contaminate our blood with their evil intent." In the next frame, which represents Anni's dream, the disfigured Jew stands directly beside a vampire. Beside both monstrous figures stands Mr. Green, a Jewish man from Anni's neighborhood. This image contrasts the actual human with both the literal and figurative monster. If Nazis are to be held accountable for acts against humanity, they must themselves be considered *human* like us—as a society and as individuals capable of choosing to commit or to refrain from monstrous acts.

Nazi propaganda depicted its enemies, including Americans, as monsters: "America's diversity became an unwieldy conflation, and all were lumped together into the feared Other. The monster was the perfect form for this composite Other...the making of monsters exploits difference, whereas the Nazi-championed quest for a master race depends on eliminating it."[55] Neither the Americans nor the Nazis were literal monsters; they were human beings responsible for the atrocities they committed. However, by conflating the Nazi with the vampire, "Sonnenblume" regrettably reproduces rather than critiques both Nazi and U.S. propaganda.

Conclusion

Rhonda Wilcox in *Why Buffy Matters* posits, "The characters in the Buffyverse do not live in the emotional world of *The Sound of Music;* [the film's] Nazis are eminently more escapable than the vampires and demons which incarnate the evil that imbues Buffy's world."[56] The historical Nazis may have been escapable for some, but resisting the ideology requires constant vigilance on the part of the individual. Through its depictions of Nazis and military ideology, the Buffyverse warns against unquestioning obedience, hypocrisy, and the justification of immoral acts as heroism or patriotism. In doing so, it proposes critical thinking as a means of defeating both literal and figurative demons. Post–Second World War and post-9/11 government propagandists have found it convenient to locate evil in the monstrous other rather than in our own coercive state apparatuses. Inciting support for conflict is easier if the enemy is clearly marked, whether by supposed racial identifiers, forms of attire, physical characteristics, or even fangs. The use of real and metaphoric Nazis in the Buffyverse range from the uncritical reproduction of Nazi propaganda to the much more problematized use of Nazi tropes to interrogate that most universal of human philosophical puzzles: how do we account for the existence of evil in the world and how do we defeat it?

Notes

With special thanks to Kathryn Barnwell for moral support and editorial suggestions on this chapter.

1. "Buffyverse" refers to the worlds of *Buffy the Vampire Slayer* and *Angel*.
2. Geoffrey Winthrop-Young, "The Third Reich in Alternate History: Aspects of a Genre-Specific Depiction of Nazi Culture," *The Journal of Popular Culture,* Vol. 39, No. 5 (2006), p. 879.

3. Gregory Stevenson, *Televised Morality: The Case of Buffy the Vampire Slayer* (Lanham, MD, Hamilton Books, 2003), pp. 73, 75.

4. This phrase is the motto of Angel's detective agency in season 1.

5. The quotation is part of the onscreen text of "Prelude to War," the first of seven films comprising Capra's *Why We Fight* (1942). The italics replace the underlining used in the original.

6. Quotations from *Buffy* and *Angel* will be cited by episode name, followed by season and episode numbers. *Buffy* aired from 1997 to 2003. Angel aired from 1999 to 2004. Both series are available on DVD from Twentieth-Century Fox Home Entertainment.

7. The translations are generously provided by Katharina Rout (Vancouver Island University).

8. "The Ethic of Expediency: Classical Rhetoric, Technology, and the Holocaust," *College English,* Vol. 54, No. 3 (1992), 263; Wolfram Wette, *The Wehrmacht: History, Myth, Reality* (Cambridge, MA, Harvard University Press, 2006), p. 151.

9. Claudia Springer, "Military Propaganda: Defense Department Films from World War II and Vietnam," *Cultural Critique,* Vol. 3 (1986), p. 152.

10. David Hoogland Noon, "Operation Enduring Analogy: World War II, the War on Terror, and the Uses of Historical Memory," *Rhetoric and Public Affairs,* Vol. 7, No. 3 (2004), pp. 348, 343.

11. Noon, "Operation Enduring Analogy," pp. 345, 348.

12. Noon, "Operation Enduring Analogy," p. 352.

13. Abbott Gleason writes that "The United States has achieved its overwhelming military power at the same time and in close connection with a revolt against liberalism, which is arguably as deep as the one that reached its climax with the establishment of the totalitarian regimes of the 1920s and 1930s." Abbott Gleason, "The Hard Road to Fascism," *Boston Review,* Vol. 28, No. 3–5 (2003), available at http://www.bostonreview.net/BR28.3/gleason.html (accessed February 15, 2009).

14. Henry A. Giroux, "Dirty Democracy and State Terrorism: The Politics of the New Authoritarianism in the United States," *Comparative Studies of South Asia, Africa and the Middle East,* Vol. 26, No. 2 (2006), p. 164.

15. Nikki Stafford, *Once Bitten: An Unofficial Guide to the World of Angel* (Toronto, ON, ECW Press, 2004), p. 322. The phrase "once again" refers to Angel's recruitment by Wolfram and Hart—the immoral law firm against which Angel fights numerous battles.

16. Wette, *Wehrmacht,* p. 158. U.S. prisoner recruitment is depicted in Robert Aldrich's film *The Dirty Dozen* (1967).

17. For a discussion of Spike and camp, see Cynthea Masson and Marni Stanley, "Queer Eye of that Vampire Guy: Spike and the Aesthetics of Camp," *Slayage,* Vol. 22 (2006), available at http://www.slayageonline.com/essays/slayage22/Masson_Stanley.htm (accessed February 20, 2009).

18. Walter Eaton, "The Military Environment," *Social Forces,* Vol. 26, No. 1 (1947), p. 89. Wette makes comparable arguments about the German military (chapter 4 of Wette, *Wehrmacht*).

19. Eugene Jarecki, *Why We Fight,* CBC Newsworld, Online Promotional Commentary for August 24, 2006, available at http://www.cbc.ca/documentaries/whywefight. html (accessed February 3, 2009).

20. Winthrop-Young, "The Third Reich," p. 882.

21. The historical parallel is the race to create a nuclear bomb.

22. Hodges (an American) refers to Angel as "some sort of super soldier, like Steve Rogers or Captain America." Captain America is a comic book hero "created in 1941…as a morale builder for the country." Adam Shreve, "'Buenos Noches, Mein Führer': A Look at Nazism in Popular Culture," *Journal of Popular Culture,* Vol. 35, No. 4 (2002), p. 108.

23. *Why We Fight* (2005).

24. Wette, *Wehrmacht,* p. 159.

25. Wette, *Wehrmacht,* p. 159.

26. Robert A. Nisbet, "The Coming Problem of Assimilation," *The American Journal of Sociology,* Vol. 50, No. 4 (1945), p. 264.

27. *Why We Fight* (2005).

28. Robert MacDougall, "Red, Brown and Yellow Perils: Images of the American Enemy in the 1940s and 1950s," *Journal of Popular Culture,* Vol. 32, No. 4 (1999), p. 66.

29. M. D. Feld, "Information and Authority: The Structure of Military Organization," *American Sociological Review,* Vol. 24, No. 1 (1959), pp. 18–19.

30. Rae, "Review of *AtS,* Episode 5.13: Why We Fight," *RTVW Online,* February 12, 2004, available at http://www.ramblingsofatvwhore.com/2004/02/12/ review-of-ats-episode-513-why-we-fight/ (accessed February 9, 2010).

31. "The Scoobies" refers to Buffy's team of friends.

32. "The Puppet Show" (1.9); "Becoming, Part One" (2.21); and "Band Candy" (3.6). Additional Nazi references are made in season 1: In "The Witch" (1.03), Buffy refers to Amy's mother as "Nazi-like," to which Willow responds "Heil"; in "I Robot, You Jane" (1.08), a student realizes his essay has been modified to argue, "Nazi Germany was a model of a well-ordered society"; in "Nightmares" (1.10), Xander explains, "I'm unruffled by spiders. Now, if a bunch of Nazis crawled all over my face—." The same episode features swastika graffiti.

33. James Page, "Deconstructing the Enduring Appeal," *Journal of Intercultural Studies,* Vol. 29, No. 2 (May 2008), pp. 193–194.

34. "Big bad" is the term applied to the primary enemy of each season's main plot arc; Tanya Krzywinska, "Hubble-Bubble, Herbs, and Grimoires: Magic, Manichae- anism, and Witchcraft in *Buffy,*" in Rhonda V. Wilcox and David Lavery, eds.,

Fighting the Forces: What's at Stake in Buffy the Vampire Slayer (Lanham, MD, Rowman and Littlefield, 2002), p. 183.

35. Buffy's high school in Sunnydale, California, is located above a hellmouth—a portal between earth and hell that attracts demons of various sorts.

36. Richard Greene and Wayne Yuen, "Why We Can't Spike Spike?: Moral Themes in Buffy the Vampire Slayer," *Slayage,* Vol. 2 (2001), available at http://slayage online.com/essays/slayage2/greeneandyuen.htm (accessed February 1, 2009).

37. Page, "Deconstructing the Enduring Appeal," p. 193.

38. Steven B. Katz, "The Ethic of Expediency: Classical Rhetoric, Technology, and the Holocaust," *College English,* Vol. 54, No. 3 (1992), p. 264. The other kind is "political expediency, motivated by a 'concern' for the State" (p. 264).

39. Michael Richardson and J. Douglas Rabb, *The Existential Joss Whedon: Evil and Human Freedom in Buffy the Vampire Slayer, Angel, Firefly and Serenity* (Jefferson, NC, McFarland & Company, 2007), p. 71.

40. Robert Skloot, "Stage Nazis: The Politics and Aesthetics of Memory," *History and Memory: Studies in Representation of the Past,* Vol. 6, No. 2 (1994), p. 72.

41. Kristen Williams Backer, "*Kultur-Terror:* The Composite Monster in Nazi Visual Propaganda," in Niall Scott, ed., *Monsters and the Monstrous: Myths and Metaphors of Enduring Evil* (Amsterdam, Rodopi, 2007), p. 81.

42. Rob Breton and Lindsey McMaster, "Dissing the Age of MOO: Initiatives, Alternatives, and Rationality," *Slayage,* Vol. 1 (2001), http://www.slayageonline.com/essays/slayage1/bretonmcmaster.htm (accessed February 10, 2009).

43. Greene and Yuen, "Why We Can't Spike Spike."

44. Breton and McMaster, "Dissing the Age of MOO."

45. Amelie Hastie, "The Epistemological Stakes of *Buffy the Vampire Slayer:* Television Criticism and Marketing Demands," in Elana Levine and Lisa Parks, eds., *Undead TV: Essays on Buffy the Vampire Slayer* (Durham, NC, Duke University Press, 2007), p. 83.

46. Richardson and Rabb, *Existential Joss Whedon,* p. 67.

47. Breton and McMaster, "Dissing the Age of MOO."

48. Daniel Greenfield, "Sonnenblume," "*Buffy the Vampire Slayer—Tales of the Slayers—*Sonnenblume, Nikki Goes Down, Tales," *HubPages,* available at http://hubpages.com/hub/Buffy_the_Vampire_Slayer_-_Tales_of_the_Slayers_-_Sonnenblume__Nikki_Goes_Down__Tales (accessed March 5, 2009).

49. Greenfield, "Sonnenblume."

50. The uniforms appear to be those of Bund Deutscher Mädel (League of German Girls). For illustrations, see "Nazi Uniforms," *German Propaganda Archive,* available at http://www.bytwerk.com/gpa/uniforms.htm (accessed March 5, 2009).

51. "The Morning after *Kristallnacht* in Berlin: Shattered Shop Windows (November 10, 1938)," *German History in Documents and Images,* available at http://

germanhistorydocs.ghi-dc.org/sub_image.cfm?image_id=1956 (accessed March 6, 2009).

52. During training, Anni receives advice from an older man: "There is evil all around us.... You must be able to recognize evil."

53. The November 9 attackers wear the traditional uniform (Traditionsanzug) of the SS. The man in charge of the operation appears to don the uniform of the *Allgemeine SS*—however, given the lack of visible insignia, his rank remains unclear. See "Nazi Uniforms."

54. This man appears to wear the uniform (*Dienstanzug*) of a group leader. See "Nazi Uniforms."

55. Backer, "*Kultur-Terror*," p. 91.

56. Rhonda Wilcox, *Why Buffy Matters: The Art of Buffy the Vampire Slayer* (London, I.B. Tauris, 2005), p. 194.

9

"Keep Feeling Fasci/nation": Neofolk and the Search for Europe

Emily Turner-Graham

> Josef Klumb (lead singer of Von Thronstahl): Warszawa! It's an honour for us to play here in Poland...because the connection between you and us is we are the underground, the true sons and sisters and brothers of Europe, of the true Europe, not the fucking EU!
> Crowd: Europa! Europa! Europa wins! Klumb: Europe means not EU, it means you and us (*indicates Von Thronstahl*)
> Crowd: We are Europa!
> *"Victoria"—a Fascist marching song—and Von Thronstahl's "Imperium Internum" then play, Von Thronstahl drinks a toast, and the guitarist appears to give the Nazi salute.*[1]

> To play devil's advocate for the most demonic movement in history is still heresy. It is like trying to redeem the swastika from its obvious associations. The moment you touch it, you play with fire.[2]

Introduction: "Music as a Medium for Something Else"

There is considerable complexity inherent in defining the musical genre of Neofolk. To the mainstream music market, it is virtually unknown. Within the Neofolk scene itself, those who claim to be exponents or fans of it cannot even always agree on exactly what defines it. Broadly speaking, Neofolk is a musical form that brings together folk, experimental, and industrial elements. But statements such as those of musicians Josef Klumb and Richard Leviathan make clear that this subculture demands attention in relation not only to its musical expression but also for its political and social stance and its representation of both historical and contemporary questions of European identity. Indeed, many of these bands "play with fire," in the words of Richard Leviathan, by invoking the symbols and the ideas of the Nazi era.

Neofolk grew out of the postindustrial and dark music scenes of the late 1980s and 1990s. Groups such as Death in June, Sol Invictus, and Current 93 are regarded as the vanguard of the genre. These groups continue to produce music and have influenced other prominent Neofolk acts such as Der Blutharsch, Blood Axis, Von Thronstahl, and Ostara. Anyone expecting the comparative acoustic gentleness of the folk musicians of the 1960s, may find themselves taken aback by much of Neofolk—and not necessarily just because of its sound. Lyrically, Neofolk predominantly focuses on historical themes, as well as spirituality, romanticism, and occultism. While some Neofolk groups such as Von Thronstahl, Der Blutharsch, Triarii, or Rose Rovine e Amanti often favor the harsh rhythms of martial drumming or electronically generated sound or "noise,"[3] others, like Ostara, Darkwood, Blood Axis, or Sol Invictus, often perform accompanied only by a guitar, a violin, or another single instrument. Groups such as Der Blutharsch, Von Thronstahl, Blood Axis, and Ostara have garnered considerable controversy for their employment and interpretation of images and ideas from the fascist era more generally and the Nazi era specifically, and it is this controversy that forms the core of this chapter. Other groups within the broad Neofolk genre completely reject this thematic emphasis, but they will be the subject of another chapter altogether.

Part of Neofolk's importance nevertheless lies in this very breadth—in the considerable variety of music and attitudes encompassed loosely by the moniker—and in the considerable capacity of the music to attract a wide assortment of fans and, therefore, in the unique comment Neofolk in all its forms makes on the world around it. Richard Leviathan, lead singer of the British-Australian Neofolk group Ostara, defines the genre as follows, highlighting at once the inadequacy of simplistic definitions, Neofolk's diversity, and its dark side:

> There were a handful of artists who, through various influences (musical, aesthetic, esoteric and intellectual), started to produce music that explored new territory beyond the limits of pop or rock....Ultimately

what we have is not a movement but the recognition of a broad and branching path that these artists embarked upon, embracing ideas and images that are inspired by a deeper awareness of history, mythology, magick, and symbolism. Ironically, the term *Neofolk* is derived from a perception that seeks to condense the peculiarities and idiosyncrasies that are intrinsic to the originality of what later constituted a genre.... The label helps as a signifier to illustrate certain similarities of approach but there is no single definition that suffices to encapsulate the whole.[4]

Despite differences of approach, all of these groups can be seen to have one thing in common with each other and their folk music predecessors: this is the music of protest. This is "[m]usic as a medium for something else."[5]

Stephanie Obodda suggests that Neofolk music performs a positive role in pushing Nazi symbols confrontationally into popular culture. By forcing its audience to consider the crimes of the Nazi regime and the dark underbelly of Europe's past more broadly, the bands involved are "dar[ing] to depict the killers themselves"[6] and in so doing "demystify[ing]" the symbol of the swastika.[7] Further, Obodda firmly points out that a distinction must be made between Neofolk groups and outright neo-Nazi bands, such as Landser and Skrewdriver, since "[Neofolk bands] do not seek the institution of a new Nazi state, nor do their lyrics advocate violence against minorities."[8] Rather, "the bands' use of the [Nazi] aesthetic... resemble the very techniques used by the avant-garde of the early 20th century—especially photomontage artist John Heartfield—against the Nazis."[9] Obodda suggests that Neofolk is part artistic expression and part societal commentary, but nothing more. In this regard, it is not relevant "to simply determine whether [or] not the artists in question are 'Nazis.'"[10] Obodda aims to move beyond the standard "finger pointing" approach that is often attached to artists who engage with Nazi or neofascist themes.[11]

In 2008, Adam Leigh went even further to argue that in Neofolk music "[t]here are no value judgments about rights and wrongs. There is no commentary at all."[12] Neofolk's connection to Nazism is little more than "just fascination." Indeed, through this music, the trauma and complexity of Europe's tumultuous twentieth century, and particularly its Nazi history, has been assuaged and, by definition, its disturbing impact on European identity has been ameliorated. Rather, Leigh argues, its still-distressing symbols have been converted into a series of evocative but otherwise emotionless props. They speak a symbolic language and nothing more. Like the images on the album sleeves, Industrial music is often oppressive and unpleasant. The dark packaging augments the dark music. The visuals relate to dark periods in recent history, including the Second World War and the Holocaust, that are hardwired into western consciousness. They require no explanation, and as such are a preexisting set of evocative references.[13]

This chapter seeks to pick up on some of these important conclusions that have thus far been drawn about Neofolk, conclusions that strike at the very essence of how one of the most devastating periods of human history—the fascist era more generally and the Nazi era specifically—should be represented and understood popularly today. How is it that the evocative and disturbing images of this era no longer require explanation? Indeed, the use of these images in any popular context requires more explanation than ever as the tumult of the 1930s and 1940s recedes further into the past but the fascination with fascism continues unabated. So too, the fact that the images and ideas of the fascist movements of Italy, Germany, Spain, and Romania have been gathered together by Neofolk groups and fans alike—and indeed by the general public as a whole in interpreting this musical genre—without particular distinctions being made between each specific case is an important one and contributes to broader arguments surrounding the definition of fascism itself. All extreme-right representations today are instantly Nazi. But *is* German National Socialism the same as Italian Fascism? And what does Neofolk's grab-bag approach to the question tell us?

This chapter seeks to broaden significantly the focus of Obodda's and Leigh's arguments. It is certainly true that "finger pointing" serves little purpose in the consideration of this controversial musical genre, but the political beliefs of the artists involved are by no means irrelevant. Similarly, while societal commentary through artistic expression partly explains the musical output and aesthetic representation of these groups, it is not sufficient to define Neofolk solely in artistic terms. The artists considered here each present a profoundly intricate weltanschauung, and in facing difficult and complex representations of Europe's tumultuous past, we are forced to reconsider our own attitudes to that past. As a result, we are confronted with the realization that rather than these symbols and the history behind them having no contemporary or nonartistic meaning, they can, in fact, tell us much about the meaning of European identity today.

Neofolk is an important window into current popular dialogues on European identity, its composition and the way in which Europe's cataclysmic past and connections to fascism and Nazism contribute to Europeans' understanding of their selves.

The key theme of protest that links all Neofolk musicians is the question of European identity, although they disagree on what that identity is and how it should be represented. Each group espouses a hidden Europe, an alternative Europe, a Europe that departs from the path of the mainstream and from Europe as it currently stands. In the words of Richard Leviathan, "Neofolk is not protest music in the sense of trying to fight for a cause. It is a romantic rebellion against the prosaic and quotidian qualities of the age, but it is not a rabid rant in the way that punk attacked the conservative establishment. It is a more subtle but no less sinister vision of the bleakness of the world."[14]

However, precisely because it clashes with established ideas of identity, Neofolk is very much protest music, but, as with the music itself, the nature of its protest—though unified in a root cause—differs dramatically in interpretation. Indeed, in defining Neofolk as a "romantic rebellion," there is much to connect Neofolk with protest movements predating the countercultural groups of the 1960s, that is, with Europe's *völkisch* circles of the late nineteenth and early twentieth centuries and their romantic visions of a white Europe.[15] The complexity inherent in the Neofolk genre is made clear in a 2006 performance by the Danish band Die Weisse Rose (the name is a clear reference to the German wartime resistance group). Dressed in uniforms reminiscent of the Hitler Youth, they stand solemnly on stage holding flaming torch lights as a recording of Marlene Dietrich singing the 1960s folk classic "Sag' Mal, wo die Blumen sind" ("Where Have All the Flowers Gone?") plays, along with a recording of an air-raid siren. Thus, they combine the voice of Weimar-era rebel Dietrich, a Nazi-era aesthetic, and a key protest anthem of the 1960s to astonishing effect.[16]

The Internet has provided a vast forum for Neofolk protest, in addition to providing a vehicle for the spreading of their ideas and gathering of their fans. Put simply, "[w]ith its global reach, [the Internet] is far more useful than putting a few stickers on lamp posts."[17] Almost all of the groups that have been considered for this chapter have a considerable Internet presence. Through personal web sites, MySpace and Facebook sites, and Twitter and Youtube, fans can maintain an ongoing presence in a community around a band, and the fanbase itself can be expanded.[18] If web presence is a gauge, popular interest in Neofolk music is on the rise, is interconnecting with an array of virtual cultural networks, and is providing a richly visual representation of a number of the contemporary arguments surrounding European notions of self. The Internet provides a valuable and highly accessible tool for spreading and maintaining the popular fascination with fascism.

In order to explore the key themes of the Neofolk genre more fully and thereby understand their connection to and interpretation of the question of Europe in the context of fascism and Nazism, this chapter explores two notable exponents of this subculture. Both bands have been selected on the basis of their professed views and their subsequent capacity to demonstrate two of the more controversial and striking strands within Neofolk in relation to an idea of Europe: Von Thronstahl represents a more politicized, extreme right-wing voice, and Ostara a highly conservative though more esoteric perspective. Both bands, while approaching the notion of Europe in their own specific way, touch upon similar themes, allowing for direct comparisons to be made.

Both Von Thronstahl and Ostara protest the course currently being taken by the modern world and, most particularly, modern Europe. Although they approach this protest from notably disparate angles, they both nonetheless remonstrate on the basis of what they see as unacceptable challenges to European national identities and cultures. In their eyes, at worst, modern Europe with the European Union at its head is becoming a mediocre, homogenized, police state, a poor cousin to and pale imitation of the United States. At best, it stands to lose key elements of what these two groups regard as its innately and importantly European characteristics.

They make this protest by using their music and aesthetic to refer back to historical figures and historical periods they believe displayed a better notion of European identity. Their historical focus is primarily on the Nazi and the fascist eras. In most regards, Nazi and fascist symbols are used interchangeably as transposable emblems of protest in the fascism-phobic post–Second World War world. As Susan Sontag points out in her renowned essay "Fascinating Fascism," fascism, or at the very least its symbols, offers "fantasies of community, order, identity ... competence ... [and] ... legitimate authority."[19] In the uncertainty of the twenty-first century, beset by ongoing wars, economic and environmental strife, and challenges to almost all of the previously understood cornerstones of western society—such as national identity, the church, and other long-established power structures—the appeal of such an apparently ordered world is clear, provided one is prepared to overlook the extraordinarily high price to be paid for such order.

Remarkably, Von Thronstahl and Ostara make their protests by reversing the symbols of the fascist and Nazi era. That is, rather than the fascist- and Nazi-era persecution of minorities, these groups claim that in the present era, *they* are persecuted because they dare to utilize assorted images and ideas that contemporary society has deemed unacceptable. By employing forbidden images, they claim to be protesting against a society that does not allow for freedom of speech and does not read history clearly because of the agenda of those in power. Josef Klumb, for example, has been regularly photographed dressed in black jodhpurs and jackboots, which he identifies as "my SS boots."[20] Von Thronstahl's CD covers bear the symbol of Die Schwarze Sonne (the Black Sun), band t-shirts display the fasces, and their songs boast titles like "Heimaterde, Mutterboden, Vaterland" ("Native Ground, Mother Soil, Fatherland," 2000) and "Das Neue Reich" ("The New Reich," 2001). Ostara, meanwhile, extensively reference the works of far-right intellectual Julius Evola and, as we shall see, take an interesting stance on the place of the Third Reich in history.

These bands use such imagery to provoke and differentiate themselves from the mainstream but also to promote a renewed consideration of the history of Europe in the first half of the 20th century. In so doing, they attempt to depict themselves in the unusual role of countercultural right-wingers—at once marginalized, alternative, and right-wing. In exploring elements of the right-wing counterculture, I pick up where Graeme D. Macklin left off in his analysis of Neofolk musician and extreme right political activist Troy Southgate.[21] It is worth noting that the idea of a right-wing counterculture played a considerable part in the success of the Nazis in the 1920s and 1930s, when they similarly portrayed themselves as conservatives striking out against the apparently wrong-headed leftist mood of their time, in many respects as an extension of the *völkisch* movement.[22]

Von Thronstahl and *der rechte Kulturkampf*

Since his beginnings as a musician in the early 1980s, the lead singer of Von Thronstahl, Josef Klumb, has carved a role for himself as a key figure in Neofolk's right-wing counterculture or, more precisely, its *rechte*

Kulturkampf (right-wing cultural struggle).[23] He has frequently caused controversy, mainly due to his pronounced interest in the fascist and Nazi eras and aesthetics, but also because of his European nationalism and, to a lesser extent, his Catholic conservatism. Klumb has been classified as a right-wing extremist by the Dokumentationsarchiv des österreichischen Widerstandes,[24] has worked with the far-right National Democratic Party of Germany's (Nationaldemokratische Partei Deutschlands or NPD) Saxon parliamentarian Jürgen Gansel,[25] is associated with the controversial record company VAWS,[26] has been lauded by American white nationalist group Stormfront as producing "good white nationalist music,"[27] and often appears dressed in a Nazi-like uniform of black or brown jodhpurs and jackboots. In 1995, Klumb and his brother, Bernhard, formed Von Thronstahl, a martial industrial group that found a place within the Neofolk genre.[28]

The band's name suggests both aristocratic symbolism by way of the prefix "Von" and also a fascistic or at least militaristic harshness in the literally translated tag "Throne of Steel." Klumb's belief in a conservative revolution during the Second World War represented by the likes of Hitler's would-be assassin Claus von Stauffenberg is also suggested in the band's pseudo-patrician name. On Cold Spring's web site (Von Thronstahl's record label), the motivation for starting the band is stated as follows:

> The main reason to form Von Thronstahl was a longing to make music & art which would be more attached to a real European heritage and not to a freemasonary, anarchic tradition of false liberty, which means lawlessness and rootlessness. Von Thronstahl should show the way back to a majestic kind of pride, with solid values.[29]

Von Thronstahl's "solid values" are represented strongly in the band's lyrics and very precise aesthetic, which reveal a concentrated focus on the question of European identity, with distinct neofascist overtones. The lyrics of "Return Your Revolt into Style" are a striking example.[30] One of the original accompanying video clips of this song opens with an image of the Italian fascist fasces with the words "Fasci[/]nation" and "Return Your Revolt into Style" superimposed over it, thus twinning historical Italian fascism with Von Thronstahl's current message and so bringing a version of fascism into the present. It then uses footage of Mussolini, marching fascist children, and surging Italian crowds to emphasize the apparent popularity and aesthetic appeal (style) of the fascist era and its ideals. There is no appearance of irony in the clip's use of these images; they are presented with a voiced exhortation to "Follow the leader/look at the leader…[and to]…walk in line." This is exacerbated by the martial rhythm enunciated in the chorus: "left right, left right." A later version of the clip shows an excerpt from Leni Riefenstahl's notorious 1935 propaganda film for the Nationalsozialistische Deutsche Abeiterpartei (NSDAP), *Triumph des Willens* ("Triumph of the Will"), which serves much the same purpose and also underlines the manner in which Von Thronstahl see Italian fascism and National Socialism as essentially interchangeable symbols of extreme right-wing protest.

The title of the song "Der Sonne Sieg ist unser Heil" translates as "The Victory of the Sun Is Our Salvation." Coupled with the use of a version of the Black Sun (Die Schwarze Sonne) on the record's cover, this strikes another note with both historical fascism but also contemporary neofascist ideas. The occult symbol, the Black Sun, was adopted by the Nazi SS.[31] It has been interpreted as three interlocked swastikas or twelve reversed *Sig* runes. For Heinrich Himmler, it was used to recall the 12 knights of the Arthurian Round Table at the SS castle, Wewelsburg. It has been more recently adopted by many neo-Nazis as an alternative to the banned swastika.[32] The use of both "Sieg" and "Heil" in the same line by Von Thronstahl also suggests that it is being used as an alternative to the banned traditional Nazi greeting (that is, rather than "Sieg Heil!"). The sun can also be seen as a symbol of renewal and rebirth, which would be viewed as fitting by neo-Nazis. Finally, reference to the Black Sun highlights Klumb's association with noted conspiracy theorist Jan van Helsing, who is particularly fixated on this symbol and its meaning.[33]

The breaking up of the word "Fascination" to emphasise separately "fasci" and "nation" as well as the word's original meaning does, however, suggest an ironic touch on the part of Von Thronstahl. They are either knowingly tapping into Susan Sontag's essay on "Fascinating Fascism" or, more likely, simply exhibiting what Sontag described: the long-standing morbid fixation many westerners seem to have with the fascist (particularly Nazi) era.[34] Sontag argued that "[u]niforms suggest fantasies of community, order [and] identity," and nowhere is this notion better embodied that in the form of the SS because "[they] seem…to be the most perfect incarnation of fascism."[35] For Von Thronstahl, concerned with precisely these issues in contemporary Europe—"community, order [and] identity"—fascism represents the perfect symbol. So it is, therefore, that they encourage a fascination with fascism—"keep feeling it"—and why? Primarily for its aesthetic appeal—it will "dress you up like victory"—and this takes on a particular significance in the context of Klumb's overall world view. You will not necessarily be victorious, but you will give every appearance of it, you will "wear the mark" of it.

Important questions that must be asked of Von Thronstahl include: are Von Thronstahl advocating a return to fascism or Nazism? Are they play-ing with its symbols in order to shock or to protest some wider issue? Von Thronstahl's seeming play-acting has been dismissed by many commen-tators on the Neofolk scene as merely a shock tactic, but there is much to suggest that "even the bones [of fascism will] do" in order to reignite seri-ous interest in fascist symbology and ideology or at least to protest against certain aspects of modern society.[36] For Josef Klumb, for example, the key figures of the fascist era were "very frank and open about their beliefs and politics, which by no means can be said about the self-proclaimed 'demo-cratic' politicians."[37] This remark at once makes a connection between the fascist era and the present, makes a favorable comparison with that time and in so mythologizing the past stokes the flames of neofascism.

In one of Klumb's essays, published on the band's web site, he argues firmly against the European Union as it stands.[38] He makes clear that he is an avowed conspiracy theorist and puts forward a number of well-worn, extreme-right, conspiracy-riddled arguments to prove that the European Union is little more than a cog—albeit a dangerous one—in the wheel of the all-powerful New World Order (NWO), and, as such, a malformed ver-sion of European identity.[39] Traditionally, this powerful and secretive group were believed to be predominantly Jewish, and as such, these sorts of ideas have been a part of many fascist, National Socialist, and neofascist ideolo-gies for a considerable length of time. Klumb's violent rejection of the Eu-ropean Union highlights his position as a pronounced nationalist, and he finds much grist for his mill in the idea of the abolition of sovereign states.

Added to this, Klumb also focuses on the idea that within the European Union, Europe is living under "A 'DICTATORSHIP of HUMANITARIAN-ISM[,]' a TOTALITARIAN SYSTEM IN the NAME of HUMANITY."[40] Into this "dictatorship," "20–50 million emigrants from Asia and Africa" are being introduced,[41] and this point makes Klumb's concerns for Euro-pean identity plain. The "dictatorship of humanitarianism" will lead to the "[d]issolution of all natural connection, [the] decomposition of all races and peoples [reduced] to a controllable mass mash."[42] In his view, European identity is pure—that is, undiluted by Asian or African input, and it is distinctive to a particular region. There are Germans, Austrians, and French before there are Europeans, for example, and claiming ethnic identity is a vital determinant of European identity. Klumb, in espousing such a racial-nationalist view, is also projecting attitudes characteristic of many branches of both interwar and contemporary fascism.

Turning to "The Occidental Dandy Pose," another of the essay sections on Von Thronstahl's web site, Klumb continues this theme by narrowing his focus from politics to more closely examine European, and more specifically German, culture, and so underline his understanding of Europeanness. In "My Homeland Is the Coffee House of Europe," Klumb argues with a certain poetic flourish that,

> In the end every human is only the T-shirt of another, and their world ends in their own four walls of bright IKEA apocalypse in oak. "ARE YOU LIVING, OR JUST EXISTING?" But which life are you living?...[t]he T-shirt, the IKEA interiors, the BIG BROTHER TV, the coffee in the paper cup, the vacation on white plastic furniture, the unaesthetic of the lack of awareness [that is present] in [a] basic existence and filling out the time between being born and dying....If the triviality of these familiar procedural sequences is not understood through the prism of one moment of that fire [of Hell], which raises and sanctifies a procedure above the worldly, then [we] do not live, rather we vegetate. If the ritual without awareness is carried out, life ends and the lingering illness begins.[43]

These notions of both a lack of awareness of the greater context of life (that is, the Christian context),[44] but also the homogenization of European—and western—culture clearly builds upon his conclusions in "Chaos, State of Emergency, Dictatorship!"[45] However, it also puts forward themes explored by other, more stridently political sections of the far-right, such as the Junge Nationaldemokraten, the youth wing of Germany's neo-Nazi Nationaldemokratische Partei Deutschlands (NPD) in the following piece,

> You [distress] are apparent all over our country! What has happened to this country over the last decades? What is happening to our German

people, our German culture, which can be seen in our country's forests, lakes and rivers? We can see it day after day with our own eyes: corruption, destruction and foreign domination...is becoming clear to everyone in our everyday lives, at school, at university or in factories!...some try their luck in a professional career, [looking for satisfaction] in consumption and prosperity, others in a brainless tavern [or] disco on the weekends, going into drug taking, into the Left camp. The idolisation of all foreigners, the national self-oblivion—the national self hate—[makes for] the indeterminable dissolution...of the German people![46]

These correlating statements of Klumb and the NPD underline Klumb's place within a neofascist milieu and also his presence in a long line of political and philosophical examinations of the imminent or actual collapse of the west, perhaps encapsulated best for the right by Oswald Spengler in 1922 in *Der Untergang des Abendlandes* ("The Decline of the West").[47] Spengler's idea that western civilization has gone through a series of phases, only to end up in the doom-laden winter of the Faustian stage, is reprised in contemporary terms by both Klumb and political groups like the NPD.[48] The answer to Faustian man's empty pursuit of the unattainable or, indeed, the ultimately vacuous, is, for Klumb and the NPD, to refocus on the pursuit of national identity, as it particularly defines it in racial terms, in the same way that interwar fascists, especially the Nazis, had similarly seized upon Spengler's ideas more than half a century before.

Klumb mourns what the west once was *and* celebrates the death of what it has become. He also makes clear what he believes to be the laudable and unique characteristics of the "true Europe," a Europe whose last great heroes were apparently the soldiers of Hitler's army.

We celebrate the fall of the West, [and] we do it consciously, from a mixed feeling of pride and mourning. We lift our cups and well-polished glasses and drink to the inevitable collapse of a world, which [falls] particularly [due] to inelegance. We drink to the Occidental dust of all the bones, those which rest under the Catalan fields, over which once the Hunnensturm broke, we drink to Tours and Poitiers, where the Arabs were stopped. And we drink to the Wehrmacht and the Waffen-SS volunteers who could not [have] suspect[ed] that the West would finally really spoil...the final collapse of good taste, between 70s exposed concrete slabs, laminated fibre furniture and coffee from the paper cup, because with the shrinking of each consciousness, the rituals became invalid.[49]

This excerpt also gives a sense of Von Thronstahl's regular thematic focus upon the past and belief that, within the context of a profound decline in Europe, a widespread and renewed reverence for what has gone before is all that will halt this collapse.[50] In this way, the band echoes the *völkisch* strands of National Socialist ideology. This is clear in another of Von Thronstahl's songs, "We Walked in Line." Although it is a cover version of a Joy Division song, Von Thronstahl have tellingly changed the title from its original "They Walked in Line," which Joy Division lead singer Ian Curtis wrote with a disgusted distance as he watched a Leni Riefenstahl film. A line from the song runs, "Dressed in our uniforms so fine...wearing the shame of all our crimes, with measured steps we walked in line."[51] So, while Von Thronstahl suggest an identification with the subjects of the song through the use of the first person plural "we," they also acknowledge the barbarity of the soldiers' actions and the resultant shame. They, as Germans, are connecting themselves with the dark recesses of the German past in a simultaneously positive and negative way. They are highlighting both the aestheticism of Nazism's "fine" uniforms *and* the moral cost for the wearing of those uniforms. The music video that accompanies this song muddies the water even further. Taken from Leni Riefenstahl's *Triumph des Willens,* it shows only the positive—lines of ordered, uniformed soldiers marching past Hitler. It does not show the Wehrmacht's plunge into the moral abyss on the wastelands of the Eastern Front. Von Thronstahl are misusing and romanticizing the Nazi past while connecting it with modern European identity.

Von Thronstahl's 2008 cover of the old Skids song (also covered by U2 and Green Day), "The Saints Are Coming," extends the notion of rejuvenating elements of Nazism as a remedy for the ills of modernity—comprising selected elements of the past with a certain reading of the present. Filmed in the alpine region of Bavaria, the video of the song shows a woman dressed in an SS-like black uniform, standing in an evocative *völkisch* alpine area and talking to lead singer Josef Klumb by way of an old telephone secreted in the leaves. Klumb is dressed in his characteristic, military-style jodhpurs and is surrounded by his band, two of whom beat Hitler Youth-style drums.[52] Once again Von Thronstahl exhibit their fascination with fascism and suggest a potential role for it in contemporary society.

"In the Springtime of Decay": Richard Leviathan and Ostara

In the group Ostara there is, by their own admission, far more ambiguity to their views on Nazism than in those of Josef Klumb and Von Thronstahl. Ostara also advocate a significantly more esoteric and complex approach to the search for European identity. Nevertheless, they too pick up and run with the notion of a hidden or countercultural Europe, and their music is also that of protest. Ostara was founded by Richard Leviathan and Timothy Jenn in 1996, following from their previous group, the provocatively titled Strength through Joy.[53] While nominally Ostara is the Germanic goddess of Spring, it should also be recalled, as Leviathan has acknowledged, that Ostara was the name of Jörg Lanz von Liebenfels's sensationalist early-twentieth-century journal of racial theory, which is said to have greatly influenced the ideological development of Adolf Hitler.[54]

So, in embracing the monikers of the pre-Nazi and Nazi eras, Leviathan claims to be attempting to "transcend...the legacy of the past" and "fac[e] the shadows of our collective memory and experience."[55] Yet in doing so, he also reveals his own historical preoccupations, the stance behind those preoccupations, and how that stance informs his understanding of Europe. Put simply, it is unlikely that a left-wing band would name themselves after a Nazi-era state-run leisure organization.

While Leviathan continues to emphasize that Ostara are "less overtly political and more lyrically ambiguous" than Von Thronstahl, their understanding of Europe is clearly right-wing in character.[56] To begin, Leviathan defines "Europe" in the following way:

> [Europe is a] spiritual homeland with which we can identify but transcending the limits of any politically constituted nationalism or ideology. It is the foundation of what we know as the collective heritage full of shared triumphs and tragedies, an epicentre of the Occidental soul that is multifaceted, disparate, differentiated in many respects yet through a vast concatenation of history has forged a kind of fractured

intersecting mosaic, a broken mirror in which each of the constituent faces can recognise what connects the parts to the whole.[57]

So although, unlike Klumb, Leviathan nominally rejects nationalism, he nonetheless states that there is a specifically "Occidental soul" and a "spiritual homeland" with which that soul corresponds. Similarly, Leviathan explains his alignment with Goth music and the Gothic subculture in general because "it is based on an aesthetic style that is central to the cultural identity of the European soul."[58] This begs the question of what exactly constitutes the nature of Leviathan's European soul.

Leviathan too believes that a decline of the west is in progress. In a 2002 interview with *FluxEuropa,* Leviathan agreed that we were "living at the fag end of Western civilization," and when asked again in 2009, he concurred with this notion.[59] But, as with Klumb, he does not argue that this decline is necessarily a negative occurrence. Greatly influenced by the ideas of Italian philosopher Julius Evola, intellectual favorite of the inter- and post-war far right, Leviathan argues that the path taken by modern western society and Europe in particular has been a misstep. There is a true notion of European identity, a holy grail of sorts, and Europe as it stands has lost sight of and turned away from this truth. The path on which western civilization should be is the one that Leviathan depicts in his music and the one that will, therefore, be described here. In Ostara's best known song, "Bavaria," Leviathan describes this final period of European decline as the "Springtime of decay."[60] That is, it appears to be a period of growth, like spring, but it is a false spring. It is one of degeneration. Nothing can stop this decline. As westerners, we all complete meaningless activities while we tumble inevitably into the abyss. Leviathan's subject sells flowers in the springtime of decay, and paints idols "[w]hile the Muses turn to grey."[61]

In this song, Leviathan represents his understanding of the true nature of European identity, "[t]he buried soul of Europe," as being in Bavaria.[62] Here "[t]he buried soul" is "[a]live beyond the breathing grave."[63] It is striking that Leviathan's notion of an ideal Europe, its essence, is located in Bavaria with its chocolate-box, stereotypically European vistas. "Bavaria" also emphasizes that the true essence of Europe is not fashionable, superficial, or fleeting, but rather is an eternal path. Indeed, Europe becomes almost otherworldly in "Bavaria," having endured the "shining [and] burning" of the world's Evola-predicted end, the protagonists emerge in the distinct, separate, and almost mythical European "Imperium."[64] Given the pointed reference to "steeples" in the lyrics and Bavaria's reputation as a staunchly Catholic state, it must also be deduced that Leviathan's understanding of European identity is, like Klumb's, a Christian one (or, at least, Judeo-Christian, given Leviathan's Jewish origins).

Surprisingly within this traditionally Eurocentric mindset, Leviathan, dramatically unlike Klumb, is sympathetic toward the existence of the European Union, stating that

> Generally I support it. Europe always was a tapestry of related peoples bound together by classic imperialism, Christian identity, cultural empathy as well as regional rivalry. These things can exist in a federal framework and be enriched as a result. Some of the bureaucratic structures of the EU can be stifling and overly biased towards economic interests but some of the social reforms and cooperative measures sought by Brussels have been constructive. The Euro is not the disaster that it was predicted to be and the idea of a single continent in which the composite nations should coexist in peace is a noble aspiration in the light of the last two world wars.[65]

But it also needs to be acknowledged that, despite this apparently accommodating stance, Leviathan defines the European Union very much within a traditionally right-wing vein, and in doing so echoes the notions of Europe currently touted by contemporary European politicians of the right. Leviathan argues that Europe was and should continue to be "a tapestry of related peoples bound together by classic imperialism, Christian identity, cultural empathy as well as regional rivalry."[66] Once more, a specific notion of Europe as a Christian and culturally exclusive state is central to his understanding. And while Leviathan nods to this structure as potentially existing within a "federal framework," his emphasis on "regional rivalry" remains. So really, Europe as a unified and, in some ways, homogenized continental entity as it might be understood in Brussels, has no truck with Leviathan. He favors the specificities of European ethnic differences.

But with a specifically defined notion of Europe, once more comes the problem of nationalism, of exclusivity, of those who are within and without a particular set of walls. Leviathan argues that "[t]he nation as a political entity is outmoded and largely depleted in spiritual terms."[67] How Leviathan explains praising and encouraging the adoption of a very particularly defined notion of Europeanness is by suggesting that European national identities "are the product of a romanticized past whose actual regional and local identities were far less simple and more ambiguous than the political ideologies that forged them."[68]

> To embrace Germanness, we have to embrace Jewishness. To embrace paganism, we cannot ignore the role of Christianity in the revival of ancient philosophy and aesthetics. It is possible to explore regional lore and traditions and adapt these to a contemporary audience but asserting this as national identity would be like trying to separate Wagner from anti-Semitism. You can't. What we can do is enjoy Wagner as a genius of German romanticism. Similarly, we can trace themes that are uniquely European or uniquely German or Italian but the real value of that identity lies in to what extent this transcends the national borders and becomes recognizable in a more universal sense.[69]

This apparently open-minded statement, which encourages the holistic embrace of both the dark and the light of history and society, promotes within the context of Leviathan's Eurocentrism four interesting elements that are also crucial to the problematic nature of Neofolk. First, in claiming that we must embrace both sides of any complex historical debate or question of identity—that is, for example, both Germanness and Jewishness—it allows for the exploration of the Nazi era without any charge of individual neo-Nazism. Second, the hitherto mostly forbidden connections between the Nazi era and contemporary European identity are made explicit. Third, the normalizing of the Nazi era is expressed by begging questions of whether the complex historical, social, and moral territory of the Nazi period should be treated with abhorrence, with distance, or simply as another part of human history, which more than anything needs to be understood. Fourth, Leviathan has also reinforced his notion that there is a core idea of Europeanness, in spite of his contrary protestations of regional differences. The "composites" of which he speaks are all variants on his understanding of Eurocentric cultural and societal themes.

Within this context, therefore, Leviathan argues that "[t]he shallow stereotypes [regarding Nazism] have to be broken down to reach the human dimension."[70] This in itself is a worthy aim—Nazism *should* be viewed and understood within a human context. The perpetrators of the Holocaust were not aliens or monsters but—more horrifyingly—ordinary people, and this acknowledgment both fleshes out our understanding of this catastrophe of human history but also increases the profoundly problematic and complex nature of the era.

Leviathan then goes on to address a key part of the complexity inherent in not only this question but also in Neofolk's own relationship with the Nazi period.

> The allure and mystique [of Nazism] has to be understood in so far as it can be understood.... Barbarism and civilisation are not opposites. Culture and philistinism are not antithetical. Music, like literature, can reach into the depths to convey the dark truth beneath these apparent contradictions. But one runs into dangerous territory when one chooses to adopt the "enemy's" disposition or symbolism. To try and represent from within the power of what is considered to be irredeemably evil, especially as far as Nazism is concerned, is to test the limits of contemporary democracy.... To play devil's advocate for the most demonic movement in history is still heresy. It is like trying to redeem the swastika from its obvious associations. The moment you touch it, you play with fire.[71]

In holding these views, Leviathan then professes considerable sympathy for the figure of Claus von Stauffenberg, one of the key participants in the July 20, 1944 plot to assassinate Hitler, and oft-referenced darling of Neofolk circles for his perceived role as a right-wing rebel. Stauffenberg also referred to a "Secret" or "Hidden Germany," one in which, as for the Nazis, Germany's mythology and history preordained a special path for them but which, unlike the Nazis, was not apparently marred by racialism.[72] In this way, Stauffenberg could be seen to support a strong (i.e., authoritarian and militaristic) German state but not National Socialism. This evidently holds appeal for Leviathan, conveniently allowing him to overlook the fact that Von Stauffenberg *was* a Nazi. In attempting to recognize von Stauffenberg as a key figure of the German resistance movement, what Leviathan fails to engage with is the fact that while von Stauffenberg and his circle sought to end Nazi rule, they looked to replace Hitler's dictatorship with a military dictatorship ruled by Germany's officer class. Leviathan evades this problem by stating:

> He was a conservative aristocrat who believed in a greater Germany that Hitler had brought to the lowest ebb. His resistance was heroic, patriotic, and born of principles of chivalry and basic moral outrage. He may not have returned Germany to democracy but the purpose of his mission was to end the treachery of the Nazi state and restore something of the dignity of the Old Germany. That may have been quixotic but he was also a pragmatist who I think would have been open to possibilities beyond a military solution.[73]

So, significantly, there is a suggestion here that democracy need not necessarily be the only or even the ideal option in Leviathan's European weltanschauung. Rather, what is important (and what needs to be returned to in Leviathan's view, in order to put Western society onto its ideal path) is the maintenance of a sort of code of conduct—an "officer's code" of "the Old Germany," even. Providing that is maintained, even authoritarian, militaristic rule is an acceptable means to an end.

Indeed, of the Nazi era in general, Leviathan hints at the notion that the core ideas of National Socialism were not necessarily erroneous, only that their application was. In indicating no outright Nazi sympathies, Leviathan, sums up the essential ambiguity of Neofolk:

> Hitler betrayed the core of the SA, the "left" who wanted a true national socialism. I [do] not argue necessarily for the intrinsic value of that movement...in order to understand it accurately, we have to realize that Hitler was one significant proponent who adapted ideas to circumstances in order to seize power. As a radical form of nationalism, Nazism was part of a collectivist spirit that also manifested itself in other countries. It had a uniquely racial element to it but we must accept that racialism was on the rise elsewhere and anti-Semitism, while particularly virulent in Germany, was rife in other countries. The Nazis applied ethnic identity to politics and sought to create a folk community in which the German spirit would be actively realized. This in itself is not evil.[74]

In making an attempt to break down the "shallow stereotypes," Leviathan makes the point that the views of Neofolk musicians are not only artistic expressions, nor are they devoid of any commentary at all. The fascination of fascism remains, and whether these bands have enhanced our understanding of this era or further mythologized it is as equivocal as the genre itself.

"They Are Doing Something European for Sure": Conclusions on Neofolk, Nazism and European Identity

It is clear that there is more to Neofolk than "just fascination" with the dark shadows of Europe's past. While the genre does make significant and striking attempts to demystify Nazi symbols and confront the continent's dark history—though it could be argued that they do more to mythologize it—Neofolk is not an artistic expression devoid of political commentary. There is, in fact, a considerable desire among groups like Von Thronstahl and Ostara to, if not entirely reprise elements of Europe's past, then certainly to radically reconsider them and, as we have seen in their music and aesthetic, to co-opt elements of that reconsideration into an alternative representation of contemporary European identity.

That Von Thronstahl and Ostara aid the integration of Nazi ideas into their depictions of a new Europe is borne out in the responses of their fans, who, thanks to the unprecedented platform provided by the Internet, make clear that this music is not being understood solely on an artistic level. On October 8, 2008, for example, following Georgia's clash with Russia over South Ossetia, "Leo-Herbsterwachen" from Austria stated on the Ritual Front site: "Georgia is down; well done, I must say well done!"[75] A friend listed on the Von Thronstahl site—"Dea" in Austria—writes "Without recollection of tradition, there is no today and no future!"[76] Finally, on the Stormfront discussion boards, "Amagaeru" makes the significance of the Neofolk fan reception clear as follows:

> I'm a neofolk/neoclassical fan, even though 70% (let's say 30% is pretty high if you compare it with others musical style) of the bands aren't "real" WN [White Nationalist]. Most of em bring some good idea about free speech and such…they are doing something European for sure.[77]

It would be wrong to claim all Neofolk groups promote neo-Nazi and fascist ideas. At Last.fm, a group has formed calling itself "Neofolk against Racism" and identifies its "mission" as follows:

> For those who feel that (Neo)folk music should be free of racism and neo-nazism, both in terms of tendencies within the scene and stigmas from outside. Neofolk music, traditional symbols, alternative pagan religions, and so forth, all have, in principle, nothing to do with racism and neo-nazism. But sadly, many neo-nazis choose to associate themselves with these things. At the same time, symbols used in neofolk and heathen music are interpreted wrongly by outsiders and anti-fascist groups. This gives members of the neofolk scene and heathens an unwanted and unnecessary political stigma...
>
> We encourage cultural pride and love of heritage, but do not condone blind hatred of other groups.[78]

Clearly Neofolk is tapping into an appealing and unique interpretation of European identity that cannot always be automatically tied to Nazism. It is protest music, protesting Europe as it has developed and using its myriad voices to depict an alternative path. However, Neofolk's form of counterculture brings to the surface complex and difficult aspects of the European past and, as a result, presents its audience with a complex and difficult picture of what European identity represents in the twenty-first century. It also reminds us that the dark chapters of Europe's past are not truly behind us and the means of popularly representing them remain a problematic issue.

Finally, as Richard Leviathan points out, once the symbols of the Nazi period—and the fascist era more generally—are brought into discussions of national identity, "you" inevitably "play with fire."[79] Irrespective of the intentions of these musicians, Nazi symbology is not devoid of meaning; they are not the empty symbols of a long-past age. Similarly, these representations cannot be read to now solely represent a means of artistic expression. They and their ideological descendants are still very much a part of political and social dialogue. The professed political stances of Josef Klumb, Richard Leviathan, and Neofolk fans themselves surely make this clear while also amply signifying why Neofolk occupies an important place in both current dialogues on the popular representation of the fascist and Nazi eras and what it presently means to be European.

Notes

The title of this chapter is taken from a lyric in the song "Return Your Revolt into Style" by Von Thronstahl from their *Return Your Revolt into Style* album (2002).

1. Josef Klumb's introduction at the Von Thronstahl concert at the Metal Cave, Warsaw, June 20, 2009. Klumb spoke in English. "Europa wins!" is a reference to the Von Thronstahl song, "Adoration to Europa," whose lyrics include: "Hail to Europa, She always wins." Plikt242, "Von Thronstahl Warzawa 20.6.2009—metal cave," available at http://www.youtube.com/watch?v=qHdH5col3OQ&feature= related (accessed May 5, 2009). The line originally appeared in The Skids' song, "A Day in Europa," from their controversial 1979 album, *Days in Europa.*

2. Interview with Richard Leviathan (lead singer of Ostara) conducted by Emily Turner-Graham, June 2009 (will be referred to hereafter as Interview with Leviathan). I would like to thank Richard Leviathan very much for his generosity with his time and with the sharing of his ideas.

3. I use the term "noise" here to specifically indicate experimental noise artists like Boyd Rice.

4. Interview with Leviathan.

5. Interview with Leviathan.

6. Stephanie Obodda, "Sordid Allusion: The Use of Nazi Aesthetic in Gothic and Industrial Genres" (unpublished BA thesis, Princeton University, 2002), p. 13.

7. Obodda, "Sordid Allusion," p. 12.

8. Obodda, "Sordid Allusion," p. 3. For more information on Landser and neo-Nazi hate-rock in general, see Warwick McFadyen, "When Music Turns to a Howl of Hatred," *Age* (October 6, 2002), p. 17.

9. Obodda, "Sordid Allusion," p. 3.

10. Obodda, "Sordid Allusion," p. 4.

11. Obodda, "Sordid Allusion," p. 4.

12. Adam Leigh, "Just Fascination: Extreme Political Imagery in Underground Industrial Music," 2008, available at http://www.unaesthetic.pwp.blueyonder.co.uk/just_fascination.pdf (accessed February 6, 2009).

13. Leigh, "Just Fascination."

14. Leigh, "Just Fascination."

15. Nicholas Goodrick-Clarke, *Black Sun: Aryan Cults, Esoteric Nazism, and the Politics of Identity* (New York, New York University Press, 2002), p. 306.

16. Die Weisse Rose, "Kyrie Eleison," available at http://www.youtube.com/watch?v=Avd7mFP54-g (accessed August 18, 2009).

17. Graham D. Macklin, "Co-opting the Counter Culture: Troy Southgate and the National Revolutionary Faction," *Patterns of Prejudice,* Vol. 39, No. 3 (September 2005), np. This quote comes from Troy Southgate, lead singer of Neofolk band

H.E.R.R. and prominent far-right activist. Regarding the influence of the Internet on youth culture, see Emily Turner-Graham, "An Intact Environment Is Our Foundation of Life": The *Junge Nationaldemokraten,* the *Ring Freiheitlicher Jugend* and the Cyber-Construction of Nationalist Landscapes," in A. Mammone, E. Godin, and B. Jenkins, eds., *Western European Right-Wing Extremism: Nature, Cultures, Passions* (New York, Berghahn Books, forthcoming).

18. See, among the many examples available, this performance by Darkwood at the famed Leipzig alternative music festival, the Wave Gotik Treffen, at http://www. youtube.com/watch?v=zncsRgeAUzE, or Von Thronstahl's signature song "Return Your Revolt into Style," at http://www.youtube.com/watch?v=gqUVWxzNMEs.

19. Susan Sontag, "Fascinating Fascism," *The New York Review of Books,* Vol. 22, No. 1 (February 6, 1975), available at http://www.nybooks.com/articles/9280 (accessed October 17, 2008).

20. Josef Klumb, "'Geliebt, Verfolgt & Unvergessen' Der Riefenstahl-Geburtstagsreport," September 2002, available at http://www.vonthronstahl.de/zigelieb.htm (accessed April 3, 2009).

21. Macklin, "Co-opting the Counter Culture," np.

22. My thanks to Dr. Maartje Abbenhuis for pointing this out to me.

23. "Dokumentation: Kulturkampf und Kommerz: Rechte Tendenzen in der schwarzen Szene," available at http://www.turnitdown.de/245.html (accessed April 22, 2009). See Mattias Gardell, *Gods of the Blood: The Pagan Revival and White Separatism* (Durham, NC, Duke University Press, 2003) for discussion of an extreme right or Aryan counterculture.

24. The Dokumentationsarchiv des österreichischen Widerstandes is an organisation that, together with the Austrian government, monitors the activities of both Nazis of the pre-war and war-time era and neo-Nazis of the current era.

25. Gerd Schultze-Rhonhof, Gert Sudholt, and Claus Nordbruch, "Kleine Textsammlung: Extrem rechtes Propagandamaterial beim 'Tag der Reservisten,'" (Lüneburg, Antifaschistische Aktion, 2004), p. 12, available at http://www.anti fa-lg.de/docs/reservisten.pdf (accessed May 7, 2009).

26. See http://www.vaws.de/.

27. Stormfront is an American web presence, which, according to its web site, professes to be a "[d]iscussion board for pro-White activists and anyone else interested in White survival." See "Good White Nationalist Music?" http://www. stormfront.org/forum/showthread.php?p=7062560 (accessed July 14, 2009) regarding Von Thronstahl.

28. Josef Klumb's career is critically assessed in Andreas Speit, ed., *Ästhetische Mobilmachung: Dark Wave, Neofolk und Industrial im Spannungsfeld rechter Ideologien* (Hamburg, Unrast, 2002), *passim.*

29. See "Von Thronstahl—Biography," http://www.coldspring.co.uk/artists/von-thron stahl.php (accessed March 3, 2009).

30. "Return Your Revolt into Style," from the album *Return Your Revolt into Style* (2002). Full lyrics can be found on the web at http://www.sturmzeit.net/vtdisco/vtlyrics/returnyourrevolt.html.

31. Goodrick-Clarke, *Black Sun.*

32. Goodrick-Clarke, *Black Sun.*

33. Goodrick-Clarke, *Black Sun,* pp. 293–299.

34. Sontag, "Fascinating Fascism."

35. Sontag, "Fascinating Fascism."

36. With apologies to Sylvia Plath, whose line from her poem "Daddy" runs, "I thought even the bones would do" in order to recreate "a man in black with a Meinkampf look."

37. Malahki Thorn, "Von Thronstahl: The Search for Truth," December 7, 2005, *Heathen Harvest,* available at http://www.heathenharvest.com/article.php?story=20051207145142661 (accessed October 17, 2009).

38. Josef Klumb, "Chaos, Notstand, Diktatur!" December 2008, under the "Aufsaëtze & Meldungen" subheading, http://www.vonthronstahl.de/zichaos.htm (accessed April 1, 2009) (Translations by Emily Turner-Graham).

39. The term "New World Order" within this context refers to a conspiracy theory that an omnipresent, covert, and elite group of globalists is conspiring to eventually rule the world through an autonomous world government, which would replace sovereign states and other such checks and balances. These sorts of ideas have always had considerable credence in far-right circles, but since the 9/11 attacks, their appeal has widened. The interconnection of the ideology of the extreme right with conspiracy theories, as well as key proponents of such theories, is explored in Goodrick-Clarke, *Black Sun,* pp. 279–302.

40. Klumb, "Chaos, Notstand, Diktatur!" Capital letters are as they appear in the text.

41. Klumb, "Chaos, Notstand, Diktatur!"

42. Klumb, "Chaos, Notstand, Diktatur!"

43. Klumb, "Chaos, Notstand, Diktatur!" "ARE YOU LIVING, OR JUST EXIST-ING?" is a play on words in the original German, between the verbs "wohnen" and "leben"—"WOHNST DU NOCH ODER LEBST DU SCHON?" It was first used as an Ikea advertising slogan. Capital letters are as they appear in the text.

44. A close analysis of Klumb's religious views will form the topic of an upcoming article. See also Michael Sontheimer and Peter Wensierski, "Zur Rechten Gottes," *Der Spiegel,* August 2009, available at http://wissen.spiegel.de/wissen/dokument/dokument.html?titel=Zur+Rechten+Gottes&id=64197213&top=SPIEGEL&suchbegriff=josef+klumb&quellen=&qcrubrik=artikel (accessed December 3, 2009).

45. The idea that mass society is deliberately being distracted by trivialities contrived by the New World Order is a common one within the conspiracy milieu. See Goodrick-Clarke, *Black Sun,* p. 285.

46. Junge Nationaldemokraten, "Wer wir sind—Vom deutschen Elend," available at http://www.jn-buvo.de/index.php?option=com_content&task=view&id=12&Ite mid=26 (accessed November 15, 2008) (Translated by Emily Turner-Graham).

47. Oswald Spengler, *Der Untergang des Abendlandes* (München, Beck, 1922). Published in a series of volumes, the first complete set of Spengler's work was released in 1922.

48. Spengler defines the Faustian civilization as one in which the populace constantly strives for the unattainable, resulting in western man becoming "a proud but tragic figure, for while he strives and creates, he secretly knows the actual goal will never be reached." See http://en.wikipedia.org/wiki/The_Decline_of_the_ West#References (accessed November 3, 2009). See also the online version of Oswald Spengler, *The Decline of the West,* fifth English edition (New York, Oxford University Press, 1991), available at http://books.google.com.au/books?id=jYjY LoGSsQgC&dq=Oswald+Spengler&printsec=frontcover&source=an&hl=en&ei =xqpuSs_BJtWAkQXGmJ3DBQ&sa=X&oi=book_result&ct=result&resnum=4 (accessed November 4, 2009).

49. Klumb, "Meine Heimat sind die Kaffee-Häuser Europas." Josef K., "The Occidental Dandy-Pose presenting: Josef K.: Meine Heimat sind die Kaffee-Häuser Europas," http://www.vonothronstahl.de/ (accessed April 5, 2009).

50. Malahki Thorn, "Von Thronstahl."

51. See http://www.sturmzeit.net/vtdisco/vtlyrics/wewalkedinline.html (accessed August 6, 2009).

52. See http://www.myspace.com/vonthronstahlmusic (accessed July 20, 2009).

53. Strength through Joy (Kraft durch Freude) was a state-operated leisure organization during the Third Reich.

54. See also Ian Kershaw, *Hitler 1889–1936: Hubris* (London, Allen Lane, 1998), pp. 49–52. Kershaw considers the extent to which Ostara truly informed Hitler's views.

55. Miguel V., "Interview with Richard Leviathan (Ostara)," January 30, 2001, available at http://www.heimdallr.ezwww.ch/Interviews/2001/ostara.html (accessed February 20, 2009).

56. Interview with Leviathan.

57. Interview with Leviathan.

58. Keith Smith, "An Interview with Richard Leviathan of Ostara," available at http://www.compulsiononline.com/ostara.htm (accessed February 22, 2009).

59. Rik, "Ostara Interview," *Flux Europa* (January 23, 2002), available at http://www.fluxeuropa.com/mn0202-ostara_interview.htm (accessed February 25, 2009).

60. Lyrics to "Bavaria" by Ostara provided to accompany a fan-produced clip for the song at http://www.youtube.com/watch?v=vxGlzBn2Ieo. Ostara, "Bavaria," *Kingdom Gone* (2002).

61. Ostara, "Bavaria," *Kingdom Gone* (2002).
62. Ostara, "Bavaria," *Kingdom Gone* (2002).
63. Ostara, "Bavaria," *Kingdom Gone* (2002).
64. Ostara, "Bavaria," *Kingdom Gone* (2002).
65. Interview with Leviathan.
66. Interview with Leviathan.
67. Interview with Leviathan.
68. Interview with Leviathan.
69. Interview with Leviathan.
70. Interview with Leviathan.
71. Interview with Leviathan.
72. Rüdiger Sünner, "Geheimes Deutschland"—die geistigen wurzeln des Hitler-attentäters Claus von Stauffenberg, available at http://www.ruedigersuenner.de/Geheimes%20Deutschland.html (accessed June 17, 2009).
73. Interview with Leviathan.
74. Interview with Leviathan.
75. Leo-Herbsterwachen, October 8, 2008, http://www.MySpace.com/ritualfront. This comment is no longer available online. Ritual Front is a Russian Neofolk band. For a précis of the Georgia-Russia conflict, see http://news.bbc.co.uk/2/hi/in_depth/europe/2008/georgia_russia_conflict/default.stm.
76. Translated by Emily Turner-Graham. This comment is no longer available online. See Dea's profile at http://www.myspace.com/tedea.
77. Amagaeru, http://www.stormfront.org/forum/archive/index.php/t-238737.html (accessed July 15, 2008).
78. "Neofolk against Racism," available at http://www.last.fm/group/Neofolk+Against+Racism (accessed February 11, 2009).
79. Interview with Leviathan.

10

Where Does Evil Sit in the Classroom? Problematizing Teaching about Hitler, Nasty Nazis, and the Holocaust

Claire M. Hall

Sixty-five years after the end of the Second World War and the downfall of the Third Reich, British secondary school history teachers face a perennial problem, namely that their students have been educated about the history of the Nazi past through the many myths that swathe Adolf Hitler and Nazi Germany in popular culture. The prevalence of such myths seems to stem from the fact that in the western world, countries labeled as the winners of the war, such as Britain and the United States, are so captivated with remembering the Nazis as evil that the triumph over Nazism and the horrors of the Holocaust are ingrained within popular culture and form integral parts of national memory. We encounter the remnants of Nazism every day, whether it is on the television, through films, news items and documentaries, or interactively through popular video games such as *Medal of Honor*.[1] In the gaming generation, players encounter these myths while engaged in fantasy battles between the powers of good (the Allies or one heroic soldier) and evil (the Nazis). In their own way, computer games, cooperate in the maintenance of collective memory, but as recently highlighted by Eva Kingsepp, these historical games consider the heroes, villains, the battle of good against evil, and the excitement they generate to be more important than the actual historical facts.[2] As a result, Nazisploitation has ensured that Nazi evil has had an impressive staying power.[3] Students have transported this captivation with all things Nazi into the classroom, leaving teachers with the task of not only locating where Nazi evil sits among their students but also busting these myths before they can even begin to teach the history of this complex past.

This chapter addresses some of the problems of teaching the history of Nazi Germany and the Holocaust in Great Britain at the secondary school level. Such subjects are often described as being armband topics, the safe option, as history teachers choose them to entertain students rather than for their intrinsic pedagogical value. Some teachers have candidly stated that "kids find the Nazi period interesting. A lot of things happen. There is plenty of violence" or "the problem with the Nazis is that they are sexy. Evil is fascinating."[4] Consequently, some history teachers are finding that their students are not learning much history about the Nazi past, leading university teachers to complain that undergraduates start their courses with only a snapshot understanding of Nazi Germany, with little or no grasp of the big picture.[5]

The British secondary school curriculum takes a simplistic approach to Nazi Germany and the Holocaust, simplicities that are mirrored in the pedestrianization of Nazism in everyday culture. Hence, there is a general tendency for A-level (the Advanced Level General Certificate of Education) students to think that they know everything there is to know about Nazi Germany by the time they leave school. This is partly because they encounter a plethora of material in the classroom, which is not always contextualized well, but also because they continue to be influenced by much more pervasive ideas about the Nazi past outside the classroom. Within the classroom, issues relating to historical accuracy, information overload (particularly in terms of course content), the static categories of learning about Nazi Germany,[6] alongside the unchanging division of the subject into chronological periods (1933, 1934–1939, and 1939–1945) dog the heels of instructors attempting to deal with the subject matter in a sensitive and historically nuanced way.

So where should the history teacher who wishes to include Nazi Germany in his or her teaching curriculum turn? In order to behead the Nazi hydra, history teachers must focus first and foremost on being good historians themselves. It is vital that they keep in touch with changes in the historiography, in the hope that they do not perpetuate more myths within the classroom and that they themselves do not succumb to the attractions of popular culture to entertain rather than to historically explain. Teachers also have an important role in putting pressure on the curriculum setters to keep up to date.

Another challenge facing history teachers is that Nazism and the Holocaust are not only history subjects, as many schools use the Holocaust in particular to teach all manner of citizenship values to students. This has stimulated a certain amount of pedagogical debate on whether the teaching of evil in classrooms is appropriate. Mike Bottery of Hull University argues that schools serve an important function in teaching about evil, as it is only through understanding its different forms (individual, institutional, societal, and global) that we can hope to combat and prevent it.[7] In contrast, those who argue against the teaching of evil in schools claim that subjects such as Nazism and the Holocaust traumatize, shock, and disturb young children, who if exposed to such subjects at an elementary level may engage in violence themselves.[8] They argue that this is mainly because young children do not possess the faculty of understanding that only comes through adulthood. It is for this reason that they believe young people should be introduced to such subjects only at university level.

There are many dilemmas and considerations to take into account when delivering such subjects as "death education,"[9] as one could argue that when history teachers classify Nazis as evil, they assist in the perpetuation of the myths of good and evil within the classroom. Problems such as this can be overcome, in part, by ensuring that the history teacher differentiates between teaching citizenship and history and uses the correct teaching aids, methods, and curriculum support. With effective structures and boundaries in place it should be possible to present the past without traumatizing students. One solution would be to present Nazi Germany and the Holocaust as acts of humanity, where human beings were capable of both great violence and great compassion, fostering "students' sensitivity to and involvement and identification with such subjects."[10] This, of course, has to be carried out alongside the task of challenging popular misconceptions surrounding Nazism and the Holocaust.

Practical Tips for Dealing with the Hitler Phenomenon

Western society believes that the Holocaust needs explanation. In many ways, this belief has fuelled an obsession with Hitler and Nazi Germany. The obsessive quest for understanding is so prevalent that, as school subjects in Britain at least, Hitler and Nazi Germany units are regularly taught from late primary through to secondary and higher education levels. In dealing with the actual practices of delivering the subject of Nazi Germany, this section analyzes some of the problems of teaching Nazi Germany, such as the impact of the large number of "sensational, fantastical and in-accurate works on Nazism,"[11] how to keep up with the constantly changing historiography of Nazi Germany, and the various pedagogical pitfalls to teaching the subject well, alongside some remedial suggestions.

Stephen Pagaard suggests in the *History Teacher,* an academic journal for history teachers, that the "Third Reich is an area of the curriculum that fascinates students and, hence, teaching it is made easier by the fact that motivation is not a difficulty."[12] In Britain, Hitler and Nazi Germany are popular choices by students taking their GCSEs[13] and/or A-Levels.[14] It is highly probable that large numbers of these students were introduced to the subject as soon as they entered secondary education and perhaps even at the elementary level. Because students tend to only skim the surface of such a vast subject, accompanied by further exposure through popular media such as film, television, the Internet, and gaming, the result is that within the classroom, the legacy of Nazi evil endures. Examples of student arguments from my own A-level classes include: all Germans were Nazis, Hitler was a good leader because he solved unemployment, and the curi-ous importance assigned to debates on Hitler's vegetarianism. These myths are not limited to the classroom of course, but seem not to be dispelled by secondary school history teaching. What Pagaard fails to comprehend is that it is not enough for students to be fascinated by the Nazi past; they have to be motivated to want to learn it correctly—not to be further in-ducted into the myths that already exist around Hitler and the Holocaust. It seems, therefore, that the first task of the history teacher is to redirect students' motivation.

Of course, myths surrounding Hitler were invented during the Nazi era in Germany and played a key part in the construction of Hitler as a messi-anic figure rescuing the German people from the disasters facing them in the late 1920s and early 1930s.[15] That Hitler was a good leader because he solved unemployment, built the autobahn, and initiated rearmament proj-ects were ways in which Hitler was sold to the masses in the 1930s and are still tropes in which he is projected in popular culture today. Of course, there are many reasons why the Nazis' economic policies worked so well, which had very little to do with Hitler or the autobahn.[16] It is essential that teachers put the fascinating personal details of Hitler's life into a big-ger context, because rather than indulging students fascination for Hitler's quirks (such as his vegetarianism),[17] teachers need to direct students to the broader propagandistic needs utilized by Goebbels to portray Hitler's asceticism. If these details go unchallenged, they serve only the purpose of feeding the Hitler myth—a myth that places supreme importance of Hitler as one individual, rather than someone who was also the product of specific historical, social, and economic circumstances.[18] Therefore, it is vital that teachers don their myth-buster caps and eradicate these widely held popular beliefs from the classroom as quickly as possible, perhaps by identifying them right at the start and explaining how irrelevant they are to understanding the subject as history.

One way to do this is to ensure that student learning is up to date, which ultimately means that teachers must keep up with the historiography. Given the sheer scale of scholarship in the field of Nazi German history, no one would expect history teachers to master all of the literature.[19] However, it is important to become familiar with the content of key texts and to pass on this knowledge to students. Yet while extracts from works by prominent Nazi historians, such as Ian Kershaw and Alan Bullock, are regularly called upon in source-based A-Level examination papers, students are required to acknowledge different historians, but they are not required to know the historiography of Nazi Germany, as this is something it is assumed they will become more familiar with at university level.[20] While this is an understandable position from the A-level curriculum board, it does limit students' ability to comprehend that there are many ways to view the past and that discourses about good and evil are not historically constructive.

Confusion about how to teach Nazi Germany in a historically appropriate way is confounded by the inability of the A-level examination board to set appropriate questions that reflect recent changes in the historical understanding of the Nazi past. For example, in a recent A-level exam, students were asked to read an extract from Hitler's press chief Otto Dietrich's *Twelve Years with Hitler:*

> In the twelve years of his rule in Germany, Hitler produced the biggest confusion in government that had ever existed. During his period of government, he removed from the organisation of the state all clarity of leadership and produced a confused network of responsibilities. It was not all laziness or an excessive degree of tolerance which led the otherwise so energetic and forceful Hitler to tolerate this real witch's cauldron of struggles for position and conflicts. It was intentional. With this technique he systematically disorganised the upper

levels of Reich leadership in order to develop and further the authority of his own will until it became a despotic tyranny.[21]

Candidates were required to use the preceding extract, alongside five other sources, to answer the question: "How far do you agree with the view . . . that in the years 1933–45 Hitler's rule became a despotic tyranny?"[22] It is clear that the individual who set the question had not taught Nazi Germany in the classroom for some time. If he had, he would have been aware that students would, first, not understand the question, as Nazi Germany is rarely referred to as a "despotic tyranny" these days. Second, the phrase is in itself a tautology, and, third, while students are encouraged to know the works of different historians, they tend not to have the skills to answer this question, as it requires them to make some form of historiographical statement. As a direct consequence of a poorly chosen question and source, the candidates, having not understood the question, produced very confused answers.[23] This example highlights how both teachers and examiners need to be equipped with current knowledge and practical tools, which will help to ensure that teaching about Nazi Germany can be successful at every stage of learning.[24]

A good example of how quickly the historiography on Nazi Germany can change and affect how we teach the subject to secondary school students is illustrated by Stephen Pagaard's *History Teacher* article from 2005, in which he draws the readers' attention to the work of historian Robert Gellately.[25] Pagaard uses Gellately to show how the idea that the Gestapo had a spy on every corner was a myth. However, five years after Pagaard's recommendations to history teachers, my own new research on the Gestapo published in the *Journal of Contemporary History* (2009) offers new insight into the debate on Nazi terror. Drawing upon recently declassified German police files, I take a postrevisionist approach, arguing that the Gestapo did in fact have several good-sized battalions of paid spies, and I qualify Gellately's self-policing idea by suggesting that the secret policy did have a "hands-on" approach.[26] This example clearly demonstrates how over a short period of time, the debate on the history of Nazi terror has changed. All history teachers, regardless of the level they teach, need to try to take such shifts into account in their teaching.

Of course, the complications of incorporating historiography at the secondary school level are heightened when inappropriate texts are used to teach this problematic past. One such problematic work is Daniel J.

Goldhagen, *Hitler's Willing Executioners,* which has, since its publication in 1996, been almost universally debunked by academic historians.[27] It would, therefore, be wise to suggest that as responsible historians, secondary school teachers should refrain from using Goldhagen in their classrooms. But to do so, they need to put pressure on the relevant examination boards that still refer to Goldhagen as suggested reading for those studying Nazi Germany and the Holocaust.[28]

Problems also exist at the beginning of courses on Nazi Germany, as some teachers battle with the problem of how to introduce it properly. Do they provide a basic overview, which can result in misunderstanding through information overload, or do they approach the subject through the use of a teaching aid such as a film or photograph, both of which are highly problematic? In an effort to identify how my students engaged with the notion of Nazism as evil within an A-Level introductory session, I decided to test their knowledge of what they already knew about Hitler and Nazi Germany. This was an illuminating exercise, as most students stated, between a few nervous laughs, that Hitler had only one testicle. Of course, this myth is widespread in popular culture. Its origins undoubtedly lie in the Second World War with the popular ditty "Hitler only has one ball, Goebbels has two but very small." The work of pseudo-psychologists, like Rudolph Binion,[29] Walter Langer,[30] and Robert Waite,[31] in the 1970s used the myth to attempt to understand the origins of Hitler's evil by claiming that Hitler was mad because he only had one testicle, that he had contracted syphilis from a Jewish prostitute, and many more fantastical, unsubstantiated claims. Today's students do not learn the myth from pseudo-science; their understanding is fed by films and Internet articles, such as "How Hitler Lost His Testicle."[32] History teachers must be responsible and avoid focusing on the voyeurism of Nazism, the tidbits of history, and the fascination of evil. Instead, this class exercise enabled me to bust a myth and steer the session in the direction of explaining more important and central tenets of Nazism, such as the rise of a very particular political community and industrial society that facilitated genocide on an unprecedented scale.

Another major challenge in teaching the history of Nazi Germany in the classroom is that most GCSE and A-Level (GCE) textbooks lack any kind of creative flair.[33] Many authors choose to adopt a bland narrative when addressing standard subtopics such as Hitler's rise to power and his consolidation of power through individuals and organizations such as Himmler and the SS state. This leads to students being spoon fed facts and figures and facing the same tiresome teaching strategies and repetitive unchanging chronological approaches that focus on specific areas and only skim the surface of them. This is a pretty standard approach that does nothing to challenge the students' preconceptions of Nazism. Unfortunately, if teachers have to adhere to the stipulations set by examining boards and in so doing coach their students to pass their exam while achieving the best grade possible, it is highly unlikely that this method of teaching will change.[34] However, a daring teacher who is willing to risk a more thematic approach could breathe new life into the subject.

Many innovative teachers have found ways to bring their subject to life and iron out any mistruths by ensuring their students attend A-Level conferences where they have the chance to listen to experts in the field of Nazi Germany.[35] Many experts choose to take a thematic approach to the topic of Nazi Germany, focusing on one particular debate, event, or person during their talk. This is fantastic in terms of student motivation, but if the visit is not accompanied by a later teacher-led session, then visits such as these do not always translate into good grades or proper understanding. By adopting a more thematic approach, history teachers can develop the way the Third Reich is taught at the secondary level to a much more satisfactory level.

University lecturers lead the way in terms of innovative courses and delivery methods, with some choosing to develop and deliver thematic courses on Nazi Germany. Even though university lecturers, similar to secondary school teachers, face constraints, they often have more freedom in designing their courses and assessment methods. The Third Reich is a feature of most undergraduate history degree programs in Great Britain, with many lecturers offering it as a third-year specialist subject.[36] This is because it is such a complex subject, and before their third year of study, history students tend not to have the necessary historical and critical thinking skills to look at the historical evidence and fully assess it. This is in part a consequence of the unchallenging course content and simplistic delivery methods at the secondary level but is also part of the complexities of teaching this complicated past. As the topic of Nazi Germany and the Holocaust are highly unlikely to be removed from the British secondary school curriculum, however, secondary school history teachers could embrace some of the methods of their university colleagues by adopting thematic (rather than narrative) approaches and utilizing a large number of primary document reading exercises in their teaching. The regular use of documents would help to foster critical thinking and encourage students to question the past, rather than subscribe to spoon-fed methods.[37]

A good example of the thematic module approach for undergraduates is that of a second-year history module titled "The 1930s," which is delivered at Anglia Ruskin University (Cambridge, United Kingdom) and at its higher education partner sites, one being University Centre Peterborough.[38] The module looks at a number of forms of rule during the 1930s and the differing responses of various political systems to economic and social crises in the decade. The tensions between democracy and authoritarianism constitute one key strand of the module, but another important strand is the various case studies (on which students present short class papers), which are based on historically significant locations or events such as the Nazi book burnings of 1933, the Nuremburg rallies, and the 1936 Berlin Olympics. "The 1930s" module is taught by a mixture of weekly lectures at the beginning of the module followed by weekly seminars lasting two hours, giving the students the chance to practice the skill of critical analysis by discussing their weekly reading from the key text. The lecturers who deliver this module attempt to motivate students by inviting Piers Brendon, author of the textbook *The Dark Valley: A Panorama of the 1930s,*[39] to deliver a special lecture titled "Truth about the 1930s." This is usually scheduled toward the middle of the module, which ensures that the students have something to work toward and something that will equally motivate them to complete the module. This is a wonderful teaching strategy because students, having consulted the key texts for months, are able to witness the book coming to life through the spoken words of its author. More importantly, an indirect encounter with Nazi Germany alongside an analysis of many other European countries, some of which embraced authoritarianism (the Soviet Union) and some which did not (France), offers yet another example of how Nazi Germany can be taught comparatively, something that secondary schools could look to adopting and incorporating within their courses.

While secondary school teachers can learn how to improve course design and adopt more appropriate pedagogical strategies practiced by university lecturers, they both share a common problem when delivering modules on Hitler and Nazi Germany. The History Channel, popularly known as the Nazi or Hitler Channel, seems much more attractive to students (at every level of education) than the unappealing book stacks of their school or university library. Joseph Coohill, an academic at Pennsylvania

Illustration 7: Piers Brendon signing copies of his book, *The Dark Valley,* at a special workshop titled "The Truth about the 1930s" delivered at University Centre Peterborough (United Kingdom), November 29, 2007. (Printed with kind permission of Karen Lawrence)

State University, draws attention to the notion of a "History Channel Generation" in a recent article, in which he details how

> Right at the beginning of my teaching career, I was struck by how many students would describe to me documentaries they had seen on the History Channel, PBS, or on other stations, in tremendous detail, not only relating the "facts" they learned, but often discussing some of the nuances and shades of interpretation presented in those programs.[40]

While Coohill acknowledges his own dislike for the "Hitler-soaked" programs of the History Channel, he does recognize the important fact that "television history is a major component of this generation's historical consciousness, and students are very used to learning things visually."[41] It is clear that visual material helps to maintain students' interest. For example, after watching the episode "Wild East" from the BBC award-winning series *Nazis: A Warning from History,* my own A-Level students grasped the division of Poland during the Nazi occupation much better than they had previously when reading a relevant academic textbook. Coohill is correct in his assertions, as it is crucial that both lecturers and teachers consider the question of television history as an educational aid and motivational tool for learning, because "if we really want students to have a dialog with the past, then perhaps the History Channel can indeed teach us something."[42] However, teachers must introduce such material with care by using it as an aid to learning and not the essence of learning about the Nazi past. Here their direction of classroom discussion and focus on student comprehension is absolutely essential.

Remembering Evil—the Holocaust

Another obvious reason why "Hitler will not go away is the Holocaust."[43] As a highly emotive and complex subject, the Holocaust is a subject we cannot afford to avoid, and it is for this reason that it has been made a compulsory part of the national curricula in Britain,[44] the United States, and Israel.[45] Holocaust memory and commemoration have come to play an important role in shaping collective memory and national identities within these countries.[46] Future generations will learn about the effects of institutionalized intolerance and genocide and prepare students to examine the role of uncontrolled racism in present-day conflicts. The establishment of Holocaust Memorial Day in Britain, in 2001, has guaranteed the Holocaust's place in British national memory.[47] Educational organizations working within Britain, such as the Holocaust Education Trust,[48] Facing History,[49] and Holocaust museums such as the Beth Shalom Centre (Laxton, Newark) and the Jewish Museum (London), as well as the Holocaust exhibition within the Imperial War Museum (London)[50] have also contributed to keeping the Holocaust within British popular memory. These museums and organizations work closely with schools in offering teaching fellowships for teachers and Holocaust educators who have the opportunity to work on a Holocaust-related project while receiving up-to-date instruction from leading Holocaust scholars.[51]

However, there is a heated debate about whether the Holocaust should be located within history or in subjects like citizenship, where it is used to deliver moral lessons, and some have gone further to question whether or not it serves any useful purpose in being taught at all.[52] As a nation, Britain continues to teach the Holocaust and Nazi Germany because these topics fascinate us, in part, because they have been mythologized. Questions abound around whether Holocaust education is actually teaching or a form of preaching, or whether moral lessons can actually be learned (or should be learned) from this event. Also being currently debated by history teachers and professionals is whether or not more emphasis is needed upon fostering a historical understanding of the Holocaust. Yet one has to question whether or not the moral issues surrounding the Holocaust impede our ability as historians to approach it, let alone teach it to students who are, in effect, untrained as historians. If questions concerning human nature and actions can never be fully answered, how can history teachers teach a subject that is in effect "unteachable?"[53]

Still, even though the moral questions surrounding the Holocaust are difficult, if not impossible, to answer or ignore, secondary school teachers cannot avoid their function of helping to shape young people into responsible adults. With that responsibility comes the need to explain extremes of human behavior, placing questions surrounding motivations within the historical context. In the words of Mike Bottery: "How society deals with the evil within it is a painful mirror into which only the most courageous dare look. Yet the moral health of societies demands that they do."[54] It is for this reason that history teachers are best placed to teach Nazi Germany and the Holocaust, as they can access the past in a responsible manner, but it is important that history teachers remain in their subject area and do not attempt to combine full citizenship lessons with history sessions devoted to the history of the Third Reich. To do so may prolong the mythologized presence of Nazi evil within the classroom.

In the late 1970s, Henry Friedlander, a noted Holocaust historian, warned that the Holocaust could lose its importance if it were to be taught again and again. The result, he felt, would be an eroding effect upon content and detail.[55] His foresight was remarkable as his prediction has, to a certain degree, come true. In secondary schools at least, the Holocaust has been over-taught in too many disciplines, including history, citizenship, and religious studies. In some countries this overkill has come under close scrutiny, which has recently led a number of scholars to question the significance and relevance of Holocaust education. Noted historian Peter Novick, for example, argues that Holocaust lessons "are empty and not very useful"[56] and that the "Holocaust is a salutary reminder of the presence of evil in the world."[57] The British historian Nicolas Kinloch has added fuel to this already heated debate by arguing that "a careful study of the successful destruction of Europe's Jews might act as an incentive for those anxious to destroy their own minorities."[58] He expands upon this by contending that the Holocaust is not unique and that "it probably has no more to teach British students than any other genocide of modern—or for that matter, medieval-times."[59] Kinloch's comments caused a significant amount of uproar when they appeared in 2001. One of those to respond to him was Geoffrey Short, a renowned British educational psychologist who has published widely on the benefits of well-taught Holocaust education. Short asserts that compulsory Holocaust education is a new phenomenon restricted to a small number of countries. He further highlights that "contrary to critics, genocides which have occurred over the past fifty years are the result of there having been too little teaching of the Holocaust."[60] He develops this argument further by pointing out that "in those parts of the world that are very different politically, culturally and economically from the twenty-first century Britain, students might derive more benefit from examining a genocide other than the Holocaust."[61] Short has done a lot to highlight the complexities of Holocaust education and has pointed out that many secondary school teachers in Great Britain are still struggling to cover the subject of the Holocaust at a satisfactory level.[62]

Hence, "teaching the Holocaust can be like trying to find one's way through a minefield."[63] It is so complex that it demands a certain level of maturity to handle its content. It is for this reason that it is not advisable to deliver it at primary school level (under 11 years of age), as students need to be able to address the bigger questions and appreciate the enormity of the subject, as well as coping emotionally.[64] If adults have difficulty comprehending and explaining the horrors of the Holocaust, how can young children be expected to deal with such a harrowing topic? However, primary school teachers in Scotland have found a way to introduce the Holocaust, and that is through the figure of Anne Frank.[65] Similarly, the case study of Anne Frank is a popular choice within British secondary schools. The story of Anne Frank retains such prominence over other stories/texts in classrooms worldwide because it is a story students can relate to. Young people connect with Anne, also a teenager, as her diary puts a human face to what is frequently presented as a faceless event.[66] In the United States, Cynthia Ozick suggests that there is a general "tendency to infantilize, Americanize, sentimentalize, falsify, kitschify and finally deny the horror that truly confronted Anne Frank," so much so that Anne is portrayed as "an all-American girl," which is something that is mimicked in most United States classrooms.[67] This kitschification has led to Anne's account becoming only a partial truth, reinforcing a simple moralism, a narrative that obscures the truth and realism of the Holocaust. Although Anne Frank's is only one story within Holocaust literature, it is the most read and constantly used in school textbooks (for all grades), with the result that Anne Frank's story *is* the Holocaust for many students.[68] This, therefore, highlights the need to stress the importance of teaching the Holocaust within a much wider framework and the notion that students need to be introduced to other faces of the Holocaust.[69] Regardless of the level at which it is taught, Anne Frank's story must not be the only Holocaust perspective students receive.

In an attempt to make figures likes Anne Frank real within the classroom, however, some secondary school teachers have adopted role play to make the Holocaust real through a learn-by-doing approach.[70] Role playing the Holocaust is a pedagogical disaster if incorrectly done.[71] Critics argue, quite rightly, that "those who have not experienced the Holocaust can never really 'know' what is was like to be in the Holocaust" and should not want to try.[72] Clearly, as Samuel Totten warns:

> for students to walk away thinking that they have either experienced what a victim went through or have a greater understanding of what the victims suffered is shocking in its naiveté. Even more galling is for teachers to think that they have provided their students with any sense of what the victims lived through and/or to think they have at least approximated the horror and terror the victims experienced.[73]

Those that have used role play in Holocaust teaching have noted how certain "surprise factors," such as the unpredictability of the victims' fate, resulted in heightened levels of anticipation and a strengthened student involvement. They have stressed that "it is difficult to imagine how these contradictory feelings were managed by participating students and what the emotional residues of this situation were."[74] Alongside the "surprise factors," some teachers also use "shock tactics" to jolt their students into the realism of the subject. Many teachers use photographs to shock their students, despite pedagogical warnings for teachers not to launch in with such pictures.[75]

There are many different ways in which students can be introduced to the topic in a historically appropriate manner.[76] While "no sensible historian would argue that using images in history lectures is a pedagogical waste of time,"[77] many would agree that atrocity photographs should be used only when there is a clear educational benefit to the students. Yet even though teachers are advised to actively refrain from using atrocity photographs in the classroom, students will undoubtedly come across them outside the classroom. Infamous images of the Holocaust such as the piles of dead bodies at Belsen and the haunting images of the "Last Jew of Vinica" have entered popular imagination and, in turn, have helped to shape the

Illustration 8: Rows of dead inmates line the yard of Lager Nordhausen, a Gestapo concentration camp, April 1945. (Photograph by James E. Meyer, April 12, 1945. National Archives and Records Administration, United States. [ARC identifier 531259])

collective memory of the Holocaust. Such images tend to dehumanize and reinforce the historical fallacy that Jews existed historically only as victims of a murderous regime, not as fully functioning human beings, a view that is held by many British secondary school students.[78]

The endless array of such images on the Internet and in television documentaries and feature films has resulted in many students becoming immune to their content. For example, when shown the photograph of rows of dead bodies within the yard of Nordhausen concentration camp, my A-Level students were not perturbed by the horrors of this image. In many ways, my students have become desensitized to the horror of the image, partly because of their overuse outside the classroom and the fact that students nowadays are used to seeing all sorts of horrors in pictorial form. As a result, showing the images does little to add to the teaching of the history of the Holocaust. If such photographs are to be used, then teachers need to remain vigilant in terms of historical accuracy, placing them well within the lesson, explaining the content of the picture, and ensuring that students attain a proper understanding of the significance of what they are analyzing.

History teachers have also called upon the use of other popular visual mediums such as feature films to deliver courses on the Holocaust.[79] Of course, films are fictional representations of the Holocaust and not the event itself, and this must be made very clear to students. The use of popular feature films, such as *Schindler's List* (1993), as teaching aids is fraught with problems. Educational expert Rich Gibson is very critical about the pedagogical value of *Schindler's List* and suggests that while teachers frequently use the film to introduce the Holocaust, they rarely step outside the internal issues of the film, which presents the "Nazi Holocaust... as having no real beginning, but a clearly defined ending, as a horrible event separate from the unfolding of the surrounding socio-political context, a moment for which everyone is responsible, yet no-one is responsible."[80] He concludes that "fascism did not fall from the sky and it was not defeated by Schindler."[81] Gibson is not alone in his criticism of the film and its director, Steven Spielberg. Documentary filmmaker Claude Lanzmann is also highly critical and believes that Spielberg produced a film that was tainted by the brush of Hollywood and its focus on a German who saved Jews, when the reality was that so many Jews were sadly not saved.[82]

Films such as *Schindler's List* are in part responsible for the creation and persistence of particular incarnations of Nazi evil in popular culture and the classroom. Film writers and directors create their own image of individuals such as Oskar Schindler or representations of an event such as the Holocaust. These representations are detached from the historical figure or the event. Filmmakers thereby perpetuate their own myths about the past, which are then projected onto society. Students encounter these myths at the movie theatre and bring them into the classroom.[83] The classroom then becomes a battlefield of sorts, where the teacher is responsible for rewriting the students' accepted version of the past. As a result, such fictionalized accounts are rarely useful within the classroom, because of issues concerning historical accuracy and authenticity.

Still, this does not mean that films cannot be used as an effective teaching aid, but as with all teaching they must be introduced and contextualized properly.[84] In an A-Level session looking at the role of Hitler in the Holocaust, for example, my students were shown a few carefully selected clips from the German film *Downfall* (2004). The students were then directed to complete a critical analysis exercise focusing on questions such as the portrayal of Hitler and the realness of the character. Student feedback on this exercise proved very positive as students demonstrated how they should approach such films and their use as historical sources (or not). With some encouragement, the students managed to identify the various faults of the film, which were all criticisms put forward by film reviewers at the time of the film's release. These included the humanized depiction of Hitler. They also highlighted how the actor, who played Hitler, Bruno Ganz, looked very similar to Hitler and spoke German, which led them to discuss the "realness of Hitler" in the film. This exercise confirmed how films such as *Downfall* continue to give life to the myth of Hitler being a seductive leader, a clear indication of how Hitler is represented in modern society.[85] If films such as *Schindler's List* and *Downfall* are to be used within the classroom, then students must be encouraged to analyze such films in a critical manner so that the myths they create and perpetuate can be dismantled by the students themselves.

Conclusion

Britons are introduced to Hitler, nasty Nazis, and the Holocaust at a very early age in elementary school, and Nazism follows us throughout our years of education. Outside the classroom, students experience a certain pedestrianization of Nazism in everyday culture. Often these popular mis-representations make their way into the classroom, where it then becomes the task of the teacher to attempt to eradicate them. Therefore, it is of vital importance that academics and practitioners work together, in a positive collaborative environment, to ensure that subjects such as these are delivered using appropriate pedagogical practices. Still, while there are many ways in which the teaching of Nazi Germany and the Holocaust can (and should) be improved in the British education system, it is one thing to help students to approach the Nazi past appropriately but quite another to ensure they refrain from embracing monstrous mythologies outside the classroom. While the monsters can often be successfully banished from our schools and curriculum, they are likely to roam at large in modern popular culture for quite some time.

Notes

I am greatly indebted to David A. Cameron and Alan Brooke who offered constructive and helpful comments on the original draft of this chapter.

1. *Medal of Honor* is a video game about one man, American soldier Jimmy Patter-son, who takes on the Nazi menace alone. His missions take the player through occupied France and Nazi Germany, where he battles against endless numbers of Nazis to destroy weapons such as the V2 rocket and a German U-boat. *Medal of Honor* (Playstation, 1999).

2. Eva Kingsepp, "Thrills of the Third Reich: Contemporary Popular Culture Approaches to Nazi Germany and the Second World War," paper presented at the annual meeting of the International Communication Association, San Francisco, California, May 23, 2007.

3. The Nazisploitation in popular culture is a trend that has existed since the 1970s. See Dagmar Herzog, ed., *Lessons and Legacies VII: The Holocaust in International Perspective* (Evanston, IL, Northwestern University Press, 2006), p. 404.

4. John Simkin comment on "Education forum," posted October 26, 2004, available at http://www.Ipbhost.com, cited in Derek Matthews, "The Strange Death of History Teaching," Cardiff University web site, available at http://www.cardiff.ac.uk/carbs/faculty/matthewsdr/history4.pdf (accessed July 2009).

5. George Chamier, *When It Happened: A Very Short History of Britain in Dates, Including the Most Important Kings and Queens, the Major Battles and Other Great Events, to Help Anyone Who Cannot Remember or Never Learned* (London, Constable & Robinson Ltd, 2006), pp. vii–viii.

6. Static categories include those such as Hitler, his character, the nature of Nazi support, resistance movements, economic, social, and foreign policy, and the Holocaust.

7. Mike Bottery, "The Teaching of Evil," *Oxford Review of Education,* Vol. 19, No. 3 (1993), pp. 319–336.

8. Those against the teaching of evil in schools often cite the following work: Albert Bandura, *Aggression: A Social Learning Analysis* (Englewood Cliffs, NJ, Prentice-Hall, 1973). Bandura has shown that children who witness violence are more likely to commit violent acts. However, there is very little empirical evidence to prove that Holocaust education has led to some young children engaging in violence.

9. See Valerie Clark, "Death Education: An Education for Life?" *Curriculum,* Vol. 12, No. 1 (1991), pp. 42–52.

10. Chaim Schatzker, "The Teaching of the Holocaust: Dilemmas and Considerations," *Annals of the American Academy of Political and Social Science,* Vol. 450 (1980), p. 218.

11. Richard J. Evans, "Writing the History of Nazi Germany," *BBC History Magazine,* Vol. 9, No. 10 (2008), p. 61.

12. Stephen Pagaard, "Teaching the Nazi Dictatorship: Focus on Youth," *History Teacher,* Vol. 38, No. 2 (2005), p. 205.

13. GCSE (General Certificate of Secondary Education) is an academic qualification that students, between the ages of 14 and 16, study for in England, Wales, and Northern Ireland. Students usually study up to 10 subjects.

14. A-Level (Advanced Level General Certificate of Education) is an academic qualification that students (England, Wales, and Northern Ireland) progress onto study after completing their GCSEs. They usually choose to study three subjects, which they will specialize in from the age of 16 to 18 when they will, if they choose, go to university to undertake a degree in their preferred choice.

15. See Ian Kershaw, *The "Hitler Myth": Image and Reality in the Third Reich* (Oxford, Clarendon Press, 1987).

16. For an excellent concise but detailed survey of the Nazi economic recovery see Richard J. Overy, *The Nazi Economic Recovery, 1932–38* (Cambridge, Cambridge University Press, 1996).

17. See Rynn Berry, *Hitler: Neither Vegetarian nor Animal Lover* (New York, Pythagorean Books, 2004).

18. Kershaw, *The "Hitler Myth."*

19. If you type "Nazi Germany" into the search field of the online store http://www.amazon.com there are over 5,000 books available. If you type in "Hitler," there are over 14,000 works.

20. See Hilary Bourdillon, ed., *Teaching History* (London, Routledge, 1994).

21. Otto Dietrich, *12 Jahre mit Hitler* (München, Isar Verlag, 1955).

22. Edexcel A2 History Paper 6526/6E, *Hitler and the Nazi State: Power and Control, 1933–45.* June 11, 2009.

23. For examples of how students misunderstood the question, see comments posted throughout June 2009 on the History Teachers' Discussion Forum, http://www.school history.co.uk/forum/index.php?showtopic=11550&st=0 (accessed July 2009).

24. Pagaard, "Teaching the Nazi Dictatorship," p. 206.

25. Pagaard, "Teaching the Nazi Dictatorship," p. 206.

26. Claire M. Hall, "An Army of Spies? The Gestapo Spy Network 1933–45," *Journal of Contemporary History,* Vol. 44, No. 2 (2009), p. 258.

27. See Richard J. Evans, *In Defence of History* (London, Granta Books, 2001).

28. Examples of A-Level examination boards that cite Goldhagen on their suggested reading for modules on Nazi Germany and the Holocaust include AQA GCE, Unit 6W: Alternative J, The Holocaust, 1938–1945.

29. Rudolph Binion, *Hitler among the Germans* (New York, Elsevier, 1976). Binion argues (drawing upon the ideas of Freud) that Hitler's development was stalled by his relationship with his mother, placing emphasis on breast-feeding and her eventual demise from breast cancer.

30. Walter C. Langer, *The Mind of Adolf Hitler: The Secret Wartime Report* (New York, Basic Books, 1972). This work originated from a psychoanalytical wartime report that Langer wrote for the OSS during the Second World War. In his psychological profile of Hitler, Langer concluded that Hitler was "a neurotic who lacks adequate inhibitions" (p. 140).

31. Robert G. L. Waite, *The Psychopathic God: Adolf Hitler* (New York, Basic Books, 1977). Waite ponders on the thought that Hitler may have had Jewish ancestors and suggests that this is something that Hitler constantly struggled with throughout his life.

32. Wim Wenders, "Historische Aufzeichnungen enthüllen. Wie Hitler seinen Hoden verlor," November 19, 2008, available at http://www.bild.de (accessed July 2009).

33. For example, see Martin Collier and Philip Pedley, *Germany, 1919–45: Heineman Advanced History* (Oxford, Heinemann Educational Publishers, 2000).

34. In 2007, 67.2% of GCSE history entrants passed with an A–C grade, compared to 61.3% in 2000. In 2008, 98.9% A-Level history entrants passed with an A–E grade compared to 89.2% in 2000. See UK Department for Children, Schools and Families web site, available at http://www.dcsf.gov.uk/ (accessed July 2009).

35. The Imperial War Museum in London offers sixth-form conferences twice a year. Examination boards organize similar conferences inviting specialists in the field to deliver key sessions.

36. For example, Professor Richard J. Evans offers a document-based special subject on the economic and social history of the Third Reich at Cambridge University.

37. See Diane F. Halpern, "Teaching for Critical Thinking: Helping College Students Develop the Skills and Dispositions of a Critical Thinker," *New Directions for Teaching and Learning,* Vol. 89 (1999), pp. 69–74; Robert T. Pithers and Rebecca Soden, "Critical Thinking in Education: A Review," *Educational Research,* Vol. 42, No. 3 (2000), pp. 237–249.

38. University Centre Peterborough is a joint venture between Anglia Ruskin University (Cambridge) and Peterborough Regional College to provide higher education in Peterborough and its surrounding area.

39. Piers Brendon, *The Dark Valley: A Panorama of the 1930s* (New York, Alfred Knopf, 2000).

40. Joseph Coohill, "Images and the History Lecture: Teaching the History Channel Generation," *History Teacher,* Vol. 39, No. 4 (2006), p. 457.

41. Coohill, "Images and the History Lecture," p. 458.

42. Coohill, "Images and the History Lecture," p. 464.

43. William Carr, "Historians and the Hitler Phenomenon," *German Life and Letters,* Vol. 34, No. 2 (1981), p. 260.

44. The Holocaust is a compulsory subject in all secondary schools in Britain for students between the ages of 11 and 14.

45. The Holocaust became a mandatory part of the school curriculum in Israel in 1963. See Hanna Yablonka ad Tuvia Friling, "Introduction," *Israel Studies,* Vol. 8, No. 3 (2003), pp. v–xi.

46. For works on school curriculum, national memory, and national identity in Britain, the United States, and Israel see Stephen Cooke, "Negotiating Memory and Identity: The Hyde Park Holocaust Memorial, London," *Journal of Historical Geography,* Vol. 26, No. 3 (2000), pp. 449–465; Alan L. Mintz, *Popular Culture and the Shaping of Holocaust Memory in America* (Seattle, University of Washington Press, 2001); Julia Resnik, "Sites of Memory of the Holocaust: Shaping National Memory in the Education System in Israel," *Nations and Nationalism,* Vol. 9, No. 2 (2003), pp. 297–317.

47. See Neil Burtonwood, "Holocaust Memorial Day in Schools—Context, Process and Content: A Review of Research into Holocaust Education," *Educational Research,* Vol. 44 (2002), pp. 69–82.

48. For more details about the Holocaust Education Trust and their work in Britain, visit their web site, available at http://www.het.org.uk (accessed July 2009).

49. For more details about Facing History and their work in the United States, visit their web site, available at http://www.facinghistory.org (accessed July 2009).

50. The Holocaust exhibition (permanent) was officially opened by Queen Elizabeth II in June 2000.

51. See the Imperial War Museum web site for more details on the Holocaust Education Fellowship, available at http://www.iwm.org (accessed July 2009).

52. See Samuel Totten, "Should There Be Holocaust Education for K-4 Students? The Answer Is No," *Social Studies and the Young Learner,* Vol. 12, No. 1 (1999), pp. 36–39; Paul Salmons, "Teaching or Preaching? The Holocaust and Intercultural Education in the UK," *Intercultural Education,* Vol. 14, No. 2 (2003), pp. 139–149.

53. Christopher R. Friedrichs, "Teaching the Unteachable: A Canadian Perspective," *Annals of the American Academy of Political and Social Science,* Vol. 548 (1996), pp. 94–104.

54. Bottery, "The Teaching of Evil," p. 329.

55. Henry Friedlander, "Toward a Methodology of Teaching the Holocaust," *Teachers College Record,* Vol. 80 (1979), pp. 519–542.

56. Peter Novick, *The Holocaust in American Life* (New York, Houghton Mifflin Co., 1999), p. 240.

57. Novick, *The Holocaust in American Life,* p. 239.

58. Nicolas Kinloch, "Parallel Catastrophes? Uniqueness, Redemption and the Shoah," *Teaching History,* Vol. 104 (2001), p. 9.

59. Kinloch, "Parallel Catastrophes?" p. 13.

60. Geoffrey Short, "Lessons of the Holocaust: A Response to the Critics," *Educational Review,* Vol. 55, No. 3 (2003), pp. 277–287.

61. Short, "Lessons of the Holocaust," p. 286.

62. Geoffrey Short and Carole Anne Reed, *Issues in Holocaust Education* (Ashgate, UK, Aldershot, 2004).

63. Paul Wieser, "Instructional Issues/Strategies in Teaching the Holocaust," in Samuel Totten and Stephen Feinberg, eds., *Teaching and Studying the Holocaust* (Boston, Allyn & Bacon, 2001), p. 62.

64. Samuel Totten, "Holocaust Education for K-4 Students?" *Social Studies and the Young Learner,* Vol. 12, No. 1 (1999), pp. 36–39.

65. See Paula Cowan and Henry Maitles, "Developing Positive Values: A Case Study of Holocaust Memorial Day in the Primary Schools of one Local Authority in Scotland," *Educational Review,* Vol. 54, No. 3 (2002), pp. 219–229.

66. See Alex Sagan, "An Optimistic Icon: Anne Frank's Canonization in Postwar Culture," *German Politics and Society,* Vol. 13, No. 3 (1995), 95–107.

67. Cynthia Ozick, *Quarrel and Quandary: Essays* (New York, Alfred Knopf, 2000), p. 98.

68. David H. Lindquist, "Guidelines for Teaching the Holocaust: Avoiding Common Pedagogical Errors," *The Social Studies,* Vol. 97, No. 5 (2006), p. 216.

69. See Michael Brown, "The Holocaust as an Appropriate Topic for Interdisciplinary Study," in Gideon Shimoni, ed., *The Holocaust in University Teaching* (Oxford, Pergamon Press, 1991), pp. 9–14.

70. Examples of the use of role play in Holocaust education can be found in the following works: Miriam Ben-Peretz, "Identifying with Horror: Teaching about the Holocaust—A Response to Simone Schweber's *Stimulating Survival,*" *Curriculum Inquiry,* Vol. 33, No. 2 (2003), pp. 189–198; Simone Schweber, "Stimulating Survival," *Curriculum Inquiry,* Vol. 33, No. 2 (2003), pp. 139–188.

71. There is a huge amount of literature on experiencing the Holocaust. For examples, see Donald Schwartz, "Who Will Tell Them after We're Gone? Reflections on Teaching the Holocaust," *The History Teacher,* Vol. 23, No. 2 (1990), pp. 95–110; Gary Weissmann, *Fantasies of Witnessing: Postwar Efforts to Experience the Holocaust* (New York, Cornell University, 2004).

72. Lindquist, "Guidelines for Teaching the Holocaust," p. 218. See also Annette Wieviorka, *The Era of the Witness* (Ithaca, NY, Cornell University Press, 2006).

73. Samuel Totten, *Holocaust Education: Issues and Approaches* (Boston, MA, Allyn & Bacon, 2002), p. 122.

74. Totten, *Holocaust Education,* p. 193.

75. Lindquist, "Guidelines for Teaching the Holocaust," p. 219.

76. The United States Holocaust Memorial Museum (USHMM) offers an online teaching guide, which details 10 useful suggestions on how to introduce the Holocaust to students. See USHMM "Guidelines for Teaching about the Holocaust," available at http://www.ushmm.org/education/foreducators/guideline/#5_guide lines (accessed July 2009).

77. Coohill, "Images and the History Lecture," p. 455.

78. See David D. Perlmutter, "Re-visions of the Holocaust: Textbook Images and Historical Myth-Making," *Howard Journal of Communications,* Vol. 8, No. 2 (1997), pp. 151–159.

79. See John E. O'Connor, *Teaching History with Film and Television* (Washington, DC, American Historical Association, 1987).

80. Rich Gibson, "Teaching about the Nazi Holocaust in the Context of Comprehending and Overcoming Fascism," *Cultural Logic,* Vol. 4, No. 1 (2000), p. 5.

81. Gibson, "Teaching about the Nazi Holocaust," p. 14.

82. Weissmann, *Fantasies of Witnessing,* pp. 189–190.

83. For an in-depth analysis of how myths are constructed and deconstructed, see Roland Barthes, *Mythologies* (New York, Hill and Wang, 1987).

84. For examples of how film can be used to foster students' skill of critical analysis, see Gregory Bassham and Henry Nardone, "Using the Film JFK to Teach Critical Thinking," *College Teaching,* Vol. 45, No. 1 (1997), p. 10.

85. For a more detailed study of how the Hitler myth is staged in film, see Judith Lechner, "Staging Hitler Myths" (unpublished MA thesis, University of Missouri, 2009).

11

From Hagiography to Iconoclasm: The Nazi Magazine *Signal* and Its Mediations

Brigitte Sion

"The deadliest weapon from the immense arsenal of Axis propaganda"[1] is how *Life* magazine characterized *Signal,* the biweekly publication of the Wehrmacht's Propaganda Department from April 1940 to March 1945. An exemplary journalistic product, this lavish publication was a model of pioneering photojournalism, professional layout, outstanding color printing, and top paper quality. Masterfully designed, *Signal* promoted the skill and artistry of Nazi Germany while disseminating its propaganda all over the world. But *Signal*'s life did not end with the downfall of the Wehrmacht. Some 50 years later, the French performance artist Christian Boltanski found a collection of *Signal* magazines in French, from which he randomly selected 20 color pages and created a collage of Nazi officers, nature, and art. His work, named *Signal,* was publicly displayed only twice, and was published in book form in 2004 in Germany.[2]

Signal then reappeared in 2008 in France, when the Historical Library of Paris dedicated an exhibit to André Zucca's photographs, called *The Parisians under Occupation,*[3] which portrayed middle-class Parisians enjoying a leisurely life. André Zucca was a solitary adventurer who was little known in the world of Parisian photography. He traveled all over the world, never belonged to an artistic or political group, and was not attached to a specific media outlet. Nothing in the exhibition material disclosed the fact that during the Second World War, Zucca was a French collaborationist hired exclusively by *Signal,* which provided him with the expensive color films at a time of war-time scarcity. Unsurprisingly, Zucca's collaborationist past was controversial. Another controversy erupted over the title and content of exhibit as well, which really showed only *some* Parisians—those who could safely enjoy fancy cafés and renowned theaters during the war—and did not represent the reality of occupation for many others.

Through this constellation of *Signal* case studies, this chapter examines the perceived aura of authenticity given to photography, curatorial practices, and the agency of display. Analyzed together, these loci illustrate how the same photographs, mediated through a propaganda magazine, an artistic installation, and a photography exhibit, can both serve propaganda purposes and memorialize absent victims of Nazi Germany.

Signal had ambitious origins. Produced by the Wehrmacht's Propaganda Department under the Oberkommando of the Wehrmacht (Armed Forces High Command) and published by the party's *Deutscher Verlag,* it was destined for Axis, neutral, and enemy countries and published in 20 different languages. The lavishly illustrated biweekly focused on German achievements in culture, sports, and technology; its circulation peaked at 2.5 million in 1943, a quarter of which went to France.[4] Each 40-page issue included mostly pictures, some text, and eight pages in color. As Bernhard Jussen writes, "The magazine was meant to show the work of the Wehrmacht in a favorable light, but without appearing to be propaganda. It was to win the confidence of the populations in the occupied territories and in neutral countries by impressing on them the achievements of German culture, the German talent for organization, and German science."[5] *Signal* prided itself on German success, from cutting-edge farming equipment, to powerful aircraft, to charming ballerinas. The photographs and articles described progress, beauty, and other qualities that would make the readers admire, and even envy, Germany's prowess, regardless of the war. It called itself "the Magazine of New Europe," as if Germany had already won the war. The articles abstained from controversy, avoiding comments about Jews and Slavs and mention of the "Great Germanic Empire." The magazine included war-related photographs, but these images never depicted combat, death, or misery. Rather, the pages displayed proud German officers, impressive gunships, U-boats and aircraft, as well as war heroes. "These pages mirror—though not by design—the fundamental conflict of interests with which the magazine lived: the Wehrmacht wanted images of weapons, technology, and warfare, whereas Goebbels and the Reich Ministry for Propaganda wanted pictures not so much of 'soldiers' but of culture and nature."[6] In other words, *Signal* was a catch-all publication wielding a charm offensive on societies that needed convincing of the worthiness of the Nazi cause.

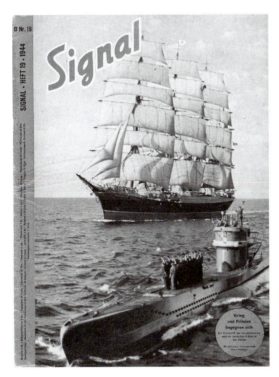

Illustration 9: Cover of *Signal* magazine, 1944, depicting the crew of a German U-boat in the Baltic Sea saluting a glorious merchant sailing ship in full sail.

The Wehrmacht's Department of Propaganda deployed extraordinary means to create a magazine like no other, a magazine that was excessive in all possible ways. Its oversized format, the bright colors on the cover and inside, the close-up portraits of handsome, strong, and joyful people, and aesthetic photojournalism contributed to promote Germany not as a bellicose country but as a modern, well-grounded, and peaceful nation. The pictures and the layout created icons that ignored some aspects of a person or object and exaggerated others. *Signal* showed only achievements in technology, the military, sports, arts, and other fields—a scene at the opera, the development of the X-ray machine, a football match, or a decorated soldier. In volume 20, published in October 1942, two young men lie under the African sun.[7] Their light-skinned bare chests are shining; their colonial hats hang loose or sit next to them; the camera caught them restfully chatting, on the grass. Their athletic bodies, light complexions, and blond hair fit the Aryan ideal perfectly and serve the Nazi ideology of racial superiority. The colonial hats symbolize the peak of German power, when Rommel and his troops invaded Africa and expanded German dominion on a second continent. This picture encapsulates Aryan superiority and military power, the most defining characteristics of Nazi ideology. The people depicted in *Signal* were overwhelmingly young, healthy, beautiful, happy, and self-confident; the close-ups take up all the space, leaving only glimpses of background scenery. At the same time, these iconic portraits obscure the realities on the ground, such as the violence of the battlefields and the persecution of natives that took place under the same African sun.

Signal was only about glory, prowess, and triumph, and promoting the benefits of war. The over-the-top images and design acted as screens that covered up the bombs, hunger, and violence of war time by providing a positive image of Germany to the general public.

Some 50 years after the last issue of *Signal* appeared, the French artist Christian Boltanski serendipitously found an old collection of French-language *Signal* magazines in a Parisian flea market. A performance artist interested both in old photographs and in memory, Boltanski set out to recycle the pages of *Signal* as an archivist would rescue and memorialize old documents. However, he questioned both the photographic medium and the people represented in *Signal* as propaganda tools. He interpreted the excess of images, color, quality, and happiness that filled the pages as a substitute for what was *not* shown, such as combat zones, destruction, hunger, persecutions, gas chambers, and dead bodies.

By dismembering the magazine and reconfiguring the pages in a new sequence, Boltanski broke the frameworks established by the Nazi order and interrupted its propagandistic narrative. By framing these photographs, he transformed the old icons into new signifiers. Photographs that were too bright, too close, too big, and only gave a partial view of daily life in war time were stripped of their deceptive purpose. Boltanski did not crop them, nor did he add captions or written commentary. Rather, he isolated color pages from the whole magazine, reconfigured them in pairs, and framed them. For example, one part of the installation depicted, on the left, a reconnaissance aircraft identified by its swastika flying over Greece, in a display of German supremacy. The white houses look very small from above; many are darkened by the aircraft's gigantic shadow. On the right page, three young women wearing swimsuits sunbathe on the deck of a yacht; one is standing and smiling, the second sitting and staring at the horizon, while the third one is lying down and sleeping on a pillow.

They embody youth, beauty, insouciance, and leisure. Next to the aircraft, however, the image of bathing women yields something disturbing, if not obscene. War against pleasure, armor-plated machine against exposed female bodies: both pictures are too beautiful and too perfect to tell the whole story. The military aircraft and the young women both display self-confidence, as well as superior social or political status; the sky in the background is blue, and the landscape is peaceful. All of it is too blue and too peaceful for a photograph taken during the Second World War.

In Boltanski's installation, the photographs extracted from *Signal* were juxtaposed in order to point to their own disjunction and dissonance, to the missing link, and to what was not in the photographs. The artist created a new narrative of absence, a memorial work to those who never appeared in *Signal* because they were vanquished or were deemed socially or racially inferior; they were skinny and hungry, they lived in fear, or had already been murdered. Boltanski used propaganda images to denounce the deceptive nature of photography and propaganda, as well as to pay a silent and implicit tribute to those people who never appeared in *Signal*.

Writing about exhibitions and museums, Barbara Kirshenblatt-Gimblett argues, "Display not only shows and speaks, it also *does*. Clues to its agency lie in the processes from which it emanates and in which it eventuates."[8] This is precisely what Boltanski's exhibition did: he used only 20 colored photographs from *Signal,* paired one with a military theme and one without, framed them, and displayed them. The fact that they originated from a Nazi propaganda magazine but were then organized in a new sequence and presented as an artistic installation gave new agency to the display and prompted a revisioning for viewers. The rearranged *Signal* photographs did not contribute to the worship of German achievements anymore; instead, they served as a memorial in absentia for the victims of Nazi censorship and ideology. The display mediates absence by questioning the particular use of color photography and by emphasizing the disconnects between the beauty of the images and the context of war.

It is at the juncture of the pictures, on the edges of the matting, that the agency of remembrance is at work, alluding to what is not in the frame: the people, scenes, and objects that were physically excluded from the Nazi worldview. By juxtaposing a fallen Nazi marshal and a bee gathering pollen from a rose, a squadron of airplanes and two oxen pulling a plow in a green landscape, helmets and lipstick, uniforms and bathing suits, swastikas and diamond jewelry, Boltanski creates dissonance, a tear in the harmonious and seamless fabric of the propaganda. His memory work is dedicated to the absent, and plays out *in absentia,* as if revealing a negative film, as if scratching a palimpsest to uncover a hidden meaning.

"My earlier work showed dead Jews, but 'Jew' and 'dead' are too close,"[9] said Boltanski in an interview. He, therefore, set out to create a new symbolic and visual language for his memorial work relating to the Holocaust. With *Signal,* the memory work takes place in two stages: the destruction of the Nazi propaganda effect and the evocation of those who are missing. Once pulled apart and taken out of context, Nazi achievements look anecdotal and mundane, the activities and people depicted seem frozen, as if they were encased in a nontriumphant mausoleum, their lives and actions exhausted from the magazine. By contrast, the glaring absence of destruction, victims, and death is emphasized. Both tasks are left to the viewer, who must engage in a remembrance process by looking at the intersection and the dissonance between images, and at the space outside the frame.

As Ernst van Alphen commented, Boltanski questions the relationship between signifier and signified; the artist dislocates the Nazi equation between the two semiotic elements and points to a different signified, to another reality that has been obscured. "These portraits do not signify 'presence,' but exactly the opposite: absence."[10] However, the absent are not named, seen, or identified in any manner. Boltanski does not attempt to capture the totality of the absence or the scope of the destruction. His signified is indirect, tacit, and embraces everybody and everything that *Signal* did not exhibit as "German accomplishments." By literally destroying the issues of *Signal,* he symbolically breaks the propaganda machine that produced the lies. He replaces the violence of war with the quiet violence of dissonance. However, Boltanski's installation is art, not counter-propaganda. It is implicit, silent, and works by association. It is somehow an elitist artwork, which has been only exhibited three times, in small spaces, for a short period of time, and not in major cultural venues. I would argue that Boltanski remediates *Signal'*s photographs as yet another attempt to memorialize unidentified and unknown victims, as he has done throughout his career.[11]

Boltanski does not only challenge the propaganda discourse of *Signal;* he also challenges photography as a medium often imbued with an aura of authenticity. This is particularly true in the case of illustrated propaganda, which uses photography to canonize self-serving images and to impose an unequivocal narrative that bears the stamp of truth. According to Janis Bergman-Carton, "bearing vestiges of 'truth,' but easily manipulated to lie, [photography] is an ideal medium for his meditations upon history's potential to diminish, rather than strengthen memory."[12] Boltanski questioned photography's authentic quality by thinking about the subjective decisions that come into play—characters posing, choreography, light, focus, background, and so forth. He did not rework the photographs or write about them; instead, he recycled, archived, organized, framed and displayed lying images and turned them into a memorial to the absent and nondepicted truth.

What is not in the pictures is precisely what unites and separates Boltanski's installation from the 2008 exhibit of André Zucca's photographs. As an artist performing memory work, Boltanski salvaged not an old Nazi propaganda magazine, but the memory of those who were excluded from the pages, never had their story told, remained censored, and died in oblivion. Zucca, as a photographer hired by *Signal,* knew what topics would be rejected by his editor, and contributed to replacing the missing people with flamboyant representations of Parisians under occupation. "Starting January 1, 1942, A. Zucca becomes the exclusive correspondent of the magazine [*Signal*]. He participates in 30 issues....After Liberation, he was convicted for collaboration with the enemy and for endangering the security of the State; the case was closed on October 8, 1945."[13] After the war, Zucca settled outside Paris and worked as a photographer for hire, under the pseudonym André Piernic. He died in 1973. Between 1942 and 1944, Zucca took over 200 color photographs for *Signal,* most of which were only exhibited for the first time from March 20 to July 1, 2008 in Paris, and reproduced in an accompanying catalogue.[14]

As a contributor to a propaganda magazine, Zucca mostly stuck to the line developed by *Signal:* healthy, happy people in peaceful settings. The exhibit and catalogue included over 200 images, but only a handful showed the harsh reality of the war. Two included yellow stars sewn on clothes, and two others hinted at economic hardship—one depicting a man in rags at a market, another giving a close-up of wedge heels as substitutes for leather and other scarce material. However, these few exceptions were not published in *Signal,* but were in the catalogue and the exhibit. The handful of negative images was largely outnumbered by those displaying wealth, enjoyment, and abundance. Most pictures focused on Parisians filling outdoor cafés, rushing to the theater, betting at horse races, meeting in upscale neighborhoods, and attending mass at the Eglise de la Madeleine; they were always dressed up—with women displaying fashionable hats and attire. Some pictures include Nazi soldiers—but they looked relaxed and often interacted with the French population. Nothing in the content of the photographs should be surprising, since Zucca faithfully adhered to his employer's agenda: life under German occupation was prosperous, leisurely, and peaceful. In Zucca's photographs, the Nazi presence seemed natural and enhanced cultural and social life.

What is alarming, however, are the ways in which Zucca's photographs were mediated, in the catalogue and in the exhibition hall in 2008. The French historian Jean-Pierre Azéma, an authority on the Vichy régime, wrote in the preface to the catalogue of *Les Parisiens sous l'Occupation* (The Parisians under Occupation), "*Signal* was a propaganda magazine, but well done, based on legible photo-reporting." He added that Zucca considered himself "apolitical" and "was required to work for *Signal,* in exchange of which he received a professional I.D., an *Ausweis,* black and white and color film for his Rolleiflex and his Leica."[15] Azéma presents Zucca as an honest worker who did not have a choice but to write for a professionally produced publication, rather than as a loyal servant whose Agfa films were sponsored by the Nazi regime. The curator of the exhibit, Jean Baronnet, wrote a two-page account of Zucca's life until 1942; "and then it will be the *Signal* period and his trial in 1944. Too late...before he was even acquitted, he was already forgotten."[16] In two lines, Baronnet understates Zucca's collaboration with the enemy, his renown as photographer, and added that many French photographers also worked for the Germans. In her afterword, Nicole Zucca, André's daughter, uses yet another rhetorical device to cleanse her father from any collaborationist stigma: "The 1939–1945 period was made of light and darkness....André Zucca walked through those years of lead on a tightrope, working both for and against the occupier."[17]

André Zucca's positive portrayal in the catalogue was built upon the fact that he was a relatively unknown photographer from a time that does not have many living witnesses left. However, his images of occupied Paris certainly clash with those of Henri Cartier-Bresson and other photographers who documented the French underground and the Nazi occupation as a period of hunger, fear, and violence. The catalogue avoids the word "collaboration" and barely mentions the nature of *Signal*. The photographs present *some* Parisians having a good time—those with the means to go to cafés and to dress up for an evening at the theater. Faithful to *Signal*'s ideology, Zucca filled the space with bright colors, with smiling people, with leisurely activities that overshadowed the lines of hungry Frenchmen in front of grocery stores, the work of the underground, the rounding up of Jews, and the general atmosphere of fear, food shortages, and violence. Zucca's photographs were a part of the Nazi colonization of Paris in the offering of a selective and uniformly positive view of the occupied city, and by putting a layer of bright varnish on war-time life. A number of photographs included German officers in uniform, flags bearing the swastika, and posters in German. The occupying forces blended naturally into the Parisian environment. German officers and men are depicted sitting in cafés, attending movies, and mingling with the French as naturally as the swastikas and the Gothic font became part of the Parisian landscape, the rows of Nazis flags photographed on rue de Rivoli for example, or the military parades on the Champs-Elysées and the reincarnation of the movie theater Marignan as a Deutsches Soldatenkino (German cinema for soldiers).

The exhibit devoted to Zucca's *The Parisians under Occupation,* was a misnomer that spread the false impression that all Parisians experienced a leisurely life between 1940 and 1944, and that the Nazi occupation was not so bad after all. The all-encompassing title was complemented by curatorial decisions that omitted any reference to *Signal* as a Nazi publication and to the propagandistic purpose of the photographs. Similarly absent were references to Zucca's collaborationist activity and subsequent trial and to historical facts about daily life for the majority of Parisians who did not enjoy such pleasant lifestyles under Nazi occupation. This remediation of Zucca's photographs helps to create a different memory about France's involvement in the Second World War; it is problematic not only because it replicates the propaganda but also because it replicates the silences and thus skews public perceptions about the past.

The exhibit was not received well by all who viewed it. A scandal erupted shortly after the opening of the exhibit, when journalists, public intellectuals, elected officials, and visitors questioned the content of the photographs and the context of the exhibit—who was this Zucca who took such complacent photographs? Why was this exhibition insultingly called "The Parisians" ["Les Parisiens"]? Where were the Jews, the hungry children, or the resistance militants? A Parisian official called the show "a spectacular failure," another spoke of "urbane revisionism,"[18] and requested that the title be changed to "some Parisians" ["Des Parisiens"] on posters and marketing material, and that an informative pamphlet be available to visitors to explain the context better. It was too late to edit the title of the catalogue, but posters were redesigned, and a soft disclaimer acknowledging *Signal*'s nature and the context in which Zucca took these pictures was displayed in the entrance—though it remained largely unnoticed.[19] The labels and captions only included the location and year of any particular photograph. They did not evoke informers, spies, anti-Semitic graffiti, closed stores, lines in front of bakeries, discrimination, collaboration, resistance, compromise, or hope. "Everything that could hint at the tragedy of a country that lost some of its honor was carefully avoided,"[20] wrote the art critic Jean Pierrard. Instead, in allowing these images to float freely only under the exhibition title, curators missed an opportunity to acknowledge French collaborationist activity and to use these photographs to document a *slice* of life in war-time Paris. By not giving the exhibition a proper context, the curators have given the opportunity for the wider public to come away with a false perception of the Nazi occupation of Paris, as a period that was not so terrible after all.

Christian Boltanski used similar images from the same source, similarly did not add labels, captions, or commentary, but by means of separation and random juxtaposition, he managed to turn propaganda on its head and create a memorial work dedicated to absence, which helped to contextualize and offer meaning to the pictures and the past. It is precisely the absence of juxtaposition—a photograph next to a label, to a didactic panel, or to other photographs—that was missing in the Zucca exhibit. The curatorial choices, from title to labels to catalogue to background information, rendered the exhibit a double propaganda machine: it appeared to condone the Nazi view of a world without Jews, communists, Gypsies, and other undesirables; it also posthumously reinstated André Zucca as a better photographer and a more honorable citizen than he actually was. The show, exhibited in a public museum and funded by the city of Paris, used colorful aesthetics to cover Zucca's politics. The issue was not the accuracy of facts—*some* Parisians did go to the theater and the horse tracks, dressed in the latest fashion, and led prosperous lives. However, the curators lied by omission by displaying conflated and partial views—precisely what Zucca and *Signal* were doing—and contributed to the perpetuation of Nazi propaganda into the next century. At the core of the tension lay the display of photographs and their presentation: is the public, according to curators, intelligent enough to not need further didactic explanation? Or is the period of French collaboration still so taboo in France that the visitors of today need to be educated in an objective manner about the small number of resistant fighters and the large number of petty collaborationists? Such curatorial decisions not only raise questions about war-time France but also about contemporary France in its handling of national myths of collaboration and resistance.

The daily *Le Monde* ran an editorial on April 27, 2008, asking the difficult question: "In this context, how can one not see in this exhibit yet another example of a country that refuses to analyze all facets of the Occupation and collaboration period?"[21] In relation to Zucca's exhibit and Boltanski's installation, it is worth noting the publicity—albeit negative—that the photographer received, while the performance artist's piece went largely unnoticed in France. In fact, an improbable coincidence brought Zucca and Boltanski even closer in the summer of 2008. While Zucca's photographs were generating a scandal in downtown Paris, Boltanski's installation *Signal* was quietly displayed for the first time in France—for a day in an elite Parisian university. It was barely reported in the media except for *Le Monde,* which called for a "longer exhibition of this work that is a powerful eye-opener."[22]

In both Bolstanski's installation and Zucca's exhibit, the focus shifted from the original *Signal* photographs to what was *not* depicted in the photographs. Whether by questions begged by those enraged at a politics of forgetting, or by design in the collapsed spaces between Boltanski's paired images, both installations drew the eye beyond the images themselves. What was ignored by Zucca's camera is remembered by Boltanski's montage. These case studies reflect two diverging preservation practices originating from the same material but serving opposite views, purposes, and representations—both of Nazi Germany and contemporary France. Boltanski acts as an archivist who salvaged documents to reveal hidden stories and forgotten victims; the promoters of Zucca's exhibit dressed his work as documenting Parisian life under Nazi occupation, only to rewrite France's war-time history as one devoid of suffering, violence, and struggle. At the core of these opposed performances of the *Signal* photographs lies the agency of display, which can turn a collection of pictures into a monument to absent and nameless victims or into a commercial nurturing national lies about war-time France.

Notes

1. *Life,* March 22, 1943, quoted in Martin Moll, "'Signal': Die NS-Auslandsillustrierte und ihre Propagnada für Hitlers 'Neues Europa,'" *Publizistik,* No. 3/4 (1986), pp. 357–400.

2. Bernhard Jussen, ed., *Signal: Christian Boltanski* (Göttingen, Wallstein Verlag, 2004).

3. *Les Parisiens sous l'Occupation: Photographies d'André Zucca* was presented at the Bibliothèque Historique de la Ville de Paris from March 20 to July 1, 2008.

4. Rainer Rutz, *Signal: Eine Deutsche Auslandillustrierte als Propagandainstrument im Zweiten Weltkrieg* (Essen, Klartext, 2007), p. 93.

5. Jussen, *Signal,* p. 54.

6. Jussen, *Signal,* p. 57.

7. *Signal,* Vol. 20 (October 1942), p. 10.

8. Barbara Kirshenblatt-Gimblett, *Destination Culture: Tourism, Museums and Heritage* (Berkeley, University of California Press, 1998), p. 6.

9. As quoted in Jussen, *Signal,* p. 50.

10. Ernst van Alphen, "Deadly Historians: Boltanski's Intervention in Holocaust Historiography," in Barbie Zelizer, ed., *Visual Culture and the Holocaust* (New Brunswick, NJ, Rutgers University Press, 2001), p. 55.

11. See, for example, *Les Suisses morts* [The Dead Swiss]; *Classe terminale du Lycée Chases en 1931 Castelgasse-Vienne* [1931 Graduating Class of the Chases High School, Castelgasse, Vienna]; *Missing House; Inventaires* [Inventories]; and *Tout ce que je sais d'une femme qui est morte et que je n'ai pas connue* [Everything I know about a woman, who is dead and whom I didn't know].

12. Janis Bergman-Carton, "Christian Boltanski's *Dernières Années,*" *History and Memory,* Vol. 13, No. 1 (Spring 2001), p. 13.

13. Françoise Dunoyelle, *La Photographie d'actualité et de propagande sous le régime de Vichy* (Paris, CNRS editions, 2003), p. 118, my translation.

14. Jean Baronnet, ed., *Les Parisiens sous l'Occupation: Photographies en couleur d'André Zucca* (Paris, Gallimard, 2008).

15. Baronnet, *Les Parisiens,* p. 7, my translation.

16. Baronnet, *Les Parisiens,* p. 13, my translation.

17. Baronnet, *Les Parisiens,* p. 174, my translation.

18. Christophe Girard, deputy mayor of Paris in charge of culture, quoted in *Le Monde,* April 25, 2008, p. 24, my translation.

19. See Luc Debraine, "Paris sous l'Occupation, Exposition Polémique," *Le Temps,* April 29, 2008 (in French), np.

20. Jean Pierrard, "Polémique en couleurs," *Le Point,* May 1, 2008, np, my translation.

21. Michel Guerrin, "La photo, la propagande et l'histoire," *Le Monde,* April 27, 2008, np, my translation.

22. Philip Dagen, "Des photographies de propagande nazie provoquent un malaise," *Le Monde,* April 12, 2008, np, my translation.

Contributors

Maartje Abbenhuis is senior lecturer in modern European history at the University of Auckland, where she teaches the history of war and peace, the history of modern Germany, and Nazi Germany and its legacies. She received her PhD in history from the University of Canterbury, New Zealand. Her primary research interests are the history of European neutrality from the Napoleonic era to the Second World War as well as historical investigations of borderland theory. Her first book, *The Art of Staying Neutral: The Netherlands in the First World War 1914–1918,* was published in 2006. In 2009, a collection titled *Restaging War in the Western World: Noncombatant Experiences 1890–Today,* which she co-edited with Sara Buttsworth, appeared.

Ahmed Khalid Al-Rawi teaches English language and literature at the English Department of Rustaq College of Applied Sciences, Oman. His research interests are mainly related to the relation between politics and literature, comparative literature, popular fiction, Orientalism, and folklore. He has several papers published in different journals such as *Arab Studies Quarterly, International Journal of Contemporary Iraqi Studies, John Buchan Journal, Journal of Colonialism and Colonial History, Bookbird, Cultural Analysis, and Folklore,* and as book chapters published by Pickering and Chatto Publishers and Brill.

Sara Buttsworth graduated with a PhD in history and women's studies from the University of Western Australia in 2004. She has been working in the History Department at the University of Auckland since 2004 in a variety of capacities, including teaching modern German history. Sara is currently teaching in the Tertiary Foundations Certificate program. Her most recent publications are *Body Count: Gender and Soldier Identity in Australia and the United States* (2007) and the collaborative effort with

Maartje Abbenhuis, *Restaging War in the Western World: Noncombatant Experiences 1890–Today* (2009) to which she contributed as co-editor and as the author of the chapter "From Bedpans to Bulldogs: *Lottie: Gallipoli Nurse* and the Pitfalls of Presenting War to the Young." At the moment she is working on Cinderella stories and the American Dream with particular reference to the vampire series *Twilight*.

Claire M. Hall completed her PhD at Hull University in 2008. Her main area of specialization is German police intelligence networks during the Nazi period with a particular focus on the Gestapo Spy Network. Her monograph, *The Gestapo Spy Network 1933–1945* is currently in preparation for publication, but an overview of her main argument on policing in Nazi Germany can be accessed in the *Journal of Contemporary History.* Claire has taught history at both secondary level and degree level within the United Kingdom. She is currently working on a part-time basis for the School of History at Nottingham University.

Marc Hieronimus is a historian and linguist. He finished his studies of German, history, and philosophy in 2000 with a master's degree on the subject of German morphology in the frame of optimality theory (OT). After a sabbatical year in France, he wrote a historical PhD thesis about the psychological, sociological, and medical aspects of the 1918 influenza pandemic in France, England, and the German Empire. He is now working on iconological aspects of history such as the power of images in nation building and intercultural dialogue, or the representation of Nazism in comics. In addition to his employment as German teacher at the Jules-Verne-University of Amiens (France), he is involved in a German-Turkish association for intercultural dialogue in his hometown Cologne. As a writer he regularly publishes essays, prose, and poetry in magazines and anthologies.

Eva Kingsepp has a PhD in media and communication from Stockholm University, where she is currently working as lecturer in the Department of Journalism, Media, and Communication (JMK), mainly within the fields of popular culture/cultural studies and philosophy of science, with a focus on hermeneutics, structuralism, postmodernism, semiotics, and visual culture. Her research interests include popular culture, memory culture, intertextuality, remediation and transmediation, myths and processes of mythification, audience research, the construction of meaning, and knowledge building.

Cynthea Masson holds a PhD in English from McMaster University. She teaches medieval literature and composition in the English Department at Vancouver Island University (British Columbia). Her academic research and publication areas comprise medieval visionary literature, medieval alchemical poetry, and the contemporary works of Joss Whedon, including *Buffy, Angel,* and *Firefly.* For her paper "What the Hell?—*Angel's* 'The Girl in Question,'" she was awarded the Mr. Pointy Award for best paper at the *Slayage Conference on the Whedonverses 3* (2008). Her fiction includes *The Elijah Tree* (Rebel Satori, 2009), a novel that combines theories of medieval mysticism with contemporary issues of faith and sexuality.

Ruth McClelland-Nugent graduated with a PhD in history from Dalhousie University in Halifax, Nova Scotia, Canada. She has taught in both Canada and the United States, where she currently is an assistant professor of history and member of the Women's Studies Committee of Augusta State University, Augusta, Georgia. Her research interests are in gender and popular culture. She is currently studying the portrayal of military women in twentieth-century American films.

Lynn Rapaport is the Henry Snyder Professor of Sociology at Pomona College. She is the author of *Jews in Germany after the Holocaust: Memory, Identity, and Jewish-German Relations* (Cambridge University Press, 1997), which won the 1998 Most Distinguished Publication Award in the Sociology of Religion from the American Sociological Association. She is also the co-editor of *Lessons and Legacies IX: Memory, History, and Responsibility: Reassessments of the Holocaust, Implications for the Future* (Northwestern University Press, 2010). She is currently working on a project on how the Holocaust is portrayed in American popular culture from the 1940s to the present day. She received her PhD in sociology from Columbia University.

Gavriel D. Rosenfeld is associate professor of history at Fairfield University (Connecticut, United States). His area of specialization is the history and memory of Nazi Germany and the Holocaust. He is the author of several books, including *Munich and Memory: Architecture, Monuments and the Legacy of the Third Reich* (2000), *The World Hitler Never Made: Alternate History and the Memory of Nazism* (2005), and the co-edited work (together with Paul Jaskot) *Beyond Berlin: Twelve German Cities Confront the Nazi Past* (2008). He is also the author of numerous articles, which have appeared in such journals as *Central European History, History and*

Memory, Holocaust and Genocide Studies, German Politics and Society, and *The Journal of Modern History.* His work has also appeared in news-papers such as the *Washington Post,* the *San Francisco Chronicle,* and the *Forward.*

Brigitte Sion is assistant professor/faculty fellow at New York University's Religious Studies Program and Department of Journalism. She earned her PhD in performance studies from NYU in 2008; her dissertation focused on the conflicting performances taking place at the Holocaust Memorial in Berlin and the Memorial to the Victims of State Terrorism in Buenos Aires. She is the author of four published books, including *Max Ehrlich: le Théâtre contre la Barbarie* (2004), about theatrical productions in the Nazi camp of Westerbork, and she is currently editing a volume on memory, trauma, and performance in Argentina.

Emily Turner-Graham is a historian. Her PhD dissertation, "'Never forget that you are a German': *Die Brücke, Deutschtum* and National Socialism in Interwar Australia," is the first detailed cultural study of Nazi ideology as it was presented to the interwar Australian public. It will be published by Peter Lang Verlag. Her research interests include German colonialism, interwar fascisms in Germany, Britain, and Australia, and contemporary extreme right activity in Austria and Germany. She has taught widely at a tertiary level in German and Australian history. She is currently an hon-orary fellow at the University of Melbourne's Contemporary Europe Re-search Centre.

Sarah Fiona Winters completed her PhD at the University of Toronto in 1999, specializing in Christian poetry. She is lecturer in children's litera-ture at Nipissing University in Canada, teaching courses in children's lit-erature, fan fiction, and the school story. Her research interests revolve around children's fantasy and theology and literature, and she is the co-editor of *Marvellous Codes: The Fiction of Margaret Mahy* (2005). She is currently writing a book on the representation of evil in children's fantasy written after the Second World War.

Index

Abu Graibh prison (Iraq), xxv
Adamson, Andrew, 68–69
Adolf (Moers), 86–87, 90
Adolf H.: Zwei Leben (Schmitt), 8–13
Adult Video News (AVN), 118
Aestheticization strategies, 2
Agent Extraordinary (Bayne), 164–65, 170
Al-Husseini, Haji Amin, 157, 158
Al-Kaylani, Rashid Ali, 156–58, 163, 166
Allied Resistance, 69
All-Star Squadron (comic book), 142, 144–47
Al Qaeda, 22
Al-Rawi, Ahmed, xxv
Alternate histories: Hitler elimination in, 7–17; of Holocaust, 2, 17–21; overview, 1–3; of World War II, 3–7
Angel (TV show): demons in, 180–88; detachment in, 186–87; fascism in, 181–82; good vs. evil in, xxxi, 179–80, 188, 189, 192, 193; military rules in, 183–85; virtue in, 180–81
Anglo-Americans, xxv, 11–12, 14, 22
Anglo-Iraqi Treaty, 156
Anti-Semitism: by Arabs, 155, 158, 161; in comics, 77–78, 84, 86; in fiction, 62; in films, 114, 125; in Great Britain, 5; in magazines, xxxiv; in

music, 217, 219; Nazism and, 219; stemming, 19; on TV, xxxi, 193. *See also* Genocide; Jews/Judaism; *Signal*
Apocalypse theme, xxvi, 35–37
Arab-Islamic culture, 162
Arab-Israeli conflict, 155, 159, 161, 163–64, 170
Arab villainy, in fiction: history of, 156–61; literary background of, 161–64; Nazi-Arab allegiance and, 169; novels and, 164–70; overview, 155–56
Arafat, Yasser, 159
Arendt, Hannah, xvii–xviiii, 54, 59, 61, 63, 65, 69
Arsllan, Amir Shakib, 157
Aryans/Aryanism, 58, 68, 253–54
Asterix and the Goths (comic), 76, 78, 92
Auckland Grammar school, xiii–xiv, xvii
Auckland War Memorial Museum, xiii, xvi–xvii
Audience studies, 39–46
Auerbach, Nina, xviii
Auschwitz, (Crocy), 85
Auschwitz concentration camp: comics about, 83–85, 92; prostitution at, 107; torture at, 58, 67, 107; Trials, 80; women in, 113